Business Alliances Guide

Business Alliances Guide

The Hidden Competitive Weapon

ROBERT PORTER LYNCH

JOHN WILEY & SONS, INC.

New York • Chichester • Brisbane • Toronto • Singapore

Library of Congress Cataloging in Publication Data:

Lynch, Robert Porter
    Business alliances guide: the hidden competitive weapon / by Robert
Porter Lynch.
       p.   cm.
    Includes index.
    ISBN 0-471-57030-3 (cloth)
    1. Joint ventures—Handbooks, manuals, etc. I. Title.
HD62.47.L97 1993
338.7—dc20   92-15341

This book is dedicated to those alliance managers who have . . .

- Had the courage to build their careers on cooperation;
- Empowered others with little desire for recognition or reward;
- Faced challenges against often daunting odds;
- Followed a vision, seen it shattered, picked it up, and tried again;
- Left a legacy for others to build their dreams on;
- Dared traverse uncharted waters with no compass to guide them;
  and
- Never strayed from their fundamental ethic of building value.

PREFACE

Everything great is just as difficult to realize as it is hard to find.

—Spinoza

Collaborative ventures are one of the oldest forms of business activity. However, very little has been written to assist those who are considering a business alliance. Many executives reflect the statement of one joint venture manager who told me:

> So little is written on the subject that it creates a real lack of structure, wasting precious time and resources—a "by gosh and by god" seat-of-the-pants approach.

So many alliances start this way, it is a wonder there are any successes. In defining civilization, John Ruskin, the father of architecture, said:

> Great nations write their autobiographies in three manuscripts: the book of deeds, the book of words, and their art. Not one of these books can be understood unless we read the two others. But of the three, the only trustworthy one is the last.

The books of deeds and words reflect interpretations and intentions; the art and architecture symbolize universal priorities in the sense that they have endured the test of time. Many of the recent writings about alliances reflect the latest, most innovative, most public attempts at corporate teamwork. Like moths drawn to a flame, journalists tend to hover around the current, the popular, the ephemerally visible—and, particularly, the failures. Although sensuously exciting, these currently newsworthy ventures are not necessarily the alliances from which to learn the true lessons of time.

We live in an age of information. Each year, more books, newspapers, and magazines are published than anyone can possibly read. Information grows by specialization; details are magnified. As specialization increases, perspective decreases—and we learn more about less. Information explosion causes content implosion.

This flood of information causes us to move from monthly to weekly to daily to hourly reports in our effort to stay current. The timeless is sacrificed on the altar of the transitory.

Instead, the older, less visible, highly effective, and often silent alliances provide the true insights to success. Granted, we tend to learn more from failure than from success, but, in many respects, corporations become paralyzed by their failures. They tend to bury the dead quickly, or hide them in closets so that professional careers can continue without the scars of lost battles obstructing their paths. Frequently, almost like a haunting refrain, I have heard this lament from executives: "My god, we tried alliances before, and they were a disaster. We wouldn't think of doing it again!"

Few companies have any incentive to spend time on completing an "autopsy report" that will provide the richness of understanding needed for future growth, and then to pick themselves up and get back into the ring.

Alliances must be viewed differently from the common and routine tasks of normal business management. Alliances are *neither internal nor external* to the corporation; rather, they are part of the "extended" corporation, and as such can be neither commanded nor controlled in the traditional sense. They operate within a different set of rules and frameworks, and we must be aware of this uniqueness if alliances are to be understood and then operated successfully.

We must deal with the extended corporation as a living organic system. It thrives on critical interrelationships and support systems, it is constructed with an inherent skeletal structure, and it is designed to have vital organs that function together to carry out a primary mission. The extended corporation will have its own unique culture, personality, and style. If these are not created through intention, they will develop helter-skelter in a less than satisfactory manner.

What is true for alliances is true as well for books about alliances: it is vital for the author to keep an objective clearly in mind. Otherwise, the book will miss the target, meander with verbosity, and disappoint the reader. My objectives are simple and straightforward:

1. To improve the chances of *obtaining excellent results* from an alliance. Unfortunately, alliances have received only superficial treatment by most authorities. Virtually no academic institutions in the world are exploring the issues at any depth, and the few that have attempted to do so are merely tackling the broad philosophical and strategic questions. Moreover, "authorities" have given alliances a very superficial review, and, based on very limited data, have created "myths" about alliances that, while appearing true on the surface, actually perpetuate misunderstandings. Key leaders who must translate theory into everyday practice, and whose personal

careers thrive or die with the consequences, are thus provided little or inaccurate guidance.

An idea is more rapidly transformed into reality when it is concisely explained—and when it contains an inner simplicity, like Einstein's Law of Energy ($E = MC^2$); thereby making the vital *core issues* and *critical decisions* extremely clear to those who will be responsible for the alliance's success or failure. I refer to this organic system as the "alliance architecture."

2. To provide *new insights* into what has been conspicuously missing in the understanding of alliances. Some recent handbooks have concentrated on the mechanics—the "nuts and bolts, bricks and mortar" outlines of the legal, tax, and functional issues. Others have been excellent compendia of strategy and patterns of development, but, because the *connecting links between strategy and mechanics have been seriously lacking,* it has been difficult to cross the bridge from the concept to the reality of alliances. To make the understanding of alliances truly actionable, we need a far better set of criteria for *choosing partners* and *negotiating deals;* sounder *frameworks for operational management;* and more effective *"process maps"* that transcend caveats and cultural points of view. I have given scores of corporate seminars and executive briefings, examined numerous successes and failures, personally experienced the frustrations and ecstasies of alliances, and spoken with countless novices and experts in every conceivable industry, from computers to paper making, nuclear energy, finance, and real estate. In all these experiences, the inner simplicity of alliance design has only become more and more clear.

This is a guidebook rather than a cookbook. A cookbook gives formulas for combining ingredients, measuring proportions, and tracking sequences. Although some cookbook elements are included (and often in great detail), the purpose of this book is to present a map of the various options one has on the journey through an alliance, the principles of design, and some of the potential consequences to expect if certain principles are violated.

My intention in writing this guidebook is to break new ground by describing this architecture: purpose, energy, style, design, engineering, and interrelationships, based on structured processes, conceptual frameworks, critical issues, key principles, early warning signals, vital signs, measurement criteria, and alternate pathways.

Success in building cooperative ventures requires more alliance architects. In this book, you will find the core materials needed to become an architect of alliances, the essential elements that make all business alliances work, whether they are with small companies or giant corporations, in real estate development or high technology, manufacturing or marketing. These principles transcend national boundaries, industry shibboleths, and corporate culture.

A successful alliance is not a happenstance occurrence related to the luck of the draw. It succeeds because it follows a *design*, a process that brings it from conception to operations and continually maintains the delicate balance of a win/win—the double win—for both sponsors. Critical to this architecture is an understanding of the "three-dimensional fit"—how corporate *strategy*, human *chemistry*, and operational *management* must all continually integrate in a win/win environment to achieve success. Managing the double win in the ever changing strategic seas is the essence of alliance management. People are responsible for producing the power of success, yet often unsuspectedly sow the seeds of destruction.

There is an inner, harmonious structure to an alliance. The architecture is as beautiful as nature itself, and, like nature, it adheres to particular principles, laws, and processes. We violate these at our own peril. Yet, inherent in the principles of design is enormous latitude for transformation and creativity.

Those who have practiced the art of alliances know how vital the architecture is; those who have not experienced the joys and pains of success and failure will rightfully analyze and question these principles. As the years progress, these precepts will continue to evolve; they will be further refined and added to until the building and maintaining of strategic alliances is as easily practiced and replicated as the building of any other organization.

Each alliance is a custom creation designed for the successful union of two or more corporate organizations. Because of the myriad of options and demands, this book cannot even begin to prescribe all the varieties and combinations of solutions. Therefore, questions and principles become more important than the answers: without the right questions and with neglect of the key principles, there is no way, save chance, to find the right answers. Although no two alliances are alike, the architectural principles presented here still apply, regardless of the companies, the market, the technology, or the location.

This architecture is not an academic statement of ideals and platitudes. Nor does it emanate from some theoretical vision conceived in an ivory-tower classroom. Rather, the architecture derives from years of competition on the playing fields of real business by experienced practitioners.

In Chapter 12 I have outlined the essence of the "secret art" of alliance management. Secret because, although cooperative ventures have been around for centuries, no one had ever developed a sound theory based on empirical evidence, capable of being used in actual in-the-trenches business. This book examines these management issues in great detail.

Caught up in so many of the technical details of alliance formation, we haven't focused on conceptualizing the fundamentals. In fact, in many cases, we haven't even determined the fundamentals.

In Japan, business leaders are three times more likely to engage in an alliance, and even more trusting of its potential for success, than are their American counterparts. The Japanese see alliances as an inherent part of their culture; Americans do not. This is truly ironic, because business alliances have always been a fundamental part of business enterprise, as we will see in Chapter 1.

Fortunately, the American Management Association (AMA) saw the trend emerging, recognized the educational deficiency, and filled the gap with a forum for hundreds of business executives throughout the United States. Their participation in dozens of executive seminars helped bring this book into being.

During the past 20 years, American business has been placed in an increasingly adversarial environment of lawyers and litigation. Heated attempts to iron out the wrinkles in our economic system have often burned holes in the fabric of human enterprise. We have many intelligent professionals who are passionately dedicated to pitting business against government, business against the consumer, and business against itself. The adversarial process of law is well-documented, and now fully embodied in our culture. Perhaps books like this, and others that follow, will provide the structure and tools to begin rebuilding our business culture utilizing an emerging architecture of cooperation.

By creating this architecture, we can create competitive cooperation across diverse cultures and disparate industries in unique forms hitherto unrealized.

Since the publication of my first book, *The Practical Guide to Joint Ventures and Corporate Alliances* (1989), I have had the wonderful privilege and opportunity to present management seminars to bright and demanding executives representing hundreds of corporations of every conceivable industry, and to work side-by-side as a consultant with both large and small companies. Their feedback, constructive criticisms, guidance, and overall encouragement have been one of the great joys of my business career. Moreover, their relentless and piercing questions, their sharing of successes and failures, and their willingness to experiment with new ideas and avenues to alliances have enabled this next genesis to evolve.

Thus, in many respects, I feel I have served as a scribe echoing a chorus of experienced individuals singing a tune. From alliance to alliance, the tune, while sung by unique characters from customized scripts on very different stage settings around the world, has a familiar melody when successful, and, conversely, a dissonant cacophony when failing. In many respects, I have served as their scribe, writing down the early lines of an epoch oratorio that has been evolving and unfolding for centuries not only here in America but around the world.

I sincerely hope that the perspectives presented in this book provide business leaders with valuable insights and a frame of reference for their personal success, and allow them to avoid the pitfalls that I and other predecessors have encountered. As the successes of business alliances continue to mount, I invite others to share their insights and experiences for future editions of this book.

Providence, Rhode Island   ROBERT PORTER LYNCH
December 1992   THE WARREN COMPANY

Contents

PART FOUR   TOOLS OF THE TRADE

PART FIVE   ACHIEVING SUCCESS

PART ONE

Introduction to Business Alliances

1

The Revolution among Us

In the decades to come, managers will either be part of an alliance or competing with one.

—Paul Lawrence, Harvard Business School

In politics, revolutions tend to arrive as violent, wrenching acts that make bold headlines and quickly turn the tide of history. In business, however, revolutions are more likely to take shape silently, in graduated steps; they remain almost unnoticed until their impact is powerful and pervasive. The revolution in business alliances, one of those silent upswellings, has caught many business leaders unprepared for its pervasive impact.

EXPLOSION OF ALLIANCES WORLDWIDE

Strong, powerful forces are unifying to drive fundamental changes in our economic, social, and business systems. The world is being reshaped along economic boundaries rather than political ones. The North American Free Trade Agreement among Canada, the United States, and Mexico is a response to the European Economic Community (EC-92) of 12 nations. Several of the Eastern European countries, formerly of the Eastern Bloc, are joining EC-92 as adjunct members, someday to be assimilated completely. Many of the countries not in EC-92 have formed the European Free Trade Association (EFTA). In Latin America, two economic blocs have been formed: The Andean Common Market and the Southern Cone Common Market. We can expect to see many major evolutions of this new economic order, especially with the worldwide collapse of communism.

1

During the 1990s, the structure of business will change dramatically as businesses adapt to the dynamics of worldwide markets. Driven by consolidation of the global marketplace; accelerated by the dizzying pace of economic reforms and sociopolitical revolutions in Europe; and fired by the economic engines in the Pacific Rim, this decade offers dramatic new opportunities for American enterprises entering the global market. In contrast, the 1980s were a decade of frenzy directed toward corporate acquisition. As commentators Donald L. Bartlett and James B. Steele described the typical sequence:

> An army of business buccaneers began buying, selling, and trading companies the way most Americans buy, sell, and trade knickknacks at a yard sale. They borrowed money to destroy, not to build. They constructed financial houses of cards, then vanished before they collapsed.[1]

This surface frenzy masked the magnitude of other deep-flowing currents. While U.S. CEOs were mustering all their resources to defend their walls against the attacks of hostile-takeover artists, their foreign counterparts were building vast empires through massive capital expansions and consequent control of global market share. Japanese and European firms acquired three U.S. companies for every company Americans acquired abroad. The number of alliances formed throughout the world multiplied enormously in virtually every industry. These alliances took the form of joint ventures, interlocking supplier alliances, franchises, and research and development consortia. For the first time in history, the 50 largest Japanese firms' research and development budgets exceeded their capital expenditures on new machinery and equipment.[2] The world had a new high-water mark for investment in long-term future growth.

The time has come for rebuilding, for an affirmation of the real underlying business values that have always grown economic wealth and prosperity, and provided value to the customer.

BUILDING GLOBAL ALLIANCES

Executives face the choice of seizing the strategic advantage or being squeezed by aggressive competitors seeking to capture more market share. A corporation's future will require tighter and closer relationships formed by joining forces with an ally, foreign or domestic, to ensure continued growth.

The "rugged individualist" image of the successful entrepreneur or corporate CEO may become the dinosaur of this century. The future leader/CEO will be more visionary, spiritual, and adaptive, able to capture opportunity rapidly, respond to changing markets, and inspire a team through a dynamic common vision and shared values rather than through commands and orders.

REVOLUTION FROM REALIGNMENTS

The 1990s will be an era of massive organizational revolutions. The past decade brought us the information revolution; the present decade will reorder our business structures. Giants of the past, to survive, will decentralize, become less hierarchical, and look and act more like small and medium-size companies, or go the way of the dinosaur. Many multinationals, such as Ford, General Motors, IBM, AT&T, and Siemens, have recognized this fact and have already begun reorienting their corporate structures to encompass multiple ventures in multiple markets around the globe.

These realignments will cause extensive relocations of people and financial power. The advantage will go to the swift and flexible companies—small and medium-size businesses—and to the large multinationals whose strength is not encumbered by bureaucracy, ego, intransigence, or adherence to once powerful, but now ineffective, operational styles.

Corporate agnosticism is not a strategic option—it is a death sentence. The commonly chosen, inwardly oriented responses selected by too many American business and political leaders, such as the verbal narcissism popularized by "Japan bashing," are ineffective misplacements of energy and responsibility.

The strategic executive of the 1990s will not futilely fight these changes, but will opportunistically seize the advantage. The best conventional strategic options are a well-known pair: "Fight 'em or join 'em." An all-out fight may be the more heroic and natural reaction, and joining them risks loss of corporate control, but a carefully controlled alliance can combine the most favorable elements of both choices.

OPTIONS FOR GROWTH

Any company in the global market must perpetually face the issue that if it is not growing, it will be expiring. Essentially, a company can grow in three fundamental ways, and all companies must choose among these options.

The first option is to *expand internally*. This requires capitalizing on superior technologies and/or expanding markets. Most firms gravitate toward this strategy, because they can control it most effectively and because, if successful, it can yield high rewards. However, the internal growth option has some considerable limitations. It is contingent on strong markets, good profit margins, and the ability to hire, train, organize, and control a continually expanding sphere of human resources. It also runs the risk of becoming inbred, and therefore inflexible or blind to important changes in the competitive environment.

The second option is growth through *acquisitions and mergers*. This approach requires large sums of cash and excellent profits, particularly if sales decline in a poor market; overleveraging of debt can cause financial collapse. Many corporations have tried this technique, and, regardless of whether it was a focused core technology acquisition or part of a diversification maneuver, the failure rates, on an industry-by-industry basis, have always exceeded the success rates by a significant margin.

Alliances, the third growth option, require leveraging precious resources and current competitive advantage in new and innovative ways. With relative rapidity and little cash, multiple alliances can be formed horizontally or vertically in numerous markets. However, alliances require new, often unfamiliar methods of management, therefore becoming inherently riskier to the uninitiated.

This last strategy has been growing with almost explosive energy in the past few years. Yet it is, for the most part, a secret and silent competitive weapon. Many of the alliances formed between corporations are not made public in newspapers or magazines, either because the sponsors want to keep their deals confidential for competitive purposes, or because journalists do not see them in the same light as acquisitions.

STRATEGY FOR THE FUTURE

The growth strategy of the 1990s will carefully combine all three strategies. However, three "tip-of-the-iceberg" indicators may be the real forecasters of this powerful trend: the Japanese *keiretsu*, franchise alliances, and Wal-Mart's phenomenal 25% annual growth rates. What these three indicators demonstrate is the combined market and economic success of strategies that create strong financial margins by linking core internal competencies with the unique capabilities of allies. The key factors in unleashing powerful growth forces are proper strategic focus and effective integration of operational functions, used in combination.

Japanese *keiretsu* relationships are vertical alliances between large corporations and their many suppliers. Frequently, the larger business takes a minority ownership (5% to 15%) in a supplier—not for financial reasons, but for business reasons. The two organizations become bonded together in a strategic partnership for their mutual gain—a double win. In tough times, both tighten their belts together, and in good times, they share the rewards.

Franchise alliances (often the orphan child of the business world because business schools don't know how to categorize them) have achieved extraordinary success in business start-ups, often with a 90% winning rate judged 5 years after the start-up. (What is truly astonishing is that franchise alliance performance is totally the reverse of the normal independent start-up, which suffers a tragic 90% failure rate after 5 years.)

Moreover, the franchise alliance system has been America's most exportable business structure, with an astounding ability to cross cultural borders into countries such as France, Japan, Thailand, and Russia, with equally successful results.

Wal-Mart's dazzling 25% annual growth rate, which brought it to the position of the world's largest retailer in record time, is attributable to far more than its founder's charismatic personality. Looking into its strategy, one discovers a finely tuned network of 5,000 supply alliances carefully coordinated with an intricate array of electronic data systems. These systems enable suppliers to work closely with Wal-Mart in a strategic, long-term manner to reduce costs of their goods.

Formerly specialty-focused, middle managers are becoming strategic business managers coordinating multifunction teams in addressing broader issues than they faced in their traditional jobs. This expanded scope has also led to an internal restructuring of old hierarchies into more streamlined, self-directed business teams.

Cooperation as a Competitive Weapon

Competition has traditionally been thought of as the antithesis of cooperation. Only recently have strategists and scholars shifted to a fresh perspective and recognized how powerful a weapon cooperation can be in playing the global competitive game.

Alliances utilize unique management methods, which, all too often, are poorly conceptualized, are seldom shared, and are almost never taught; managers usually learn by trial and error. Experienced venturers tend to hand down do's and don'ts lists or a few word-of-mouth techniques. Further, most journalists and deal makers are totally bored by proper management practices, leaving the alliance field barren of good management information.

OPPORTUNITY OR DANGER?

Today's global market makes the cooperative venture an essential element in the successful pursuit of global business. This course of action conserves capital and corporate energy while it builds a more powerful force with which to face competitors on their home ground. A strong competitor that already enjoys a profitable position in its own market can become a fierce ally. Better to fight the competitive battle alongside an ally than to face this same competitor in open combat. For example, Honeywell's long-standing alliance with Yamatake helps keep other Japanese competitors at bay.

Joined corporate forces have accelerated market changes, resulting in, at the same time, both greater instability and greater opportunity.

Alliances may also diversify dependence on domestic markets by gaining an immediate position in foreign markets. According to Jerry Wasserman, Vice President of Information Industries at Arthur D. Little:

> Strategic alliances are no longer a business luxury, but have become a necessity to compete in the global marketplace. No one is self-sufficient any more.[3]

Jean Pierre Ergas, Chairman of American National Can, has observed:

> The years of closed shops, of closed companies are over; worldwide strategic alliances are evolving. The years of hard-nosed negotiating to extract the most financially out of our suppliers are over because it has produced a battle of win/lose. Win/win is the only realistic approach. We meet with suppliers to work in tandem, in an open exchange; we now share information on technology with suppliers.[4]

THE FUTURE ISN'T WHAT IT USED TO BE

Small and large corporations alike are faced with critical choices. Ford Motor Company determined years ago that no auto maker could remain competitive in the future on its own: a company with global aspirations would need a partner, through either an acquisition or an alliance. Ford has used its alliance with Mazda, of which it owns 25%, to initiate joint sales in Japan and joint production in Europe (to ensure a more secure position for EC-92) and in New Zealand. Ford and Central Glass of Tokyo shook hands to build a production facility in the United States to supply glass to Japanese makers of autos at U.S. locations. Ford became, in effect, a supplier to its competitors.

Ventures with international partners can provide companies with gains from access to excellent applications engineering and technology refinements, while securing an unwavering commitment to strategic growth. Michael Bonsignore, President of Honeywell's International Division, states:

> As the global marketplace emerges as a powerful force, we will see more strategic alliances. American companies will have to become more comfortable with cooperative ventures as a way of doing business in the increasingly competitive environment of the future.[5]

In the past, smaller companies could establish several sales agency agreements abroad, be content with managing the relationship, and watch sales grow. Developing foreign sales agents may be an excellent way to establish an initial beachhead overseas, but today it should be considered a short-term strategy. Many of these small agency agreements may not survive the tremendous competitive onslaught spawned by competitive realignments in overseas markets.

Think Globally, Act Locally

It will be important to customize products for specific national, regional, or demographic market niches. Products will need to be more highly differentiated and of higher quality, and will typically have shorter life cycles. We are seeing increased requirements for flexibility and tighter linkages among suppliers, manufacturers, market distribution systems, and the ultimate customers. New partnerships in business are being forged to meet these demands. Already, according to the National Association of Purchasing Managers, the term "vendor" is becoming obsolete and the favored term, "supplier," is rapidly being expanded to embrace "supplier alliances."

Multinational combines are emerging in the form of strategic alliances, joint ventures, mergers, and acquisitions—often with the active support of the public sector. An example is Airbus, a consortium of German, French, British, and Spanish businesses initially subsidized by government investment, which is now one of the world's major aircraft competitors.

Ultimately, these new combines will have their sights set on lucrative U.S. markets, following in the steps of the Japanese. Nestlé's, the Swiss food giant, nearly doubled its U.S. candy market share with its acquisition of RJR-Nabisco's candy divisions. Unilever, the Anglo-Dutch conglomerate, has made over $2 billion of acquisitions in the United States, staking out the number three position in the cosmetics market.

American companies are finding overseas investments far more lucrative than domestic business. Capital investment overseas is growing at twice the rate of domestic investment by U.S.-based multinationals, because their after-tax return on assets of foreign affiliates averages over 14%—in striking contrast to U.S. divisions, which average only a 2.5% return.

TRENDS

Some industries are moving in the alliance direction with extreme rapidity. According to a 1991 survey, by Dataquest and Arthur Young, of over 700 CEOs of start-up and fast growing companies, nearly 90% had begun forming alliances, up from 81% in 1990 and 73% in 1989. Partnering arrangements are fast becoming an integral part of corporate strategy.

Despite such trends and forces, other industries are moving to the future more grudgingly. Outside of the electronics industry, American managers show an amazing reluctance to change. A 1988 Booz-Allen & Hamilton survey showed that only 17% of American business executives saw alliances as effective, compared to 74% of their Japanese counterparts. Nearly one-third of the American CEOs thought alliances were "dangerous," compared to only 1 out of 25 Japanese CEOs.

While the U.S. trend is clearly increasing, the Japanese move forward rapidly with alliances worldwide. According to Peter Schavoir, IBM's Director of Strategy, nearly 25% of the new equity and cash flow of Japanese corporations is invested in alliances, and the remainder is invested in new plant and equipment and in research and development (R&D).[6] He asserts that this investment process is critical to capturing market share, and that strategic alliances are vital for overall efficiency and market coverage.

While large American corporations were playing the acquisition game, a powerful alliance form—the franchise alliance—captured the hearts and souls of smaller businesses on a massive scale, both domestically and internationally. In the retail sector alone, in 1980, franchises accounted for $325 billion in trade in the United States. By the end of the decade, this had leaped to $720 billion and was growing at a rate of nearly 8.5% annually. Essentially an American device for using far less capital, the franchise alliance also proliferated around the world with a phenomenal success rate, especially when compared to the acquisition disasters of the same era.

ALLIANCES AND THE AMERICAN TRADITION

The trend in alliances is not just the model of the future; it is deeply rooted in the past and can be traced to the great global ventures of the 18th and 19th centuries.

Indeed, the 20th-century "globalization of the marketplace" is not really a new phenomenon. It has been a continuous wave of history that was interrupted only by the Dark Ages. It began 2,500 years ago with the Phoenicians, continued with Alexander the Great, and was expanded in the Roman Empire. After a 1000-year hiatus, it began again with the voyages of Columbus, the Spanish conquests of the Americas, the rise of the Dutch and English as great world traders, and the great colonial empire building of the 1800s. We must look at what is happening in today's business from the perspective of the past, to understand the major trends and how they relate to present and future strategies.

Market expansion—and even globalization—as a phenomenon has been inextricably linked to cooperative ventures for dozens of centuries. The first joint ventures were formed in ancient Egypt and Phoenicia, when merchants cooperated in their commercial activities. After the European discovery of the Americas, a new era in market globalization spawned significant collaboration, often with the government's sanction, support, or sharing in the risks and rewards. Unlike their Spanish counterparts, the English settled the American colonies not to conquer land, but as venture merchants, collaborating with merchant bankers, trading companies, and even the royal crown, to further their business interests.

U. S. entrepreneurs continued this English tradition unabated in America after the Revolution.

Cooperative ventures are not new in the United States, yet it is truly unfortunate that American business has such a short memory. Harvard's Professor Jay Featherstone has said that we live in the "United States of Amnesia." Our collective business memories tend to last only about 60 years—the longest terms of the business careers of our eldest business mentors. In the 1990s, few wise leaders recall the lessons that created the boom and bust of the Great Depression; nor do we remember the strategies for growth during that severe and prolonged economic downturn. There are virtually no professional business historians in the academic world to transfer management knowledge, models, and processes across the progression of time. Few understand how deeply business alliances played a role in this country during its formative industrial years, and how profoundly that tradition has become ingrained in our business structures in a variety of forms.

Roots in Shipping

Today's alliance framework finds its roots in the shipping industry, where management of risk was essential to reap the lucrative rewards of trading. In the 18th and 19th centuries, the United States entered the global market by sending trading expeditions to such faraway destinations as China, as early as 1784.

The first documented joint venture in the United States occurred just as the treaty was signed with Britain to end the American Revolution. No sooner had the British troops departed for England, in November 1783, than a group of prominent Philadelphia and New York shipping merchants immediately laid out a daring venture. The British West Indies, once a preeminent market for colonial merchandise, were now inaccessible to American shipping. The colonies' shipbuilding industry was decimated, and overseas trade relations had fallen into such disuse that it would take years to recover. A swift and dramatic act was necessary.

In a bold move the merchants authorized the construction of a ship named *Empress of China,* to compete with the more powerful English cargo ships. This swift new vessel, designed with the most advanced hull of its day, was built to make the voyage to China in record time. It was to be a intrepid voyage across poorly charted seas to a land halfway around the world, where no ship under the American flag had navigated before.

The only exportable commodity of any value from America, in the eyes of the Chinese, was the ginseng root, used as a highly prized medicinal herb. An expedition by the promoters, into the hills of western Virginia and Pennsylvania, quickly brought back a quality crop. The *Empress* was laden with this domestic cargo for delivery to the Orient in exchange for silks, spices, teas, and porcelain.

Before the *Empress of China* was ready to set sail, its owners made sure that both the ship and its cargo were insured. However, there being few established insurance entities in the new country, the merchants turned to another joint venture in France.

The French consortium, consisting of 41 individual underwriters, insured the vessel for a premium (typically 7% to 8% of its value), with 97% coverage upon total loss and no payment if losses were less than 5%. (Throughout the early decades of the next century, insurance companies frequently relied on the joint venture format to underwrite insurance policies for U.S. shipping.) An agreement was written into the insurance document for appointment of an independent arbitrator in the event of contestation of payment for losses.

Risk Management

To reduce risk of loss on the voyage, the insurance consortium insisted that the captain receive strict orders from the owners regarding the ports where the ship could call; any deviation from those orders were grounds for canceling the insurance.

Aboard the ship were two attorneys (called supercargoes) who acted as the business managers and agents for the merchant-owners. The attorneys were assigned the responsibilities of paying for any repairs needed to the vessel, overseeing the ship in any ports-of-call, and, more significantly, negotiating any trade deals with foreign merchants. While at sea, the captain commanded the ship; while in port, the captain answered to the authority of the supercargoes.

Commercial alliances in the days of early America were far more elaborate than we might believe today. An international web of interconnecting relations was the norm. Merchants maintained close business and financial relationships not only among their fellow entrepreneurs on the Atlantic seaboard, but also throughout France, Spain, Italy, Portugal, the West Indies, and, later, again with England.

Rather than leave such a risky venture precariously undercapitalized, additional financing for the *Empress of China* venture was necessary. A mortgage (called bottomry) was taken out on the ship with a Parisian merchant banking firm, to leverage whatever finances were available without diluting existing shareholders.

While the ship was on its voyage, mortgage payments were due regularly. The race was on—the ship must sail for China via the Cape of Good Hope, trade its cargo, and return safely, before the mortgage payments depleted the preciously limited funds of the American merchants.

In a classic foreshadowing of a common modern business malady, the deal was overleveraged. One of the joint venture partners ran into serious financial difficulty in another venture while the ship was at sea, causing him to have severe trouble keeping up with his portion of payments to the bank, and forcing other partners to mortgage further business interests in order to satisfy the bank. Eventually, the solvent partners had to advance more than double the stock stipulated in the dead of co-partnership, as the joint venture agreement was then called.

Fortunately for American business interests, the voyage of the *Empress of China* was fantastically profitable. Further voyages to the Orient were organized from virtually every seaport in the new country, and the beginnings of American trade dominance were established.

Several decades after the China trade began, American whalers, using the joint venture organizational framework, built a vast industry which, by the 1840s, dominated 75% of the world market. This massive enterprise used a very sophisticated alliance management structure between the shipboard captain and the landbound investors to limit risks. It also included profit-sharing plans with all the crew members, as well as government mandated (though primitive) health care.

Joint Ventures in Mining, Oil, and Gas

The American shipping industry was not restricted simply to ocean craft; it quickly expanded to include railroads and canals. All these ventures required large amounts of financial capital and use of new, developing technologies, in the highly uncertain boom-and-bust economic environments that characterized the 1800s.

The ability to move coal from Pennsylvania to the eastern seaboard by canal boat, coastal schooner, and rail enabled coal gasification technology to begin to supplant whale oil as a relatively more efficient form of lighting by 1850. It was not surprising to find the shipping and whaling interests investing in the laying of gas piping in entire cities and towns in the early 1850s. Naturally, these gas utilities used the joint venture as a means of minimizing the risks of building an infrastructure that might take years to repay them for their investment.

With the discovery of oil in Pennsylvania in 1859, the whaling era came to a close. Petroleum supplanted whale oil as a lubricant. The whaling merchants of New Bedford averted potential financial disaster by converting their whale oil refineries into crude oil refineries and by transforming their source of oil from ocean-based whaling to land-based drilling. Adapting their highly successful whaling-industry method of spreading risks and rewards through the joint venture, they commissioned oil explorations using the same organizational structure. To this day, numerous oil and gas explorations go forward as joint ventures.

As the West was being tamed, the joint venture was utilized extensively by wealthy East Cost financiers to build railroads and to mine gold, silver, and copper in the Rocky Mountains. Today, joint ventures are still the dominant mechanism for the aluminum mining industry, as well as being a major form in other aspects of mining.

The Franchise Alliance

Franchising was also a natural spin-off of the cooperative venture, enabling an alliance between a larger, more developed company (the franchisor) and numerous independent, smaller, more tightly managed companies (franchisees). The first franchises were in the railroad and utility industries in the mid-1800s. Railroad companies would offer "franchises" to ranchers and homesteaders to create towns along the railroad rights of way. In return, the towns would have access to shipping and commerce, and, of course, provide business to support the railroad's investment in track and equipment.

Elias Howe, creator of Singer Sewing Machines, used franchises in the 1860s to promote the phenomenal growth of both his own manufacturing empire and the apparel industry. In 1860, Singer was selling 110,000 sewing machines a year.

The Early Technology Alliances

Alliances have tended to be used extensively to spur on new industries, because of the extensive risks involved. Connected through interlocking licensing agreements, the franchise alliance contributed to the rapid proliferation of products and services into numerous global markets, by utilizing local management talent and capital investment. The franchise alliance overcame the organizational problems of setting up subsidiaries or the extensive time and money headaches of acquisitions.

Naturally, as the electric and telecommunications industries burgeoned in the 1880s, with Edison's development of the light and power generation systems (emerging as General Electric) and Bell's creation of the telephone (resulting in AT&T), the cooperative venture structure was used to divide risks.

Edison's creative genius required tackling a triple risk threat: *new companies* entering *new markets* with *new technologies*. After Thomas Edison had demonstrated the technical success of the electric light and of complex power generation systems in New York's financial district in the 1880s, he set up a series of exclusive franchise licenses throughout the metropolitan area, for power generation technology. The metropolitan utilities became franchisees, committing themselves to purchase the equipment—dynamos, meters, circuit boards, and so on—from Edison's company. Many of today's utilities, such as Detroit-Edison and Consolidated-Edison, still bear testimony to his legacy.

Edison General Electric was formed in 1889 as a corporation composed of a consortium of investors, corporate partners, several of Edison's businesses, and Edison himself. Several members of the consortium are recognizable today, including Deutsche Bank of Berlin, Siemens and Halske, and General Electric Company of Germany. By 1891, through a subsequent merger, the corporation became General Electric, the parent company we know today. Many of the existing gas companies became the natural vehicle for the electric franchises offered by Edison General Electric, and the resulting utilities, to this day, still offer combined gas and electric services.

Later, in the motion picture industry, Edison faced numerous patent challenges to his movie projector. In 1909, in an arrangement that ended a long battle of legal challenges to patents and a period of ruinous competition, Edison, as inventor of the motion picture projector, joined forces with his legal adversary, the inventor of the motion picture camera, forming a 50/50 deal by placing both patents into a joint venture.

In the deal, Edison's ally, Eastman Kodak received exclusive rights to manufacture film. George Eastman, Kodak's founder, had a long-standing supplier alliance with Edison, dating back to Kodak's development of flexible film in the 1890s. Eastman also gave Edison the technical formulation for celluloid, needed by Edison's phonograph company for the successful creation of commercial recordings.

Nippon Electric Company (NEC) of Japan, today the $25 billion electronics and telecommunications giant, was formed in 1899 as a joint venture between two Japanese businesses and Western Electric, a subsidiary of AT&T. NEC is now part of the vast Sumitomo complex of alliances and itself heads its own network of affiliates, alliances, and subsidiaries.

Into the Automotive Industry

In the early 1900s, auto manufacturers established franchise alliances with exclusive dealer-franchisees, rather than setting up expensive corporate-owned dealerships. In the 1920s, this system was extended into the oil and gasoline industry, and licensed dealers proliferated throughout the United States.

When the automotive industry exploded, strategic alliances developed between auto manufacturers and their suppliers, as an alternative to expensive vertical integration. One of these was the once long-standing OEM (original equipment manufacturer) relationship between Ford Motor Company and Firestone Tires—a relationship augmented by the personal friendship between Henry Ford and Harvey Firestone.

In 1924, General Motors sojourned into a corporate partnership with Esso (now Exxon). The newly formed Ethyl Corporation made and sold tetraethyl catalysts to Esso's competitors, who were reluctant to purchase directly from Esso itself. Having General Motors as a co-owner of Ethyl Corporation made their purchases legitimate, because General Motors was a user of many of Esso's competitors' products.

Later, Ethyl formed a joint venture with Dow Chemical to enable Ethyl to have a constant source of supply of bromine. Dow has been involved in numerous joint ventures, such as Dow-Corning, a highly successful venture to produce electrical insulating resins, greases, and silicones. This venture has taken on a total life of its own, and the sponsors of the venture spend virtually no time managing the alliance; they simple reap the rewards. Corning, no stranger to the joint venture process, has created alliances in genetic enzymes, fiber optics, hollow glass building blocks, and—probably its most renowned joint venture—Owens-Corning, which virtually controls the fiberglass insulation market.

In the early 1980s, Goodyear supplied money to Chrysler in the auto maker's darkest hours, so it is no wonder that Chrysler is loyal to Goodyear as a supplier of tires.

Early Retailing Alliances

The alliance process began a period of rapid growth in the retail sector in the 1920s. Wholesalers and retailers began linking up with franchise alliances. To compete against the big retail chains, such as Woolworth's, Ben Franklin stores were established as franchises in 1927. During the Great Depression, Pepsi, Coke, 7-Up, and Royal Crown, all faced with a shortage of capital, used franchises extensively to establish bottling dealerships. This was followed by Rexall and Walgreen drug stores; IGA (Independent Grocers Assocation) to compete against A&P; Western Auto (originally a mail-order house); and Hertz car rentals.

By the 1950s, franchise alliances had exploded. Today, they are responsible for hundreds of thousands of jobs in the United States alone, and account for fully one-third of all retail sales.

In the 1920s and 1930s, Sears (then Sears, Roebuck and Company) established numerous strategic equity partnerships in companies such as DeSoto Paint, Standard Arms, and Whirlpool. Sears took a 20% equity interest in their suppliers, to solidify their long-term relationship, in lieu of a contract for more than 1 year.

The considerable increase in the number of alliances since 1980 reflects the fact that corporations, both large and small, are now becoming more amenable to cooperative strategies, and are again realizing potential that had been demonstrated for many decades before. David Beretta, former Chairman of Uniroyal comments:

> Alliances keep rolling over, taking new forms, transitioning to account for new situations. Corporate liaisons must change to reflect the changing global conditions.[7]

Alliances have evolved into numerous industries throughout the world. The development of the franchise system, the formation of high-tech research and development consortia, and the emergence of supplier strategic alliances are evidence of the progression and evolution of the original joint venture form.

THE JAPANESE *KEIRETSU*

Japanese business culture is rich with formal and informal business alliances. The Japanese have both formal *(keiretsu)* and informal *(shudan)* alliances. The *keiretsu* hold formal legal status. Essentially, they are vertically oriented structures dealing with complex products such as autos and electronics. They lack firm centralized control and rely instead on informal but close coordination for decision making. The head of the *keiretsu* guides the affiliates (the affiliates are not subsidiaries), which supply parts, financing, and marketing. These are organized much like the shipping industry ventures in America during the first half of the 19th century.

The *shudan* are broad-based, informal groups established in trading, industry, finance, and real estate; examples are Mitsui, Mitsubishi, and Sumitomo. Cross-ownership of shares and interlocking directories are common. These strategic alliances demonstrate mutual involvement (but not control) in each other's business, with informal coordination of policy and strategy. *Keiretsu* and *shudan* result in tight working relationships at top echelons, where mutual benefit is understood. Control takes the form of coordination, not subservience.

Assuming a wide variety of relationships, the *keiretsu* and *shudan* are an integral part of most Japanese companies, and they provide a rich opportunity to access additional resources and working relationships.

The difference between the Japanese *keiretsu* and the American alliances is that our liaisons are not structured as tightly as those of the Japanese, who have an advantage in the tight business linkages through which strategic and tactical maneuvering becomes easy. Close personal relationships between top executives in Japan, a fundamental factor in the success of Japanese business, are an important element in the functioning of Japanese alliances.

Coordination in Japan is orchestrated like a fine piece of music—so well orchestrated, in fact, that one American CEO told this story about his experience with a chemical-industry venture in Japan:

> In Japan, there was never excess production capacity. When it was our partner's turn to expand, we did. There was nothing written down, it wasn't in the books, there was nothing official, it was just decided it was our turn—unlike the unstructured competition in this country, where we all expanded at the same time and created a glut on the market, dropping prices, ruining margins, and creating headaches for everyone in the industry. It kept the suppliers happy, it made things economically viable. No wonder Just-In-Time-Inventory works—the Japanese are so coordinated.[8]

WHY NOW—AGAIN?

Why are we seeing such a proliferation of alliances? Many forces are aligning, and this combination of factors is becoming the driving motiviation.

Globalization of markets is certainly one of the important forces at work. Companies are faced with a critical question: Should we form an alliance now and attack our foreign competitors on their turf, or face their army of alliances on our home ground in 3 years?

Numerous companies are answering this question with an aggressive response rather than a defensive posture. Often, their decision is accelerated when local markets stagnate and greener pastures are seen overseas.

Rapid changes in markets, technologies, product life cycles, and competition have caused instability in the strategic environments of many industries. These instabilities increase the element of risk, consequently requiring companies to keep many options open, to allow them to adapt to the winds and tides of change.

The Failure of Mergers and Acquisitions

During the 1970s, U.S. companies were falsely led by the illusion that diversification would be the answer to the control of their destinies. When it became clear that diversification was a dead end, the 1980s acquisition mania followed. Spurred by investment bankers with sources of quick cash, some companies seemed to be buying nearly everything in sight.

Now, the results are in, and the aftermath of acquisition mania has left symptoms of a dreaded disease: overleveraged businesses, indigestion, and a pronouncement by numerous authorities that more than 80% of the deals should never have taken place. Frederick Withington of the management consulting firm of Athur D. Little says, "The vast majority of acquisitions of high-technology companies by large corporations have ended in disaster."[9] One study of acquisitions by General Electric's director of planning, who surveyed a number of acquisitions over the past decade, came to the conclusion that 95% of acquisitions displayed disappointing results. "Most have died of corporate culture shock," adds Withington. The entrepreneurial attitudes, and the speed and flexibility of decision making—the very advantages the large corporation sought to exploit—are often quickly exterminated soon after the acquisition.

Driven by these disasters, many companies are looking toward an alliance as the best alternative. Unfortunately, however, far too many businesses are also viewing alliances as a "quick fix," thereby sowing the seeds for their cooperative ventures to fail for the very same reasons their diversification and acquisition strategies met their demise. However, for the moment, the rush is on, for better or for worse.

Procurement as a Strategic Weapon

An additional motive is the startling fact that, in the past 50 years, goods and services procured from outside vendors have almost tripled, from 20% to nearly 60%, as a proportion of total sales price.[10] Vertical integration has diminished significantly.

Increasingly, companies have learned that technological and production innovation is harder to manage through broad corporate bureaucracy. Smaller and middle-size business entities tend to manage innovation better than behemoths. Highly vertically integrated industries, such as steel and automobiles, became petrified in their ways and faced extinction or change. This ultimatum has led to the strengthening of alliance ties with suppliers, as companies have recognized the strategic value of procured goods and services. In addition to price, speed of delivery, quality, and customization features have become vital factors in the competitive war.

A Cooperative Mood

There are many other relevant factors, as will be discussed in later chapters, but a general spirit of cooperation—a more subtle, less quantifiable influence—seems to be emerging. Beginning in the late 1970s with the growth of quality circles and the quality of working life movement, and then augmented by a decline in labor strife and the reorganization of many companies into more flexible team-oriented operating units, the past decade has produced a stronger acceptance of cooperation as an effective tool for improved performance. Further, with the demise of communism worldwide, we are seeing the end of an era that cast labor, management, and government in a never ending, self-perpetuating trilemma. With these changes, capitalism will no longer define itself in juxtaposition with its opposite, and will take on new and innovative organizational forms.

The combination of the diminution of labor strife and the growth of global competitive forces has also caused governments to reconsider the restrictive use of antitrust litigation. By defining markets as global entities rather than limiting them to national borders, the concept of antitrust has eased the redefinition of corporate cooperation.

THE FUTURE FOR ALLIANCES

Since the late 1970s, the quantity of cooperative ventures and partnerships has increased dramatically, not only in numbers but in scope. What was once a trend limited to a few industries has become increasingly common in virtually every segment of business. Strategic alliances are an important alternative to outright mergers and acquisitions, an alternative that can avoid many problems inherent in these two approaches.

More and more frequently, the strategic alliance is being used as a preacquisition move, a test of the waters on a limited scale to see whether a future acquisition would be beneficial, and, if not, a way to win nevertheless. By taking a small equity position in an ally, a corporation can position itself for a friendly takeover, or, if judged ill-advised in the future, the corporation can simply sell the equity in return for cash.

The decade of the 1980s saw a tenfold increase in the number of cooperative alliances established, according to Venture Economics, which tracked the formation of over 5,000 alliances in 1991.[11] However, they estimate that at least twice that amount were unreported to maintain the hidden competitive advantage. Itsunami, a California alliance tracking firm, saw a $2^{1}/_{2}$ times growth in software partnerships between 1986 and 1990, and similar rates of growth in other high-tech industries.[12] The healthcare industry tends to spawn over 550 alliances per year.

The cooperative process is now redefining the very concept of competition. Collaboration is increasingly replacing confrontation, and a new language of cooperation is being communicated between former antagonists.

New Perspective Needed

Peter Drucker, considered perhaps the world's foremost business authority, has predicted that cooperative partnerships will become the dominant form of business in future decades. These massive changes in the way the world does business require a new way of thinking about business, as well as innovative methods of management.

Business leaders must overcome the tendency to view alliances as simply an adjunct of deal making, a quick fix to plug a hole in a strategic plan, or a new twist on improving vendor quality control. Alliances are part of the "extended" corporation, neither internal nor external, but intimately connected. As such, cooperative ventures need to be treated from a new perspective.

2

Understanding Alliances

Understanding and belief are the first steps toward effective action.

Although business alliances have existed for years, they remain relatively misunderstood. In America, for the most part, they have been the choice of last resort among most CEOs.

THE "CONTROL" FACTOR

In an informal survey of nearly 1,000 top-ranking executives, conducted from 1989 to 1992, representing a cross-section of industries and geographic distribution, the overwhelming concern about alliances was a perceived loss of control.[1] These executives reflected the underlying passion that characterizes the U.S. corporation and differentiates it from many of its European and Asian counterparts. This informal survey similarly reflected a strong aversion to 50/50 joint venture deals, again because of the perceived inability to maintain control. Foreign companies, however, show far less concern about this factor.

Why the fear? Are there any realistic methods of dealing with this dilemma? The answers are intertwined in both corporate cultural traditions and our lack of understanding of the architecture and operational methodologies of the "extended" corporation. For example, because of the overlapping of roles and responsibilities in the Japanese corporation, the Japanese manager is more adept at managing a diverse interdisciplinary team of people than the American manager, who is steeped in a tradition of departmental fragmentation.

A bad experience can easily sour an entire company, especially when all the managers draw the conclusion that alliances just don't work. Corporate culture is not in the business of conducting autopsies on failed ventures, especially when careers may be put on the line once the finger of blame is pointed in someone's direction. The problem is always compounded when neither of the partners has had any significant experience in managing cooperative ventures. The real answer to the control issue is multifaceted, just as the problem itself is multidimensional. Several approaches must be taken:

1. There needs to be a thorough *conceptual understanding of the architecture of alliances* based on the systematic interrelationships among its strategic and operational functions;
2. Executives must clearly grasp the *unique managerial elements of controlling the "extended" corporation,* especially as they are differentiated from traditional control processes;
3. Both companies must enter into alliances with a *mature level of understanding and expectations;* too often the sponsors enter into major league ventures with Little League capabilities;
4. Regardless of the type of alliance, it must be seen as its own *unique organizational entity,* and those charged with its leadership must be familiar with the resources it will require and the nature of adapting it to the winds and tides of changing strategic and operational environments;
5. The process of formation must *not fragment the deal makers from the alliance's operational managers,* and both sponsors must have a clear understanding of the *results they expect,* along with a reasonable *method of measuring* those results on a frequent basis.

These five thrusts should form the basis of any business's strategy to enter the alliance ring and win. Subsequent chapters will address these critical five approaches and provide the bases for effective action.

ALLIANCE ADVANTAGES

Why construct an alliance? What are its real advantages? What factors should a company consider when teaming with another? Peter Drucker maintains that alliances are the most flexible instruments for making "fits out of misfits." But misfits don't have to be the mainstay of alliance creation.

Criteria for Forming Alliances. Companies should enter into alliances in order to concurrently:

Achieve strategic goals;

Reduce risks while increasing rewards;

Leverage precious resources.

If an alliance fails to meet these three criteria, the alliance may not be strategic, nor successful, nor efficient. Alliances created solely for convenience, or operational efficiencies, or to buoy sinking finances, will yield unsatisfactory results.

If an alliance meets these criteria, then the alliance format has numerous advantages over an acquisitions approach, as Figure 2.1 indicates. In fact, in the time it takes to put together one good acquisition, companies can form several alliances and not run the risk of incurring additional debt loads or suffering from an acquisition's most common malady: indigestion caused by incompatible corporate cultures.

Alliances offer certain significant advantages that may not be available through other mechanisms:

- Synergies, by combining strengths from diverse corporate resources;
- Increased speed of operations, particularly when large corporations team up with smaller companies;
- Risk sharing, enabling companies to tackle opportunities that might otherwise be too risky;
- Transfer of technology between companies, to maintain a competitive position in their separate marketplaces;
- Tying up competitors on their own turf without expending enormous sums of money waging a battle;

Figure 2.1   Advantages and Disadvantages of Alliances (Compared to Acquisitions)

ADVANTAGES

- Quicker to form
- More flexible to operate
- Less risky
- Require less cash
- Drain fewer resources from sponsors
- Are relatively easily established
- Enable stretching of financial, managerial, and technical resources

DISADVANTAGES

- Require new control methods
- Require unique management skills
- Require commitment of resources

- Increase in sales by gaining critical market intelligence, access to larger markets resulting from new distribution channels, and closeness to new customers—an aid in product planning;
- Infusion of capital into smaller companies by a larger corporate partner's investment in either stock or research and development contracts;
- Protection of equity in each company, because the many alliance forms do not involve equity dilution investment;
- More rapid adjustment to new technological changes as a result of better access to engineering and marketing information;
- Increase in marketing domains, either vertically or horizontally, by enabling entry into new and otherwise impenetrable markets.

When alliances are managed skillfully, the partners have a wider range of strategic flexibility than when they go it alone.

ALLIANCE DRAWBACKS AND PROBLEMS

As with any business strategy, the alliance has limitations that must be carefully weighed. For most managers, control factors weigh the heaviest, tending to dominate the hearts and minds of most corporate executives. Their ultimate control mechanism—the ability to hire and fire—is totally absent in an alliance.

However, the control factor is really no more than a perception problem, and is not necessarily a reality. With the proper management systems in place, the control problem is easily surmountable.

Because the differences between managing the internal corporation and the "extended" corporation are seldom analyzed, and less frequently taught, they are referred to as the "secret art of alliance management." In Chapter 12, we will explore the methods of controlling an alliance and show how control through coordination can be highly effective.

The most difficult drawback in the alliance process is also the largest problem in acquisition: finding the proper partner. The mating game is very critical, because the wrong match will yield poor or negative results. Fortunately, the process of alliance development, when properly executed (as will be discussed in later chapters), can ensure a high level of certainty of the right match. This process will examine the three dimensions of "fit"—strategy, chemistry, and operations—plus the ways to maintain a win/win environment over the course of time, through proper management techniques. Unlike the accepted methods for making acquisitions, which often have built-in failure mechanisms, alliance development can have an extremely high success rate.

Beyond the control issues and the rules for making decisions, there are several other factors that must be considered:

Competition. Most alliance agreements will stipulate that your firm will not compete directly with the alliance. This may be prudent when the agreement is signed, but your strategic position may change dramatically in the future.

Technology derived from one alliance, unless properly protected, may subsequently be used by a partner for its own purposes or in another alliance with a major competitor. This occurred when Savin split up with Ricoh, and when Canon parted ways with Bell & Howell. Some companies hold on to their newest, most advanced technology, using the prior-generation methods for the alliance until the partners have had sufficient time to build high degrees of trust, thereby inhibiting a poisonous competitive move.

Insurmountable Risks. Although an alliance is designed to reduce the element of risk, some risks are insurmountable, regardless of the care taken in formation of the agreement. This is one of the principal reasons for the failure of technology development ventures. McKinsey & Company has reported failures in this area to be as high as 50%. This percentage seems extraordinarily high, but one must consider that the risk factors were exceedingly high also. As Thomas Edison said after 9,999 attempts at perfecting a filament for the light bulb: "Failure? Why, man, I've gotten a lot of results. I now know several thousand ways that won't work."

When explorations into *new technologies* are coupled with the development of *new products* for *new markets*, it is like solving a triple simultaneous equation with three unknowns. In many technology alliances, the alliances themselves did not necessarily fail; instead, the challenge of the technology was insurmountable, and then the alliance no longer served a purpose.

Strategic Shifts. Alliances are created when two companies recognize that they have inherent weaknesses that are complemented by the other's strengths. After a period of time, one company's weaknesses may no longer exist, and the underpinnings of the alliance may be withdrawn, requiring dissolution or buy-out. Other strategic changes occur as competitors enter or withdraw from markets, or as political, economic, or technological movements occur.

Operational Effectiveness. In one respect, alliances are like any other business venture: Once the right strategy is in place, their success depends on the effectiveness of operational managers. If the selection of managers is wrong, the venture will fail. In an alliance, one partner can be easily lulled into believing the other partner will handle all the problems effectively, especially when the problems are believed to be within the partner's specialized area of expertise and, in fact, they are not.

The biggest operational trap is that CEOs have no idea how sophisticated the operational process will be. Too often, they assume an alliance will either be no different from managing one of their own internal divisions, or will not require much management time at all. They will cut a deal and turn it over to one of their general mangers, who will play it by ear. Then, six months later, when everything starts to unravel, the CEO and general manager will say "Alliances don't work."

Your car wouldn't work if you let it run out of oil and put water in the gas tank. How can anyone expect an alliance to function when it receives no attention or the wrong ingredients? If you want an alliance to work, you've got to give it support and you've got to make commitments. Halfhearted efforts are doomed to failure before they start.

Any alliance will only be a reflection of its sponsors. When teamwork is not functioning internally within one of the sponsors, it will dysfunction within the alliance because the alliance is plagued with a weak foundation.

DISTINCTIONS AND DIFFERENTIATIONS

With the proliferation of alliances has come a very unfortunate confusion in terms. Business magazine writers will refer to a "joint venture" when, upon closer examination, the arrangement is seen to be not a joint venture at all, but something else. It is important to understand the distinctions and differentiations among various alliances, in order to identify the advantages and disadvantages of each form of alliance. Figure 2.2 is a simplified reference guide that will help to clarify these distinctions.

The strategic alliance is the most basic, simple, and straightforward form of cooperative venture. All variants of the strategic alliance—joint ventures, equity partnerships, and franchise alliances—are built on the operating foundation of the strategic alliance. What is absolutely essential to understand is that the basic and fundamental principles for operating any consortium are the same, regardless of the form or the nature of the legal agreements. The nature of the enterprise undertaken, not the form of agreement, determines what type of alliance exists. Many strategic alliances are very informal, having no legal standing other than perhaps a contract to supply a product, components, or services. Frequently, they are consummated with only a simple handshake.

Several key factors must exist for a relationship to be considered an alliance:

1. There must be a *tight operating linkage* between the partners.
2. There must be a true *vested interest in the ally's future*. Each company must recognize that its future growth is intimately connected to the success of the partner.
3. An alliance is fundamentally a *strategic affair*, with long-term time horizons and significant competitive advantages. Organizational relationships for tactical purposes are not alliances.

Figure 2.2 Differences among Ventures

ALLIANCE DEFINITIONS

Strategic alliances, the most simple and basic of all alliances, are informal business relationships characterized by:

- Tight operating linkages, such as cross-training, product development coordination, long-term contracts based on quality, not just price;
- Mutual vested interest in each other's future;
- Long-term strategic orientation;
- Top-rank support; frequency of contact at top and middle levels;
- Reciprocal relationships sharing strengths, information, and mutual advantages;
- Coordinative management styles organized around collaboration, not hierarchical power.

Equity partnerships are one level more involved than basic alliances. They have all the characteristics of a strategic alliance, plus either:

- Minority equity stakes (usually 5% to 15%, sometimes larger), often with options or preemptive rights for more stock purchases, *or*
- Informal joint ventures, which legally establish a third independent entity but operationally do not form a separately managed organization.

Franchise alliances are systems of multiple alliances in which the partners are linked together through interlocking license agreements (the typical form is a parent with multiple smaller geographic franchisees or two equal cross-licensors). The agreements grant:

- Rights to offer, sell, or distribute goods and services, often with the cross-obligation to purchase goods in return;
- Master licenses that provide long-term implementation assistance, plus access to new products and future technologies.

Joint ventures are formalized alliances uniting two or more separate organizations and resulting in:

- The creation of a new separate business entity;
- The allocation of ownership, operational responsibilities, and financial risks and rewards to each sponsor, while preserving their separate identities/autonomy;
- Staffing by a separate management team.

"Acquisition joint ventures" are a hybrid version whereby one company purchases a 50% interest in an existing subsidiary division of another company, which is then spun off as a separate joint venture corporation.

4. There must be *top-rank support* for an alliance to truly exist. Alliances formed solely by middle management tend to be relatively short-lived, tactical in nature, and ineffective. Additionally, there must be frequent contact between the top ranks and the middle ranks.
5. With some notable exceptions, the management style of interaction tends to be *highly coordinative* and *collaborative*. Unless the venture is commanded by one superior company with the consent of the other, sharing and codetermination tend to be the predominant style.

Alliances can take on many forms during their lifetime. For example, Honeywell had an equity partnership in Japan's Yamatake dating from 1922, with a brief hiatus during the Second World War. Recently, Honeywell sold its equity at a handsome profit, but maintains a very close, strategic working relationship with Yamatake.

OEM Relationships.   Frequently, the question is raised: Are OEM (original equipment manufacturer) relationships strategic alliances? The answer is: Sometimes. Figure 2.3 demonstrates some of the differentiations between OEM and strategic alliances. Most OEM arrangements start off as tactical relationships, with purchase contracts that may run for a year. Often, the following year, the contract will be renewed with new terms

Figure 2.3   Original Equipment Manufacturing (OEM) Relationships

O.E.M. TACTICAL RELATIONSHIPS vs. STRATEGIC ALLIANCES

Factor	Tactical Relationship	Strategic Alliance
Time Frame	Short/Indefinite /Renewable	Long Term
Relationship	Superior/Subordinate Purchaser/Supplier	Leader/Teammate Purchaser/Supplier
Information Flow	One Way	Two Way
Product/Service Improvement	Defined by Contract	Ever-Changing, Fluid
Control	Traditional Hierarchy	Multi-Disciplinary "Teamwork"
Primary Objective	Price	Quality, Price, Timing
Profit	Buyer Controlled	Mutually Controlled
Benefit	Win/?	Win/Win

and conditions, and, after several years of working closely, the OEM arrangement begins to transform from a tactical relationship to a strategic alliance. Once strong top- and middle-level interaction occurs and the purchaser looks to the supplier for more than price benefits, an alliance is emerging. However, it is always best for both companies to acknowledge this relationship and guide its direction, rather than let it unfold unsystematically, with a strong possibility that unmet expectations might arise between the partners.

Sales Reps. Sometimes referred to as a strategic partnership, the relationship between many small manufacturers and their sales representatives is more often than not a tactical relationship operating from year to year. Some dealer/distributor networks qualify as strategic alliances if they are truly strategic, long-term relationships aimed at using the manufacturer's engineering and production strengths and the dealer/distributor's marketing and sales strengths.

Financial Investments. A strategic alliance is not created by simply making a passive capital investment in another company. Money is not strategy, and effective strategy does not necessarily translate into financial returns. Only when the investment bonds two companies together in a mutually beneficial strategic union is an alliance formed. Therefore, investors and venture capitalists seldom qualify as true alliance partners. Nor do contractor/vendor or contractor/subcontractor arrangements qualify as alliances. In a similar manner, alliances are not necessarily related to such internal strategies within large corporations as "internal venturing," "intrapreneurship," or "strategic business units," unless there is a clear alliance formed.

FRANCHISE ALLIANCES

McDonald's has a very wide variety of thoroughbred alliances in its stable. The McDonald's strategy is to build a presence in a broad cross-section of global markets. McDonald's spent years establishing a site in Moscow, which was structured as a joint venture. The company vertically integrated in Russia, as it had done in Australia, by owning its own farms. In Thailand, the Golden Arches were created through a joint venture with a Thai investment group. The joint venture holds the master franchise license, thus enabling McDonald's, as co-owner of the joint venture, to exert greater control over the fast-food sites because it is an active participant. The result is stronger quality control in a region that is unfamiliar with franchise management methods.

McDonald's has had a long-term strategic alliance with Martin Brower, a food purveyor, dating back to the early days when Ray Kroc needed

---

Trap

Watch Out When Referring to "Partnerships": Avoid using the term *partnership* unless you truly mean it. The word has very strong legal implications regarding your ability to incur legally binding commitments on the part of your partner, and vice versa.

Recently, one very large U.S. corporation had told one of its suppliers that it wanted to engage in a cooperative partnership with its vendors. The supplier made major capital investments based on this commitment. When the market changed unexpectedly, the large corporation canceled its orders and the supplier successfully sued based on the supposition that a partnership existed. Use the term *alliance* instead.

---

help starting his business. It is reputed that there are still no written contracts; McDonald's trusts Martin Brower and expects that all food will be the highest quality, at the lowest price, and delivered on time.

In many countries, it is expected that the franchise alliance leader will participate more as a joint venture partner than as a hands-off licensee, according to Jack Hellriegel, President of International Franchise Management. Many foreign banks will insist on the franchisor's co-guaranteeing such things as finance notes for the franchisee's purchases of equipment, further fusing the bond between the partners.

The typical retail-style franchise alliances are among the most sophisticated of all alliance structures, according to Hellriegel. He states:

> It is inherently an American device which has been effectively exported throughout the world. The Japanese, for example, have embraced and embodied the American franchise alliance very easily. Now there are hundreds of different American franchises in Japan, with over 4,000 7-Eleven units in that country, and hundreds of Mr. Donuts and Dunkin' Donuts, among many others. . . . because of the clarity of roles and responsibilities between the parent and the individual alliance units, the system is relatively easily managed, no matter what the international culture. Teamwork, effective communications, and a long-term perspective are paramount. Success is built on the premise of mutual independence, capitalizing on the parent's organizational, technical, marketing, and financial strengths, and the franchisee's willingness to contribute capital, entrepreneurial energy, and share of risk taking. What is truly exemplary about the franchise alliance is the mutual commitment to each other's success and growth. The foundation of the franchise is a permanent win/win orientation.[2]

Other forms of franchise alliances tend to be more balanced. Instead of having a parent and numerous franchisees, they have cross-licensing agreements between relatively equal partners. These agreements might cover exclusive rights to products, and territories for expansion of product lines, in return for noncompete terms. In the high-technology industry, value-added resellers (VARS) are another variant of the franchise alliance.

JOINT VENTURES

When a new, separate, independent business entity is formed, this is properly called a joint venture alliance. The joint venture can be a totally new business unit, or a joint acquisition, or a jointly owned spin-out of an existing division, or a jointly owned merger of two spin-out subsidiary divisions. An example of the latter was the "dual spin-out" of General Motors' hydramatic transmission division and Chrysler's spin-out of its four-wheel drive division into a jointly owned, merged corporation.

Of all the alliances formed, less than 10% tend to be joint ventures.

PREACQUISITION ALLIANCES

Often, an alliance will be part of a long-term exit strategy to sell a business unit or to exit from an industry. For example, when Wells Rich, an advertising company, and France's BDDP formed a strategic equity partnership in 1989, they exchanged minority stock positions in the two companies. This gave the French a strong entry into the American advertising business for their French clients, and gave the American company a reciprocal advantage. A year-and-a-half later, it was made known that Mary Wells, one of the American partners, was retiring from the business and Wells Rich was acquired by BDDP, after testing the issues of operational integration.

THE STRATEGIC SPECTRUM

In my work with companies, too often the first question heard is "How do we structure this deal?" Quickly, deal makers want to jump into a form or structure, without adequately understanding the driving strategic imperatives or the operational functions. In an alliance (and in most other deals, for that matter) the first questions about structure should seek to

---

Tip

Alliance Similarities: Regardless of the form of the cooperative alliances, they are all part of the "extended" corporation; as such, their strategic and operational management principles are all similar.

---

match the right strategic and operational "fit" to the right structure. I have examined too many failed joint ventures and acquisitions where the deal should have been structured as a simple licensing agreement, or as a contracting manufacturing agreement, or as a basic strategic alliance. In the rush to lend a faulty air of sophistication to the deal, it was designed with the wrong structure, with often tragic results.

One of the central reasons for the wrong choice of structure is an inadequate method of conceptualizing organizational form to match corporate strategy. Methods are often, at best, a rough-hewn, helter-skelter approach akin to reaching into a grab-bag for the appropriate structural option for a deal.

To counteract the grab-bag methodology, the strategic spectrum was created which groups all structural options into a range of related forms (see Figure 2.4), from "external" relationships to "extended" alliances to "internal" organizations. In our work with U.S. companies, executives have said this is one of the most helpful frameworks for matching *form* to *functional objectives* and for understanding how to design a *flexible transition* from one form to another related form.

The strategic spectrum is a very valuable tool. It groups various business structures into families with similar characteristics, and it guides the strategist into easy transitions from one structure to the next. Moreover, it becomes clear to managers where the internal corporation ends and the "extended" corporation begins.

The understanding of the strategic spectrum can be put into another perspective when we examine the way in which a company progresses through its stages of growth. For example, a small, local business typically begins expanding internally and then couples the internal expansion with a series of external relationships, perhaps establishing vendors and a network of sales representatives in various territories. As the company continues to grow, if it has some valuable technology or process, it might license its proprietary process in return for cash to

Figure 2.4   The Strategic Spectrum

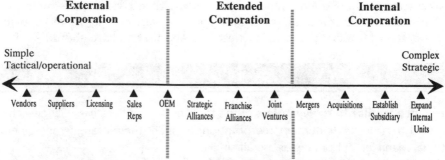

fund its expansion, even though it may be mortgaging its future. These are simple, if somewhat tactical moves. The left side of Figure 2.4 shows this process.

However, rather than continue the growth process incrementally across the spectrum, many companies are induced to jump rashly across the spectrum, such as purchasing another company, in a deluded drive toward diversification. Or, they are induced to invest in a subsidiary, set up by a foreign government to have great financial attractiveness, without really understanding the culture, or the markets, or the way business is conducted. The results of these quantum jumps are, more often than not, quantum disasters. (I made this mistake myself, after wiser souls had advised me not to—everyone was into acquisitions, and it looked so attractive, especially with 90% financing.)

Saner minds may opt for an incremental approach, moving only a step or two across the spectrum, and then testing the integration of the companies, and learning the new markets—digesting rather than gulping.

MANAGING THE EXTENDED CORPORATION

Peter Drucker was perhaps the first to foresee this silent revolution and describe the "extended" corporation. In 1982, he predicted that, in future decades, the business world will see a proliferation of autonomous corporate partners linked in a confederation rather than through common ownership. Businesses forming these confederations will need to deal person-to-person, rather than level-to-level, to compensate for the cultural differences between partners. These partnerships will be highly

Figure 2.5   Style of Operations

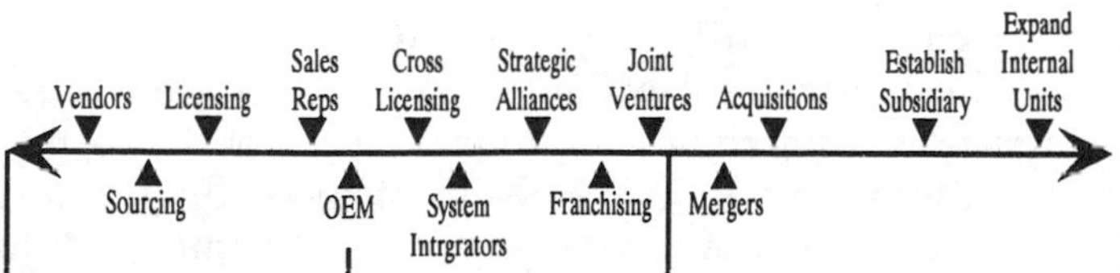

Spectrum of relationships (left to right):
Vendors, Licensing, Sales Reps, Cross Licensing, Strategic Alliances, Joint Ventures, Acquisitions, Establish Subsidiary, Expand Internal Units

(below the spectrum): Sourcing, OEM, System Intrgrators, Franchising, Mergers

	External	Extended	Internal
TYPE OF INTER-CORPORATE RELATIONSHIPS	External	Extended	Internal
CONTROL STYLE	Legalistic & Contractual	Collaborative & Flexible	Commanding & Directive
MANAGEMENT STYLE	Formal	Coordinative	Hierarchical

specialized in a narrow range of products, ensuring that the people involved talk a similar "language," regardless of their corporate or national cultural backgrounds. Drucker added that, because no one company will be the owner or sole parent, no one will be in total control. The relationship will be one of mutual dependence rather than domination or subordination. The critical skill in managing these companies will be the ability to coordinate rather than command.[3] Clearly, his prediction has become reality.

Figure 2.5 illustrates the differences, along the strategic spectrum, of the style of operations for each of the configurations. Each of the three modes of organization—internal, extended, and external—requires a shift to a different method of management or leadership, a new perspective on the business, and a major shift in values.

THE BOUNDARIES OF THE "CORPORATE CASTLE"

Joseph Badarocco, author of *The Knowledge Link*,[4] compares the traditional corporation that arose in post-Second World War America to a "citadel," a medieval fortress. At the center of the citadel exists a sphere of managerial authority, which has defined four boundaries between the interior of the citadel and the outside world. Those four walls are: (1) administrative procedures defining lines of hierarchical authority; (2) financial mechanisms to define assets, profits, and flow of funds; (3) social cultures that have prescribed values, behaviors, and reward structures; and (4) contractual procedures with external suppliers, based on legalistic approaches that sharply define rights and obligations. With the increased transfer of knowledge in an information-based economy, the walls of the citadel have become increasingly permeable.

The concept of corporations with castlelike boundaries is changing with the proliferation of a variety of new alliances. The term *extended corporation* bridges the gap between the internal and the external. The movement from the traditional bimodal (internal–external) corporate concept to a trimodal (internal–extended–external) concept requires a fundamental reconstruction of our traditional model of the corporation.

To achieve success in the realm of the extended corporation will require a new vision of the purpose of management. Middle managers, familiar with the bureaucratic departments in the corporate castle, must become team coordinators, both internally and externally and, more importantly, their role must shift from being essentially *tactical* to being more *strategic*. Furthermore, the new, innovative methods of control must be designed to manage an informal network of organizational relationships based less on power and financial clout and more on knowledge and flexibility.

3

How to Use an Alliance

The only impossibility in this world is gaining access to a closed mind.

—Anonymous

Choosing among the three growth strategies—internal growth, acquisitions, and alliances—is not easy, and there is no single approach that outweighs the others in all circumstances. To prescribe an alliance for every situation would be lunacy. Dow Chemical knows that fact well; Dow only chooses an alliance when there is no better alternative.

PRECONDITIONS FOR SUCCESS

The checklist in Figure 3.1 will help the strategist to sense whether the climate is supportive. If the partners can answer Yes to the characteristics in Figure 3.1, their alliance has a reasonable chance of success. Remember one key rule: The higher the future ambiguity, the higher the probability of failure. Alliances are the stepchild of uncertain risks and opportunities. Uncertainty breeds ambiguity, and ambiguity is the seed of business failures. Do everything possible to reduce the risk of the unexpected's ruining your success.

CHOOSING A GROWTH STRATEGY

How does a company make a decision as to what form its growth should take? There is no single right answer for every company. But there is a method to attaining the best, if not the right decision.

Figure 3.1   Checklist: Preconditions for Success

Alliances are most advisable when conditions are right both within your company and within your target industry. The more "yes" answers you can give to the following statements, the better your chance of success.

Company Conditions

_____ Our company has something very valuable to offer to a prospective partner *and* our company has something valuable to gain from another company.

_____ Our company has a cooperative corporate culture.

_____ Our company has insufficient resources *or* our company has prominent but not debilitating strategic weaknesses.

_____ Our company desires a leadership position in the marketplace.

_____ Our company knows that pursuit of a strategic objective is too risky to undertake independently.

_____ Our company is very doubtful of its ability to complete an important project or to obtain customer acceptance of a new product without the support or name recognition of another company.

Style of Operations

_____ The prospective partners have similar goals, rewards, methods of operations, and corporate cultures.

_____ Both companies have a similar style of decision making.

Support

_____ The chief executive officers of both partners are in full support of the alliance.

_____ There is no threat of unfriendly takeover, which could jeopardize trust and a cooperative working relationship. (This should not prevent discussion of a buy-out of the venture by one of the partners.)

Industry Conditions

_____ High capital costs result in the need to share financial risks.

_____ Rapid changes occur in technology, customer traits, and the need for product differentiation.

_____ Decline or maturation of a industry requires consolidation to protect market share.

_____ High entry costs or entry risks make risk sharing advisable.

_____ Major competitive realignments (mergers, acquisitions, foreign entry into the market) are occurring or there is uncertainty about potential responses by major competitors.

_____ The market is expected to respond positively to the "best product," which can only be produced by a superb team combining excellent resources.

_____ There is a need for rapid market entry and acceptance.

Time Perspectives

_____ Both prospective partners take a "long term" view.

Financial Goals

_____ The goals of the alliance are not driven primarily by quarterly earnings.

The strategist must examine a range of strategic options, which then should be measured in terms of their related risks and rewards. Rewards can be measured in a variety of ways—market share, cash flow, variety of product line, or organizational growth, to name a few. Risks generally include political, monetary, technological, partner, and market risks, among others.

For many large companies in the 1980s, there had been an implicit assumption that the best growth strategy was through mergers, acquisitions, and establishing subsidiaries. This scenario, promoted more by investment bankers than by careful strategic planners or sharp business managers, imagined or assumed that the risk–reward relationship, when plotted graphically (see Figure 3.2), would provide greater rewards for acquisition deals, despite the marginally increased risk.

However, the risk-reward relationship for every deal will have its own unique "signature," differing dramatically in reality, from company to company, from market to market, and from industry to industry.

Other examples of possible risk–reward scenarios are demonstrated in Figure 3.3, where a mid-spectrum cooperative strategy would be best,

Figure 3.2   Risk–Reward Analysis

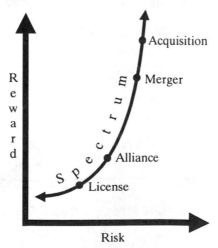

Using the STRATEGIC SPECTRUM
Example 1

In a theoretical environment, the risk-reward relationship might look like this:

This analysis favors choosing a merger or acquisition

Figure 3.3   Risk–Reward Analysis: **Figure 3.4   Risk–Reward Analysis:**
Mid-Spectrum Cooperative Strategy   **Low-Risk Licensing Strategy**

Using the STRATEGIC SPECTRUM   Using the STRATEGIC SPECTRUM
            Example 2   Example   3

   In this example, an alliance   In this example, a low-risk licensing
strategy would be best.   strategy would be best.

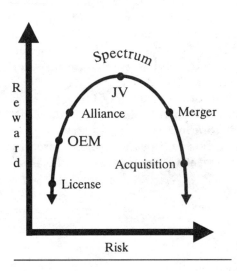   

and Figure 3.4 which points to a simple license agreement as the most
effective strategy.

   The corporate strategist must consider the risk–reward scenario that
most accurately describes the interaction among the company, the competitive advantage, the customers, and the value of various strategies. The
proper strategic objective is to choose the option yielding the highest reward for the least risk, given the available resources and the relationships
between the companies. This approach takes into account *risk, reward, resources,* and past *relationships.*

   What are some of the pros and cons of alternative strategies other than
alliances?

THE SEDUCTIVE LURE OF A START-UP SUBSIDIARY

The establishment of a start-up subsidiary can be a costly and time-
consuming gambit requiring a developed product line and distribution
systems that are properly matched in advance to local market tastes. For
years, economic development officials, courting U.S. corporate executives

on the idea of establishing subsidiary companies, have advocated the building of efficient new plants subsidized heavily by government loan guarantees and staffed by local workers whose pay is underwritten by job tax credits.

This seduction strategy is as alluring as the sirens' song in Homer's *Odyssey* and is equally fraught with risk. It makes sense only if a substantial amount of corporate revenue now comes from a specific overseas market. Intel, an American corporation that is strong in the European computer and semiconductor market, has chosen to build a plant in Ireland. The reason: 25% of Intel's current revenue already originates from Europe, and Intel knows Europeans would rather buy from local manufacturers.

For many companies, a new subsidiary is faced with very difficult problems, usually unanticipated. Market tastes in one country can be totally different from those in another. Levis at first made a splash in Japan, but soon a Japanese competitor recognized that the Oriental physique is different from the Western, and jean dimensions could be improved on. The American company quickly lost market share when it failed to respond to the difference.

Similarly, Europe, while it is becoming a unified economic system, will remain a tremendously fragmented set of markets, for generations. The French will not like the instant coffee the English prefer, nor will the Germans change their tastes in engineering. Consider the experience of Nypro, a $100 million U.S. plastics manufacturer. In 1975, Nypro went into France with a 100% acquisition. According to Gordon Lankton, Nypro's CEO:

> It wasn't long before all our French customers were letting us know they weren't about to do business with an American subcontractor. Furthermore, the French labor bureau began informing us that the rules were different in France. If a business downturn occurs, the French labor bureau calls the shots.[1]

Ultimately, Nypro expanded globally with a series of alliances in Europe and Asia. Langton explained:

> Nypro has learned that there is a big world out there. It's a world we need to be a part of, but we can't do it alone. We only have $100 million in sales. If we could afford a staff of experienced international lawyers, financial analysts, and multilingual business executives, we might be able to do it alone. But I doubt we would want to.[2]

TRYING A MERGER OR ACQUISITION

A merger might make a great deal of sense when two companies can have a much more dominant share of the market and take advantage of economies of scale by joining together as one. But, as many executives have learned, mergers may be far more successful on paper than in reality. Corporate identity means far more than ego gratification to a CEO. Corporations are often wise to protect the highly successful culture that has made them profitable. Changing corporate culture is a far more difficult, costly, and time-consuming process than most strategists can conceive. On the other hand, an alliance seeks to capitalize on cultural differences and can often protect a winning corporation from diluting its effectiveness.

In instances when a merger might trigger an antitrust case, the alliance may serve as an equally effective alternative.

Acquisitions can be an effective tool if the strategic and operational "fit" is correct, and if the acquiring company has the ability to control the "aftershock." Acquisitions may also be a preferable alternative when one company needs better locations for distributing its product or service, larger facilities for production, additional resources or sources of supply, greater opportunities for expansion, and so on. The deciding condition is frequently the need of one company to completely control the resources of another.

When major strategic and operational overlaps make the two companies more similar than they are different, and when the corporate cultures can be assimilated, the acquisition makes great sense. However, if a smaller acquisition target is driven by a motive to double or triple sales in a relatively short period of time, and the acquiring company is substantially larger in sales, such energy and enthusiasm for growth may likely end in frustration for the small company and minimal impact on the bottom line for the larger corporation.

When one company has the financial resources to acquire another company and make a bold strategic move for market leadership as well, the acquisition alternative may be worthwhile; but if financial and human resources are limited, an alliance is advisable.

Generally, acquisitions make the most sense when in your core business, but alliances are better when entering new markets or new technologies, or fields outside the core business. In the chemical industry, U.S. companies are twice as likely to form a joint venture with a foreign partner than they are to make an international acquisition. They are, however, even more likely to select another U.S. company for total acquisition.

Large corporations that have stock selling well below book value, and are highly leveraged in debt, are often positioned out of the acquisition market. For them, the alliance strategy has the clear edge.

Many CEOs have learned that the alliance strategy is a good preliminary step prior to an acquisition. In the rushed momentum of trying to consummate an acquisition before a competitor moves in, many acquisitions have been abject failures suffering from indigestion and lack of effective integration.

If an alliance will not work, it's more than likely an acquisition would not have worked. But the lesson costs far less with an alliance. Typically, the cost is only 25% to 35% of the cost of a doomed acquisition. When Arco's joint venture with Sweden's Ericsson was unsuccessful in penetrating the

Tip

Alliances Are Less Risky: If an alliance fails, it probably would also have failed as an acquisition. But the lesson will be learned far less expensively with the alliance, and the process of recovery will be far more rapid than with an acquisition.

office products market in the mid-1980s, the losses were so small that the press hardly bothered to report it. Compare this with Exxon's disastrous office products acquisition and integration strategy during the same period, which eventually cost over $1 billion in losses before abandonment. Exxon learned to its dismay that no amount of gold could successfully integrate 15 high-tech companies in a market Exxon knew little about. To add insult to injury, the press had a field day broadcasting the failure.

All too often, we read of an acquisition that looked good on paper, only to learn several years later that the acquisition failed to meet the financial performance standards established initially. In such cases, an alliance with a future buy-out clause might have been a more desirable course of action. (This would be highly unrealistic in the case of a hostile takeover, however.)

Critical Flaw

Those who choose to pursue the acquisition mode should beware of one critical flaw that is inherently built into the acquisition process. By design, acquisitions in publicly held companies purposely exclude middle managers from active engagement, to limit the chance of insider trading problems. As will be seen in Chapters 7 through 9, the right architectural design process for an alliance actively *includes key middle managers,* who serve as one of the best insurance policies imaginable to check operational "fit."

LICENSING AS AN OPTION

Licensing enables a company that owns proprietary technology or know-how to sell its knowledge to another company.

Generally, a licensing agreement stipulates what specific knowledge is being sold, the locations in which this knowledge can be used, and for how long the knowledge is authorized for use. Typically, a licensing agreement will be purchased for an up-front fee paid by the acquirer, who will then pay royalty fees in the future, based on a percentage of future sales. A great deal of technology and know-how can be licensed very simply.

Most companies will arrange for consulting and training assistance to be included in the licensing fee. For smaller companies with proprietary technology, a licensing deal with a large corporation can enable the smaller company to recoup its investment rather quickly.

Many companies have learned the hard way that licensing agreements are often instruments to mortgage their future away, especially when a foreign company purchases the license, then improves on the technology, lets the license expire once they have created their own processes, and eventually enters the original licensor's market territory as a competitor.

Most licensing agreements are one-way sales agreements, not true alliances. Licensing can become a cooperative venture, particularly when there is a *cross-licensing* and/or *cross-marketing* agreement that commits both companies to sharing risks and rewards for mutually strategic purposes, thus preventing the licensee from becoming a future competitor.

Many alliances that have started with one-way licensing agreements or OEM agreements have later advanced into strategic alliances as the next stage of cooperation.

THE OEM OPTION

The term *original equipment manufacturer* (OEM) was originally coined in the auto industry, among suppliers of equipment to the auto giants. An OEM, such as Goodyear, would capitalize on its unique relationship as vendor to the car manufacturer by advertising the relationship in the auto after-market.

Many manufacturers looking to increase sales will serve on an OEM basis for a large marketer. Under an OEM agreement, the manufacturer produces the product, and the marketer uses its own brand name. Sears is a notable example of a purchaser of OEM products. Appliances are branded with the Kenmore name, tools with the Craftsman name, and auto batteries with the Diehard name.

An OEM normally begins as a vendor or subcontractor relationship for tactical purposes. However, after a period of close cooperation and coordination, the OEM relationship can grow into a strategic alliance.

A problem can arise when one of the companies in an OEM relationship sees the arrangement as a vendor arrangement and the other sees it as a strategic alliance. In one case I was asked to unscramble, the expectations of the two companies were so different, and personalities had become rubbed so raw, that the vendor nearly lost their contract in an honorable attempt to serve the purchaser better by trying to act as an alliance partner, which the purchaser didn't want.

This conflict illustrates how an OEM arrangement can be either an *external* vendor relationship or an *extended* strategic alliance. The important point is that both companies should be clear about the nature of their cooperation.

TACTICAL RELATIONSHIPS

A number of cousins of the strategic alliance bear a resemblance to alliances, but do not qualify because they do not serve in a strictly strategic manner. For the most part, they are *tactical relationships,* much like the early stage of the OEM relationship. Over the course of time, some tactical relationships between companies grow to become true strategic alliances.

One of the oldest and simplest forms of tactical relationship is between a manufacturer and an independent manufacturer's sales representative or agency. Both parties sign an agreement outlining the principles, commissions, supply schedules, support, and so on. The manufacturer spreads the risk by paying the rep a commission only when the product is sold, and the rep is rewarded handsomely by a sales commission, usually ranging from 6% to 10%. Rep agreements are generally cancelable on 30 days' notice, and are written to stay in place for 1 year; however, many have remained in existence for over a generation as family-owned manufacturers have maintained an ongoing relationship with the next generation of manufacturer's reps.

Pall Filter Corporation, founded after the Second World War, uses technology first developed for nuclear weaponry. Pall began its growth utilizing manufacturer's sales representatives. However, given the very technical aspects of the sales process, plus the need to customize many orders, the sales force became more and more specialized, and dedicated exclusively to Pall.

Over the past 40 years, Pall has grown to be a $600 million company, with consistently high levels of profitability. Rather than abandon its relationship with this highly qualified group of dedicated independent sales reps, Pall has continued over the years to build their capabilities with commissions that are far superior to any they would receive from competitors, coupled with strong technical training. Gradually, these sales reps have dropped other lines and become exclusive dealers and distributors of Pall's products. What began as a tactical relationship has now taken on all the strategic and operational characteristics of a franchise sales alliance.

There are numerous other forms of alliance in virtually every industry, from health care to real estate to accounting to insurance. Creativity is rampant when alliances are the goal.

COOPERATION: AN EFFECTIVE COMPETITIVE WEAPON?

Cooperation can be a highly effective form of competition, as General Electric has realized with its CFM aircraft engine joint venture with France's Snecma. CFM International not only has orders worth billions of dollars from European customers, but also holds major contracts with the

U.S. military. The cooperative venture's competitive edge cuts advantageously on both sides of the Atlantic.

Inherently, many foreign business cultures are more amenable to the cooperative venture as an initial overture than to the acquisition. Better to have a positive trading relationship first, assess the business's real potential, and gain the confidence and understanding of current management, without the risk of a costly acquisition. Britain's Jaguar was far more receptive to General Motors' proposed equity alliance than to Ford's hostile takeover. Later, if signs are positive and both sides are willing, the alliance can be transformed into an increased investment share or an acquisition.

Triggering Conditions

Every industry in the world is undergoing realignments as a result of the globalization of markets and revolutions in technology. Major realignments have occurred in the telecommunications field, and a phenomenal number of new alliances now link partners in telecommunications, publishing, computers, and banking.

For years, chemical companies, such as Dow, Hercules, Olin, and Arco, have used the joint venture to build new plants throughout the world. When shortages of raw materials threaten their future production, it has been common practice for them to form a joint venture to secure future sources of supply. Figure 3.5 describes the typical conditions that trigger alliances.

Figure 3.5   Alliance-Triggering Conditions

When is the right time to begin moving into the global market? Typical conditions triggering the decision to form an alliance are:

- When a company is ready to penetrate a foreign market more fully, but lacks the management resources, capital, or full product line to start an overseas marketing company;
- When overseas competitors are positioning themselves to capture a greater market share;
- As a preemptive move to keep a foreign competitor tied up on its home turf, so that it cannot move into the domestic market;
- To create a permanent distribution channel without expending exorbitant amounts of cash;
- When foreign government policies prohibit control of their domestic corporations by a U.S. corporation, or when foreign regulations require local content, forcing a full or partial shift of production overseas to hold market share;
- To establish an off-shore production site to offset costs of shipping, exchange rate fluctuations, or to become closer to sources of material supply.

Impact of Currency Valuations

Changes in international valuations of currency often stimulate strategic realignments through alliances. When the value of the U.S. dollar began falling relative to the value of the Japanese yen in 1986, Japanese products became more expensive in America, and, in the U.S. tire market, Japanese tires quickly lost their competitive edge. However, these changes also made it more affordable for the Japanese to purchase *both* U.S. goods *and* U.S. companies.

Bridgestone tire, a Japanese firm, lacking an effective U.S. source of retail distribution, approached its competitor, Firestone (which owned a worldwide manufacturing network as well as 3,500 independent tire dealers) with a joint venture that had some characteristics that resembled both a merger and an acquisition.

The first step in forming the venture required Firestone, whose business was divided about two-thirds in the tire manufacturing business and one-third in diversified rubber products and retailing, to transfer its tire assets to a subsidiary corporation.

Firestone then sold 75% of its interests in the tire subsidiary to Bridgestone, making the subsidiary a joint venture corporation, owning and managing Firestone's worldwide tire business. In return, Firestone received $1.25 billion in cash. Sixty percent of the cash ($750 million) came from Bridgestone, and the joint venture borrowed the other 40% ($500 million).

Upon the conclusion, Firestone received an infusion of $1.25 billion, while retaining 100% of its diversified product divisions and 25% of its Tire Division. Bridgestone acquired a 75% interest in a much-needed worldwide tire manufacturing and distribution system.

Whenever the dollar is strong, American companies are at a disadvantage in selling overseas because their prices are not competitive. Under these circumstances, it is often more profitable for the American company to send its raw materials to the processing plant of its Asian, Latin American or European partner, where they may be converted into a finished product and ultimately sold at a more competitive price. The American company then receives a further benefit of the alliance because the product can be sold on the European market as a European-made product—a real advantage in a culture where business prefers to support its brethren!

When the dollar is weak, the American partner in the alliance has competitive price advantage with its foreign sales force.

Multiplying Your Impact

An international alliance generally enables a company to establish a marketing, manufacturing, or service delivery presence in a foreign country. Knowledge of government regulations, the ability to cut through red tape, and access to local markets permit the foreign corporation to combine its sales savvy with the expertise and resources of its partner, to produce success.

Whether a company is small or large, this strategy can be used to create multiple international alliances rapidly enough to capture otherwise unattainable markets. As an example, Tri-Wall Corporation, a manufacturer of corrugated paper boxes, is a small corporation located in upstate New York. Tri-Wall was doing $3 million in sales in the mid-1960s. Its chief asset was an excellent triple-layer corrugating technology that would withstand pressures greater than those exerted on wooden crates. With only limited funds, Tri-Wall first tried licensing its technology for 1 year to the industry giant, International Paper. Bernard Roth, then Tri-Wall's Vice President of Marketing, commented:

> We thought with all their size, money, manufacturing plants, and marketing clout we would be very successful. But we met nothing but frustration. International Paper had a very large sales force that was used to selling bulk quantities of paper. As a commodity-oriented company, they knew nothing about selling a specialty product in a niche market. They rejected our offer to help train their sales force. And in the first year, they couldn't sell a single box. We had to take the license back and look for an alternative. Given our limited financial resources, we began establishing a series of joint ventures.[3]

Roth traveled the roads of Europe, the Middle East, and Asia in search of partners. He looked for smaller, niche-market companies with local manufacturing capability, to match with Tri-Wall. Eventually, he established six deals, covering the major markets across the world. Tri-Wall provided the technology and sales support, and local manufacturers provided the knowledge of local markets and production. Rapidly, Tri-Wall penetrated market after market with partners in England, Germany, Israel, Japan, and Australia.

For its niche product, profits were more than double the average for Tri-Wall's commodity competitors. Sales quickly doubled, then tripled, then quadrupled. Within 10 years, Tri-Wall's sales had grown eight times, and, despite a series of hostile and friendly acquisitions within the industry during the 1970s and 1980s, each of the joint ventures survived, even when direct competitors ended up owning the parents of the alliance.

Capitalizing on Economic Policy

Political–economic development policy has also spurred the use of the international venture. In Japan and Mexico, for many years, the joint venture was the only form in which these governments would allow a U.S. corporate presence. Japan and Mexico no longer require local investment, but dozens of other Latin American, African, Eastern European, and Asian countries still operate under commercial policies of this type. Rather than being viewed as restrictive, the impact of these economic development policies can be highly positive in creating driving forces for companies to unite for their common interests.

Uniroyal, for instance, combined with a local Mexican firm to enter the Mexican petrochemical market. Mexican government regulations at that time required that domestic firms control 60% of each company in the petrochemical industry, hardly surprising in a country whose economy depends very heavily on oil. Uniroyal was still able to reap 40% of the profits while it developed critically important knowledge of the Mexican market through the joint venture arrangement. Acquiring knowledge is clearly reflected in an observation of Alexander Giacco, former Chairman of Hercules Chemical:

> With traditional domestic joint ventures, you banded together only if you were not large enough to do something that required huge outlays of capital, or if pooled technology led to lower costs. With an international venture, you're also looking for cultural savvy, for a partner that has knowledge of the local market and operating conditions.[4]

Hercules Chemical, a frequent participant in joint ventures, formed a partnership in Taiwan to build a polypropylene plant. Although begun a year after Hercules commenced building its own plant in Canada, the Taiwan plant was completed a year sooner than the Canadian plant. Giacco saw an advantage, in that the principals of the Taiwan investor group knew the local conditions:

> We were profitable from day one. Our Taiwan partners knew how to make the venture's financing work in Taiwan. And they understood the training that was needed and what had to be done to get the plant built on schedule.[5]

Giacco used the joint venture extensively in building Hercules. In the middle 1980s, Hercules was faced with a cyclical downturn, with the polypropylene division suffering a $9 million loss. In addition, the introduction of a new competitive technology developed by a joint venture between Italy's Montedison and Japan's Mitsui threatened to reduce manufacturing costs by up to 30%. This technology was capable of destroying Hercules's market share and customer base and of making obsolete the heavy investment in plant and equipment. Giacco knew he had a real "pig" in his portfolio and took immediate action.

Deciding that Hercules should eventually exit the polypropylene industry because it was inherently a cyclical, price-competitive commodities business, and faced with a potential decline in value of its plants because of the new competitive technology, Hercules proposed to join forces with Montedison rather than face ruinous competition.

Hercules combined its existing plants and international sales force with Montedison's smaller plant and sales capacity, and new technology, in a 50/50 joint venture called Himont. Three years later, after selling some of the stock in Himont in an initial public offering on the stock exchange, Hercules sold its remaining interests to Montedison and realized a $600 million profit, thus disproving the old adage "You can't make a silk purse out of a sow's ear." As Peter Drucker has said, the joint venture is the best mechanism for making "fits out of misfits."

Today, Himont is extremely successful. It holds a major market share internationally, and has grown to be a larger company than Hercules, which is concentrating on highly profitable niche markets. Had Giacco not taken swift action, other industry forces would have made life miserable for Hercules.

To gain more effective market penetration, Union Carbide used a joint venture with Mitsubishi. It spun out its $700 million carbon products division and sold a 50% share to Mitsubishi. The alliance is still headed by Robert Krass, formerly of Union Carbide, and now the president of the joint venture corporation, which rents office space for its headquarters from Union Carbide. The venture provided cash for growth for Union Carbide and made for effective use of Mitsubishi's worldwide marketing network.

WHAT IS THE BEST STRATEGY?

There is undoubtedly no "best" growth strategy to fit all circumstances. The corporate strategist must determine the best architecture for the risks, rewards, resources, and existing relationships. Given the 80% failure rates of acquisitions in the past decade, critical questions must be asked about the viability of this approach. The key to the acquisitions game, as well as the alliance process, is *operational integration*.

Integration is a key management concept that not only links together the core competencies of differentiated organizations, but also unleashes their synergistic power. Unfortunately, operational integration is one of the least understood and most poorly executed of all management skills. The alliance architect must view integration as a pivotal factor in strategic design.

The next chapter begins to address the alliance architecture, the factors underpinning success, and the methods of integration to create a long-term winning condition.

PART TWO

Alliance Architecture

4

The System of Success

Good architecture passes the universal test: the passage of time.

Roy Bonner, a recently retired IBM senior executive and one of its top troubleshooters, has made this analysis of alliances:

> There are a lot of good mechanics and technicians out there in this alliance business, and a few good deal makers. But there aren't any true architects. In fact, there really isn't even an architecture for alliances. Until there is, alliances will not be as successful as they should be. It's a shame.[1]

Bonner had been responsible for managing some of IBM's most sophisticated computer development projects. Bonner knew that, just as a good computer system must have a coherent design, so must any properly functioning organizational system. Bonner challenged me to seek the underlying design for alliance architecture.

WHY THERE HAS BEEN NO ALLIANCE ARCHITECTURE

When a sports team performs poorly, the root cause is usually poor execution of the *fundamentals.* When businesses fail, again the cause is usually failure to get the fundamentals right. Similarly, the underlying problem for the failure of alliances is poor understanding and implementation of fundamentals.

However, with alliances, there has been a more profound obstacle: the fundamentals have not been adequately formulated. There has been no real alliance architecture. Four factors are to blame for this empty space on the business landscape:

1. Lack of systematic models and processes;
2. No shared vision from conception to implementation;
3. Inadequate metrics and diagnostics;
4. Lack of input from operational managers.

There have been no systematic models to follow, no processes that linked theory to practice, strategy to operations, structure to implementation, and mission to accountability. Furthermore, there has been no coherent management theory for alliances.

As one top executive from a very prominent electronics company told me: "We know how to negotiate the deals, but we simply don't know how to manage the deals after we sign the legal agreements." The frequency with which I have heard this comment, from numerous companies, has led me to doubt that the deals were negotiated well, when there was no close linkage of the strategic purpose with the legal structure and practical operations; typically the "front end" of the deal was divorced from the operational "back end."

Alliances often have too many technicians (lawyers, accountants, financial analysts), deal makers, and mechanics (day-to-day implementors), with each seeing the alliance from a singular perspective. They have become like the three blind men who visited the elephant house at the zoo. One happened to grab an elephant's trunk, one an ear, and one a leg. Afterward, they sat on a park bench to discuss their experience. Each described a radically different animal, and none of the three had comprehended the magnitude of the whole elephant.

To understand success, one must also understand failure. In the alliance field, there has been no effective auditing process and no systematic autopsy process. Most audit methodologies have been designed to determine financial accountability in the internal–external relationships of the traditional corporate-castle style of company. The unique nature of the extended corporation exists not in the company's procedures manual.

To conduct a good autopsy of a failed alliance means embarrassing the perpetrators of the failures and putting careers at stake. It's far easier to herald success than to dissect failure. Corporate disasters tend to be excised and quickly discarded, or disguised to look like successes, or put into locked closets whose keys are soon lost.

Interconnections between Theory and Practice

The most effective people in the alliance business are the on-line operators—the experts in the trenches, who know through practice and intuition exactly how to join theory with reality and make the deals work. However, these down-to-earth individuals have been limited in their conceptualization by their narrow range of experience. Seldom would these managers write down their understandings and pass them along to others; they yearned for a scribe. As one senior executive from a large international paper company told me: "I've done a superb job building and managing alliances all over the world; now I need more managers to do the same thing, but I have no idea how to train them, no idea how to translate what I did into words."

THE ELEMENTS OF ALLIANCE ARCHITECTURE

Many managers have asked me: "Why all the emphasis on architecture of alliances? All I want to do is make my deal work! Just give me enough understanding so I can get on with the show."

The answer is quite simple. If one does not know the principles of designing an alliance, one cannot properly construct, or effectively manage, or systematically evaluate an alliance, for success or failure. Similarly, without good architecture, the roles of the strategic designers, the deal makers, the technicians, and the mechanics are ill-defined, resulting in chaos and confusion. No actor can play a part well without reading the full script and seeing the role in the context of the entire production.

Good architectural principles transcend industries, cultures, and corporations. Because so many alliances bring diverse, rather than similar, strengths and weaknesses together, often from countries and industries with widely differentiated perspectives, the very process is potentially fraught with conflict and must be carefully orchestrated. This is not unlike architecture for buildings: one must integrate into the design the talents of the mason, the electrician, the plumber, and the carpenter. Poor integration will result in an inferior building. The principles of alliance architecture must apply to all circumstances; these must be the *core issues*. The master architect holds the broad insights and makes those visions clear to others.

Fortunately, from studies of hundreds of alliances, there emerges a grand design that does work, regardless of the country, the industry, or the corporation. One does not need to be an architect to appreciate, understand, or use architecture. My purpose is not to insist that all who are involved in alliances become master architects, but only to become aware of the underlying laws and the available utilities.

The architecture of alliances is composed of a number of critical elements. These include: key laws, principles, practices, strategies, structure, systems design, management processes, roles, interrelationships and interfaces, conceptual frameworks, critical issues, early warning signals, vital signs, and alternate pathways.

It is not enough to say that alliance architecture should have an inner truth or a harmony and balance. While important, such measures are too

Figure 4.1   Twelve Standards for Alliance Architecture

1. **Applicable:** Does the principle have applicability to nearly all situations, regardless of industry or culture?
2. **Actionable:** Will the principle truly work in practice, or is it just a nice theory?
3. **Understandable:** Can the principle be simply communicated to those involved?
4. **Verifiable:** Can changes be clearly observed when the principle is put into place?
5. **Measurable:** Is there a method of measuring the principle's effectiveness in action?
6. **Controllable:** Will the principle enable more effective control of direction, intensity, speed, and other similar characteristics of the alliance?
7. **Diagnosable:** When a problem occurs, can it be seen clearly? Is there a way to recognize misapplication of the principle?
8. **Prescribable:** If an element is missing, can the principle be injected into the system to effect a cure?
9. **Replicable:** Can a positive result be recreated time and again?
10. **Trainable:** Can operational managers successfully acquire the skills and knowledge required for implementation?
11. **Valuable:** Is the principle really essential, or merely a superfluous nicety?
12. **Predictable:** Can the positive or negative results be foreseen in advance?

vague and ethereal to be used effectively in the business world. Instead, good architecture should be universal, capable of indisputably discerning the good from the bad, without reference to style, energy, or cultural taste. Therefore, as Figure 4.1 indicates, a set of 12 standards has been established to test all the elements of alliance architecture.

All the principles, concepts, and frameworks addressed in this book have been tested against these standards for universal applicability. These approaches have been derived empirically from analyzing the successes and failures of scores of alliances. The practical application of these standards in hundreds of cases has withstood the test of time. As your company begins developing an alliance, testing the underlying assumptions about the alliance against these standards may make the difference between success and failure.

THE DEADLY SINS: CONCLUSIONS
FROM THE AUTOPSY REPORTS

From examination of scores of ventures that were less than satisfactory (some of which I knew intimately from personal experience), a number of conclusions can be drawn. Many examples of failures will be illustrated in the following chapters. A full examination of the failures is worthy of a volume of its own; however, because of the confidential nature of the information, much detailed data must be generalized here. Yet, no matter what the type of alliance, the autopsies show the same distinct patterns.

The "six deadly sins" that were identified as tending to undermine at least 80% of the failed deals are discussed next.

Deadly Sin 1. Sowing the Seeds of Destruction Before the Legal Agreements Are Signed

This deadly sin is the most frequent killer of alliances. Typically, before any legal agreements are signed, the orchestrators of these alliances have violated numerous key principles and processes, generally because they are seduced by the euphoria of courtship, are pressured into closing the deal, and have dollar signs dancing in their heads. The deal makers who fall into this trap unwittingly violate key rules when they should instead turn and run away.

Often, this sin results from avoidance of addressing the most basic business fundamentals, such as doing a rudimentary market analysis, looking into the financial condition of a partner, being sure government approvals will be given for certain technologies, and the like. All too often, familiar assumptions are made: "My partner's strength will take care of those things," or "We'll let the operational managers take care of the details."

Some executives fall into their own trap by assuming that a good strategic "fit" implies a good operational fit. As AT&T found out with Olivetti, a strategic match made in heaven can end up in a divorce hell. Some executives want a deal so badly, they will do anything to get a signed document. Instead, they should take the time to carefully write out an operations plan. With the prescriptions in the following chapters, you will be able to avoid this problem with utmost certainty.

Deadly Sin 2. Focusing on Peripheral versus Core Issues

It is surprising how many alliances get started on the wrong foot by getting caught too soon in the secondary details of legal and tax issues and the intrigue of international affairs. When the peripheral issues become the driving factors, the alliance negotiations are headed for trouble; the principals might as well be blindfolded and driving a car in rush-hour traffic. Core issues are often obscured by the peripheral questions.

This sin is usually brought about by overzealous lawyers, accountants, consultants, and foreign economic development officials. These technicians fill an executive's time and mind with the details, and put the *pivotal architectural issues—strategy, structure,* and *operations—*on the back burner until the deal is signed. By then, it is too late.

Don't get trapped in the converse of this sin, either. By neglecting the peripheral issues, you can overlook critical factors that could haunt you later. As a general guide, use the "80–20" rule: Spend 80% of your time on the core issues, and 20% on the periphery.

Deadly Sin 3. Negotiating the Deal "Six-Gun Style": Ready . . . *Shoot* . . . *AIM!*

When it comes to negotiating deals in international circles, Americans have a reputation of being the world's most "trigger-happy" participants. In their haste to notch one more victory, many executives count their success on the speed of closing and the quantity of deals, rather than on the follow-on success. Typically, this sin is committed when a vague strategy and shotgun negotiations are quickly consummated in an agreement without careful strategic or operational planning.

This sin is characterized by the middle managers who lament: "Oh no! The boss just got back from a business trip and pulled off another deal. If he had only asked me, I could have told him the difficult problems he's not aware of. Now I'm the one he's going to ask to manage this thing."

Deadly Sin 4. Failing to Gain *Both* Top- and Middle-Rank Commitment and Support

Make no mistake about the *dual support* implied by this sin. I have been guilty of this mistake, as have thousands of others. Leaving middle management out of the deal making is standard practice in the mergers and acquisitions game.

Particularly in publicly held companies, middle management is often completely left out of the deal-making process. Investment bankers and lawyers are, on the surface, concerned that middle management will breach the confidentiality required under insider-trading laws. Underneath this fear is an additional concern that middle management might kill the deal and ruin lucrative commissions. Judging by the scorecard of failures in the acquisition game, it is clear that middle management would have found many reasons why a deal that looks good on paper would crash upon takeoff. Knowing what makes a good operational "fit" is the daily domain of middle management, not outsiders.

The converse is also a problem: alliances conceived strictly at the middle management level, without the blessings of top management, are destined for difficulty, if not failure. Middle managers cannot leave their bosses out of the loop, even when the bosses say they are too busy. Alliances are *strategic* in scope and *must* have top-rank commitment.

Deadly Sin 5. Closing the Deal Without Operational Planning

Management of operational interfaces is essential for fulfillment of strategic goals. However, all too often this element is either overlooked or poorly handled, for several reasons. First, managing the "extended" corporation requires special management techniques that are different from the control methodologies that typify the "internal" corporation. The specialization is exacerbated by the lack of a coherent alliance management theory in any of the books or articles written on alliances. Second, because operational integration is often so deeply neglected by strategists and deal makers until after closing a deal, most managers are flung into alliances totally unprepared for their duties, which then become an ordeal and a negative experience.

The critical operational issues, the "how to" questions, address planning, personnel selection, coordination, communications, and joint decision making before the legal agreements are signed. If these issues are sidestepped, conflict may occur without proper mechanisms in place to handle the situation. The Japanese are masters of the art of spending time making sure that a venture is right the first time, and they pride themselves on their facilitation skills. Their American counterparts would be wise to learn this lesson. The rush to closing too often neglects this domain, with predictably poor results.

Deadly Sin 6. Failing to Maintain a Win/Win Environment

A lot has been said regarding win/win in the negotiations stage of deal making. Unfortunately, there is a strong tendency to see win/win as strictly a negotiations technique, and to overlook the more fundamental functions of win/win.

The win/win perspective is not just a negotiations tactic; it has very critical strategic implications during *both* the negotiations period and the subsequent continued operations. If the win/win mentality ends upon finalizing negotiations and signing legal agreements, then the deal is headed toward the grave.

Another missing element is the critical *strategic role* middle management plays in managing the "extended" corporation. However, most often, middle management is not equipped by corporate strategists to understand the important shifts in the strategic atmosphere. When one of the alliance sponsors experiences such a strategic shift, the alliance must adapt, and the alliance managers must become creative and resourceful, to realign the alliance and maintain the win/win perspective. If the operational managers are not flexible and cognizant of their strategic role, they will blindly maintain a course leading to failure when strategic conditions change around them. (Chapter 8 outlines several new approaches to the win/win negotiation process, and Chapter 12 addresses the issues of managing the winds of change.)

It is crucial not only to avoid these mistakes, but also not to substitute other lesser evils in their place. Knowing the right approach is as important as being aware of the pitfalls. The processes, models, and frameworks that compose successful alliance architecture are designed to avoid these deadly sins and to provide the foundations for excellence.

The proper alliance architecture, encompassing an understanding of three-dimensional fit and the alliance development pyramid (discussed later in this chapter), will enable a company to avoid these deadly sins.

THREE-DIMENSIONAL FIT

Those acquainted with the procedures of mergers and acquisitions know how much importance should be placed on having *both* strategic fit and operational fit. This is equally true for alliances. However, there is one additional fit that *must* be included in the formulation of an alliance—the "chemistry fit." Chemistry is a measure of the *quality of the relationships* among the people involved in operating the alliance. Chemistry is essential, according to virtually every veteran of successful alliances. (Chapter 7 addresses this unique factor in great depth.)

Insisting on these three fits is like purchasing a good suit; it must be the right size, style, and material. The suit is not a good buy at any price if the size is wrong, the style is outdated, or the material won't last.

Role of Alliance Manager

Maintaining the three-dimensional fit is inherently a dynamic process because each of the three elements is always changing as the conditions that affect each of the three environments are recast. For example, in the strategic environment, competitive forces are continually thrusting new players into the arena and discharging old ones. Market forces are ever evolving, and political forces can create critical advantages for emerging industries. In the operational environment, the fit is affected by changes in technology, costs of materials and production, costs of financing, and new processes for manufacturing and engineering. The chemistry fit is equally fluid as new personnel enter the alliance, CEOs are promoted, alliance champions retire, and new organizational values are spawned by new managers and new trends.

In this dynamic alliance world dedicated to obtaining results, the role of the alliance managers must be to continue to remold the three-dimensional fit to achieve a win/win condition—not an easy task for an inexperienced manager or a rigid thinker. For some alliances, there will be times when it will be difficult, if not impossible, to adapt the alliance without *transforming* its structure into some other form, such as a merger, acquisition, or tactical relationship.

ALLIANCE DEVELOPMENT PYRAMID

The "six-gun approach" to alliance formation began with an all-too-vague strategy, and then proceeded to move through legal documents to a closing, with no real thought about operations. When the six-gun model is explained to executives in alliance seminars, there are always several groans from the participants, along with the comment: "Yeah, we just had one of those rammed down our throats." The six-gun is fired too often.

The proper alliance development process is quite different as illustrated in Figure 4.2. The genesis of an alliance is the parent company's mission, goals, and strategy, which form the basis of an alliance strategy. From strategy, the process ideally calls for seeking the right partners—a

Figure 4.2 Alliance Development Pyramid

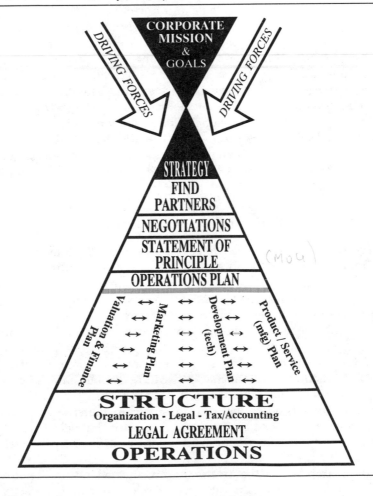

proactive posture—rather than reactively responding to whatever deal comes in "over the transom." Seeking the right partners implies having a clear understanding of the profile of a good match. Negotiations can then proceed with some assurance that the potential for the alliance might be realized.

Form Follows Function

Once negotiations have proceeded to outline the basics of an alliance, many deal makers are tempted to "structure the deal" by jumping immediately into detailed legal agreements. This step should be carefully avoided at this stage. Instead, a very brief Statement of Principle (SOP) or Memorandum of Understanding (MOU) should be generated to outline the fundamentals of the union, including the strategic fit, the presumed operational interfaces, and the goals and objectives.

Then, following the principle that *form (structure) follows after determining functions,* an operational plan should be *mutually* created by the prospective partners to ensure that the gears of the alliance mesh properly. By writing the operational plan together *before* the legal agreements are signed, the prospective partners can test the teamwork at the operational level, thereby having some level of insurance that the middle managers will be able to maximize their capabilities once operations commence.

Only *after determining the functions* of the alliance should the *form and structure be decided.* Equal emphasis should be placed on organizational structure as the legal issues are resolved. At this point, contractual documents are in order.

Averting an Impending Disaster

In one recent case, I was asked to review the legal documents for a $20 million joint venture between a $1 billion Australian mining company and a $100 million American chemical company. The companies had never had any previous business relationships together. Each was planning to invest $10 million to build a new manufacturing plant in Australia, utilizing a technology being developed by the American company.

I learned quickly that the technology had yet to be demonstrated beyond the test-tube stage. If the new process could not be perfected fully, at the old production price, the market would be about half the projected amount. It soon became obvious that a potential disaster was unfolding. The legal documents were just days away from being signed, thereby committing both parties to construction of a plant that very likely, before it was put into operation, would need a refit costing the potential partners millions of dollars.

To make matters worse, the American company had not developed a clear strategic plan for its own international development and, consequently, jumped at the first real chance to enter the Pacific Rim when the Australian company presented the deal. The Americans had no strategy to test the opportunity against—they were reactive, not proactive. By invoking the process called for in the alliance development pyramid, the deal was quickly put back on track.

Ultimately, the Australian–American deal was quickly transformed into a simpler, less costly, and less risky strategic alliance. The two companies agreed to a dual collaboration: each contributed $100,000 to joint R&D, to determine whether the engineering technology could be upscaled to handle high levels of production economically, and they agreed to establish a joint distribution system, linking their agents and distributors to achieve a far better penetration of the Pacific Rim area. They concurred that, should both the collaborative efforts be positive, they would take the plunge into the originally conceived joint venture. But this time their plan would be far more realistic and less risky, and they would have had the advantage of a relationship of trust built on actual experience working together.

About six months later, the two firms had failed to upscale the technology (which would have rendered their proposed plant inoperative), but they were able to continue R&D work together and to integrate their sales and distribution networks.

Had either of these two companies followed the process outlined in Figure 4.2, they never would have come so close to a potential disaster. The alliance development pyramid is an absolutely essential and pivotal *process map* for alliance development. It is fundamental to understanding the architecture of any alliance, and it will prevent most of the deadly sins while maximizing the chances of successful implementation. The details of the alliance development pyramid will be discussed in subsequent chapters.

PATTERNS AND DESIGNS

Alliances are, by their very nature, customized entities crafted by creative individuals who tailor the fit of the partners to the unique characteristics of the parent companies' culture and of the forces of the strategic environment. In all alliances, there are three basic patterns relating to markets, products, and technology. Virtually all alliances are derivatives of one or more combinations of these three elements, as Figure 4.3 indicates. (An alliance is best defined by its "purpose"—i.e. marketing—rather than by its components or its structure.)

There are many examples of "pure and simple," single-purpose alliances, but, over the course of time, many companies tend to develop multi-dimensional, multipurpose alliances. For example, one company may first market the products of another; the alliance may then evolve

Figure 4.3   Basic Patterns and Functions

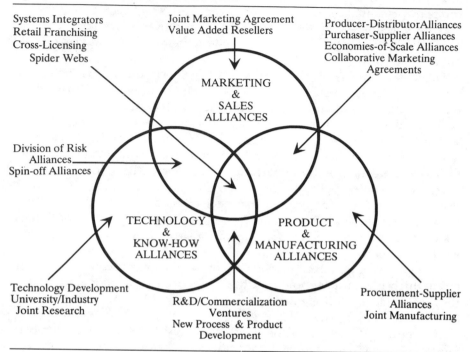

into a cross-marketing agreement to sell each other's products. After successfully working together, the partners may engage in a joint production agreement for development of a new set of products. When alliances become multidimensional, with mutual interdependencies, the relationship tends to become cemented more strongly; each company really becomes more and more reliant on the other, forming a true extension of the corporation. Watch for these transitions as alliances develop over time, because, although they tend to help ensure success, they also require more commitment of resources.

Because of the unique customization required, a particular alliance may be somewhat different from these patterns. Don't be afraid to be creative and develop your own version of the available options. (The following sections look at some of these options in more detail. The coverage is not intended to be a definitive list of variations, but it is an adequate sampling of some of the possibilities.)

Marketing Alliances

The basic marketing alliance utilizes the distribution system of one company to increase the sales of a partner that is providing a product or service, but lacks an effective distribution mechanism and sales force. For example:

- A small dairy owns a proprietary cheese formula and has growing customer acceptance seeks a major supermarket chain with an extensive distribution network.
- A foreign manufacturing company seeks entry into the American marketplace through a well-established retail chain.
- An American manufacturing company forms a joint venture with a Korean company, to gain credibility and governmental approval to operate in a different market where tastes, as well as economic, social, and political environments, are very different.

The basic strategic purpose of the marketing alliance is quite simple and straightforward: by increasing sales, without new investment or substantial increases in overhead costs, profits increase dramatically. By gaining entry into new markets, the alliance establishes customer loyalties as a protection against competitive incursions. Many companies have found they can double or even triple sales using the marketing alliance process. Approximately one-third of all nonfranchise alliances are marketing-focused.

Product Alliances

The product alliance links purchasers with their suppliers to achieve just-in-time deliveries, to improve the quality of materials and components, and to reduce costs. Procurement managers have found they can increase quality, reduce scrap, and lower costs 5% to 10% with long-term contracts to suppliers. When procured materials and services are a large part of cost of goods sold, small decreases in costs have very heavy leverage on improving profits.

Another variation of product alliances is the joint manufacturing venture, where, because of scale costs, it makes economic sense to build a plant of large capacity, but no one company's market demand can support the entire production capacity. Or, smaller companies may find their volume/size of operations does not ideally fit the type of process required for cost-effective production. For example:

- A small chemical R&D company invented and patented a new chemical refinement process, but required a multimillion-dollar chemical plant to manufacture the product, and a large-volume user to justify the size of the plant. A joint venture with a major chemical producer satisfied both requirements.
- Two competing companies have product lines serving stable customer demand, but are suffering from intense price competition from foreign sources. They join their production facilities into a joint venture, eliminate overhead, and utilize the combined R&D staffs to develop

more modern, cost-efficient production technology to compete more effectively.

Technology Development Alliances

The development of new technology is both risky and expensive. Joint ventures and equity partnerships are used extensively by technology-based companies to develop products that would require more capital than they could conceivably generate internally. Many new concepts, systems, and technologies are so intricate and futuristic that huge sums of capital are needed to commercialize their potential. Moreover, such ventures are often highly risky and expensive, and have many potential dead ends.

For example:

- A small electronics firm with a new sensor/control device for the utility industry forms a joint venture with an instrument company, which pays for the R&D in return for the manufacturing rights and an agreement to divide profits.
- A small laser optics company uses its technology in a joint venture with a large hospital supply house to create a new diagnostic instrument. The laser company contributes its patents and technical know-how to the venture; the supply house provides developmental capital and receives the exclusive rights to the U.S. market.
- In the oil, gas, and aluminum industries, a chance of a "strike" in raw material exploration is often increased through the use of joint ventures, whose greater resources permit exploration of multiple sites. If nothing is found, only a small portion of each company's investment is lost.
- In the development of new high-speed integrated circuits, more than a dozen world-recognized U.S. corporations form a joint venture and contribute their best engineers and technical know-how to find the next generation in technology.
- Three computer firms join together to research a new computer-chip technology. Each contributes equally to the research process, providing human and financial resources, and each shares equally in the resulting information. None of the participants is prohibited from continuing with individual research, and none is prevented from competing with the others in using the future applications.

It is estimated that approximately 25% of all nonfranchise alliances are R&D-oriented.

Over time, the single-purpose alliance will often migrate into a multi-dimensional alliance, creating new and often very innovative joint technology, product, and market linkages. A technology–marketing alliance is an excellent way for a small technology company to enter a market, particularly when the "window of opportunity" is nearly closed and the market entrance costs are quite high. Typically, one partner has technology expertise—patents, know-how, manufacturing plants, a special service, or production skills—and the other partner, often much larger in size, has marketing abilities—sales force, service support, distribution channels, reputation, and credibility.

The technology–marketing alliance is not just a one-way street for the betterment of small technology companies. Large corporations recognize that technology development can absorb huge amounts of cash to achieve the critical mass necessary to be successful on a global level. Studies have shown that smaller companies can develop a new technology for far less than their larger corporate counterparts. In the pharmaceutical industry, the average cost of bringing a new drug to market exceeds a quarter-billion dollars. Stephen Doran, CEO of Immunex, a Seattle biotech company, states: "[R&D] moves quickly. There's less bureaucracy." Immunex has succeeded in delivering seven products to market for under $85 million.

What surprises many technicians is that, once development is completed, costs of gearing up for production and bringing the new product to market may far exceed the technology development costs. For smaller technology companies, which seldom enjoy brand-name recognition, severe difficulties can be encountered in closing sales. With a larger marketing partner, sales can happen almost instantaneously.

In one case, a small electronics company had invented a very good high-speed telecommunications data multiplexer. Although the device worked extremely well, the sales closing rate was poor, resulting in an awful cash-flow picture. The company was on the brink of doom, when a larger, well-known electronics company made an equity partnership investment, relabeled the product with its brand name, and opened its channels of distribution. Within two weeks, prospects who had been balking at buying clamored in line to purchase the product. The larger partner's excellent name and reputation had brought to the product a credibility that no amount of advertising could provide.

New Opportunities

Medical technology is a particularly fertile ground. During 1986, over 430 joint ventures and strategic partnerships formed in health-related industries, and the number has grown each year. The focus has been on marketing distribution, product development, and licensing arrangements. For example, Electro-Nucleonics Inc. (ENI), a small instrumentation company, entered a strategic partnership with Pharmacia AB. In return for an equity investment in ENI, Pharmacia received access to ENI's instrumentation skills. ENI gained access to Pharmacia's expertise in medical chemistry, for future instrumentation development, as well as immediate profits from Pharmacia's business with doctors.

The electronics industry is also prime territory. In the late 1970s, for instance, Siemens, the European electronics megaconglomerate, established a strategic partnership through the purchase of 17% of Advanced Micro Devices (AMD). The two companies set up a separate joint venture company, of which Siemens held 60% and AMD held 40%. Siemens gained access to the U.S. market and to advanced technology; AMD gained capital and important worldwide marketing channels. A combined joint venture and strategic partnership of this type offers a superb way for a medium-size company to thrive in the rapidly changing high-technology market, where tremendous amounts of capital are needed for marketing and systems development.

The union between IBM and Apple represents an opportunity to integrate different technical design standards, create a universal system with broad market appeal, and solidify the IBM–Apple customer base against incursions by Asian and European competitors. It also helps reduce cutthroat competition that erodes R&D budgets and profit margins. Because the cultures of IBM and Apple are radically different, the alliance encourages the two companies to carve out smaller project development teams that can establish their own independent culture. In this way, Apple managers and engineers are not engulfed in a barrage of the bureaucracy so frequently essential to the operation of a larger corporation, such as IBM. Decisions can be made and actions can be taken in a rapid manner.

Compare the IBM–Apple approach to the alternative of making an acquisition. When electronics giant Raytheon acquired the smaller, swifter, and more fluid Lexitron, Raytheon's lumbering corporate bureaucracy crippled Lexitron's wide-open entrepreneurial style. Report writing, Raytheon's lethargy, and complex decision-making processes ruined Lexitron's morale. One Lexitron engineer boasted a sign on his office wall that read: *THE RAYTHEONS ARE COMING.*

When a strategic alliance is managed skillfully, it can avoid the type of corporate culture clashes exhibited by Raytheon and Lexitron. IBM had made a similar mistake in its acquisition of ROLM several years earlier; the result was a divestiture shortly thereafter. With Apple, IBM is determined not to repeat its costly mistake. Only time will tell.

Research and Product Development Alliances

Alliances of this type are used to reduce the risk of developing a new technology and then applying the new technology to product or process development. In the joint *research* venture, which may have a dozen or more members, sometimes including a university, the results of the research are disseminated among the partners. In the *product* development venture, it is customary for no more than two or three companies to team together and jointly share the rights to market the product.

A research and product development alliance often starts with a written agreement forming a strategic equity partnership as a forerunner of a possible technology/marketing joint venture. Should the quest be successful, the technology developer may choose to continue to make refinements to the technology, and the other partner may decide to focus on the marketing within the joint venture.

Some R&D can cost so much that, even considering the disadvantages of sharing facilities and information, alliances remain an efficient strategy. In the oil industry, for example, drilling an oil well that has a meager 10% chance of producing oil may cost as much as $20 million. Oil companies are almost forced to cooperate, to manage the tremendous risks associated with drilling.

Technology companies also cooperate to develop products. MCC (Micro Computer Technology Corporation) was established as a consortium of 20 partners representing such major American corporations as Digital Equipment, Honeywell, and Rockwell International. It was the purpose of MCC to pool the partners' technological expertise in order to effectively compete against "Japan Inc." Using engineers, money, and technology from the partners, the new company develops new computer software technologies and makes this knowledge available to any of the partners.

A similar consortium of 14 high-tech companies formed another partnership called Sematech (Semiconductor Manufacturing and Technology Institute) to develop high-speed computer-chip technologies that would be competitive with Japan's recent manufacturing advances. Sematech is funded by the founding companies and the federal government, and the shareholding companies have rights to the knowledge developed by Sematech. In the spirit of cooperation that typifies most alliances, Sematech quickly announced it would coordinate its efforts closely with computer science research at MCC.

Research and development alliances thus illustrate some classic reasons for cooperating: high risks and high costs. If those can be spread among several firms, then large, risky projects, impossible to manage individually, may be feasible. Other agreements call for the funding of research and the purchase of certain licenses, technologies, and quantities of product.

Spin-Off Ventures

In our entrepreneurial business environment, many large corporations have watched experienced and creative engineering leave their companies to form independent start-ups. These companies often invest in their spin-offs, preferring to link up with promising, highly motivated young companies rather than face them later as fierce competitors.

Xerox watched key personnel leave and decided to do something positive about it. "If he's leaving the company, then let's get a piece of the action," proclaimed Richard Hayes, Director of Corporate Business Development for Xerox.[2]

SmithKline Beecham believed its molecular linking technology for delivery of site-specific drugs could best be developed outside the company. So it licensed the technology to its own spin-off, Zynaxis, made an equity investment in the new company, and then Zynaxis financed further development costs through a $20 million public equity offering.

In another variant of the spin-off, larger companies use it as a mechanism to license technologies that are too small in scope, but make eminent sense as a foundation from which a smaller company can grow. The arrangement still provides a return to the larger corporation in the form of royalties. In this way, a dormant asset can provide cash flow to the larger corporation with no risk and without intense management responsibilities. Frankly, more large companies should look through their corporate archives for dormant assets that can be spun off as alliances.

Spider-Web Alliances

Spider-webbing refers not to one single alliance, but to an intricate array of interconnections among companies, often across international and industrial lines. These interrelations truly blur distinctions between competitors: one can often see the same two companies competing in one arena and collaborating in another.

The spider-web technique is used for several purposes. One goal is to intertwine an industry so completely that no competitor can dominate. This was JVC's strategy when it went head-to-head with Sony in the battle of VHS versus beta formats for videocassette players. Using a spider web of alliances, JVC was able to encircle and dominate the industry against a much larger and more powerful competitor.

Another use of spider webs is to ensure that no one competitor ever gets so far advanced in a particular technology that it can make the technologies of other industry competitors obsolete. This technique came about when older, vertically integrated companies failed to upgrade the technologies in their supply chains, were left out of new breakthroughs, and watched other competitors develop superior production processes. By having multiple connections throughout the world, a company's chance of overlooking a new innovation is diminished. IBM has used this technique extensively, with strategic alliances, equity partnerships, and joint ventures in numerous industries and technologies.

Spider webs can also be used in the multidimensional manner found in the automobile industry. The automotive spider webs provide production capacity, distribution outlets, technology development, parts supply, and financial support. To do justice to the automotive spider webs would require an entire book on that topic. The phenomenon is impossible to diagram completely, because of the sheer quantity of connections, and new ones are constantly being formed. Currently, there is not a single auto company in the world that does not have multiple strategic alliances with other companies.

As an example, General Motors owns: a 38% equity partnership in Isuzu in Japan; 50% joint-venture shares of Daewoo in Korea and Saab in Sweden; R&D ventures with Ford and Chrysler; and a joint transmission plant with Chrysler, which supplies manual transmission and four-wheel-drive components to both manufacturers. Honda is supplied with suspension components through a supplier alliance with GM for assembly in Spain, and GM provides axles for Renault. GM markets Isuzu cars in the United States through its GEO dealerships; Isuzu markets GM's European Opels in Japan; and both supply each other with components and engines. GM owns a 5.3% equity partnership interest in Suzuki, and the two companies jointly own an assembly plant in Canada. Cross-marketing agreements enable GM to sell Suzuki vehicles in the United States, and Suzuki markets Pontiacs and Chevrolets in Japan. GM has a 50/50 joint venture with Toyota to build cars and trucks in California, and another 50/50 deal in Australia which merges the Toyota and GM manufacturing plants. A comparison with Ford, Volkswagen, or any other major automotive company would show a similar pattern.

Another style of spider webbing uses a team of companies against another formidable competitor. For example, a massive joint venture was assembled to bid against AT&T on the $4.5 billion contract with the U.S. Government for the Federal Telecommunications System, a nationwide voice, data, and video network, designed to become the largest single private telecommunications network in the world. The bidding alliance was led by Martin-Marietta, an aerospace conglomerate seasoned in joint ventures, and the prime contractor to the Federal Aviation Agency's upgrading of the nation's air traffic system. Martin-Marietta would be responsible for the venture, providing integration, management, and network control. Teammates would be the regional Bell Operating Companies (formerly subsidiaries of AT&T until the divestiture), providing local communications services and local access to national networks; US Sprint (initially created as a joint venture between GTE and United Telecom), providing long-distance carrier service; and Northern Telecom, an American subsidiary of a Canadian firm, and its Canadian research arm, Bell Northern, providing network design, technical support, and software development.

In Japan, IBM has modeled itself after the Japanese *keiretsu*, teaming up with a plethora of suppliers, technical distributors, and marketers. IBM's highly successful Japan division has linkages for distribution with Ricoh, systems integration with Nippon Steel, financial systems marketing with Fuji Bank, integrated manufacturing with OMRON, and telecommunications networking with NTT, among numerous others. There are reputed to be nearly 1,000 such connections to IBM's functional area in Japan.

This has been just a sampling of the many varieties of alliances. The designs may be different, but the principles used to ensure proper functioning are all the same.

THE ESSENTIALS FOR SUCCESS

In any industry, regardless of whether the partner is domestic or foreign, a well-conceived cooperative venture will have a set of common essential characteristics. The eight essentials for success are fundamental building blocks of all alliance architecture. Elimination of any one or more of these factors will reduce the likelihood of a successful venture. Each of the essentials will be the subject of a subsequent chapter.

- **Critical Driving Forces.** Every company exists in its own unique strategic and operational environment, as defined by its relationship to itself, its customers, and its competition. Consequently, there are critical forces compelling the company to act, react, or not act at all. Moreover, no company has unlimited human and financial resources, nor does any company possess strengths in every dimension. An effective alliance is held in place when the driving forces—strategic and operational—for both companies are complementary.

- **Strategic Synergy.** A company should look for complementary strengths—strategic synergy—in a potential partner. To be successful, the two partners should have more strength when combined than they would have independently. Mathematically stated: $1 + 1 = 3$, or more. Potentially good partners will have strengths that complement each other's weaknesses. Mutual advantage must exist; if it does not, the venture will eventually unwind.

- **Great Chemistry.** Each company in an alliance must have the managerial ability to cooperate efficiently with the other company, and they must share an equally cooperative spirit. Veterans of alliances reiterate the importance of "chemistry," pointing out that partners often have to treat divisions of their partners' companies as if they were their own company. Chemistry is the result of positive, team-oriented, trust-filled relationships between key sponsors. A history of past working relations is very beneficial; management can then build trust and communications on an existing foundation.

- **Win/Win.** The operations, risks, and rewards must be fairly apportioned, to prevent internal dissension that would corrode and eventually destroy the venture. The dynamics of the global marketplace are like shifting sands beneath a stormy sea; risks and rewards, like the tides, are ever changing. As though they were sailing a boat, the partners must maintain a very flexible course, trimming the sails of their agreement in order to navigate through changing winds and

tides, and readjusting again when the strategic or operational environment changes. Partners must be willing to address new risks, be
committed to flexibility and creativity, and be ready to transform
the alliance structure.

- **Operational Integration.** The style of operations and methods of
  management should be compatible. Companies with aligned goals,
  rewards, methods of operations, and corporate cultures tend to make
  better partners; otherwise, the relationship is akin to mixing oil and
  water. Differences in national styles and methods of handling problems can become very thorny if managers are not selected for their
  multicultural understanding or are not properly cross-trained.
- **Growth Opportunity.** The alliance, by its very nature, should create
  an opportunity for positioning the participating company in a leadership or growth condition to sell a new product or service, or to
  secure access to technology or raw material. At least one of the partners should be uniquely positioned with the "know-how" and reputation to take advantage of that opportunity. This typically will
  create an excellent reward/risk ratio. With a partner, the likelihood
  of success must be significantly higher. If the chance of success in
  achieving growth is only marginally higher, an alliance may not be
  worth the additional complexity it requires.
- **Sharp Focus.** Excellent clarity of purpose is one of the most frequently cited reasons for the success of an alliance. It is not enough to
  have high levels of trust, energy, and communications. Ventures with
  specific and concrete objectives, timetables, lines of responsibility,
  and measurable results are best suited for potential success. Companies must learn to avoid alliances where the partners cannot clearly
  delineate results, milestones, methods, and resource commitments.
- **Commitment and Support.** Leadership is essential. Companies
  tend to reflect the attitudes of their president. Without top-level
  support, middle managers devote energies to other priorities, which
  they believe may lead to their promotion. There must be a corporate
  "meeting of the minds" at the CEO level, to ensure that the proper
  attitude filters to the lower managers. To maintain an international
  alliance, CEOs must interact with their counterparts in the alliance;
  if they do not, a signal is sent to all subordinates that there is inadequate support, coordination, commitment, and communications.
  Similarly, middle management's support is vital, because people
  will support what they have helped to create. Further, support must
  be backed up by the commitment of resources to get the job done.

The following chapters show, in detail, how to build an alliance based
on these eight essentials for success.

5

Critical Driving Forces

No man really becomes a fool until he stops asking questions.

—Steinmetz

How does an alliance come together in the first place? How does it stay together over the long term? These are important questions, because the answers reveal how powerful forces can keep certain alliances together for decades, yet others disintegrate rapidly.

WHAT ARE THE DRIVING FORCES?

The key to these questions is an understanding of the driving forces that keep pressure on the partners. (See Figure 5.1.) Poor understanding of these forces will result in defective alliance architecture, and the venture will not endure the winds of change. Imagine these driving forces as pressure clamps or a vise gripping the two companies; they will not naturally stay together for long unless there are sufficiently strong driving forces to keep them in alignment. These forces are a major component of understanding the essence of strategy formulation "fit."

When determining whether it makes sense to commence an alliance, the driving forces for both companies should be assessed. Are they sufficient to hold the structure together? What is the expected duration of these forces? Is each company aware of the forces that affect its prospective ally? Are these forces truly strategy forces or are they more tactical

Figure 5.1   Keeping an Alliance Together

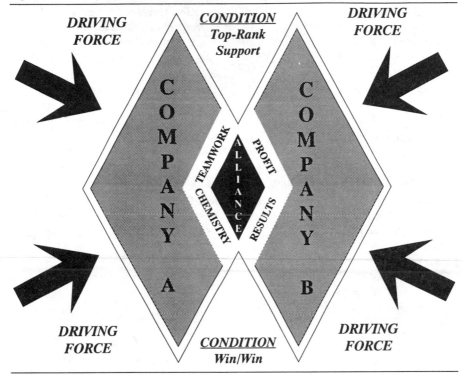

and operational in nature? Figure 5.2 lists some examples for each type of driving force.

The forces can be many, or they might be few; the important factor is that they must be powerful, they are interwoven with strategy, and they can be expected to be somewhat permanent. Some companies, such as General Electric, will not begin thinking about an alliance without first identifying the significant drivers.

Every company exists, at any single moment in time, in a particular strategic and operational environment. One thing that can be predicted with utmost certainty is that this environment will be different in the future. For some companies in dynamic markets and technologies, the future atmosphere may be rather stormy. For those in mature markets, it may be cyclical, with feasts followed by famines. Companies involved in commodities may be subjected to great fluctuations in prices and supplies.

Therefore, both the orchestrators and the operators of the alliance must be keenly aware of these forces; the ever changing pressures will require the alliance to have the flexibility of a willow's branches. If the sponsors are unaware of approaching storm clouds, the alliance will be

Figure 5.2   Examples of Driving Forces

Strategy Driven:	**Regulation Driven:**
World-class company goals	Government prohibitions
Leverage resources	Legal requirements
Vertical integration	Taxation
Resource Driven:	**Production Driven:**
Management resources	Control/Lower costs of supplies
Technology resources	Improved quality and reliability
Capital resources	Design for manufacture and assembly
Technology Driven:	**Finance Driven:**
Hybridization of technology	Downsizing
Development of new technology	Lower production cost
Commercialization of technology	Increase profits
Market Driven:	**Threat Driven:**
Globalization of markets	Loss of market
Access to markets	Competitor-predator
Closeness to customer	Hostile takeover
Risk Driven:	
Economies of scale	
Share risk of capital expenses	
Share operational risks	

uprooted when socked by an unanticipated gust from a major shift of wind in the strategic atmosphere, such as a large corporate takeover or a major exit of a competitor from the market.

Or, just as unfortunate, they will have built an inflexible edifice, a Maginot Line incapable of adapting to new conditions and likely to be outflanked by the competition.

During negotiations, critical questions should be asked of both companies regarding their driving forces. And it pays handsome dividends to partake in a bit of future forecasting. What will these forces look like in 3, 5, or 10 years? Strategists should look to uncover any hidden opportunities for additional driving forces in order to build greater structural strength into the alliance. All those who are involved in operations once the alliance is underway must remain keenly aware of these pressures, because they are vital to the continued understanding of and commitment to the alliance's mission and purpose by both sides of management.

An international marketing manager for a well-known automotive exhaust parts manufacturer recalled a very unfortunate example of this type of problem. The U.S. manufacturer had sought a joint venture with a Brazilian investment company that had just bought a local exhaust system manufacturer. A joint venture was consummated, and the U.S. firm left the basic business operations to the Brazilian partner. The U.S. head of international operations would fly to Rio for their quarterly meetings,

Driving Forces Goal: Maximize the number or the strength of driving forces on *both* sides of the alliance.

but did not do a credible job of keeping track of the venture or of the forces acting on the partner as conditions changed.

Suddenly, without notice, the Brazilians announced they were withdrawing from the automotive parts business, leaving their American partner with the venture. It took some time to find an adequate replacement suitor, and the U.S. company has yet to make a profit from this venture.

Do your homework, ask tough questions, and have a foresighted management staff that stays aware of strategic issues, not just mechanics. This is a new role for many middle managers, but it unquestionably goes with the territory of alliances.

THE NATURE OF THE FORCES

Not all driving forces are created equal, and neither are they all imbued with the same powers. Often, many of these forces are not understood within the companies driven by them, much less being understood by their allies.

It is useful to differentiate "opportunity driven" forces from "problem driven" forces, and then to separate those forces that are internal to the company from those whose origin is external (Figure 5.3).

In each of the four quadrants, the forces work in very different ways and tend to change over time, for very different reasons. It is valuable to understand the intensity and longevity of a strategic driver, as well as its source. Less intense drivers will have a lower effect on the commitment of top management to the alliance.

A strategic principle states that people (and therefore organizations) are relatively more invigorated by external threats from competitors—the

Diminishing Drivers: If the driving forces on either side of the alliance *diminish,* then beware: The alliance may need restructuring or renegotiation.

Figure 5.3   Strategic Drivers

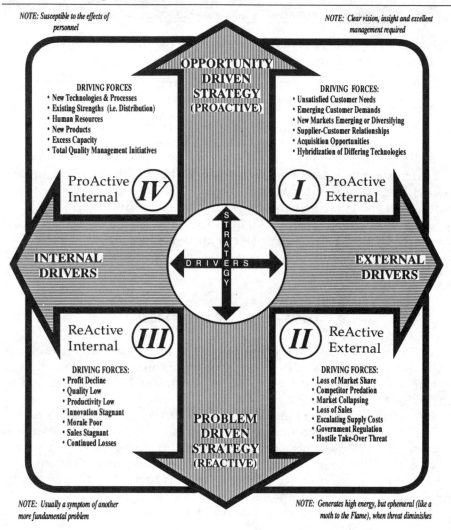

NOTE: *Susceptible to the effects of personnel*

NOTE: *Clear vision, insight and excellent management required*

OPPORTUNITY DRIVEN STRATEGY (PROACTIVE)

DRIVING FORCES
• New Technologies & Processes
• Existing Strengths (i.e. Distribution)
• Human Resources
• New Products
• Excess Capacity
• Total Quality Management Initiatives

DRIVING FORCES:
• Unsatisfied Customer Needs
• Emerging Customer Demands
• New Markets Emerging or Diversifying
• Supplier-Customer Relationships
• Acquisition Opportunities
• Hybridization of Differing Technologies

ProActive Internal **IV**

I ProActive External

INTERNAL DRIVERS

STRATEGY DRIVERS

EXTERNAL DRIVERS

ReActive Internal **III**

II ReActive External

DRIVING FORCES:
• Profit Decline
• Quality Low
• Productivity Low
• Innovation Stagnant
• Morale Poor
• Sales Stagnant
• Continued Losses

DRIVING FORCES:
• Loss of Market Share
• Competitor Predation
• Market Collapsing
• Loss of Sales
• Escalating Supply Costs
• Government Regulation
• Hostile Take-Over Threat

PROBLEM DRIVEN STRATEGY (REACTIVE)

NOTE: *Usually a symptom of another more fundamental problem*

NOTE: *Generates high energy, but ephemeral (like a moth to the Flame), when threat diminishes*

"warrior instinct"—than by customer needs or internal improvements. This phenomenon occurs in quadrant II.

Unmistakably, competitive threats bring out strong fears of organizational annihilation or extinction. Threat of external aggression was the prime motivating technique of Churchill and Hitler during the Second World War, as it was for Eisenhower and Krushchev during the Cold War. Pepsi and Coke wage their battles on this same principle. The fear of loss is always a stronger motivator than the opportunity for gain, as every insurance salesperson knows. Kenichi Ohmae, Japan's management strategist, states in his book, *The Mind of the Strategist:*

> The deterioration of a company's position relative to that of its competitors may endanger the very existence of the enterprise. When striving to achieve or maintain a position of superiority over a dangerous competitor, the mind functions differently from the way it does when the object is to make internal improvements. . . . It is the difference between going into battle and going on a diet.[1]

However, as every general and soldier can testify, the heated energy for battle wanes rapidly as soon as the threat retreats or is conquered. It takes a stronger form of leadership to motivate when fear is absent—a leadership based on vision and values. Competitively driven strategies are only one dimension of the strategic picture.

Strategy drivers must be more than just concepts; devoted "champions" must sponsor and guide their organization's response. Strategy drivers without champions are, like lightning, unharnessed energy without direction or use. Quadrants I, III, and IV require far stronger leadership, guidance, commitment, and sense of purpose than does the fear-motivated quadrant II.

As we continue the evolution of the global economy, companies will need to communicate their strategic game plan far more effectively to *both* their middle management personnel *and* to their alliance partners, or else run the risk that none will be in synchronization. Competition, markets, and technology are all changing at a pace far too rapid for any company to control; therefore, there is a need to be well coordinated, to stay tuned to the flow of change, to respond rather than react, and to capture opportunities rather than catch up after being clobbered.

DEVELOPING THE ALLIANCE STRATEGY

The first question that must be addressed is: Do we need an alliance? If you have internal resources, or control is the most important factor, then perhaps an alliance is not needed. Assuming an alliance makes sense, what should its objectives be? Figure 5.4 demonstrates a case example of a corporation seeking to be a low-cost, high-quality producer. In each sector are various strategic options and directions.

The understanding of driving forces must reflect the interrelationships among the market, the company, and the competition. Understanding the competition is essential in the business game. As the ancient Chinese warrior-strategist Sun Tzu advised: "Don't begin battle until you know your competitors' strategies and their alliances."

Figure 5.4   Example: Different Objectives and Courses When Using an Alliance

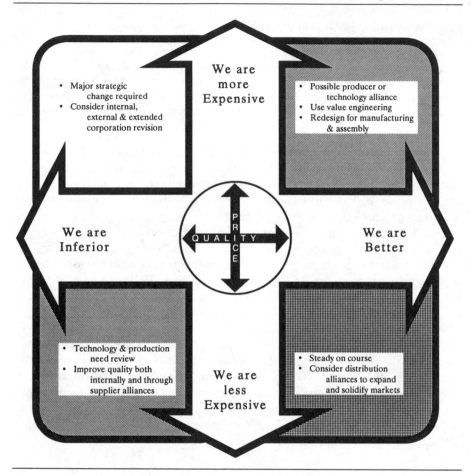

Periodically, someone makes the brash comment: "I'm lucky, I don't have any competition." Somehow, I can't help but wonder whether a market is lacking entirely, or whether this poor soul is ready to be crushed by a blind-side attack?

Critical driving forces affect every company uniquely because of its own particular relationship between its customers and its competition, which defines inherent obstacles and creates specific opportunities. A company seeking an alliance will look for a partner that can maximize the results it gains from these opportunities, a process referred to as "strategic synergy."

Strategic synergy is the outcome of having, between allies, an excellent strategic fit that can be then translated into effective operational action. The next chapter describes this process in some detail.

6

Strategic Synergy

Coming together is a beginning;
Keeping together is progress;
Working together is success.

—Henry Ford

How should today's company respond to strategic threats and opportunities? First, it is generally better to fight the competitive battle overseas now, rather than face the alternative: an attacking alliance on the company's domestic turf in 5 years. Second, timing is critical. Waiting too long to formulate strategy will let strategic advantages slip further away. Napoleon said he could always make up lost ground, but could never make up lost time. Third, an aggressive strategy must be well-conceived, maximizing the leverage of resources without incurring excessive risk.

WEIGHING THE STRATEGIC OPTIONS

Of the three growth options—internal expansion, mergers and acquisitions, and alliances—only the latter option has the real advantages of speed, breadth, and minimal depletion of resources. The first two options require start-up subsidiaries or expensive outlays of cash, often risky maneuvers in unknown foreign markets. A number of acquisitions may be necessary to cover the breadth of the global market. Finding the right acquisition targets with the proper strategic and operational fit could take years—too long, in a rapidly emerging marketplace.

Smaller companies have normally opted for more simple arrangements: licensing and sales agents. As first steps designed for operational convenience—to eliminate difficult-to-manage and expensive in-house sales forces or to recapture development costs—these may be excellent because they generally require relatively minimal resources for implementation. However, they seldom offer long-term strategic advantage. In the relatively stable marketplaces of the past, where competition was not overly threatening, these arrangements were far more advisable than in today's dynamic competitive marketplace.

THE STRATEGIC ALLIANCE GAME PLAN

Although there is no one "right" plan for every company, a pattern is common when beginning an alliance strategy.

Eight-Step Basic Alliance Game Plan

1. Preparing
2. Beachheading
3. Digging in
4. Networking
5. Exploiting the network
6. Supporting the core
7. Strengthening the customer base
8. Leveraging resources

Preparing. The first step had better be internal preparation, a step that is often overlooked or underrated. Establishing alliances requires certain internal organizational realignments, resource commitments, new or additional responsibilities, and a clear understanding of the unique management aspects of the extended corporation. Form a core team of people committed to developing a successful alliance strategy.

Beachheading. Next, a careful "beachhead" approach should be mapped out, starting with a few alliances. I know of one company that had never engaged in a single alliance and then set a goal of having ten in operation by year's end. I told the planners to pare back the objective so they wouldn't have indigestion and failure. Start with one or two, do them well, then expand from there. An overly aggressive game plan is an invitation to disaster. Usually, the best beachhead partners are those with whom a company has already had some working relationship or those with a good track record in alliances.

Digging In. Once beachheads are in place, a company can begin attacking competitors on their home turf, rather than wait for a need for a defensive alliance against a foreign aggressor's attack. Another variant of this step is to build or penetrate new markets where competitors are weak or sleepy. The Japanese are excellent at moving into a small niche market, perhaps at the low, unprofitable end, or into a new, emerging, but as yet unfulfilled market.

Networking.   The next step is to weave a web of alliances and spread new, improved, higher-value products vertically and horizontally in the market. These networks can be technology R&D programs, distribution alliances, or supply alliances. The spider web prevents any new technologies or products from slipping through and possibly leaving the company vulnerable, without the right product in the right market at the right time.

Exploiting the Network.   Once the network is in place, the company can begin exploiting it vertically and horizontally with an invasive diffusion strategy. This means invading with newly developed technologies, expanding markets, and procuring carefully to ensure the position of high-quality, low-cost producer.

Supporting the Core.   Technological renewal, state-of-the-art knowledge, advanced processes, and an empowered organization are the core internal competencies of business success. By using the alliance network extensively, the internal core is continually revitalized. Ford learned this art well in its relationship with Mazda, bringing new design systems and quality techniques back to Detroit. (Be careful not to let an alliance dilute core competencies.)

Strengthening the Customer Base.   A strong internal core stays healthy on a steady diet of customer responsiveness. The techniques used to build alliances with suppliers and distributors are the very techniques that cement loyalty in the customer. When the customer truly becomes an ally, there is little room for a competitor to tread.

Leveraging Resources.   While tackling these steps, the resources of the alliance network should be utilized to accelerate technological and market development and to effect cost leadership, spending as little cash as possible.

This generic game plan can be adapted to each company's own needs.

DEVELOPING STRATEGY

Each of the potential partners must have a clear strategy before moving to form an alliance or even to seek partners. Constructing a strategic alliance begins with gaining a grasp on the company's own strategic position, and then proceeds to a strategic plan that encompasses a potential partner. If a company does not have a sound strategic plan, the venture will be built on a weak foundation. Indeed, "if you don't know where you're going, any road will get you there."

Defining your company's strategic position can be tedious; but it is a vital step in forming a strategic alliance.

When companies have first analyzed their own corporate strategies, some have discovered that the proposed alliance was structured to cover weaknesses that could and should be firmed up *internally*. The alliance was unnecessary!

If, on the other hand, internal weaknesses are too difficult to overcome alone, then it is wise to proceed. For example, as the auto market became more globalized, American Motors (AMC) knew it would need a European or Asian partner if it was to continue operations. Mounting losses were undermining the underpinnings of the corporation. Renault was faced with a similar predicament.

The joint venture between AMC and Renault was aimed at helping both companies supplement weaknesses in marketing and technology. Renault needed, and acquired, the broad distribution network of AMC auto dealers. The French company's optimistic claim at the outset of the venture was that AMC was the ideal partner because its dealers were

Figure 6.1   Strategic Alignment

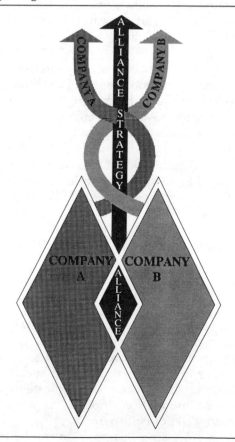

accustomed to selling smaller cars. AMC, on the other hand, needed cash and the technical resources for the expensive task of developing a new line of smaller cars, if it was to compete against the big three industry giants at a time when smaller cars seemed to be the trend. It also needed to meet U.S. government fuel economy regulations quickly—and did so through technology it gained from Renault.

As history has shown, the small-car trend did not continue when oil prices fell, and North American consumers never have been won over to French autos, as Citroën and, later, Peuguot learned. AMC stayed alive long enough to be an attractive acquisition for Chrysler, which wanted AMC's Jeep line, its new version of luxury Eagle cars, and its extensive dealer network. In this case, the joint venture was successful, but some of the market changed, requiring a transformation of strategy.

Once a company is clear about its own strategy, it can begin examining the issues of strategic fit. Allies seldom actually share the same strategy, but they must be going in parallel, or intertwined strategic directions, as Figure 6.1 demonstrates. Alliances with divergent strategies will eventually fail.

WHAT IS STRATEGY?

What exactly is strategy? How does one develop a good strategy? When I wrote an earlier book on alliances, I used the following definition of strategy:

> Strategy is a long-term, competitive, and systematic program of action that allocates precious resources to take advantage of specific emerging opportunities, resulting in positioning the company for future market strength, organizational security, and profitability.[1]

I thought it was a good definition at the time, but when I tried to remember it during my corporate seminars, I consistently forgot some of the key pieces. If I couldn't remember all the elements, how could I expect anyone else to remember them? It was a great definition for business schools, but not for the real world: it focused on *concepts*, not *results*.

Lack of Strategic Measurement System

Other executives I spoke with experienced their own versions of the problem I had. Often, alliance managers complained about how difficult it was to translate "strategic value" into some measurable framework or to bring down the highly elusive issue of "strategic synergy" to day-to-day reality.

Still other managers were disenchanted with auditing teams that performed an annual financial audit on an alliance well before it was designed to turn a profit, causing the consequent anguish of trying to explain the lack of profitability to a boss who was bottom-line-oriented. As one manager said, "Our alliance is one year old and performing extremely well. However, because it isn't profitable yet, we don't have any way of measuring success."

The problem is also faced by financial experts. A chief financial officer of a $4 billion division of a large multinational corporation complained that he saw too many deals that looked great when the financials were analyzed, but he knew instinctively (and his fears were later proven justified) that the deal was not good enough. There was no acceptable mechanism for analyzing the deal except for the normal return on investment (ROI), discounted cash flow (DCF), and net present value (NPV) routines. His gut reaction told him that the financial analysis tended to skew the answers toward the near term and diminish the value of longer-term, strategic divisions.

This financial officer's auditing team had similar concerns. They were perplexed about how to deal with their corporation's myriad alliances. The standard financial audit mechanisms didn't fit such unique creatures as an R&D alliance or a cross-marketing agreement.

A top executive from a financial services firm was deeply concerned that his company's joint ventures and acquisitions were performing poorly. "The numbers always work out before we close the deal, but the deals never seem to achieve their strategic objective," he lamented.

New Measurement System for the Extended Corporation

The lack of an adequate strategic performance measurement system for alliances is the result of trying to apply the measurement and control systems designed for the internal "corporate castle" to the "extended" corporate realm of alliances. What is needed is a new system designed for the extended corporation. To be effective, this new system should:

- Be simple and straight forward enough to be used and understood by top and middle managers;
- Challenge underlying assumptions about an alliance;
- Focus the efforts of the alliance on measurable performance criteria;
- Examine the interplay of strategic factors for synergistic effects;
- Link strategic issues and leading indicators to financial returns;
- Determine whether standard financial analysis supports or diverges from other strategic goals;
- Enable both alliance partners to jointly develop performance criteria and then tailor an *operational* audit to the specific intercorporate objectives;
- Adapt to changing strategic needs in a rapidly changing world, thereby enhancing flexibility, speed, learning, and adaptability;

- Provide insight on *leading* indicators of performance, rather than *lagging* indexes, such as financial evaluation.

STRATEGIC RETURN ON INVESTMENT

The concept of Strategic Return On Investment (STROI) has emerged as a measure of five basic areas of strategy. Figure 6.2 represents the five elements.

Notice that financial gain is only one of the five dimensions. Because the primary purpose of an alliance is *strategic*, its rewards must be more than financial. Four elements (market, organization, innovation, and competitive advantage) are *leading* indicators, and the financial element is a *lagging* indicator. In some respects, financial gain is not just a *result* of strategy but also a *measure* of the combined strategic success of the other four elements.

Describing the five dimensions enables the measurement of strategic results. The partners then know whether the alliance is achieving its strategic goals; they can look for the key strategic benefits and can then measure these returns against their "investment," which can be one of time, people, technology, or money.

Figure 6.2   Strategic Return on Investment (STROI)

The STROI Dimensions

Some amplification of the strategic return on investment (STROI)* elements is in order. Figure 6.3 shows a sample.

Market Strength.   A company's strength in its market can manifest itself in several ways. The Japanese will typically view this as market *share,* top line (versus bottom line) management. Other approaches include expanding into new markets, capturing niches that show promise of future growth, locking up key distributors, pumping more product through existing distribution channels, and becoming more responsive to customers. The possibilities are as broad as the driving forces and inspirations of the alliance creators.

Organizational Capability.   The dimension of organizational capability has many possibilities. Ultimately, all organizational strength is based on its ability to marshal its human resources, not simply on the money in the company's coffers nor on its technology. Strength is not measured in the numbers of people, but in the effectiveness of its people. When asked what Thomas Edison's greatest achievement was, the curator of the Edison museum commented that it was Edison's ability to organize technical talent.

Components of this organizational element of strategy can include new knowledge, heightened loyalty and commitment, teamwork, new career opportunities, adaptability to change, and utilization of resources. For example, Ford's strategic partnership with Mazda has yielded Ford many additional organizational capabilities, ranging from Mazda's lead in designing Ford's small cars to Mazda's high-efficiency accounts payable system. These programs eventually have a powerful effect on Ford's bottom line, but a traditional internal financial audit might not validate their potency.

Innovative Capacity.   Peter Drucker has said that there are two basic functions of a business: marketing and innovation. Without innovation, there is no adaptability for the future. Innovation can take a variety of forms—new technical capabilities, development of better manufacturing processes, service delivery capacity, new products, better quality, and higher productivity, to highlight a few. Alliances where there should *not* be an expectation for achieving new forms of innovation are few in number. The biggest problem with this element is that it sometimes eludes measurement. However, the corporation that does not see continuous

---

* The Latin verb *struere* means "to build." Its antithesis in English is "destroy." Unfortunately, there is no English equivalent of the positive form, which would be, if it existed, "stroy." I've used STROI in a dual way: as an acronym for Strategic Return On Investment, and to indicate the "building of value."

Figure 6.3   Measuring Strategic Return on Investment

SAMPLE STRATEGIC RETURN ON INVESTMENT ANALYSIS

Strategic Element	Measurable Return Expected	Resources Invested (Time, Money, Material, and People)
1. Market Strength	Double sales. Increase share from 10% to 20%	Existing sales force plus $150,000 for promotion
2. Organizational Capability	Increase sales with no rise in fixed costs	8 individuals (100% dedicated)
	Shorten new product development cycle to six months by November 1994	Assign 3 engineers & 1 technician
3. Innovative Capacity	Initiate joint product development program	6 individuals (50% dedicated)
	Introduce 3 new products in Year 1 and 5 in Year 2	1 design engineer
4. Competitive Advantage	Lock up key distributors before competition enters market	$100,000 (variable costs)
	Hold position of highest quality, lowest cost producer	$50,000 in new equipment plus TQM
5. Financial Gain	Double return on sales Lower unit-marketing-costs	Total of above

improvement as a fundamental component of its business strategy will soon be overrun by the fast-advancing armies of international competitors.

Competitive Advantage.   All strategy must give a major consideration to competitive advantage, if it is to be successful. Seldom is there ever a single "best move"; strategy is all relative to the response of the competitor. Numerous alliances have been formed as a barrier to entry for other competitors, creating efficiencies of scale that made market entrance costs excessive. Other joint ventures have created a new corporation to operate at arms length from its sponsors, thereby enabling competitors, who would not buy from the sponsor, to buy from the joint venture offspring. If there is not a competitive advantage component to the alliance, one must ask whether the venture is truly strategic.

Financial Gain.   Notice that this dimension does not necessarily measure *return*; it measures *gain*, which is a broader factor. Financial results can be garnered in a variety of ways through an alliance. Probably the area most ripe for harvesting in the American corporation is procurement, where

Figure 6.4   STROI Checklist (Sample)

Rewards from an alliance may be measured in numerous dimensions. Generally, rewards should not be strictly financial. How each reward is evaluated will be custom tailored for each venture. This sample checklist covers typical STROI issues.

SAMPLE ISSUES

Market Growth
_____ Penetration into new market niches
_____ Expansion of market share
_____ Broadening of product line
_____ Access to best lines of distribution
_____ Faster responsiveness to customer needs
_____ Higher customer satisfaction
_____ Greater sales closing rate/shorter sales cycle time
_____ Development of strong brand recognition

Organizational Capability (not necessarily measured in quantities of people)
_____ Organization of talent, service delivery capacity, better teamwork
_____ Higher productivity/shorter product development cycles
_____ Lower absenteeism, higher morale
_____ Broadened and deepened knowledge/specialized capabilities
_____ Capacity to convert ideas into new product
_____ Faster/more accurate decision making
_____ Higher levels of synergy between business units
_____ Greater commitment, teamwork, and vision
_____ Improved service delivery capacity

Innovative Capacity (more than just technical)
_____ New/broader technical capacity, state-of-the-art knowledge
_____ Better manufacturing processes
_____ Financial innovations (e.g., new financial tools or mechanisms)
_____ New product innovations/continuous improvement
_____ Systems integration for added value

Competitive Advantage
_____ Status as "Best in Class" competitor
_____ Creation of new barriers to entry/exit
_____ Position as highest-quality, lowest-cost producer
_____ Enlargement of market to maximize production efficiencies
_____ Early market entry, control market niche
_____ Brand recognition
_____ Fight on competitor's turf

Financial Gain
_____ Faster cash flows
_____ Decreased overhead costs
_____ Improved return on sales, equity, or assets
_____ Lower production costs, greater efficiency
_____ Increased gross profit margins
_____ Decreased marketing costs on a per-unit basis
_____ Maintenance of industry cost/price structure
_____ Prevention of ruinous/cutthroat competition
_____ Leverage of fixed costs

outside goods and services make up nearly 60% of all final sales costs. Cutting supplier costs can dramatically increase profits in many corporations. Becoming a low-cost producer can increase profits, or it can break loose cash for new strategic investment.

CEOs must be sure their strategic planning and financial officers are in synchronization with the operational managers involved in the alliance. Both alliance partners should develop a STROI matrix similar to the one in Figure 6.3. By developing the STROI analysis together, the allies become unified in their goals and in the methods by which they will be gaining their return on investment. All too often, the auditors begin tearing the alliance apart after the alliance is underway, forgetting or not understanding its original purpose or the concept behind measuring its success. STROI not only sets the criteria for evaluating results, but also becomes the framework and underpinning for an annual audit of the alliance.

STROI also creates a linkage between strategic and operational fit. Once STROI objectives are identified, the alliance partners can then write an operational plan to test the achievability of the objectives. Figure 6.4 is a sample STROI checklist.

SYNERGY REQUIRES SYNTHESIS

One of the most vexing tasks encountered in alliances (or any other organization for that matter) is the creation of synergy. The difficulty stems from our inherent propensity toward the *analytic* process. We tend to analyze issues, situations, and conditions first, breaking them down into their component parts, and then, maybe as an afterthought, hope synergistic results will be achieved.

Traditionally we begin by conducting a detailed financial analysis, examining every factor in detail, seldom translating these pieces into a wholistic strategic view. *Synergy requires synthesis precede analysis.* By envisioning the results of the end-state—the five elements of STROI—the whole picture is formulated first; and then the alliance architect can subsequently address the design of *both* the parts *and* the appropriate measurement systems.

During the next decade, alliance architects will concentrate more effort into this crucial issue of designing synergy.

ANALYZING OPPORTUNITIES

After reviewing your own company's strategic position and getting a clear understanding of the expected STROI, the next step is to identify and analyze the existing strategic opportunities: entering a new market, a new field, or a new industry; bringing a new technology or a new product into an existing industry; or making a major capital investment that will enhance your company's ability to become dominant within its industry or region.

The highest risk exists when new products with new technologies are brought into new markets. To reduce risks to more acceptable levels, it is best if both (or at least one) partners know the dynamics of the industry, the intricacies of the market, and the real potential for attaining market share.

Change is present in every industry, and every change brings about a unique opportunity as well as new risks. Changes in technology, market preferences, and investment perspectives provide new potential for the right venture to achieve prominence.

Within each industry, however, certain companies will be better poised and more willing than others to enter strategic alliances. Rather than re-acting to the first suitor that comes knocking on your door, seize the opportunity to form an alliance by creating a profile of a strong ally (see Chapter 13). If, for example, a marketing alliance is in order, what are the characteristics of the ideal partner? How would you measure those characteristics? You might want a partner with excellent channels of distribution, and your measurement might be how many retail consumer outlets it has, or the size of its sales force, or the number of its customers.

In the past, the company with the largest share of the market would not have been an inspired alliance candidate in that market; smaller companies were usually preferred for acquisition. The trend is now changing; market leaders such as General Motors, AT&T, and IBM are securing and maintaining their positions through alliances. The market leader might be a good prospect for a venture into a *new* market. (However, thriving companies in troubled industries are more likely to use a growth strategy of acquisition rather than alliances.)

In the construction industry, Gilbane, the seventh largest firm in America, has been using joint ventures extensively for over 30 years, often with competitors as partners. One of Gilbane's executives commented:

> Very seldom do companies compete for a given project or development with the same perceived benefit. Many times, right after we have been successful in getting a contract, we sit down with our [local] competitors.
>
> A case in point was our Watertown [shopping mall] which is a 500,000-square-foot marketplace. We were designated to be the developer, and after we were awarded the contract, I think we shocked three or four of our competitors, because we invited them all to a meeting.
>
> We began by outlining Gilbane's strengths—construction management, track record, and large size. Of the other groups at the table, one had strength in leasing retail malls, another company was strong in management of malls. The other was our lead tenant, who, along with the others, became partners in the joint venture we proposed. It has been very successful.[2]

Within any given industry, two small companies with marginal market share may become allies in order to achieve better competitive position.

Tip

Consider "Knocking Yourself Off":   If you are worried that a competitor will decide to produce your products in a country that has low labor rates, consider establishing a joint venture that will actually compete with your company, but perhaps at a lower price and quality point. You can then have some element of control over your competition and reap the rewards as well.

Rather than let the television picture tube market fall prey to lower-wage Korean competition, Corning formed a highly successful joint venture with Samsung, which preserved a market base for Corning and prevented ruinous competition. American companies should consider this strategy in Mexico.

When they join forces, they often take on a new market segment within their industry, which neither is currently able to exploit alone.

For example, a marginal software company might profit from the managerial expertise of an established computer hardware company. Or, an undercapitalized producer of fast-food restaurant equipment might find a nationally established fast-food franchiser eager to invest capital in a venture, to ensure a constant source of quality equipment at the right price.

One major real estate development company enters into a cooperative alliance to bid on, construct, and manage large construction projects. If the field of competitors is narrow, and the company is strong relative to the competition, the company will refrain from alliances. If the converse is true—the company is not strong and the field of competitors is wide—the company will elect the joint venture.

STRATEGIC SYNERGY

Without question, the focal point of the strategic fit picture is synergy; a cooperative venture cannot survive without it. Strategic synergy ensures that the weaknesses of one company are offset by complementary strengths of the other. (See Figure 6.5.)

In other words, while the *strategic directions* of both companies should be *similar*, the *operational strengths and weaknesses* should be *dissimilar*, thereby creating a unified whole that is stronger than the sum of the parts—"1 + 1 = 3."

Alliances are formed because of weaknesses offset by strengths. Real synergy requires that a company cannot achieve alone what the venture could achieve. Make a chart, and rate your company's strengths and weaknesses.

Figure 6.5   Strategic Synergy: The Prototypical Alliance, Strengths Offest by Weaknesses

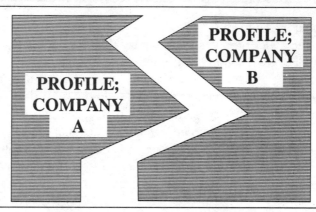

Then, confidentially, have several other people do the same. Let your top management team make an evaluation, and then let your directors or management consultant do it independently. The result will be a profile of your company. Do the same for a potential partner. If there is a complementary match, an overture for courtship might begin.

Figure 6.6 is a generic listing of corporate assets and resources that will help to identify dissimilar strengths. Companies with identical strengths have a high likelihood of disagreement over the value of their contributions to the venture; partners with identical weaknesses will suffer from a critical lack of essential resources. Two companies forming a marketing alliance can have strong marketing capability in the broad sense, but each should be different in that each has differing (but complementary) product lines, customer niches, or geographic distribution channels.

The best partners will have what you don't have, and vice versa. Ideally, your partner should not be strong where you are strong, and weak

Figure 6.6   Elements of Strengths and Weaknesses—Profile

Company A	Company B
Market Access	Market Access
Management	Management
Technology	Technology
Capital	Capital
Materials	Materials
Manufacturing	Manufacturing
Customer Service	Customer Service
Product Lines	Product Lines
Distribution	Distribution

Trap

The Strategic Synergy Sin: Be careful about how strategic synergy is used. At Union Carbide, synergy is no longer considered a factor in evaluating alliances. In the excitement of creating deals, managers tended to overstate the expected synergies to the extent that it distorted their better judgments.

Synergy is real, but it tends to create a narcotic euphoria. Like "hope," it can be a phantom, unless it can be measured. The appropriate method of measurement is strategic return on investment (STROI).

---

where you are weak. Proper construction of the synergistic relationship will build mutual respect and trust, and will prevent bickering, second-guessing, and devastated expectations at a later date.

EVALUATING YOUR PARTNER'S
STRENGTHS AND WEAKNESSES

Before actually courting a partner, a careful evaluation of a prospect's strengths and weaknesses is valuable. Do a value analysis, listing the value elements you can provide and the value elements you expect the prospect to provide. Be sure your prospective partner is sufficiently different to make an exciting match, but has enough similarity to permit a harmonious working relationship.

At Corning, where 35% of its net income is derived from its 22 collaborative ventures, partner analysis begins years before formal negotiations commence. Corning managers know from their extensive background research what to expect about their prospective partner's financial condition, strategic motives, corporate culture, technology, and core competencies.

Ask the cynical questions: What could go wrong, at every stage? How would the potential partner deal with the problems? How would you deal with them? Trust your intuition. If everything looks right on paper but doesn't "feel right" in your stomach, trust your stomach.

In the case of one European gourmet pasta company wanting to use a joint venture to enter the U.S. market, the attempt was not satisfactory. The pasta company could not enter the U.S. alone, for it did not have the proper distribution channels or knowledge of the U.S. market. Yet its attempts to link with an American pasta company proved unsuccessful, mainly because the Italians were unable to prove that their technology complemented that of the American company.

Make Strategy Exciting: Strategy must embrace energy, commitment, and spirit. People are the implementors of strategy; they must get excited about it for it to succeed.

If strategy is either boring or is something that *has* to be done, but has no sense of urgency, imagination, or challenge, it will fail to capture the hearts of those responsible for its success, with obvious consequences.

The Americans saw in the Italian company an interesting but not entirely unique product, one that might even compete with their own. The European company was not clearly offering a supplementary strength to the American company.

The Italians should have either looked for different partners with different strengths, or considered another channel to enter the market. A close examination of strengths and weaknesses would have caused the pasta company to seek a partnership with a wholesale distributor or grocery chain with excellent geographic distribution, rather than considering another manufacturer.

CLARIFYING THE ALLIANCE'S STRATEGIC GOALS

Finding a partner with strategic synergy is not enough, however. Like any company, the alliance itself must have a clear, well-defined strategy of its own. It must have meaning and purpose if it is to have value to those committed to its future success. It is around this greater purpose that the champion focuses energy and commitment. This principle applies to all alliances, however, strategists very seldom consider this important factor.

An alliance without good strategic foundations will be lost in the competitive marketplace, and no amount of "chemistry" will save it. Unless strategically driven, alliances become tactical devices, taking on a moment-by-moment flavor, failing to produce the desired results, and eventually unraveling.

Before moving forward, any corporate strategist must honestly and candidly face the critical issues of strategy. This is often a difficult task, for it is too easy to idealize the strengths, underestimate the weaknesses, and fantasize the readiness of a partner to enter an alliance. All too often, in my experience, when two companies begin discussing an alliance, they have very different meanings about what an alliance really is. The strategic expectations must be clarified before the legal agreements are signed, if the partners want to have a prosperous relationship. Figure 6.7 is a checklist to help executives address several of these important questions.

Figure 6.7   Strategic Questions Checklist

It is imperative that critical strategic questions be asked of both your own management team and the prospective venture partner's team. Both parties' answers should be in harmony. Remember, however, that, although inherent differences between companies may result in one member's playing "rhythm" while the other plays "melody," the combination may well be in harmony. The strategic questions that must be considered include:

_____ What competitive profile must we have in order to be winning 3 to 5 years from now? Does the plan have both a long- and a short-term focus?

_____ What are the strategic objectives of the alliance?

_____ Is the strategic plan based on marketing and product strategies or financial strategies?

_____ Is the mission clear, direct, and realistically targeted to the marketplace?

_____ Can this plan be effectively communicated to our own staff as well as to the executives of a partner?

_____ What are our major strengths and weaknesses compared to: those of our partner, the alliance itself, and the remaining competitors?

_____ Are we being honest and realistic in our assessment? Has it survived devil's advocacy by outside experts?

_____ Which major trends must we recognize as forming a potential opportunity, and which trends may represent a potential threat?

_____ What key events or actions could critically damage the plan? What alternatives could counter or deter such an event?

_____ What information exists that will enable us to take advantage of a desirable economy-of-scale action?

SHORT- OR LONG-TERM VIEW

Some alliances are designed for only a short-term duration, to bridge an interim condition until future circumstances force the alliance to change direction or form. Others are open-ended, with a long-term view toward continuity. Strategic imperatives *will change* as the competitive cycle changes. Generally, the cycle progresses from initial introduction of technology and knowledge to market penetration, to cost/quality leadership, and finally to market consolidation. As the competitive cycle continues to rotate, and particularly if each of the partners is in a different stage of the competitive cycle, then the strategic imperatives will be different and changing. Therefore, strategic "fit" may have to be continually adapted.

Some Japanese corporations, such as Mitsubishi, have 100-year plans, broken down into 20-year increments. The Japanese place a particularly strong emphasis on the value of market share, recognizing that, in the long run, market share will bring far greater profit than a shortsighted earnings statement. Corporations with heavy emphasis on quarterly earnings statements will not be sympathetic to the long-term strategy of many business alliances.

Cooperative Competition

Most importantly, look for a "lean and mean" partner who is accustomed to the competitive battleground. The strategy for success in the dynamic, fast changing global market will be to transfer core competencies into new markets and to innovate with new technologies and methods of delivering value to customers. Move early, penetrate where opposition is least, and catch local competitors while they sleep. Use economic downturns to lay the foundation for a future thrust. Don't put all your eggs into one partner's basket; several alliances may be necessary in the global area.

The future is indeterminate and ever changing. Your corporate strategy should be very flexible. Be prepared to thrust and parry, wait and hide, defend and advance, fight and join forces.

Ultimately, the key to managing strategic fit is knowing your expected strategic return on investment, and knowing your partner's expectations.

7

Great Chemistry

A fool may be known by six things:
  Anger without good cause
  Speech without profit or direction
  Change without progress
  Inquiry without object
  Putting trust in a stranger
  Mistaking foes for friends.

—Arabian Proverb

The first time I met Bill Silvia, Union Carbide's recently retired president of their catalysts and services division, who had been involved in at least a dozen joint ventures and strategic alliances, I asked him what he considered the most important thing about a cooperative alliance. Without thinking twice, he responded: "It's *chemistry!*"[1] His answer was very similar to dozens of others, such as that of Herbert Granath, president of a joint venture between the American Broadcasting Company and the Hearst Corporation: "I know it sounds cornball, but the most important element for a successful partnership is chemistry."[2]

Chemistry is seldom given its due position as an essential component in the architecture and processes of alliance development. As we shall see, chemistry underpins the *human* side of alliance enterprise. Chemistry defines and describes the *quality of the relationships among the people* in the alliance. It is one of the three essential "fits"; take it away and the structure of the alliance will collapse. Although intangible, it's an essential ingredient in the "glue" that holds the two partners together.

Bernard Roth, former Vice President of Tri-Wall, was the orchestrator of numerous successful joint ventures in the paper industry, which propelled his company into a massive globablization strategy. He has stated:

> Chemistry is the glue, but it is also the "grease" that allows the differing cultures to work together. Cultural integration, whether between domestic companies, different industries, or social cultures, is virtually impossible without excellent chemistry.[3]

Without chemistry, the energy, vitality, and trust of the alliance will be missing, and no matter how good the strategy or operations, the venture will fail. Chemistry is the psychological contract; it is far more important than the written, legal contract.

INTANGIBLE BUT REAL

Chemistry is *not* quantifiable, tangible, or visible, nor can it be created, codified, legalized, or contracted. If you want to drive your lawyers crazy, tell them how important chemistry is, and then challenge them to figure out how to put it into a contract. Chemistry is one of the few elements in alliance architecture that defies the rules of measurability.

What exactly is chemistry? Many successful executives have been asked this question, and their responses describe a clear pattern:

Trust in the other partner.

Faith that your partner will do the right things—strategically and operationally.

Knowing that the other party will live up to the unwritten terms of the agreement.

Unfailing commitment to a win/win arrangement.

Cherishing a reputation as a hard but fair dealer.

Respecting integrity.

Doing what you say you will.

Predictability under pressure.

Creativity in the face of adversity.

Some of these responses may sound like apple pie and motherhood, and in some respects they are. Successful cooperative ventures are built on old-fashioned values; which is why the structure has endured for so many centuries. As Stephen Covey has stated in *The 7 Habits of Highly Effective People:*

> . . . there are principles that govern human effectiveness—natural laws in the human dimension that are just as real, just as unchanging and arguably "there" as laws such as gravity are in the physical dimension.[4]

Figure 7.1   Basis of Trust

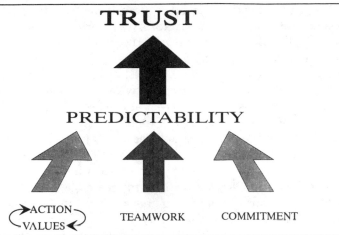

How can one determine whether the chemistry is "there"? Past experience may be the best answer, but, in the event that a prospective partner is not well known to you, how can you tell?

Chemistry is by no means black magic. It cannot be scientifically measured, but it is composed of three separate and distinct elements, and all must be present for the chemistry to work: commitment, teamwork relationships, and action-values—"walking the talk." Taken together, they add up to *trust*, which is based on predictability. (See Figure 7.1.)

The three must work in harmony. Take one element away, or pit one against the other, and the chemistry can become destructive or corrosive.

TRUST AND ETHICS: DO THEY STILL LIVE?

Several times in my early career, I was badly burned in alliances because the people were not right. Although the strategies were perfect, nevertheless the deals came apart, and I lost money, time, and confidence.

Determined never to make the mistakes again, I began interviewing successful alliance builders who had had more experience, understanding, and success. I sought counsel with a friend and wise business advisor, the late A. A. T. ("Pete") Wickersham, an investment banker, venture capitalist, and strategic consultant for the healthcare industry. He commented: "Who you do business with is just as important as having the right business strategy." William Norris, the architect of Control Data's numerous joint ventures, advised that "no matter how inspired the strategic alliance, it is the people who ultimately will make or break the deal."[5]

After interviewing scores of successful business leaders and listening carefully to the questions asked in days of negotiations with European and Asian joint venture orchestrators, two "core" questions arose that are common to virtually all cultures and the vast majority of those individuals who had a repeatedly good track record. (See Figure 7.2.)

Fairly early in the dating and courtship stages, at some informal moment (such as over dinner or a glass of wine), I recommend asking the top executive of your prospective partner at least these two critical questions, in your own words. The answers to these simple questions will yield great insight into the nature of an executive's underlying motives within his or her own organization, and will warn of a bad chemistry fit.

The answer most often given by successful alliance builders to the first question is: "The people who work on my team have made us successful." There are many variations of this answer, but they all lead to the same conclusion: *the executive valued people above all else*—one of the prime secrets of good chemistry. This type of executive is an excellent judge of character, selects high-quality people, and can focus their energies to build a team environment. It also indicates a healthy ego makeup for the CEO. It is uncanny how many top executives involved in cooperative ventures give this reply without hesitation. Companies must understand the value of their personnel, and must know how to delegate authority, how to gain loyalty, how to keep commitments, how to be fair, and how to work together as a team. All of these characteristics are critical to the success of an alliance.

Reputation is the accumulation of continued respect for integrity, successful accomplishment, management, and leadership. Those who do not value their reputation are not likely to have the respect of their subordinates, who, in turn, will probably not support their boss's decisions regarding the alliance.

While conducting the search for a partner, carefully probe your prospective partner's reputation. William Norris, Control Data's pioneer in cooperative ventures, had a far more subtle method of judging whether

Figure 7.2   Two Questions That Will Save Thousands of Dollars

1. What single most important factor has contributed to your business success?

Answer: If the answer is "I'm a pusher," "I work hard," "I am tough with my people," "I can squeeze a buck," "I watch the bottom line," or something in that vein, then more likely than not, there will not be enough chemistry to make the alliance successful. The answer given by most successful venturers told of their ability to build an excellent high quality team of capable people.

2. How important is your reputation?

Answer: Unless the answer runs along the theme of: "It is the most important thing I have—it's worth more than money," beware.

chemistry was present. He used this method when a joint venture was proposed with the Romanian government. Cynics told Norris the Romanians would bleed Control Data of its computer peripherals technology, and then dump the venture. To better understand his prospective partners, Norris decided to go on a fishing trip with them on the Danube. He "became convinced these people were straightforward and they meant what they said. . . . We signed the agreement," which, according to Norris, was mutually profitable.

Dick Girard, Vice President of Marketing at Elmwood Sensors, a subsidiary of Hawker Siddley, has negotiated a number of successful ventures. He advises: "Don't even consider signing an agreement with your potential partner unless you can trust their handshake."[6] He knows from experience that no legal document is worth anything unless someone's word can be trusted.

There must be a good personality fit as well as a strategic fit. Honeywell's International Vice President, Michael Bonsignore, states:

> The number-one factor in achieving success. . . is establishing good personal relationships. The most copious legal document is not worth the paper it is printed on without trust and understanding between the partners.[7]

If you don't trust the ability of your partner to perform, don't take upfront money as an insurance policy. Taking it would imply a weak agreement and can eventually become grounds for "getting even" later. Gut intuition can also be a good judge of whether the chemistry exists. One joint venturer will not enter into any business partnership unless his wife meets the prospective partner. He says his spouse has far better intuition about chemistry and is accurate more often than he.

Ego security is another factor. Insecure people tend to need too much nurturing and attention, and make poor venture partners. Yet, on the other end of the spectrum, those who feel too secure tend to lack the aggressiveness and energy to break through barriers and overcome hurdles. Finding the right balance is very important.

CAN THE JAPANESE BE TRUSTED?

The question of integrity is always raised regarding Japanese, Korean, and Chinese alliances (or *any* foreign ventures, for that matter). While the Japanese trust the United States more than any other country, Japan ranks only eleventh among countries that Americans trust, and both Japanese and Americans trust each other less now than 5 years ago, according to a recent Gallop poll. Why do we not trust the Japanese? What occurs between companies of different cultures that harbors distrust? A. T. Cross Writing Instruments' Vice President of International Marketing, John Lawler, suggests:

All too often the Japanese partner is not invited over here to know our families, see our homes, to understand our values as we would do with an American partner. Japanese seem quiet and withdrawn, they aren't made to feel welcome, we treat them differently. At Cross Pens, we treat our Japanese partners as family—our management is close to its employees and we treat the people from Japan like that too.[8]

Commenting on the joint venture with Japan's Sumitomo, Uniroyal's former chairman, David Beretta, said:

We found Sumitomo to be honorable people, and we relied on that trust extensively. The ever-changing market for petrochemicals necessitated a system of constant renegotiation. If we did not deal with people who considered honor and trust paramount, the venture would have been ruined.[9]

Americans underrate foreigners' acumen, to a large degree, because we don't understand them. This leads to fear and lack of trust. According to successful venture leaders in country after country, *the question of culture is supremely significant,* and both sides must come to terms or the venture will fail.

Culture is not just an international issue for alliances. It varies not only from country to country, but between local regions, between industries, between companies, between divisions of companies, between departments. Clarify suspicions up front. In both international and domestic ventures, the other corporate culture's definitions of honorable and trustworthy are not the same as in your culture.

Tip

Negotiations, Japanese Style: The Japanese are excellent at understanding the chemistry issue. Anyone familiar with Japanese negotiating knows how they spend great amounts of time with their American counterparts, dining, visiting temples, and reading tea leaves. Americans think they are wasting precious business time. Instead, the Japanese are reading our values, wanting to understand the chemistry, trying to gain insight into underlying motives, and getting a reading on the "predictability" question.

Ultimately, they are principally looking for:

Work ethic	Persistence
Long-term commitment	Predictability in crisis
Stability of personnel	Ability to communicate
Corporate values	Cultural respect
Innovation	

If you truly want to make a deal work, don't rush this process. Go with the flow. Let it unfold.

TEAMWORK AND HUMAN RELATIONSHIPS

Can a company work well with your company? Can you create a real team? The answer lies, first, in a company's possession of its own internal teamwork. If dissension is high between departments, if management is fighting labor, if edict is the principal means of leadership and control, teamwork is probably lacking. How can a company that has poor internal communications and coordination maintain the level of external teamwork necessary for an excellent alliance? The answer is self-evident; a company cannot have good external harmony unless it has achieved it internally. During the due diligence process, be sure to check this dimension. (See Checklist, Figure 8.6.)

The expectation for teamwork must be realistic, and matched between the two partners. If one company uses hierarchical methods of coordinating and communicating, a good match would be another company using essentially the same process. However, the matching of hierarchical versus participatory styles will typically result in missed communications, out-of-phase decision making, and high levels of anxiety.

INTERNAL AND EXTERNAL TEAMWORK

Gates Energy is an OEM manufacturer of Ni-Cad rechargeable batteries for companies such as Radio Shack, GE, and Rayovac. Several years ago, intense bidding competition from Panasonic and Sanyo threatened Gates's very existence. Mitch Carr, Manager of Corporate Purchasing, knew his competitors had a different relationship with their suppliers. At the time, Gates was organized in the traditional department style, and each independent specialist sought his or her own separate objectives. Quality Control only wanted better technology and fewer defects; Scheduling just wanted the product on time, and so forth. Carr commented:

> Everyone looked at what their individual needs were, but failed to look at the *business needs*. We never looked at the *big picture*. We realized that we couldn't do things well externally if we didn't work well together internally.[10]

Carr needed to get top management to buy into the new partnering process and to formalize this process into Gate's operating procedures. He described the sequence that was employed:

> Once we got everyone together, we could decide on what we needed together as a team. As a result of our alliance program, we've found benefits to our own internal teamwork as well. We recently surveyed our departments, and learned our internal relationships have never been better. If you want to create alliances, you've got to be committed and patient—but it pays off in the long run.

International Etching, Inc. (IEI) is a young, fast-growth company in a highly competitive marketplace: providing high-technology chemical milling, principally to jewelry manufacturers. Linda Brunini, CEO,

Figure 7.3   Teamwork (From International Etching, Inc.)

- Teamwork is the key to providing good service to customers.
- Teamwork means thinking about your other teammates as much as you think about yourself.
- Teamwork is the only way to succeed when you are under pressure and customers need attention.
- Teamwork is not just a nice word, it is the fundamental value upon which good service is built.
- Teamwork requires high levels of cooperation, consideration, and communication—you must value these immensely to achieve the expectations of our guests and your fellow teammates.
- Teamwork may not come naturally—it is an art requiring practice, thought, discussion, planning, and more practice.
- Teamwork means being vocal about your expectations for your own performance as well as the performance of others—and very carefully listening to the expectations of your teammates.
- Teamwork means doing whatever is necessary to get the job done, regardless of position or job description.
- Teamwork means professional performance, and true professionals always give 100% effort, not because they are paid for it, and not because others expect it of them, but because they expect it of themselves.

recognized the need to establish closer linkages with her customers, and set on a course to establish downstream alliances. Observing that her company needed internal improvements in teamwork before IEI could maximize its value to its customers, Brunini beefed up her effort to instill the right team values as part of the architectural foundation of her alliance strategy. Figure 7.3 outlines those team values. The results have been noteworthy—improved internal morale, increased productivity through better coordination, and increased sales and service despite a severe downturn in the economy.

CREATIVE TENSION

The purpose of teamwork in an alliance is to create a harmony among its members. This harmony is not a peaceful, relaxing bliss; rather, it is a harmonious tension, like that put on a stringed musical instrument enabling it to produce a resonant sound. This tension fuses the requirements for achievement, challenge, creativity, commitment, and human energy into an optimum team experience as the alliance gains control of its activities and begins to master its fate.

One of the key elements of good teamwork is predictably. Can you expect your partner to react in a particular way under a set of difficult conditions?

Knowledgeable baseball fans appreciate descriptions of the classic 1900s double-play combination of "Tinker to Evers to Chance," three infielders of the Chicago Cubs who perfected the timing of a double play with precision and consistency. A double play must be executed without the slightest hesitation, even a tenth of a second, or the attempt will fail to get both baserunners. The shortstop and second basemen make their throws to where the receivers will be. They don't even look at or for the receivers; they expect them to be there at the right time; they *know* they will be there. They have practiced their timing to perfection.

Pure harmony, teamwork in action, is a joy to watch under any circumstances, but it is even more exciting when it is executed in the pressure of the moment. Predictability under fire is the essence of chemistry. In the words of Mihaly Csikszentmihalyi, in his book *Flow, the Psychology of Optimal Experience:*

> When it happens, we feel a sense of exhilaration, a long cherished sense of enjoyment that become landmark experiences for what life should be like. It is what a sailor holding a tight course feels when the wind whips through his hair, when the boat lunges through the waves like a colt—sails, hull, wind, and sea humming a harmony that vibrates in the sailor's veins.
>
> Moments like these, the best moments of our lives, are not passive, receptive, relaxing times, . . . they usually occur when a person's body or mind is stretched to its limits in a voluntary effort to accomplish something difficult and worthwhile.
>
> Optimum experience is thus something we make happen. In the long run, optimal experiences add up to a sense of mastery—or perhaps better, a sense of *participation* in determining the content of life—that comes as close to what is usually meant as happiness as anything else we can conceivably imagine.[11]

This form of control, whose purpose is to master the coordination of strategic tension between two extended corporations, must supplant the older forms of hierarchical rule if the alliance is to attain its optimum success. This becomes one of the alliance leader's primary tasks.

STABLE RELATIONSHIPS: AN ESSENTIAL FACTOR

Good teamwork is built on many factors. One of the most essential is the stability of personnel. For example, in international deals, even the largest Japanese firms often find more comfort dealing with smaller, more stable, family-run companies. Sony's joint venture with Tecktronics has existed since 1964. One of the key elements to its endurance has been the stable relationship between the top echelons, particularly between the two entrepreneurs who founded the firms. According the Akio Morita, Sony's founder, cooperative ventures fail unless the partners are picked carefully and there are stable interests controlling both sides of the partnership.

The Nature of Values: Do companies with mediocre values make good part-ners? The answer is an emphatic NO.

Mediocre values indicate an underlying lack of commitment to the customer, to the technology, and to the company itself. 1 + 1 will only equal 2.

Mediocre values usually indicate mediocre management, which will react in uninspiring ways as soon as the first crisis occurs. The chemistry between the companies will not be sufficiently intense to make the match successful in the marketplace. Two companies committed to mediocrity will probably end up raping each other for financial rewards.

One Japanese-American joint venture was floundering, and, upon quick investigation, I found that the U.S. CEO had not been to Japan and had not spoken with his Japanese counterpart in 2 years. No top staff personnel had been assigned to work with the alliance. CEOs should always know each other face-to-face.

Many publicly owned companies are simply too volatile to withstand a cooperative venture. Long-term strategy is supplanted by a variety of other pressures—the latest fad, the last quarterly earnings report, a new president, a bad press report, or some change in the economic forecast. Rather than being leaders, or masters of their own destiny, U.S. CEOs often act like weathervanes responding to the winds of change. They are so anxious about stock analysts and hostile takeovers, they are left frustrated, insecure, unhappy, worried about being knocked off, and consequently less able to deal with such important issues as strategic alliances. In addition, high personnel turnover at the middle levels make it difficult to build the operational relationships necessary to maintain trust over the long term. If a corporation suffers from nearsightedness—obsession with short-term profits—it cannot be truly committed to long-term strategic returns on its investment.

ACTION VALUES

"Action values" demonstrate whether the corporate culture's *deeds* are in harmony with its *words*. Can it "walk the talk?" Organizational schizophrenia is a common malady in companies that espouse one set of values, often highly commendable ones, but act in other, incompatible, and often contradictory ways.

Values make up the essence of a company's inner core. If values are nonexistent, vague, contradictory, or not coherent with actions, there sim-

---

T i p

Find a Spirited Partner: Don't let an alliance become a mechanism to dull the competitive spirit. Watch out for partners lacking the motivation and desire for leadership positions in the marketplace. Their energy and strategic vision will be insufficient for a long-term relationship.

---

ply can be no trust, and therefore no chemistry. After all, how can anyone trust something that is inherently ambiguous, contradictory, or incoherent?

Action values are not simply intellectual values, nor are they simply philosophical values, although they may have a sound intellectual or philosophical structure. Action values must be more than puffery and window dressing. The mission statements of some multibillion-dollar corporations are often examples of such fluff, and their flaccid financial performance reflects what they are. Look for an intense company with a passionate mission, like Federal Express or Celestial Seasonings. The major importance of a strong set of values cannot be understated, because it is one of the main premises for the proper function of the alliance. Successful alliances are built on the foundation of an ability to both *create and maintain* a win/win condition. As Denis Waitley has said in *The Double Win:*

> Those committed to the "double win" create other winners without exploiting them. Those who practice the win–lose way of life ultimately must exploit others because others exist to be made use of in one way or another. . . . Unless you have internal values, you have nothing to give *to* others. Lacking in internal values, you need to take value *from* others.[12]

Each alliance should also develop its own clear mission statement, because, like any company, the alliance is its own entity; it must have meaning and purpose for it to have value to those individuals committed to its success. Should a strong set of core values or the win/win condition be lost during the course of the alliance, no trust can exist. Without trust prevailing, there will be no loyalty and no teamwork—no chemistry and, consequently, no alliance.

Successful people make up successful alliances. Their personal value structure is their inner core, their personal driving force. As Stephen Covey has emphasized:

> Whether it rains or shines makes no difference. They are value driven; and if their value is to produce good quality work, it isn't a function of whether the weather is conducive or not. . . . The power to make and keep commitments to ourselves is the essence of developing the basic habits of effectiveness. It is in the ordinary events of every day that we develop the proactive capacity to handle the extraordinary pressures of life. It's how we make and keep

commitments. . . . It's how we view our problems and where we focus our energies. It's the language we use.[13]

Most Americans are frustrated with the amount of time spent in protracted negotiations in Japan, "visiting temples and reading tea leaves." If one looks under the surface, it is more than just a technique designed to drive Americans crazy. Like most things in Japan, there is a purpose.

These negotiations are not drawn out, from the perspective of the oriental mind. Asians devote precious time to scratching below the surface, to learning their potential partners' values, their contradictions, their predictability in a crisis, their essence. Corporate marriages are taken seriously. Gaining the support of a large team of people who will eventually engage their counterparts at every level in the organization is essential to long-term success.

In the process of structuring a strategic alliance between a large Fortune 500 corporation and a fast-growing technology company, an executive of the larger company complained to me: "We have a great mission statement, and an almost spiritual values statement, but our bosses don't really adhere to those statements; we violate them all the time." Needless to say, that alliance is not performing up to its expectations. To paraphrase the words of William George Jordan and James Allen:

> Into the hands of every corporation is given a marvelous power for success or failure—the silent, unconscious, unseen mastery of its destiny. This is simply the constant radiation of what an organization really is, not what it pretends to be. Companies do not receive and attract what they *want*, but that which they *are*. Only when ideals and values harmonize with goals and actions are a company's objectives truly gratified.[14]

Actions communicate far more than words. In the final analysis, one cannot build long-lasting trust and teamwork in the vacuum of the negotiating table (although it may start there); they are manifested through joint action over the course of time on the playing fields of business. Trust emanates from the right corporate culture. Culture can neither be bought

---

Tip

Promote Your Values: International Etching's CEO, Linda Brunini, says:

We give our values statements to customers, suppliers, alliance partners, and employees. Then we ask all of them to expect our company to perform and behave in accordance with our values. This empowers us by helping reinforce these values; to hold us to the ideals we have set. If we violate one of our values unintentionally, we want to know.

through acquisitions or manipulations, nor can it be short-circuited by quick fixes or edicts from above. Cultural integrity comes from integrating values with actions.

Many companies now publish their values statements on a business card. During alliance negotiations, I challenge the negotiators to distribute their cards to their prospective partners, and then say: "I believe in these. My word is my bond. These values are my contract with you. You may hold me to them." I'm surprised at how many firms balk and shrink from the challenge.

Values and trust become the internal guidance system that lets the alliance achieve its goals and keeps the partners in congruent alignment. Without clear and mutually held values, the alliance partners will tend to act independently in their own separate interests, and will eventually betray each other's expectations. The presence of *commitment, teamwork*, and harmonious *action-values*—the three foundations of trust—makes a partner *predictable*.

Another way to predict how a company will act is to develop a mutual contingency plan during negotiations. Without the contingency plan, neither party has really committed to what will happen in the event of a problem.

BEWARE THE CORRIDORS OF CRISIS

Corporate culture is also manifested through the style of corporate decision making and the levels of hierarchy. There's a story about how SMC (Slow Moving Corporation) had a great joint venture with GMC (General Meetings Company). It seems that their corporate styles were in perfect harmony. They both instinctively knew how to navigate the other's turf, and both moved at the same snail's pace.

However, if a fast, young, aggressive smaller business is matched with a more lethargic, staid, bureaucratic corporation, beware of the corridors-of-crisis syndrome. This is exactly what happened to Ross Perot when General Motors acquired Electronic Data Systems.

Ford, in several of its alliances, found its internal decision making was too cumbersome. Managers could not coordinate with their counterparts without having to navigate the corporate ladders, a slow and difficult process. By giving middle managers more authority, and encouraging managers to see the larger picture of how shorter design cycles enabled Ford to become more competitive, the alliances became far more effective.

The "corridors of crisis" can be predicted and prevented by a quick analysis of how chemistry is affected by the style of management of a company. When these conditions occur, the slower moving company must split out a quick-decision team, to prevent the alliance from becoming bogged down in corporate bureaucracy.

THE GREAT EXPECTATIONS TIME BOMB

I was helping negotiate a deal with a U.S. sales corporation to distribute a Japanese paper company's products. After several days of discussions, Mr. Arakawa, the chief Japanese negotiator for Mitsui, the trading company representing the paper company, began to explain exactly what he expected from his American counterparts. He expressed the terms, conditions, and concerns. He said he needed trust and prompt communications. He wanted to know his partner was very strong—at least in the top third of its industry. He was concerned about having a good credit rating so that Mitsui would not suffer if its partner incurred a financial failure, because his company operated on very thin margins.

I was delighted at what a fine statement he had made, and asked him to please put those issues down on a piece of paper so that the prospective American company could be clear about the expectations for the alliance and communicate them to the rest of the company. He looked at me with a most puzzled look, and asked: "Why? These should be just understood." The Japanese culture is much more homogeneous than the American stew-pot; their expectations and values are subtly interwoven into their cultural fabric, while ours must be emblazoned on our shirtsleeve to be remembered.

The most elemental, but also the most overlooked, of all expectations in alliance building is: Exactly what do we expect of ourselves and of our prospective partner? This may seem very basic, but too many companies jump directly into the marriage without even the slightest discussion of the type of commitment an alliance requires. They may not even have the same understanding of an alliance. For example, one of the reasons the alliance between AT&T and Olivetti fell apart was because of very different expectations of what one party needed of the other. It exploded when Olivetti spoke of these frictions at a press conference, something the more conservative AT&T would never dream of revealing in public.

At the commencement of an alliance, on the surface, expectations may seem euphoric, glory filled, and optimistic—new products, new markets, new opportunities. However, underneath this positivism may be deep concerns and apprehensions—questions about job security, unknown risks, partnership loyalty.

Expectations are most useful when they are stated directly, up front. Unfortunately, human nature tends to create problems with expectations, because, almost invariably, an expectation is either unstated or vague—or both. Therefore, by their very nature, expectations are volatile "time bombs" ready to explode as soon as they are not met. As unstated expectations fail to be met, the underpinnings of trust begin to erode, the downward spiral commences, communications become ineffective, heated disagreements are likely, each side blames the other, and the participants' worst fears drive them toward more drastic measures.

The best approach is to follow these two rules:

1. Expect only what is specifically asked for and granted by each party to the venture. Clear expectations will yield clear results.
2. Surface all unstated expectations, put them out front, and either throw them away if they are unrealistic or unreasonable, or convert them to goals and put a clear plan into effect to make them actionable.

Prospective partners should think through their expectations up front, continually clarifying them, and taking care to agree on the value of their respective contributions.

Expectations should be high, because, as Roy Bonner, former IBM executive, put it, "High expectations yield high results." James Vaughn, involved in a number of ventures, echoed these thoughts humorously when he said, "If you shoot for the moon, you might miss and only reach a rooftop, but if you shoot for your foot, you'll surely hit it."

In a typical mining joint venture agreement, many expectations of the partners will be clearly spelled out: expected rates of production for the mine; expected transfer prices when products or services are transferred from one partner to the joint venture, or vice versa; expected time schedules and milestones; expected expenses; and expected distribution of earnings and financing of losses.

PARTNERS TO AVOID

Avoid partners with reputations for skullduggery, conniving, deceit, and winning-at-all-costs. A properly selected partner gives the alliance a safe harbor from economic piracy. The reason is quite simple: In a high-risk environment, there is no way success can be achieved by partner assassination.

Several other types of partners are unlikely to have the right chemistry, no matter how good the strategic plan:

- **Those not into "partnering":** Some people just do not have the good luck, expertise, or desire to enter into partnerships of any sort, no matter how well the deal is structured. Their experience and motivation require their sole control of the venture. Neither the CEO's personality nor the corporate culture lends itself to a cooperative approach.
- **Dependent companies that need you to survive:** A company that is on the decline and needs you and the alliance for survival will make an impossible partner. Companies that latch onto an alliance to stay afloat might be better off being acquired. Small, growing companies can be an exception to this rule. Equity partnerships often serve the dual purpose of both short-term survival and long-term gain. But this

dependency at an early stage of partnership will turn on warning lights in the executive chambers of a large company.

- **Overdominant egos:** The ego makeup of corporate CEOs can be a very critical factor in success. Every good CEO will have a strong ego. But an overdominant ego may not be able to generate cross-corporate teamwork, or it may create one-upmanship, or not hear feedback that enables the alliance to make midcourse corrections.

  A good potential partner with a strong ego can be differentiated from a poor one with a "big" ego. One experienced manager understood this differentiation well when he said: "A strong-ego leader knows his strengths and weaknesses well and is willing to deal with them openly. The one with a big ego has a 500-pound ego and a 600-pound insecurity complex."

Investors and Profit Maximizers

Marriages between investors and companies are really not strategic alliances: they lack the fundamental strategic focus. Conflicting objectives will inevitably cause frustration and probably divorce, unless the desire for short-term profit is put into perspective. Union Carbide Corporation experienced this in a joint venture in industrial gases with an investment group in Spain. Within the first year, the investors wanted to see dividends. Fortunately, UCC was able to convince the investors it needed to reinvest profits to grow the business. Within a few years, the investors were far better rewarded than if they had opted for the premature harvest.

Nepotistic Family-Run Businesses

Alliances tend to be stronger and longer term when the partners represent companies that are professionally managed rather than nepotistic. If the president's wife, brothers, cousins, and children are protected in the organization, the alliance will always be subjugated to the personal gain of the family. (Some family owned businesses are professionally managed.)

Tip

Try the Incremental Approach: If you are not sure a partner is the right match, trust your intuition and back off. If the signals are mixed, then try the incremental approach: become involved in a smaller venture first—maybe a licensing agreement, or sharing technical or marketing research. If a small venture succeeds, then consider a more involved alliance.

A corollary to this condition is the owner-dominated company, where there has been no true line of succession once the owner leaves. Instead, look for a professionally managed company, which is more likely to have a corporate culture that will endure for years. Professionally managed companies usually have deeper and more skilled personnel in the middle ranks of the organization who greatly assist in the communications and coordination of an alliance.

A corporate alliance is an intricate agreement that is susceptible to failure, and ignorance is no excuse. It is the responsibility of those who establish the venture to ask the right questions before signing an agreement.

Like buying shoes or a new suit, an alliance must be the right size, style, and color, it must fit. Should one of the "fits" be wrong, the alliance will chafe, snag, or tear. Just as a cheap price does not buy a good set of clothes, a great price from a supplier or a cheap licensing agreement does not make a great alliance. All three fits must be right.

Chemistry is the critical dimension that successful alliance managers understand dearly, but that the professional deal makers, mechanics, and technicians consistently overlook or underrate. Good chemistry is essential to augment the strategic and functional fits. When chemistry reins, the alliance and its partners are "tuned and in synch."

Chemistry, like mortar between bricks, fills gaps between imperfect strategic and operational "fits" and helps keep the partners glued together when the alliance is under stress. Great chemistry provides flexibility when the alliance needs to change its function and form to adapt to new strategic and operational demands. If the alliance strategy fails the acid test of reality or the operational plans show themselves to be faulty, the chemistry factor is then the pathway to use to rebuild, reorient, restructure, and reform the alliance. One can count on markets changing, technology becoming obsolete, manufacturing processes being superseded, political forces intervening, and any number of unexpected occurrences interfering with the alliance. Without excellent chemistry, no amount of strategic planning or crisis management can substitute.

8

Negotiating for Win/Win

We cannot negotiate with those who say: "What's mine is mine, and what's yours is negotiable."

—John F. Kennedy

The definition of *negotiations* is to *bargain, mediate, intervene, deal, transact, or trade*. None of these terms really applies accurately to the process that occurs in creating an alliance. Unfortunately, however, there is no word in the English language that really describes the process properly. Therefore, I ask you to see the word *negotiations* in a new light, to view it in terms of the *functions performed*, rather than in terms of its past inferences.

PRINCIPLE AND PROCESS OF WIN/WIN

Intertwined into the negotiations process is the concept of developing a win/win condition. The double win is not just a nifty *negotiating technique*. When win/win is considered a technique, managers think of it in terms of game theory, like a chess match with no losers. Creating the double win is far more than a technique; it is both a *principle* and a *process*.

As a *principle*, the double win mandates alliance negotiators and managers to continuously seek *flexible* solutions that *maximize gain and value* for both partners. As a *process*, the double win establishes methodologies that *seek to expand the pie*, to *strive for creative solutions*, to *provide new pathways of opportunity*.

Mutual commitment to the dual nature of win/win—both principle and process—enables the alliance to adapt the architecture of the three-dimensional fit—strategy, chemistry, and operations—to the alliance's ever changing long-term needs.

Two cases in the chemical industry illustrate the critical importance of the double-win principle and process. Ashahi and Dow formed a joint venture in Japan about the same time Sumitomo linked with Uniroyal. Both ventures proceeded successfully for a number of years, until there were major fluctuations between the value of the dollar and the yen. Ashahi and Dow could not work out their differences as to who would manufacture the product, and how adjustments needed to be made to keep the long-term production needs of Ashahi meshed with the cash-flow demands of Dow. The alliance unraveled, and Ashahi purchased Dow's 50% portion of the venture. In contrast, Sumitomo and Uniroyal were able to make these transitions, essentially tearing up their original agreement because it did not envision the dollar–yen fluctuations, and crafting a new, more flexible, Japanese-style arrangement.

The double-win principle/process must be initiated in the negotiations phase, then continued, supported, and instituted during the follow-on operations phase. Negotiating the win/win is a unique phenomenon for many negotiators.

There is no such thing as a successful win/lose arrangement in an alliance. If both parties do not see the alliance contributing to their self-interest, the venture will quickly degenerate into a lose/lose as the losing company attempts to extricate itself from an untenable situation. Once one company loses, the alliance itself will also lose.

The mandate of the double win as both principle and process is not really any different than what happens in a good marriage. The partners must continually adapt as the changing needs of career, age, family, finances, and personal aspirations. Those committed to the double win succeed; those who don't, fail or live in sadness.

THE THREE-STAGE ALLIANCE NEGOTIATION PROCESS

Negotiating an alliance should be thought of as a design process rather than a bargaining process. There are three stages in the process. The first resembles negotiations in that two parties attempt to find a common ground on which they can gain value for themselves. Then, to successfully move forward toward future operations, there is a definitive shift in style and approach marked by the Statement of Principle, the second stage which encapsulates the alliance concept.

The third stage is dedicated to operations planning.

Trap

Legalized Negotiations: Be careful not to introduce legal documents (other than confidentiality agreements) too early in the negotiations phase. Otherwise, your counterpart will be forced to provide a legal response, which will introduce elements of distrust that may poison further negotiations.

Stage 1: Negotiations

During this stage, standard negotiating techniques are frequently used. A large amount of time may be spent jockeying for improved position, enhancing bargaining power, and performing the due diligence process. This stage is characterized by a lower level of trust and openness than the following stage, because both companies are protecting themselves against the possibilities of an unethical partner or a bad deal. It is imperative, during this first stage, to gain a clear understanding of the needs of the other company, and not to be so notoriously demanding in the negotiations as to cut off all opportunities for the negotiations to progress toward a real alliance. At this stage, the two companies must be sure that their strategies will be compatible within the alliance.

This first stage should result in a genuine win/win, not in one company's dominating or beating the other. *The alliance itself will become the extended corporation,* and standard tight-fisted negotiating techniques are insufficient to produce the desired results, because the alliance must be built on a foundation of openness and trust.

Stage 2: Statement of Principle

A shift between the stages of negotiations is signaled by the writing of a Statement of Principle, a ritual that changes the demeanor of the negotiations. The Statement of Principle (sometimes referred to as a Memorandum of Understanding) signifies the intent of the companies to join forces, to hold hands, to work cooperatively in an environment of trust and mutual benefit.

The Statement of Principle crystallizes the concept of the alliance, enables the two companies to make sure there is ample internal support and understanding for the venture, and summarizes its fundamental operations and structure. It also provides an important map for any legal documents. (These concepts will be covered in greater detail later in this chapter.)

To develop the alliance, the sponsors must engage in a process of operations planning—finding the $1 + 1 = 3$ formula, which includes building, structuring, creating, planning, synergizing, envisioning, and project planning.

Keep Lawyers Informed: Keep your lawyers informed and advised during the early stages, but keep them on the sidelines. More important than legal documents is the "due diligence" process, which looks behind the negotiating facade to ensure that your prospective partner has a reputation for fair play.

All too often, however, these stages are overlooked, and deal makers jump into "structuring the deal" to end the negotiations stage. Herein is a major mistake that differentiates cooperative business alliances from external dealings with vendors and from acquisitions. The architectural profession has the right approach with the concept of *form following function*. The design of the structure of the alliance must follow the operational functions that the alliance will perform.

Negotiators who are experienced in acquisitions know "structuring" as the process of valuation of an existing entity. However, in alliances, structuring cannot and should not happen until after it is determined what the existing entity will be. Critical questions must be answered before making that determination. Who is providing what ingredients, in what proportion? How is the entity going to be prepared? How long will it take? What is the value of the ingredients? In other words, one cannot structure the legal and organizational elements of an alliance until the alliance has been fully conceived and engineered. Any attempt to structure the deal too early will be like trying to take a car trip without wheels, gasoline, and a map.

The next stage of negotiations engineers and charts the functions of the alliance and checks the chemistry fit to ensure that the structuring process will integrate the strategic fit with the operational fit.

Stage 3: Operations Planning

Once the Statement of Principle is signed, the negotiating process changes dramatically. Unfortunately, there is no single word in the English language that describes this change in process accurately, but the differences can be described.

Alliance Champion Role. One critical element in this shift concerns how the alliance champions and managers regard their role. At this point, they should no longer see themselves *solely* as representatives of their parent companies, but *also as representatives of the alliance itself.*

In a joint venture, a separate joint venture corporation is created, and the venture manager naturally plays this role. But it is easily overlooked in a strategic alliance because a separate business entity is not created, and therefore no one is designated to represent it. A conscious effort must be made in strategic alliances in envision and experience the alliance as a separate, distinct, and real department or division of the extended corporation.

Creation of Double Win.   Crucial to the development of the alliance is the creation of a genuine win/win condition. By advocating, planning, and fighting *for and on behalf of the alliance itself,* the alliance manager ensures that the alliance will have a good chance of surviving and thriving, and that the sponsors will also be in a winning condition. In essence, this creates a *triple* win—for the two sponsors and for the alliance too.

Win/win is the very process of creation. It requires trust and an ability not to divide the pie as in traditional negotiations, but to create a larger pie.

Walt Disney coined the word *"imagineering"* to describe the science/art of putting the imagination to work to create new wonders, successes, and dreams to fulfill.[1] Paul Moffat, Vice President of Material at Texas Instruments, stated in elegant and simple language how this process works:

> I was initially a project planner, so when I put alliances together, I didn't know anything about fancy negotiations. I just worked with our suppliers and our customers to design a program that made sense for all of us.[2]

One of the fundamental reasons for success in the $1 billion Du Pont–Merck joint venture is a strong commitment to a balanced outcome, where neither party will benefit at the expense of the other.

Personal Relationships.   During this third stage, the operational managers of the two companies must come together to build their personal relationships (assuming that the two companies had no prior personal relationships). This relationship building is essential to the building of trust, understanding, and commitment. *Companies* only ally with each other *in theory; in practice, people* are the bricks that are cemented together with trust to form the structure of the whole alliance. This interpersonal trust building is absolutely essential to success. Time must be built into the process for social relationships to evolve, for people to test their value structures, build teamwork, and create avenues of understanding, thereby enabling the operational managers to begin the process of managing the chemistry fit that keeps the alliance energized.

Operational Integration.   Wonderful strategy and fantastic chemistry in an alliance will not be sufficient if the "nuts and bolts" are the wrong size. The operational fit must work well. Essential questions must be asked: Will our computers talk to each other? Do we write engineering specifications using the same measurement systems? Can our inventory system supply you in the time frames needed? These may seem like elemental issues, but they are frequently overlooked in the rush to consummate a deal. (Chapter 9 addresses this issue of operational integration in greater detail.)

Unlike the traditional American style of jumping right into structuring a deal, European and Asian allies consider the negotiations stage a crucial time to learn what to expect of their prospective partners. Negotiating a deal will probably take three times longer in the overseas environment because prospective partners will want to learn, in detail, each other's motives, resources, weaknesses, past experiences, expectations, skills, operational requirements, and methods of communications. Their success rate with alliances is clear evidence that doing some homework during negotiations pays excellent dividends in the long run. By the time negotiations proceed to the point of legal agreements, the potential ally has been heavily screened.

Ted Ramstad, Vice President of Procurement Processes at Scott Paper, does extensive homework before he even proposes an alliance. He learns his potential ally's market, checks its reputation in the industry, and has a good understanding of its operating practices well before his first contact to suggest an alliance.[3]

OPERATIONAL DIFFERENTIATION

No matter what the situation, negotiations are always a unique process requiring an approach customized to the particular perspectives of each of the companies. Every company has its own individual frame of reference, based on its corporate culture, its industry, and the culture of its physical location. Figure 8.1 illustrates this uniqueness by creating an operational differentiation profile. The frames of reference all have a major effect on the negotiating environment. The greater the differentiation between each pair of factors, the greater the need for people who can integrate, bridge the gaps, and translate from one frame of reference into another, in order to be effective during negotiations. The ten factors shown in Figure 8.1 should be carefully considered, as explained in the following sections.

1. Time Orientation.   Every culture has its own time perspectives. The Japanese view the long-term as decades and centuries; Americans see it as 3 to 5 years. Americans tend to be very time-conscious and punctual. Asians and Europeans are less so, and, for Latin Americans, being punctual is a strange thing. Differences between the east and west coasts of the United States regarding use of time are significant enough to create frictions. The more radically different the time perspectives, the greater the possibilities of increased friction.

Figure 8.1 Operational Differentiation Profile (Sample)

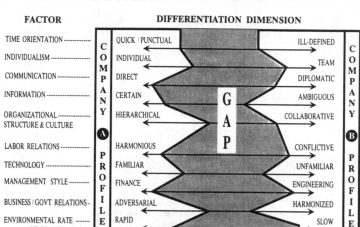

INDUSTRY & CULTURAL FRAME OF REFERENCE

2. Individualism.   Americans will respect individualism far more than will the team-oriented Japanese. The Hindu Indian may impose the hierarchical caste system perspective. Team-oriented cultures will take longer to make decisions because they must build internal consensus.

The team orientation will have a bearing on the size of the negotiating team. Richard Lembo, GenCorp's Director of International Ventures, knows how it feels to negotiate in Japan, where he was alone for five days with 10 Japanese negotiators.[4] It would be hard to imagine Lembo being able to keep track of all issues, when he was so outgunned. Many U.S. corporations like to cut costs by sending in a single negotiator against an army. Later, they wonder why they got the short end of the stick.

3. Communications.   The Japanese are far more diplomatic in their interpersonal communications than Americans, preferring never to say "No" because it might offend. Social norms create pathways for communication that can confound those not familiar with the nuances of gestures and language. The social values and norms may differ widely. Are there major language barriers? Are there strong personal relationships between individuals within the alliance that might overcome barriers?

4. Information.   Are the industries of the partners similar or radically different? Is the available information clear, precise, and specific enough for decisions to be made in a crisp manner? If one company understands the implications of the alliance well and the other company views the information as ambiguous, uncertainty will arise.

5. *Organizational Structure and Culture.* How different are the organizations of the parent companies? Do they differ significantly from each other in their values, rewards, levels of hierarchy, methods of decision making, or leadership styles? The greater the differences, the greater the opportunity for negotiations to be prolonged, strained, or distrustful.

Western cultures tend to emphasize the content, rather than the form of the negotiations. According to GenCorp's Lembo, Japanese and Korean negotiators will be more concerned about how the process develops. Because the United States is much more legalistic than Korea, for example, our contracts cover every element in minute detail; in Korea, policy rather than law is the driving force, and contracts are less detailed.

6. *Labor Relations.* A great deal can be learned about how an alliance will work by viewing internal labor relations. If the labor relations are strained, there is a likelihood that the alliance negotiations will reflect the same style—lawyers, haggling, posturing, and the like.

7. *Technology.* Are the technologies and areas of specialized competence between the partners similar or compatible? Do the experts within each of the sponsors understand the other's technical language? Again, the greater the differences, the more the need for people on the negotiating team who are multilingual in the technical vocabulary of the alliance.

8. *Management Style.* A company whose top management tends to be selected from a marketing background will reflect this approach in their negotiations; a financially oriented company will be looking for "the numbers"; an engineering company will concentrate on technology. If this is the case, more "integrators" who can bridge the differences should be on the negotiations team.

9. *Business Government Relations.* What type of governmental environment does the company work in? Companies that work closely with government will not exhibit the same fears as those who work in an atmosphere of legal strife and regulatory animosity.

10. *Environmental Rate of Change.* Is there a significant difference between the partners, regarding the speed with which their technological or market environments change? Will the joint venture's environment differ significantly from that of the partners?

By carefully analyzing these ten dimensions, the designers of an alliance can quickly determine the level of *differentiation*, and the level of *integration* needed to make the venture most effective. These frames of reference will remain in place after the alliance is formed, and must be adroitly managed after signing the legal agreements.

ALLIANCE NEGOTIATIONS MODEL

The larger the gap between the two companies, the greater the strain on negotiations. Figure 8.2 illustrates how the operational differentiation gap affects the negotiations. If there are substantial differences between the companies' industrial and cultural frames of reference, it is common for negotiations to take a legalistic turn, to compensate for the ambiguity and misunderstanding. While legal technicalities may seem to momentarily fill the ambiguity gap, they only serve to diminish trust, and consequent negotiations begin taking on an increasingly adversarial style. Instead, negotiators should examine the causes of the difficulties and attempt to bridge the gaps with increased communications and deeper levels of understanding. Many opportunities are embedded within these differences, because difference represents a unique perspective, or a new way of doing things. If companies are highly differentiated operationally, the negotiating team should be very carefully selected so that they understand their prospective partner's unique reference points.

Figure 8.2   Alliance Negotiations Model

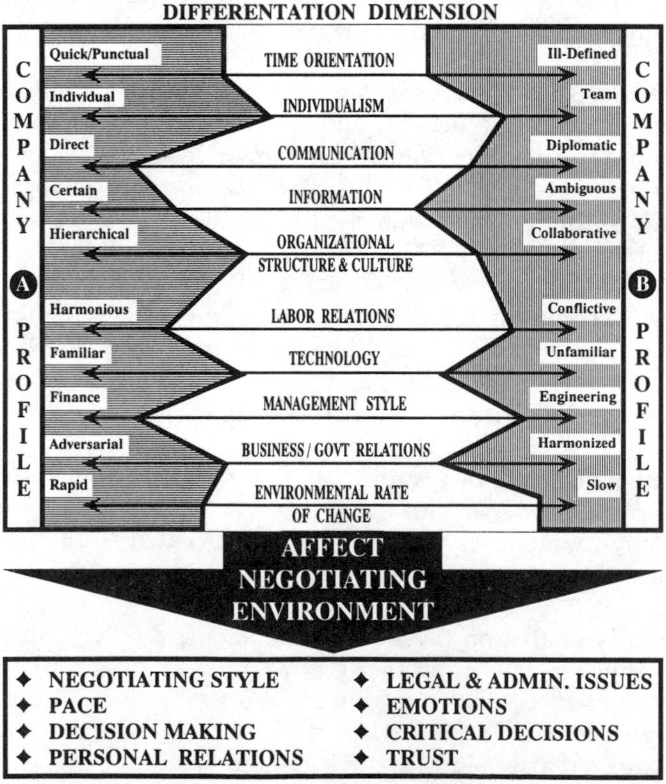

TOP-RANK SUPPORT

Negotiations should initially be established high rank to high rank, to ensure proper commitment and support. This critical element is too often overlooked, with very sad consequences. Unless the top echelons are supportive of the alliance, it is, by definition, *not* strategic, no matter how much the architects conceive it to be. Only when the high priests of the organization have sprinkled their holy water on the alliance does it become blessed.

With this high-level support, whether from a CEO or divisional manager, the alliance and its champions become empowered. I have personally seen too many alliances fail because one boss was engaged to the other company's middle managers, but his or her counterpart was ensconced high in the parapets of the corporate castle, too involved in other issues to become intimately supportive of the alliance.

In one case, events proceeded comfortably in this condition for months, but when the first minor problem occurred that strained a customer relationship, the estranged boss said: "We must immediately distance ourselves from the alliance." This was exactly the opposite of the correct response. Had the boss known of the potential power of the alliance, he would have invoked its capacity to design an elegant solution to the problem. A strictly middle management linkage between two companies is simply a tactical relationship; it only becomes a holy alliance when it receives the top-rank blessings.

THE ART OF THE DEAL

Negotiations should be used as a design process enabling an alliance to function effectively to achieve its strategic mission. Fundamental to this design process is an inner structure for the way each team approaches the negotiations. If the negotiators see the process as a technical evaluation, then that is precisely how it will be approached. If it is seen as a legal and financial procedure, then negotiations will be focused around contracts and number crunching.

During the mergers and acquisitions (M&A) heyday of the 1980s, one of the bywords of deal makers was "Let's structure a deal." Wall Street buzzed with investment bankers, lawyers, and accountants who couldn't wait to create some new "deal to structure."

By the 1990s, it became evident that M&A were only 15% to 20% successful. Moreover, the junk bonds that had fueled the fiery M&A madness had dried up. With a diminishing market, many M&A professionals have tried to retread themselves into the alliance game. For the most part, the results have been very poor.

When one examines how the M&A process works, it should be very evident that virtually nothing that was part and parcel of the M&A process is translatable into the alliance design process. Designing an alliance is a process of creation. The M&A process is one of valuation and takeover.

The principal reason M&A deals fail is that their process is fundamentally flawed in two ways. First, two critical dimensions of three-dimensional fit—chemistry and operations—are inherently left out of the process. The very essence of an M&A deal excludes the middle managers from participation, ostensibly to prevent any insider trading of stock.

Middle managers control the domain of operational integration. Because they are left out, the critical details are not effectively considered. Simple little things relating to operational fit, such as the interface of inventory procedures, or management information systems, can be extremely difficult to integrate. The operational fit problem has been encountered in every industry, from airlines to banking to retailing. How many times have managers seen their bosses come back from business trips after "cutting a deal," knowing that there were severe technical and operational problems that would result in excessive unexpected costs?

Second, many of the people who orchestrate a deal—the lawyers, accountants, investment bankers, and even the internal corporate deal makers—run away from the deal as soon as it closes, demonstrating not a single iota of responsibility for its success in the aftermath of their efforts.

Even the terminology of the M&A deal stands in stark contrast to the alliance. M&A refers to battle terms and war strategies, such as conquering, hostile takeovers, and white knights. The alliance process refers to partnering, marriage, and trust. If your intention is to make love, the conqueror's warrior-game plan will not work.

The alliance process stands in contrast by building middle management into the checks-and-balances of the design. Further, the alliance champion who conceives and believes in the venture should be attached to the alliance for its full term, rather than bolt madly to the next deal.

Trap

Wrong Techniques: Avoid getting into an offer–counteroffer game with your potential partner, particularly by phone or mail. Alliance negotiations are always best done face-to-face. An "over-the-transom" approach is neither spontaneous nor synergistic, and therefore fails to create a double-win condition.

Similarly, a "technique" style advocated by many negotiations seminars fails to address the critical need to creatively address the systems needs that alliance architecture demands. More importantly, standard negotiating techniques are tactical in nature, and thereby fail to address critical strategic issues—the *total* picture—that underpin the alliance.

KEEP CHAMPIONS GLUED TO THE DEAL

When IBM negotiates a cooperative venture, it insists that the deal be initiated at the operational level, then supported by corporate expertise. This belief comes from years of experience and recognition of how vital human relationships are in the alliance. The negotiations stage is simply the commencement of the chemistry and trust that must act as interconnecting threads from the past through the present and into the future, to attain success.

When Tri-Wall's Vice President, Bernard Roth, championed six global joint ventures in the paper industry, he remained the interconnecting link to each alliance, although not involved in daily management. At one point in the negotiations of a deal in England, which required a concession in work rules from the normally stubborn English unions, the deal began to fall apart because his British counterparts were at odds with their union. Roth, recognizing the value of personal relationships and trust, asked to talk with the unions. After several days of discussions and trust building, he convinced them of the value of the venture in preserving their jobs and creating more economic vitality in their depressed community. He spoke at a union meeting, gained their endorsement, and the deal was signed. When Roth revisited the British venture, he would always make it a point to spend time with the union leaders.

Stanley Bostitch, a manufacturer of pneumatic industrial fasteners, has had a strategic alliance with Max Corporation of Japan since the early 1970s. John Poccia, Senior Vice President of Engineering, who manages the relationship, observes:

> I personally visit Japan 2–3 times per year, and we have many exchanges of engineers and sales managers. It is critical to push for face-to-face meetings and to keep current on future plans. In some cases we elect not to cooperate on the development of a tool, in other cases we work hand-in-glove.
>
> We'll go to the trade shows together to assess new products and customer needs and analyze the opportunities together.
>
> Some negotiations have been pretty tough, but we know each other; there is a lot of good will that helps out. No one would throw away a 27-year relationship for a few minor irritants; we care about each other too much.
>
> Only two or three people have been responsible for managing the relationship since its inception 27 years ago, so we inject a lot of stability into things. The Senior Vice President of International Marketing used to handle the job, but we found technical issues were on the agenda more than marketing ones.
>
> The presidents meet twice a year, once in Japan and once in the U.S. My counterpart and I both report directly to our respective presidents and we speak for them. This top-level commitment is critical.[5]

The Japanese are most particular about preserving these relationships after negotiations end. Authors Timothy Collins and Thomas Doorley comment:

In the event of later difficulties, it is the managers who presided at the birth of the partnership who are likely to be consulted by the Japanese partner, even if they have moved on to quite different lines of responsibilities in their own companies. Their responsibilities as architects of the partnership remain. A move by a key executive to another company—common in the West, but virtually unheard of in Japan—creates considerable uncertainty, and an immediate effort must be made to rebuild human relationships between partners.[6]

ASSEMBLING THE NEGOTIATING TEAM

Once a prospective ally has been identified, informal discussions should commence with top-echelon knowledge on both sides that an alliance is being initiated. These communications can be verbal or written, but there is no need for formal legal documents at this point. Strategic and financial issues will most likely be the focus of initial discussions.

The core of the negotiations team should be the future alliance operations team—they must "own" their creation and be committed to it so strongly that they are willing to see it through birth, adolescence, and maturity. Because the core players on the negotiations team will continue on to operate the alliance, they are using the negotiations process as the first step in developing the personal linkages that make future functioning effective.

There are several excellent reasons for using a negotiating team rather than a sole deal maker:

- Slows down the process to make sure all the details, contingencies, and opportunities are thought through;
- Enables the middle managers to get involved, ensuring better operational integration;
- Does not commit either company too early to something it may regret later or cannot adhere to in reality;
- Provides an opportunity to gain full understanding and commitment among all those who will have to be involved in structuring and operationalizing the alliance;
- Provides opportunities for experts within the organization to examine the alliance and determine whether it makes sense from a multitude of perspectives;
- Builds the foundation for future teamwork;
- Allows internal experts to view multidimensional aspects of the alliance for evaluation and commitment.

Despite these compelling reasons, it is surprising how many seasoned managers wait in trepidation for their bosses to return from a business trip, expecting the terrifying pronouncement "I've just cut a deal!" These managers often know the deal that was cut by the boss should really have

Gaining Commitment: To gain commitment, remember that *people support what they help create.*

been sliced, diced, and mashed instead, but for the boss's sake they will have to make it work. It is just this type of approach that contributed to the high failure rate among acquisitions.

Anyone who has ever negotiated a deal outside of the United States will be struck by the fact that seldom do other countries ever use the "Lone Ranger" approach to negotiations (which often results in "six-gunning" a deal—Ready, *Shoot, AIM!*"). By emulating the more adroit foreign negotiating style, a far better deal will be struck for both companies.

Next to the alliance champion, the most important person on the team will be the individual designated as the alliance manager, who will be handling day-to-day responsibilities. Very early in the negotiating process, be sure that the alliance manager is designated by both sides. Failure to designate this individual during the early negotiations will invariably result in his or her not knowing the intent of many of the team's decisions. Without ownership of these decisions and an ability to influence them, a future alliance manager will, at best, be terribly disadvantaged, and more likely will be uninformed, uncommitted, and unenthused.

Involve the key operational managers who will be responsible for implementing the decisions of the negotiations team; their early commitment will be essential later. These operational managers will be a good barometer of whether the right chemistry exists beyond the CEO level. In orchestrating the highly successful Du Pont–Merck joint venture, Business Development Director Jim Wells ensured that core people from the negotiations carried over into the implementation, because only they knew the real intent of the agreement.

Senior managers will be focusing on strategic and financial issues in the venture; the operational managers will be measuring operational fit—timing, cost controls, communications, engineering, allocation of personnel, and day-to-day problem solving. Both levels should be assessing chemistry. Use a negotiating team well versed and educated in the foreign culture of the potential partner.

The larger the negotiating teams, the longer the negotiations. However, time will be saved ultimately because, once operations commence, operational managers will "hit the ground running." Figure 8.3 illustrates a typical alliance negotiating team.

Do not try to finalize an alliance during the first few meetings; all that is needed is a brief outline of a basic strategy and concept of operations,

Figure 8.3   Typical Negotiating Team

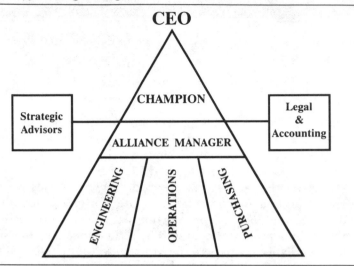

which can be rewritten as a 2- to 5-page Statement of Principle. Once the Statement of Principle is approved by both companies, then the last stage of negotiations—operations planning—can commence.

Don't change negotiating team members unnecessarily, otherwise the chemistry factors will not be recognized accurately. But don't be afraid to change players if the chemistry is wrong. *Never* try the "good-guy/bad-guy" negotiating routine in an alliance; it will kill any trust as fast as a speeding bullet.

ROLE OF THE SKEPTIC

Every negotiating team should have a resident skeptic, to ensure the venture does not get caught in the euphoria of synergy without having its feet firmly anchored in reality. There is an almost natural tendency among those considering an alliance to begin romancing the future, much like

Tip

Memories Fade: Protect yourself and your partner by writing down your agreements, even informal ones. It will be valuable to refer to at a later date to understand why certain decisions were made, especially after key individuals rotate out of the alliance into new jobs.

entrepreneurs idealizing the potential of a new gadget. Experienced venturers understand the requirement for at least one person to play the role of the cynic, to counteract these romantic tendencies. Humphrey Neil, author of *The Art of Contrary Thinking,* states:

> When everyone thinks alike, everyone is likely to be wrong—at least in their timing of events. . . . Contrary thinking is responsible for [preventing] the delusion of projecting today into tomorrow without thought of what might happen during the night.[7]

Neil goes on to say, however, "it is far easier to be contrary . . . than it is to create original thought." Skepticism alone, while providing a balance for optimism, is not enough. Use skeptics to create a dynamic tension with optimists, yielding original, unique solutions.

Don't confuse skeptics with cynics and deal killers. Skepticism is healthy; cynicism is purely negative. There is a fine line between skeptics and cynics. One definition of cynics is: "When they smell roses, they think of a funeral." Or, as Oscar Wilde suggested: "Cynics know the price of everything and the value of nothing."

The skeptic's role is not to kill the deal, but rather to look at realities, details, and things that could go wrong. The skeptic should not be a person who is threatened by the alliance. "Deal killers" are those in the company who are threatened by the alliance. They fear their job or esteem will be diminished by the resources that are being brought by the extended corporation.

When negotiating, look for cynics and deal killers on the other side. You can sometimes tell the difference because skeptics are negative but *objective,* and deal killers are negative and *subjective.*

Trap

Time Allocations During Negotiations: When deals fail, executives lament that, during negotiations, they spent:

> 100% of their time on legal and tax work; selecting products to produce, market, or develop; and on strategic issues;
>
> —but—
>
> 0% on building trust and teamwork; operations planning; management and personnel selection; developing a strong alliance team; practical decision-making procedures; and maintaining good communications between partners.

To avoid this, allocate time during negotiations for these discussions, and designate key team members to take individual responsibility for each of these factors.

To critically evaluate the venture, some companies appoint two groups: an advocacy team and a devil's advocacy team. One supports and the other opposes the alliance. Their combined opinions enable the CEO to avoid being seduced by the thrill of courtship.

MUTUAL ASSURANCES AND CONFIDENTIALITY

Do not reveal any information you consider to be propriety or confidential until both parties have entered into a mutual Confidentiality Agreement. Some large, multinational corporations refrain from Confidentiality Agreements because their organization is too large to know who might already be working on a similar field in a laboratory in some remote corner of the world. Needless to say, however, some sort of assurance that confidential material will not be used adversely is important to have at this stage.

In lieu of a formal Confidentiality Agreement, a letter agreeing not to use confidential information adversely may be a good fall-back tactic if the players are trustworthy. If your potential partner does not have an impeccable reputation for maintaining confidentiality and/or balks at signing a Confidentiality Agreement, it might be advisable to find another partner.

When highly technical, sensitive, and proprietary technical information must be shared between the parties before a decision can be made to seriously consider an alliance, a Noncompete Agreement may be in order. One company may fear that the disclosure of sensitive data would give the prospective partner an opportunity to use the negotiations to exploit the information, then abandon the idea of an alliance, and subsequently become a serious competitor. The prospective partner, however, may need to evaluate the claims, to be sure the technology can truly be used in the commercial applications envisioned by the alliance.

In Canada and certain other countries, information disclosed in pre-alliance meetings will be held confidential and may not be exploited adversely.

Tip

Confidentiality: Loose lips sink ships, and engineers, in particular, love to talk about their technical exploits and concepts. Inadvertently, they can give away very critical information, that, should the alliance not be consummated, could be very damaging.

Train your negotiations team in confidential usage. Joseph Soviero, president of Union Carbide's Specialty Chemicals Division recommends allowing only one person from each company to be exposed to technology during negotiations, and those persons should be signed to maintain secrecy.

HOW TO USE LAWYERS

Do not let lawyers act as the key negotiators; negotiating is the role of management. Lawyers should advise. Foreigners are wary of the U.S. legal system's propensity for choosing litigation instead of problem solving, and even the hint of an appearance of a lawyer too early in negotiations can sour an international or domestic deal.

Similarly, the introduction of an unwieldy or ill-drafted legal agreement too soon will only result in the other party's becoming frightened by adversarial or punitive language, then resorting to an equally impactful documentary legal counterpunch. As trust unwinds, the negotiations quickly spiral downward, fear replaces creativity, and the alliance unravels.

Alliances never fail because of the quality of their legal agreements. A good legal agreement protects against downside risks in the event of a failure, but does not prevent failure itself. Ultimately, any cooperative venture's success lies not in its legal documents, but in the success of its strategy and day-to-day operations.

Why are there so many problems surrounding legal issues in alliances? There are several reasons.

The Acquisition Mentality. Those who have had tremendous experience with mergers and acquisitions know the pivotal importance of legal documents. Lawyers and deal makers who bring this experience to alliance negotiations do not realize the critical shift in perspective that is needed. Instead of working with designing the architecture of the alliance, they do what they do best—focus on the technical details.

The Rush to Do a Deal. People who view themselves as deal makers receive no professional gratification until they get a signed document in their hands, making the agreement official. Instead of concentrating on being sure the systems interface properly and the problems have the right solution, they see their success in the form of a piece of paper.

The "Exit Strategy" Myth. Lawyers have said for years that no alliance should be created without first focusing on how to get out, should the deal fail. There is enough wisdom to this advise to make it palatable.

However, it carries its own seeds of destruction, especially when too much emphasis is placed on it early in negotiations. By overemphasizing the exit strategy, it becomes preeminent to the negotiators, pushing other more critical strategic and operational issues into the background, and it creates insecurity and fear within the two potential partners. It is far better to discuss *transformation* options, one of which is the exit strategy. Transformation looks at the strategic spectrum of options and provides various alternatives, in case the alliance has to adapt to new strategic and operational conditions.

The Substitute for Good Planning.   Probably the worst reason for excessive legal documents is not caused by lawyers. Too many times, I have seen an ill-conceived back-of-the-envelope piece of paper given to the corporate lawyer with vague instructions about converting it into a legally sound agreement. A lawyer's primary purpose and most valuable role is to protect clients against unreasonable risks. However, when presented with a vague idea of what the alliance is all about, instead of asking strategic and operational questions, which are really needed to fill the void, the lawyer will plug the many glaring gaps with the legal equivalent of nuclear weaponry. Naturally, the client is pleased with the warrior instincts of the lawyer and presents a portfolio of paperwork to the alliance partner, who sees it as tantamount to a full-blown declaration of war. Managers should carefully review and weigh any legal advice privately before introducing such rough edges into the negotiations. Negotiators must have specific clarity of purpose in their goals and plans. The Statement of Principle, discussed at the beginning of the next chapter, is designed to achieve this goal.

Effective Use of Attorneys

Some alliances have never gone beyond the negotiations stage because lawyers began asking the difficult questions about the real risks and how those risks would be minimized. Overly zealous or very conservative lawyers may occasionally protect their clients right out of an alliance, but, more often than not, the probing analysis of a good legal counsel has saved an idealist from a poorly conceived venture.

There is little need for attorneys to be present during the early stages of the negotiation, but they should be consulted to draft confidentiality and noncompete agreements, to protect against Securities and Exchange Commission (SEC) violations, and to ask hard questions about commitments and contingencies so the business participants can prepare solutions.

Needless to say, one should avoid bringing an attorney to the bargaining table as a negotiating agent. It only encourages the other side to do the same, and then the negotiations may turn into an adversarial process, with each lawyer protecting his or her client right out of the venture.

At a recent joint venture seminar, one businessman boasted that he never used a lawyer in putting together his "deals," because lawyers knew little about business and should not be involved in "mucking up a good business deal." Although this attitude might express frustration with some lawyers who tend to obfuscate issues, this businessman allowed his frustration to replace wisdom! Lawyers have a very real role in negotiating alliances, although that role is often largely behind the scenes.

Robert Edwards, an experienced business lawyer for the firm of Tillinghast, Collins, & Graham, stated a far more intelligent perspective when he said:

Trap

Use of Lawyers as Surrogate Champions: Be alert for deals where there is no real business champion for the alliance, and the gap is being filled by a zealous lawyer who creates the illusion of a real champion by strong posturing.

Beware of competitive, overly aggressive attorneys who, when in a room with their equally competitive counterparts, tend to dominate discussions, pick deals apart at the last minute, debate minutiae, and attempt to protect their clients from any and all risks. Instead, find a seasoned legal counselor. Contentious lawyers generate large legal fees but cannot sacrifice their own egos for the well-being of their clients.

> You negotiate the business deal, and I'll protect you from the worst possible legal circumstances. You are the businessman, and therefore you make the business decisions.[8]

If a business deal goes too far down the road without an attorney's input, a businessperson could find that he or she crossed some illegal boundaries or made commitments that were not legally sustainable. Think of an attorney as a coach on the sidelines—involved, but not an active player on the field during early negotiations.

At one recent deal closing, the lawyers for each of the prospective partners began a series of entangling debates about contingencies, termination clauses, and other details couched in legalese. The prospective business teammates were confused and out of the mainstream of the discussion. One businessman nodded to his prospective partner, and they both stepped out of the room, unbeknown to the rivaling lawyers. Outside, the two made whatever arrangements they thought were fair, walked back into the room, and announced their decisions to the lawyers, who were left dazzled.

HOW TO CONTROL LEGAL COSTS

When choosing a lawyer, look for one who is not litigious, one who may be confrontative yet diplomatic. Be sure the lawyer has more than just a foggy notion about the concepts and premises of the "extended" corporation. Do not pay for your lawyer's education by choosing someone who is moving from one area of expertise, such as acquisitions, into alliances, at your expense. Ask what other clients the attorney has done alliance work for. Check references and get a "not to exceed" cost before engagement. Pass along a copy of a book on alliances so that the lawyer has a feeling for the subject matter, and ask that it be read "off the meter."

Drafting Documents: Smaller companies negotiating alliances with larger corporations are often wise to let the larger corporation initiate legal documents. Most of these corporations have in-house counsel. Legal jargon will generally be kept to a minimum, and agreements will have a familiar format.

Often, the larger corporation that is given the lead will feel more in "control," and legal costs for the smaller company will be reduced.

If the alliance is somewhat complex, such as a joint venture with a large corporation, it will be wise to choose a lawyer from a firm with some depth in both corporate and tax law. Sole practitioners may not have the experience or time to handle difficult issues that might arise in the course of negotiations with larger corporate attorneys.

When dealing with large corporations, be careful that their negotiators do not get too far ahead of or out of tune with their legal department, particularly if the legal beagles are not alliance-oriented. If the corporate attorneys still see alliances as a new twist on sales reps and OEM manufacturing contracts, you will have to pay the price.

There are several additional ways to keep legal costs from escalating during negotiations, including:

1. Keep lawyers on the sidelines (like coaches in a football game), involved and advising internally, but not directly negotiating at the initial stages of alliance formation.
2. Develop a clear and concise Statement of Principles to use as a foundation for the drafting of the documents. Otherwise, the lawyers will attempt to limit their client's risk by drafting lengthy documents to cover their own uncertainties of what the

"Boilerplate" Legal Documents: Several times I have encountered larger corporations asking their in-house counsel to draw up legal documents without input from the alliance negotiators on the purpose and structure of the deal.

The in-house counsel began by using an off-the-shelf form of sales rep agreement, services contract, or licensing agreement. These agreements seldom fit the unique characteristics of a particular alliance.

Be sure the lawyers use a Statement of Principle (agreed to in advance by both alliance companies) as the foundation for their legal drafts.

---

real business concept is. These documents will undoubtedly appear onerous to the other side, who will respond with less openness, poor trust, and an equally unwieldy set of legal documents.

3. Limit the amount of time the lawyers may take for their review. Give them guidelines on how many pages they may use for the documents. If they balk at the time or length limitation, it will provide the basis for an enlightening discussion. However, without such limits, businesses run the risk of having the legal process expand to disproportionate limits. Get a firm grip on the cost for legal review. Indicate that under no circumstances will you pay for more legal costs without advanced discussion. Follow the example of General Electric and Bechtel, who were building a plant for Susquehanna Power. The project had very tight time frames. Ground had been broken and $1.5 million had already been spent, but the lawyers were still bickering about language. Finally, the two joint venture partners told the lawyers to have the agreements ready in 48 hours or they would be fired and not paid. The deal was ready for signatures the very next day.

AVOIDING FUTURE LITIGATION

The fundamental rule in avoiding legal problems is to have partners who want to make continual adjustments to keep the double win in place during the alliance. However, to make litigation a very unrealistic possibility, stipulate in the legal agreement that:

1. Prior to litigation, the CEOs of both companies (*not their designated representatives*) will meet face-to-face to attempt to resolve the problem.
2. In the event that the joint CEO meeting fails to achieve resolution, both companies agree to submit the problem to alternative dispute resolution (ADR). Alternative Dispute Resolution functions on these premises:
   - Most business disputes are best resolved privately, by agreement.
   - A dispute is a problem to be solved, not a contest to be won.
   - Third-party arbitrators and mediators should be used only after executives have attempted unsuccessfully to solve the problem themselves.
3. In the event that steps 1 and 2 fail and the conflict winds up with a filing of suit, the party who loses the suit will pay all court costs.

Using this three-step method, the chances of litigation will be extremely small.

No matter what the punitive language contained in a legal agreement, an alliance will not succeed or fail based on the quality or quantity of the legal documentation. It will succeed when the sponsors make a long-term commitment to a double-win arrangement that continually adjusts the three dimensions of fit—strategy, chemistry, and operations—to the needs of the alliance.

FLEXIBLE AGREEMENTS

The American legal profession still grows contracts from their English roots, which date back to a medieval time, when contracts were carved in stone, the world was stable, and change was measured across centuries— not in months or weeks, as it is today. In the Middle Ages, contracts did not need flexibility.

In contrast, Japanese contracts are fluid; often general rather than specific. Much of this approach is the result of a transfer of Asian philosophies of strategy to the business world. Consider the strategy of Lao-tzu (500 B.C.), whose writings are still studied ardently in the East:

> When two great forces oppose each other, the victory will go to the one that knows how to yield. This is called going forward without advancing. Rather than advance just an inch, it is better to retreat a yard.

Another of Lao-tzu's offerings teaches flexibility in relationships:

> Men are born soft and supple; dead they are stiff and hard. Thus whoever is stiff and inflexible is a disciple of death. The hard and stiff will be broken; the soft and supple will prevail.

These principles are demonstrated in the martial arts of karate and jujitsu, as well as in the Japanese treatment of alliance partners. When Japan's Sony Corporation first began introducing transistor radios into the U.S. market in the late 1950s and early 1960s, Sony's CEO, Akio Morita, was astounded by the difference in contract law between Japan and the United States:

> The first thing that puzzled [American] lawyers and accountants was that many of our contracts specified that if, during the life of the contract, conditions changed in a way that affected the ability of either side to comply with the terms, both sides would sit down and discuss the new situation. This kind of clause is common in Japanese contracts, and many companies do much or even most of their business without any contracts at all. . . . The Americans could not understand how we could sit down together and talk in good faith if the two parties were having a major disagreement.[9]

Keep the legal agreements very flexible and think of them as a "beginning," recommends Jim Wells of Du Point–Merck. This keeps the relationship dynamic and ever evolving.

Especially when dealing with countries that do not use English law as the basis of their legal structure, consider writing a flexible agreement that can be adapted as strategic and operational conditions change.

U.S. lawyers who have no background in international agreements will have a very difficult time with this approach. As a case in point, I was involved in negotiating an alliance in the energy industry. One very large U.S. corporation was finalizing negotiations with a fast moving high-technology company overseas. The three dimensions of fit were perfect, and the opportunities for growth, both short- and long-term, were excellent. Operational teams from both companies had met for three days to ensure that technology development would be well integrated.

The terms of an agreement were hammered out between the champions of the large corporation and the CEO of the smaller company. Everyone was ready to operationalize the alliance. The technology codeveloped by the two companies would be owned by the large company, which would use it exclusively in its propriety markets. The smaller company would receive an exclusive license for all the other markets, and would pay a royalty to the larger corporation.

Because we could not determine exactly what amount of work would be necessary to bring the new technology to the point of final field tests, it was decided to leave the final royalty payment flexible, and all agreed that, for now, a rate of 3% to 5% would be a "fair and reasonable" range.

However, the lawyers for the U.S. corporation would have nothing of such a "loose-ended" agreement. They thought it provided too much room for litigation. They maintained that the corporation never did things like this before. They regarded the granting of all the nonproprietary markets to the alliance partner an insupportable position.

The lawyers had been left out of the negotiations loop. Normally, they preferred to be intimately involved in the negotiations process, as they had been in the mergers and acquisitions heyday of the 1980s. Not only were their egos bruised, but now they were prepared to torpedo the deal rather than seek the win/win solution. It did not matter that killing this alliance would rob their company of a highly valuable competitive weapon.

The lesson here was not that lawyers are deal killers, but rather that we should have spent several days educating the lawyers regarding alliances, being sure they understood the alliance process, and confirming their roles in bringing alliances from conception to fruition. What's more, the corporate lawyers should have received a signal from higher powers regarding their role in alliances.

HOW HARD BARGAINING CREATES SUCCESS

The major problem for an alliance negotiations will be not in the *differences* in positions between the two companies (often an advantage in the alliance), but rather in the *conflicts* of their interests, needs, desires, concerns, and their fears.

Figure 8.4   Checklist for Measuring Your Bargaining Power   ☑

Several key issues should be analyzed in measuring bargaining power:

_____ How strongly does your prospective partner want an alliance?

_____ What resources are contributed by each partner?

_____ What is the relative urgency for each partner?

_____ What other alternatives exist for the partners?

_____ How highly does the other partner regard your strategic and operational strengths and weaknesses?

_____ Does the other partner think that your involvement will be essential to success?

_____ Are the expectations for performance realistic?

_____ Can you actually meet your commitments? Can your partner?

_____ Are you and your partner willing to frankly and openly assess each partner's individual strengths and weaknesses?

When pressure is put into the early stages of negotiations, the conflicts will tend to surface; they will not be driven underground during the joy of courtship, only to come back to haunt the alliance later, when it is under great stress. Conflicts will emerge better in the first stage of negotiation, when there is still a quasi-adversarial atmosphere. They will tend to be submerged in the rather blissful and cooperative air of the last stage of operations planning. A good rule is: Identify the conflicts early, but formulate their resolution in the last stage, when trust is stronger.

The Japanese like to use protracted negotiations to learn about how their prospective partner will work under stress. If there is insufficient commitment to make the alliance work, it will be learned by seeing whether the prospective ally meets deadlines, keeps promises, and responds positively in ambiguous situations. Find out how your partner will react to the first crisis.

Sweat the details. Fuzzy goals should be converted into clear expectations. Broad generalities are open fields for confusion and misinterpretation. Go beyond the euphoria of synergy and chemistry to see whether the alliance really has substance. (See Figure 8.4.)

IBM AND THE GOLDEN RULE

During negotiations, it is vital to understand the value system of your partner. Values form the basis of trust. Businesses that do not prize the value of their reputations generally do not make good partners. Figure 8.5 illustrates a statement of some of the values that work in alliances. Roy Bonner, former senior executive at IBM, has said,

A handshake is a deal—as defined by the other party. The partners must consider their reputations as their most important possession. The *real* Golden

Figure 8.5   Alliance Values

IBM'S CODE OF CONDUCT[10]

IBM issues a "Code of Conduct" to all its employees. The following excerpts are noteworthy because they are clear representations of a value structure conducive to strategic alliances:

- Don't make misrepresentations to anyone you deal with. If you believe the other person may have misunderstood you, correct any misunderstanding you find exists.
- Honesty is integral to ethical behavior, and trustworthiness is essential for good, lasting relationships.
- Never use IBM's size itself to intimidate, threaten or slight another person or organization.
- Everyone you do business with is entitled to fair and even-handed treatment. This is true whether you are buying, selling, or performing in any other capacity for IBM.

Rule was the foundation for Thomas Watson's growth of IBM. He believed he would succeed in direct proportion to the trust customers had in IBM.[11] When the Golden Rule is ignominiously referred to as "He who has the gold, rules" or "Do unto others before they do unto you," we will all be done harm.

Watch carefully to see whether actions and values are in harmony, and whether corporate value structure is of the highest standards. Anything less than the best will create opportunities for disappointment.

USING YOUR BARGAINING POWER

Negotiating an alliance is not like buying a house or a car; it is more like arranging a marriage. It is far more important to determine whether $1 + 1 = 3$ than to squeeze the last concessions out of an opponent. Your objective is to create a win/win, not a win/lose, condition. In alliance negotiations, it is far more important to unleash creative powers, to formulate an expanding pie, than to dicker over the crumbs. By expanding the pie, creativity spawns more creativity, and both parties gain value. Each realizes a bigger piece, rather than worrying who got the biggest piece.

You will have to rely on your partner to help solve problems when they occur. Make sure your partner is in sync with you, and not seeking to regain perceived advantages that were lost in the original negotiations. When the partners have created an expanding set of opportunities, if their original plans are unsuccessful, they can fall back on many other alternatives.

This style of negotiating does not imply weakness. "Sell" your company and its strengths. Show your partner you are a strong player. Don't be afraid to strike a hard bargain on your behalf—as long as it is fair. Push hard for more, for both you and your partner. Demonstrate your vested interest in seeing the alliance win. Don't accept second best; don't take less; *seek more for each.*

WATCHING FOR CRITICAL SIGNS

During the preliminary negotiations, check whether the preconditions for a successful alliance are present. Is there sufficient support to sustain an alliance over the long haul?

As people at other organizational levels of your company begin working with their counterparts in the other company, there will be a critical opportunity to begin watching for indications of whether the venture has a decent chance of achieving its potential.

However, if negotiations drag on, if deadlines pass, if meetings are continually postponed, very probably nothing will ever happen.

Negative responses may seem disappointing, but the critical signs are a pretest of the stark realities of whether the alliance is more than a creative imagining of its designers. Watch, listen, and evaluate how these signs are reflective and indicative of the future. It is far easier and less expensive to transform or exit from the alliance at an early stage than after beginning full-fledged operations.

Chemistry and Trust

In additional to top-notch performance, the other critical issue to be checked at this stage is the underpinning of chemistry. Without high levels of trust, there will be no chemistry, and without chemistry the venture is doomed.

Alliances are usually risky ventures. Difficulties are bound to arise, and if communications are not excellent, good problem solving will not occur to address the difficulties. Inevitably, in an environment of low trust, there will be blame setting rather than problem solving; the venture will then be on its way to oblivion or divorce.

A dramatic example of the desired type of trust involved a joint venture among Fleet Bank (one of the Northeast's largest banks), Nortek (a Fortune 500 company), Gilbane (one of the nation's 10 largest construction firms), and Hinkley, Allen and Comen (a regional law firm). The four firms were involved in a joint venture to build a costly ($63 million), 25-story office complex to house the corporate offices of Fleet, Nortek, and Hinkley, Allen, and Comen. Construction was complete and tenants were moving into the building. At the ribbon-cutting ceremony, one of the partners commented: "Shouldn't we be signing the joint venture agreements pretty soon?" Until that time, the partners' commitment was bound only by their handshake, mutual trust, and long-standing working relationship.

TIMING

There is no hard and fast rule that states how long it should take for an alliance to be consummated. Tactical relationships, such as those between manufacturers and their independent sales reps, are so traditional and easily replicated and formalized, that they often begin and are consummated in less than a week.

Strategic arrangements, because of the greater number of levels of involvement, the large stakes, and the more complex analyses, tend to take longer. If large expenditure or very detailed analysis is required, such as in the construction of a major chemical plant, negotiations may take a year or more to complete.

The opposite extreme is also a problem. Shot-gun marriages, even with the right strategic fit, may not work operationally. Avoid pressures to sign an agreement until key operational managers have had a chance to review the venture and meet with their counterparts. It is better to back off or say "No," than to be railroaded into an ill-fitting alliance. Consider using the strategic spectrum to evaluate exactly what relationship works for the level of trust and commitment that is available. For example, if a joint venture is not appropriate at this time, perhaps a narrower strategic alliance or even an OEM relationship would be more appropriate. Later, should the levels of cooperation generate sufficient synergies, a transformation to a more complex arrangement may be appropriate.

Like babies, alliances are usually born within about 9 months. The time frame can become longer if the internal decision-making process of the sponsors is more complex. Smaller companies with streamlined decision making can be frustrated by large corporations until they become educated to the bureaucratic process. Without a good understanding of who has the authority to make decisions, the smaller company may withhold critical information necessary to trigger a positive decision, accidentally undermining the large corporation's key advocate of the venture.

Dana Callow, a partner in Boston Capital Ventures, which has an alliance with Prudential Bache, said:

> It took us 12 months to structure our relationship. We were careful to meet with a lot of people that might be involved—people with decision making authority and control of budgets. What is important, though difficult, was educating our partner on how we must operate, especially since our prospective was long-term and theirs short-term.[12]

Foxboro Corporation's Ernest DeBellis, Manager of International Joint Ventures, recommends:

> Get the operational management issues clear before signing the legal agreements. Know how you will measure achievement. It's easier to build these into the alliance on the front end rather than try to fix the problem later on.[13]

PERFORMING PROFESSIONAL DUE DILIGENCE

Caveat emptor—the buyer beware—applies to alliances. The best basis for judging trust is a successful past relationship. If you are entering into a new alliance in a foreign country, or with a supplier with whom you've only had a vendor relationship in the past, how can you be sure that you won't be married to a thief, a dilettante, or a wastrel? Figure 8.6 is a checklist to use when trying to answer these kinds of questions.

Due diligence is the technical term for looking into the background of a potential ally. It means doing more than a credit check. It maximizes the chances of a successful venture and avoids entering into a deal that will eventually sour. Corning performs a basic level of due diligence *before proposing* a venture. In that way, they screen out unsuitable companies without expending resources on negotiations, travel, and lawyers.

Figure 8.6   Checklist for Performing Due Diligence

HARD DATA

_____ Financial statements—Do they ensure a capacity to uphold financial commitments?

_____ Relations with vendors/customers—Do bills get paid on time?

_____ Court filings—Is the company always involved in legal hassles?

_____ Board of directors—Does the board support the decision to form an alliance? Will it support or undermine the CEO?

_____ Agreements with other companies—What licenses, alliances, etc., are currently relevant?

SOFT DATA

_____ Industry reputation—Is it for quality?

_____ Quality of the top managers—Do they have a good track record? Is there high turnover?

_____ Critical strategic decisions in the past—Does the company have a record of excellent judgment?

_____ Core organizational values—Do you like the company's integrity, reputation, teamwork, tough-mindedness, loyalty, discipline, adherence to commitments, entrepreneurship, human resources, and similar characteristics?

_____ Relations with vendors—Do suppliers like doing business with the company? Do problems get solved easily?

_____ Code of conduct—Is there one? Does it stick?

_____ Longevity of management—Is there stability or is it a revolving door?

_____ Win/win culture—Does the company know how to continually expand opportunities for its employees and customers?

_____ Strategic alliance track record—Is there a successful history of working with other companies in an alliance framework?

In foreign deals, the commercial service officer in the American embassy located in the country with which you are dealing will help perform some of the due diligence function by going through official channels to look for potential problems. (This individual is a U.S. Department of Commerce official.)

Savvy managers will ask around to find out who is capable and has a good reputation. Two independent confirmations will usually ensure that the reputation is valid.

There are some informal ways of conducting due diligence that can be very effective. I was once negotiating a potential alliance, but did not feel very comfortable with the CEO of the other company. Over dinner, he had just one glass of wine too many, and let it slip that he had had some dealings with an individual with a known criminal record. The price of that dinner was a small fee for what would have inevitably cost me a lot of money.

In another situation, I was not as adroit. I entered into a joint venture with an individual who, I later learned, tended to settle all disagreements by employing lawyers and lawsuits. When there was a difference of opinion on how to handle a matter, I learned to my dismay, either he won or I went to court. Before taking a legal settlement route, I learned that, in the past, he had usually lost in court but would habitually file an appeal.

Given the current court delays, there would be no resolution for several years. Those less financially endowed who won the first round in court would usually settle on less than favorable terms rather than be bled by time and additional legal fees. It was an expensive and hard-learned lesson. Proper due diligence would have steered me elsewhere.

Would a tight legal agreement have solved this problem? Probably not. A lawyer might have advocated the value of strong legal language, but the deal was inherently flawed by not having the right chemistry in the first place. The partnership was not founded on the principle of a commitment to perpetuating a double win. No legal language could ever fill this critical hole.

PREPARE TO SHIFT GEARS

The first stage of negotiations should be focused on gaining a basic understanding of what the alliance should be doing. The goal is not a formal legal agreement, but a Statement of Principle, which will communicate simply what the alliance is all about. The next chapter provides details on the Statement of Principle and on the operational planning steps that follow its acceptance.

9

The Power of
Operational Integration

I thought my partner was responsible for that!

—Lament of a failing alliance

Drafting a nonbinding Statement of Principle is one of the most critical steps in formulating the alliance architecture. Its primary purpose is to move the negotiations beyond initial talking stages, where the verbal understandings may be somewhat vague or conceptual, to the stage of a clear description of the nature of the alliance. The purpose of the Statement of Principle (sometimes referred to as a Memorandum of Understanding or Philosophy Statement) is to begin to codify the discussions, clarify ambiguities, and ensure that the two parties are aiming at the same objectives. The Statement of Principle serves as a convergence point where concepts coalesce; it marks the beginning of translating strategy into reality.

The document is not a formal legal agreement—that occurs later. Its purpose is to outline, in laypersons' terms, the fundamentals of the alliance.

In some cases, according to attorney Paul Broude:

[The statement] may become the basis for beginning the parties' operating relationship even before the final agreement linking the companies together is concluded. In one situation, our American company client agreed to do product development for a Swiss company providing funds. We wound up putting together a very detailed letter of intent that served as the basis of the working relationship for more than a year, until the final papers were completed and signed.[1]

STATEMENT OF PRINCIPLE

The Statement of Principle should be drafted mutually by the key negotiators of each of the companies, without lawyers present (but probably after having consulted with them). Later, if a legal agreement is necessary (most purchaser–supplier alliances, among others, do not require legal documentation beyond the normal contracts), the lawyers will translate this basic document into the final binding legal agreement.

The Statement of Principle should be brief and to the point; usually two to six pages are all that is necessary. (If it is any longer, no one will read it, and it will therefore become useless.)

Frank Little, retired architect of many of Union Carbide's alliances and acquisitions, is very articulate regarding the nature of the Statement of Principle. He states:

> The Statement serves as a road map for the alliance. It sets goals for the venture and establishes broad principles for action. Most importantly, it is written by businessmen for businessmen; but it is not a legal document.
>
> The intent is not to be controversial. It's really a tool, a means of communication, both in-house and between partners. It opens lines of communications between staff and line personnel, and the respective legal counsels. It enables people to air their concerns regarding what further issues should be included before negotiations are finalized.
>
> Whereas legal documents have a negative, protecting tone, this document deals with the alliance in a positive tone. Legal counsel is then provided with clear mandate for drafting agreements based on management's position on key basic issues.
>
> Later, once the alliance is underway, the statement will provide a background for new staff coming on board and for settling minor interim disputes.[2]

The Statement of Principle is brought to top management for approval, revision, or rejection. The alliance negotiations team has the current position confirmed or revised and is given a clear direction for the next stages of decision making. In addition, should any newcomers join the alliance team, the Statement of Principle serves as a position paper to short-circuit posturing and last-minute outside influences.

Trap

Statement of "Intent": Beware of using the term Statement of Intent at this stage in negotiations. It can be ruled as a legally binding agreement in some jurisdictions, such as New York.

Stay with less legalistic terms, such as Statement of Principle, or Philosophy Statement, or Memorandum of Understanding.

Once top management has signed off, the Statement of Principle can serve as a discussion paper with lower-level managers—a means of communicating the concept and gaining critical input before the final commitments are made and details are readied for implementation. The Appendix contains the framework for the document (p. 322).

If some issues remain somewhat vague, do not be overly concerned; these will be thrashed out later, when the Statement of Principle is translated into a legal agreement.

How can all these issues be stated in just two to six pages? Keep the issues simple and straightforward; if necessary, append some of the minutiae. Leave the details and complexities for the next phase, to be resolved by the operational planners, lawyers, and accountants. If the Statement of Principle is too long, it will not be read or understood, will not achieve buy-in from top and middle management, and will be fair game for snipers, deal killers, cynics, and second guessers.

John Margherio, Director of International Marketing at Olin Corporation, advocates including critical dates for key milestones, along with a "drop dead" date for signing the Statement of Principle. This ensures that the alliance doesn't wallow in the halls of corporate bureaucracy for too long without ever getting started.

Many times this critical step of creating a Statement of Principle is left out of the alliance development process, usually with awkward, if not disastrous results. When the process is short-circuited, the result is usually to prolong the negotiations, to increase the legal costs, to start the alliance without critical upper or middle management support, or to create a false start with the partners pulling in the wrong direction.

When these things happen, the initiation of the alliance is handicapped with a cloud over its birth.

Once the Statement of Principle receives management's sign-off, the final stage of alliance negotiations—operations planning—commences.

Tip

Termination Clauses: Lawyers may want to add an exit clause. The exit process is important, but an exit clause is itself negative and can sour a relationship unnecessarily. Instead, talk in terms of the broad issues of *transformation*, which include: exit or termination, future growth opportunities, and evolution into other forms.

WHY AN OPERATIONS PLAN IS IMPORTANT

Writing an operations plan is the last litmus test to predict the validity of the alliance. It is an insurance policy that accomplishes the following critical functions:

1. Checks to see whether all the "gears will mesh" before the actual launch of the alliance. It puts the alliance into a preliminary "shakedown cruise," to gain a very accurate idea of whether the alliance will work in reality, prior to formalizing any legal documents.
2. Checks the operational fit and serves as a barometer of whether good chemistry exists within and between the middle ranks of the partners. Those who will eventually be running the alliance should be given the opportunity to test ideas and working relationships before the alliance is formally launched.
3. Establishes the proper systems of leadership, responsibility, and control. If there are conflicts over control, if leadership is not present, or if there are ambiguities over which partner will have key responsibilities, then these issues will become very evident before they can blow the alliance apart.
4. Utilizes the form-follows-function phenomenon. Having defined the operational functions, all final structuring issues—organization, legal form, and tax issues, if any—will become evident.

Teamwork Test

The *process* of developing the plan is just as important as the *content* of the plan. The process tests the partners' intelligence, common sense, and ability to solve problems together. Far better to go through this process before the alliance begins, than to deal with such surprises afterward.

The operations plan should be written as a "mini-joint venture" between the operational managers of the prospective alliance. If the appointed operational managers cannot write the details of the plan together, they have slim hopes of managing the venture together. The teamwork test enables operational managers to troubleshoot the plan, check chemistry and trust, smoke out unforeseen personnel problems, determine whether the "not invented here" syndrome will smother innovation, and, if it has not yet happened, isolate the deal killers from the skeptics. The process secures organizational support and clarifies future roles and responsibilities.

I strongly recommend a very structured process that puts a group of key operational managers from both companies in a room for three days, and emerges with a very specific plan that covers all the design issues for proper functioning and integration. At the end of the session, a plan should be produced that provides a specific course of action for the next 120 days, tied to key tasks and individual responsibilities.

Why three days? Because it takes that long to write the plans, see how well two teams can work together, understand each other's frames of reference, and test their chemistry under pressure. Don't be tempted by the false lure of the "over-the-transom" method of developing an operations plan, with each team writing its own portion of the plan independently. There will be no test of the synergies of being able to create a larger pie; the chemistry test will not occur; real operational integration will not be tested; and in the long run the process will take longer, with a far less telling result. Writing the operations plan together is part of the courtship process; it must be done face-to-face, not by telephone or fax machine.

For those involved in developing new process technologies or new products, this teamwork test will seem familiar. It is analogous to a ramp-up trial of a new production line. When scaling up from a single prototype model to full production, there are hundreds of things that can go wrong. Often, companies will build a midscale pilot plant or assembly line to test functioning and integration and to work out the bugs before committing to full production.

It is truly amazing how many problems surface—and are solved—during a three-day operational planning session. For example, in one session, after the second day, it became very clear that a deadline for getting a very scarce, expensive, and volatile chemical for shipment across the Atlantic for processing was so tight that a shipping order had to be placed within 12 hours or the deadlines for production and delivery would be missed. By taking immediate action, the alliance was able to successfully meet the deadline. If the over-the-transom approach had been used, the deadlines would have been missed by at least two weeks. Commitments were made to operationalize the alliance at that point in time, with the legal agreements to follow later.

In another example, while estimating the cost of a newly designed product, the manufacturing partner of a marketing–manufacturing alliance found the costs were going to be 50% higher than expected, given the specifications. By changing the specs and the designs in the session, the original projected financial returns were achieved, thus establishing the foundation for success before the alliance started.

Some of the other problems that might surface during those three days are: alliances without champions, champions without passion, hidden deal killers, personality mismatches, alliances with little or no top-level support, and totally different conceptions about the meaning of an alliance. Nearly all these problems can be fixed because the alliance is still in the negotiations phase, a time of learning and a graceful period of adjustment. The cost of these changes once the alliance had been launched would have been far greater.

Commitment Check

One reason for failure of some alliances is middle managers' lack of commitment to make the venture work. By engaging both top and middle management in the process of formulating an operations plan before the venture begins, commitment is gauged and, even more important, top management will get its first glimpse of what will happen when the middle managers engage the gears joining the participating companies.

Success comes when strategy can be transformed into operations. This requires a commitment to "sweating the details." If one of the allies does not want to engage in the details, beware of a fatal flaw in the alliance. William Silvia, former president of Union Carbide's Catalysts and Services Division, suggests:

> Top management is best when they deal with the strategic issues. But the middle managers know how to handle the real life nuts-and-bolts problems. When they say the alliance will work, then I know we have a potential winner. . . . The Statement of Principle may be broadly defined, but it should be backed up with a tight operations plan that contains concrete objectives, specific requirements, and attention to the details, with periodic reviews.[3]

Getting middle management's commitment for the alliance is a safeguard that ensures a higher possibility of success before full engagement and commitment of resources. Specifically for this reason, alliances have a higher success rate than acquisitions, which, by design, tend to leave this critical dimension unattended.

The operations plan is a fundamental piece of the negotiations. Without it, there is no way to know how you will create a larger entity; there is only a dream, with no connection to reality. The operations plan tells you the ingredients, the proportions, and the sequence. Roy Bonner, former IBM executive, is as tough as a drill sergeant when it comes to operational plans. He asserts:

> Don't tell me you don't have time to write an operations plan. Proceeding without one is like going to a gambling casino and rolling dice. That's not what business is about. . . . I want to know the full architecture—the broad design as well as the small details. If you run out of answers before I run out of questions, you haven't thought the plan through carefully.[4]

Tip

"People Support What They Help Create": This is one of the most important commandments for everyone involved in alliances.

WHAT ISSUES THE PLAN MUST COVER

Because every venture has its own unique circumstances, the operations plan should be tailored to the specific needs of the venture. It should be written as a joint effort by those who will be implementing it. Each plan will be unique to the needs of the alliance, but virtually all plans have common threads covering operational, administrative, and policy issues. Figure 9.1 is a checklist of the more frequent elements in the plan.

SWEAT THE DETAILS

It is surprising how many executives who are enamored of deal making lack any interest in the details that make their deals work. Deal makers often leave a trail of deals behind them without thinking through how to make them operationally successful; they expect the operational managers to clean up the mess they have left behind.

One large U.S. corporation left just this type of trail during the 1980s, with a series of joint ventures and acquisitions in Europe—one in England, another in Spain, another in France, one more in Italy, then onward like Marco Polo into Asia. Woefully, the details were never tied down; presumably, "synergy" would fill in all the ambiguities. Not long after the deals were closed, money invested, and plants built, each deal began unraveling unceremoniously.

In each case, the details had not been thought through. The English venture lost money because no one considered doing a simple market analysis to determine whether anyone would buy the product. In France,

Figure 9.1   Checklist for Operational Planning

_____ Key Objectives and Milestones
_____ Financial Forecasts Summary
_____ Critical Success and Risk Factors
_____ Product Performance Specifications
_____ Service Support
_____ Competitive Analysis
_____ Management Procedures and Personnel
_____ Marketing Plan with Sales Projection
_____ Manufacturing/Production/Engineering Plan
_____ Implementation Schedule
_____ Contingency Plan
_____ Operational and Administrative Responsibilities
_____ Prices, Payments and Ordering Procedures

the deal was so one-sided in favor of the French that, when the market changed, there was no flexibility for adapting the venture to the new conditions without the French feeling they would lose their inherent advantages. Because the chemistry between the French and the Americans was so bad, there was no trust. The U.S. company ended up selling its investment to the French partner.

The Italian deal fared worse. The American company controlled the Italian venture 70/30. A plant was fully constructed pending approval from the Italian government before the technology could go into production. Bureaucratic delays held up the venture for several years. The Italian company went belly-up and the Americans sat on a nonperforming asset.

WHAT WE CAN LEARN FROM FRANCHISES

The franchise alliance, the most formalized type of cooperative venture, has one of the most successful track records, both domestically and internationally. Jack Hellriegel, president of International Franchise Management, comments:

> One of the reasons the franchise alliance is so successful throughout the world is because it provides a template for developing the operational details. The process has become formalized—there are checklists, formats, forms, and procedures that both parties must commit to before the alliance is created. A franchise alliance has a built-in framework for planning the operational details well before anyone commits to accepting substantial risks.
>
> Once in place, each knows their role, what is expected of them, and what to expect of their alliance partner. Because there is so much advance attention to the details, there just aren't as many ambiguities to create additional risk.[5]

This attention to operational detail is one of the principle reasons why the American franchise alliance system has been so successfully imported into Japan, while other forms have had less than stellar results. Whereas Americans are enamored of deal making, the Japanese pride themselves on their ability to manage the detailed operational issues. To be an engineer or a production manager is a proud honor. They love to sweat the details. This extra effort may mean it takes longer to start the alliance, but once it starts, the success rate is far greater.

Too often, the deal makers who negotiate the alliance are not the same people who will be its managers. Then, after the ceremonial handshakes, the moment of truth arrives as alliance managers are thrown together with virtually no guidance by the strategists. Having been given little direction, day-to-day authority is jeopardized by the lack of both clear leadership and teamwork. Frustrations and faulty communications are followed by failures, which accelerate tensions between the allies, driving the alliance into a downward spiral of increasing distrust and broken expectations.

Ultimately, the primary objective of the operational planning element is to be sure the alliance management team is staying out in front of the problems—that it is dedicated to action, not reaction. Rather than become convulsive in the face of the first crisis, the alliance must plan for contingencies.

The more complex the alliance, the greater the need to have a detailed operations plan, to avoid confusion and prevent critical items from slipping through the cracks. Operational managers should ensure that the plan is clear, and the partners should agree on the program without hidden reservations. The plan need only contain enough information to ensure that the practical realities of the alliance will work.

MEASURING REALITY

One of the first rules of managing alliances is: *If you can't measure it, you can't manage it.*

This is also usually the first rule of management that gets violated in alliance development. I suspect that when executives leave the internal security of their corporate castles to commence their crusades on the newly opened fields of alliances, they lose their bearings quickly. They know they cannot use their trusted command-and-control systems in the alliance, so they work totally on instinct, trust, and faith. Without a familiar map, compass, and yardstick, navigation is a lot trickier.

The manifestation of this problem is everywhere. Many alliances have fuzzy goals, no clear planning, inadequate understanding of strategy, only a broad conception of the desired results, and insufficient commitment to success. The answer to the problem lies not in forsaking all attempts at management control, but in using a control system appropriate to the perspective of the architecture of the extended corporation. The components of the system are described in the following sections.

Define the Strategic Return on Investment

STROI, discussed in Chapter 6, contains five elements—market, organization, innovation, competitive advantage, and financial return—that should be defined in specific, measurable terms. The operational plan, in turn, should be designed to provide definitive resources to achieve the strategic returns. The normal financial measurement systems used for the internal corporation may be very inappropriate for this task because they were designed to measure everything by converting to monetary standards. This will work for some things, like cost of materials, but will be thoroughly inadequate for other things, such as organizational strength, innovation, and competitive advantage. For these issues, the alliance partners may have to develop their own individualized methods of measuring a win.

Know the "Elements of Victory"

To do this effectively, you must know the critical units of measure: How many? How much? How often? How soon? For example, innovation may be measured in the number of new product introductions, the reduction in new product development cycle time, or the number of new patents. Organizational strength can be measured in terms of increases in productivity, larger spans of influence, greater satisfaction with teamwork, or shorter approval times. Competitive advantage can be gauged by market penetration, customer satisfaction, or relative growth rates.

Establish a Management Information System

An efficient system enables the alliance to learn quickly and easily about its progress. Operational managers dread the overburden of extra reports; the system chosen should follow the line of simplicity, flexibility, and rapid response. It is better to know quickly the few key indicators than to have cumbersome details that take months to gather and are questionable in interpretation. When you can ask three poignant questions and know where you stand, you've probably got a good system.

An effective monitoring system keeps energies focused on the plan, rather than being diverted to dozens of other fascinating potentialities. Particularly in technology and product development, engineers may begin designing their next version before the first is complete. Similarly, budding entrepreneurs, in their typically expansive manner, find innumerable uses for their products and technologies, failing to focus on immediately achievable targets, such as distribution systems, applications engineering, and cash flow. Note, however, that the measurement systems most effective in the *internal* corporate environment may not provide the best tools in the *extended* corporation.

Trap

Dual Reporting Systems: Tremendous amounts of confusion arise when dual reporting systems are used. The two partners may be thinking in two different operational languages. When logistical or technical problems arise, there will not be a common method of defining the problem, let alone solving it.

CONTINGENCY PLANNING

During negotiations, the partners may have been lulled into thinking that sales may be greater than reality will bless, or that now, with a partner, all the production problems that plagued them will suddenly halt.

We all want the future to play into our plans, but fate is seldom so kind. Every alliance must navigate turbulent waters as well as calm seas; the forces of change are ever present. Today's technological advantage will soon be replaced by tomorrow's distribution advantage, which then succumbs to cost competitiveness before the cycle repeats. The architecture of the alliance must provide a design for these cyclical changes. An alliance that has only fair-weather thinking sets the stage for future animosity or failure.

Evaluating Sales Forecasts

Not long ago, a real estate developer came to me with an opportunity to solve a problem. A building he owned had a restaurant that had gone out of business. Bank financing had become very tight, and buyers for the restaurant were nearly as scarce as bank financing. He found an excellent chef who wanted to start his own business. Together, the chef and the developer proposed a partnership that would reopen the restaurant under joint ownership. They had put together a plan, and had drawn up a first draft of a legal agreement; they were very nearly ready to shake hands on a deal.

Trap

Forecasts: Beware of the optimistic sales forecast, especially when done on a computer spreadsheet. Sales forecasts are only as good as the assumptions that underpin them. Many forecasts are nothing more than dreams unconnected to reality.

Be sure the forecast is built on accurate data that can be verified. Ask the critical questions:

How many units will sell?
How quickly can they be sold?
How many sales calls must be made to sell one unit?
How often will there be repeat business?
What will the promotional costs be on a per-unit basis?
Will the customer really pay money for the product or service? How do you know?

When they asked me to review the venture, the first thing I zeroed in on was the plan's financial forecast. From my own sometimes traumatic experience in start-ups, I knew that the most tenuous element of any plan is the sales forecast. Dun and Bradstreet's analysis of small businesses indicates that nearly 70% of all the failures are traceable to sales and marketing problems.

Sure enough, the sales forecast was done in monthly segments expressed in dollars of sales per month. I asked for a breakdown in a weekly format, with each day of the week expressed in terms of the number of customers per day (based on seating capacity) multiplied by the average check for lunch or dinner for that day. Based on those customer counts, what was the realistic staffing plan for serving that number of people?

When the partners expressed the sales and labor expenses in this revised format, it became clear that their sales forecast was a fantasy. The business, even in the best seasons, would not break even. They had almost trapped themselves into a dream that soon would have become a nightmare ending in failure and possible bankruptcy.

Avoiding Divorce

Lawyers try to handle the downside risks by emphasizing termination clauses, divorce provisions, and exit strategies. There is nothing inherently wrong with this legalistic approach, but it misses the mark: the lawyers are focusing on the effects of not having a good contingency plan. Before even thinking of divorce provisions, it is far more important to discuss the kinds of circumstances that would cause such a split and how to prevent them.

Only one thing is ever certain about the future: it will not be what we have expected. Even with the best predictions and forecasts, any alliance exists in a risk-prone environment. Therefore, it is wise to have contingency plans in place to handle the unexpected.

Surviving Crises

Contingency plans are a key factor in building excellent chemistry and maintaining a win/win condition. Because they provide a predictable course under adverse conditions, the partners know what to expect of each other and can therefore take action quickly. The late A. A. T. ("Pete") Wickersham, an experienced alliance developer in the healthcare industry, said:

> All alliance will go through at least three major crises that can jeopardize its very existence prior to landing on stable ground. Before launching the venture, try to predict the crises which might be encountered.

Tip

Have a Contingency Plan: A contingency plan performs several vital functions:

1. Provides a **predictable course** when conditions change, thereby building trust;
2. Enables **downside risk** analysis to determine whether the plan is workable, even under adverse conditions;
3. Builds in **flexibility** while prescribing, in advance, a win/win position, even under adverse conditions.

And beware of misjudging time, the ever-present enemy of all good intentions. Most alliances fail on this point. Delays are usually unplanned, and therefore translate into the need for more money. Think of time as an alliance thief.[6]

An alliance must be flexible enough to change when the uncertainty of the future commands. Try developing three plans for the alliance: an optimistic plan (what you think and hope will happen), a pessimistic plan (what will likely happen if there is any slip-up), and a "Black Sunday" plan (the crisis plan). Always knowing the alternatives, in the event something might go wrong, enables the venture to keep ahead of the problems, anticipating difficulties before they occur. When partners create a team composed of flexible problem solvers, their chances of forming a highly successful alliance improve dramatically.

OPERATIONAL INTEGRATION

Often, *the better the strategic fit, the more difficult the operational fit.* Excellent strategic fit matches one company's strengths with another's weaknesses; what one has, the other wants, and vice versa. However, these very differences mean that, operationally, the prospective partners may have a very frustrating experience working together to achieve their goals, because their strategic differences are manifested in very disparate corporate cultures.

For example, when AT&T formed a strategic partnership with Italy's Olivetti, it looked like a strategic match made in heaven. AT&T wanted to enter the global office products market and find a method of penetrating the computer market. Entrepreneurial Olivetti had global distribution and wanted AT&T's technology and telecommunications processes. AT&T brought financial resources, superior technology, systems expertise, network operations management, and the U.S. market. To complement this offering, Olivetti brought an entrepreneurial spirit, marketing skills, speedy product design, and the European office market—all of which AT&T lacked.

AT&T purchased 22% of Olivetti's stock for $260 million. Several years later, AT&T pulled up its stakes and sold its portion of Olivetti for $635 million—a 145% gain, an excellent profit. But the alliance had failed. Olivetti's fast-paced, market-oriented culture clashed headlong with AT&T's slower moving, operations-oriented mentality, which had functioned for nearly a century and was accustomed to long product cycles and belabored decision making.

The match made in heaven failed to account for the issues of operational integration. The excellent strategic fit was a poor operational fit. Had the deal makers empowered the alliance with the proper integrating mechanisms, this could have been both a financially and strategically successful venture.

ORGANIZATIONAL MANAGEMENT STYLE

Companies in relatively stable and mature industries, where there is little change and a pattern of highly routinized work, tend to use hierarchical management more frequently. On the other hand, fluid industries needing rapid adaptation to change will tend toward the more collaborative style.

Figure 9.2 illustrates some of these critical differences. The two styles should not be seen as distinct, but as a spectrum or continuum. Many companies will, in fact, be some combination of the hierarchical and the collaborative styles.

The farther apart (or differentiated) the management styles of the partners, the greater the chance of having an oil-and-water mixture. And, as in the science of chemistry, some form of "bonding agent" will be necessary to make these mix. At the points in the organization where groups with major stylistic differences must interface (work together), there are bound to be conflicts. At the interfaces, individuals with good integrative and communications skills should be mediating. Also, effective integrating mechanisms must be put in place to enable the two companies to work together at those interfaces. (This process is covered in greater detail in Chapter 12.)

The style of the alliance will generally be a blend of the organizational management styles of the partners. However, it is essential for managers to discuss precisely how differing styles will be integrated. This is too important to be left to chance. The alliance should *opt for the fast and flexible*, not the slow and dogmatic.

Figure 9.2   Organizational Management Spectrum

Dimensions of Management Structure	Internal Corporation Stable Environments ◄──── Hierarchical Approach	Extended Corporation Dynamic Environments ────► Collaborative Approach
Authority:		
Guidelines	Policies, procedures, rules	Standards of behaviors, values, driven
Leader role	Guides work unit	Builds mutual trust, support & cohesion
Influence	From leader to group	From work unit to its members
Direction	Leader directs work unit	Work unit directs its members
Decision making:		
Interpreted as	Precise	Guidelines for work
Binds the individual to	The leader's decision	The work unit's decision
Power for implementation	Leader or organization	Work unit & its cohesion
Enforced by pressure	From leader & organization	Within work unit
Communication:		
Listening	To leader's ideas	To work unit's ideas
Sensitivity	Toward leader	Among work unit members
Directionality	Downward by instruction/advice	Lateral by mutual influence
Conflict:		
Disputes are controlled by	Leader	Work unit members
Resolved by	Leaders or policy	Work unit, by consensus
Activities determined by:	Leaders	Consensus between leader & work unit
Competence located in:	Leaders	Work unit membership
Planning & evaluation done by:	Leaders	Work unit
Commitment is to:	Leader's tasks/needs	Work unit's tasks & needs
Primary relationship between:	Leader and sponsors	Leader & work unit
Roles are:	Fixed or constant	Flexible, depending on situation

EMPOWERMENT THROUGH INTEGRATION

Empowerment, a critical process in the architecture of an alliance, involves establishing seven mechanisms to achieve the functional integration required to attain the partner's goals:

1. Leadership
2. Teamwork/Role Clarification
3. Control by Coordination
4. Policies and Values
5. Consensus Decision Making
6. Resource Commitment
7. Lateral Liaison.

Every successful alliance establishes an empowerment process to develop the clout that will accomplish its goals. Empowerment can come in a variety of ways, and there is no best way. The right time to determine empowerment is during the operational planning process.

Individuals, companies, and cultures will have very different views toward control in an alliance. For those who have relied on hierarchical power to maintain control of their corporate domains, control will be a far more important factor than for those in more fluid companies.

Control, to some companies, means a full range of authority, responsibility, leadership, and decision making. When a company says it needs "control" of an alliance, it is using the term in the broader context of full authority for everything.

For other companies, control is defined as a much narrower authority; it is simply a mechanism for keeping informed and for preventing people from going off in too many directions. For our purposes, the latter, narrower perspective is how the term is used.

An alliance is based on the ability to *share power*. During the negotiations phase, if one company tends to overemphasize the issue of dominance, it is probable that this dominance will permeate the alliance, placing one member in the superior position, and relegating the other to the inferior position. The long-term consequences are obvious. Strong egos are too tough to stay in an inferior position for long.

This does not imply that all alliances should be 50/50 deals. There can (and often should) be a controlling partner, but there must be a good reason for the division, and both sides must believe it is fair. It is imperative for the more powerful member of the venture to be sensitive to the needs, values, and style of the other, and for the subordinate member to respect and appreciate the position of the other member.

The opposite condition—when power and control issues are not dealt with sufficiently—is also a problem. It may forewarn a lack of interest or motivation, or indicate that the partners, not wanting to offend one another, are treading too cautiously. The alliance itself must be aggressive if it is to be successful. Discuss specific operational issues in detail, as part of the operational planning process. The mechanisms of integration listed are:

Leadership.   Without a clear understanding of the leadership roles in the alliance, there will be no guidance and direction. Joint ventures often solve this problem by having one partner take a majority interest, thereby "commanding" the alliance. However, many joint ventures are 50/50 arrangements; they are not commanded, but are led by strong individuals with deep commitment to the alliance and to their parent company.

Leadership implies a strong passion for the very mission of the alliance; it is not the same as management. Each company should have a champion for the alliance, a person committed to seeing the alliance succeed. Edwin Martin, of the law firm of Hale and Dorr, is one of the exceptional attorneys who understands the critical importance of leadership in an alliance. He states:

> Probably the single most important factor for success of a corporation partnering relationship is an individual, for each sponsor, who believes in the project, has the confidence of the principal executives of the other partner, has an understanding of the project and the technology involved, and has clear access to and the confidence of his own CEO. This individual also needs to have enough time to work within his own company and closely within the partner's company on the project.[7]

If the champion is not going to handle the day-to-day operations of the alliance, then designate an alliance manager prior to finalizing the operations plan.

Teamwork/Role Clarification.   Because alliances cannot be commanded in the traditional sense of the term, coordination is absolutely essential to success. Therefore, each company must place a heavy emphasis on teamwork.

The team-building process begins during the development of the operations plan. Each operations team should be given a chance to get to know each other socially, to understand the frame of reference from which they operate. Site visits to each other's facilities can be invaluable.

Teamwork takes practice that will be refined in actual operations, but it is vital that each company and each individual know their specific roles

---

Tip

Champions: Before considering an alliance, be sure you have a champion who will pioneer the cause. The champion is not an appointed position. The champion steps forward because of belief in the alliance's value, not because his boss says he must be a champion.

Tip

Teamwork and Communications: The two keys to excellent coordination are teamwork and communications. No alliance ever failed because of too much of either. Many have failed for lack of one or both.

---

and responsibilities. Responsibility charting is an excellent tool to achieve clarity of roles. (See Chapter 12.)

Control by Coordination.   Establishing a strong communications system in an alliance is one of the most critical elements, if coordination is to be effective.

Good communication is very dependent on a full understanding of the other company. Because each company has its own culture for communicating, it is essential to understand that culture. The more differentiated the companies, the more difficult the communications and the greater the risk of problems.

During the operational planning phase, the partners must delineate the key issues that must be communicated, their frequency, and their criticality. Alliance managers typically agree to talk with each other at least once a week. Some form of management information system must be established for reporting purposes. Many alliances are using Electronic Data Interchange (EDI) systems to enhance the accuracy of their technology exchange, production scheduling, and engineering specifications.

When managing an internal corporation, much of the control comes from the ability to command, to hire and fire, to direct, and to say "No." In an alliance, none of these is available; instead, one of the best tools is good project management techniques. An outline of key responsibilities, milestones, time deadlines, financial commitments, essential tasks, and required support is valuable.

Policies and Values.   Being clear about the ultimate mission of the venture is vital to focusing the energies of the alliance partners. A mission statement for the alliance, developed jointly by the team developing the operations plan, should be prominently displayed and branded into the minds of all involved. Post it on the walls; focus attention on it. It is a unifying element that contributes to integrating the differentiated cultures and objectives.

The mission statement should be supported by a statement of the values the alliance members stand for. In an alliance between General Electric and Sweden's Eurosim, the partners developed a set of values focused on maintaining a win/win environment, ethical dealings, frequent communication, creative problem solving, and probing for expanded opportunities. By placing a set of values into the alliance, future decisions have a frame of reference based on honesty and integrity.

Consensus Decision Making. Without a decision-making process, the alliance cannot function. Because unilateral decision making is inappropriate in most key alliance decisions, joint decision making is the rule. Most alliances will establish a steering committee composed of members of each company. If it is essential for one company to staff the committee with a majority, in order to "control," then this should be agreed to and supported far in advance of signing any agreements. Most foreign companies prefer to have a 50/50 relationship, making each party equally committed to the venture.

Americans, however, tend to prefer 51/49 arrangements, giving more control to the company with the greatest risk or exposure. Some authorities have tried to tie success or failure factors to either 50/50 or 51/49 deals, but I do not think any of the analyses focus on the most critical issues. *The real key to success is the skill of both parties to carve a double-win course in a changing world, not the proportion of imagined control.* The double win is not an inherently easy process. The issue is not just *how* decisions are made, but *who* makes them and in whose *interests* they are made.

Resource Commitment. An operations plan cannot work unless adequate resources are committed to carry it out. The plan should make clear the resources that will be needed; there should be no surprises once the alliance is launched. If there are any concerns regarding the return either company will receive for its resource allocations, renegotiate—before the alliance commences. Partial commitment at this point can be disastrous. John Lawler, Vice President of International Operations at A. T. Cross Writing Instruments, warns:

> Once you get over the trust issue, you've got to open up and fill the bond of trust. You can't go in halfheartedly. You can't inch along when you should be taking leaps and bounds.[8]

Lateral Liaison. Two companies brought together into an alliance present the same difficulties as the joining of any two dissimilar materials. Glass doesn't naturally adhere to plastic, wood doesn't bond to rubber, nor does fabric join to metal. Special adhesives must be used. The same is true with alliances. The more differentiated the companies, the greater the functional integration required. According to Harvard Business School's Professor Paul Lawrence, a pioneer in integration management:

> Organizations faced with the requirement for both a high degree of differentiation and tight integration must develop *supplemental* integrating devices, such as individual coordinators, cross-unit teams, and liaisons whose basic contribution is achieving integration among other groups.[9]

Essentially, lateral liaison makes more effective use of lower levels of expertise, thereby empowering more middle and lower management levels to act. If the previous six mechanisms are put into place, the lateral liaison can be effective because it receives the proper guidance regarding functional integration. Without the other six, lateral liaison can cause confusion.

One very effective lateral liaison technique is cross-training. When Pall Filter Corporation set up an alliance, it established a series of training seminars with its alliance partner, which reciprocated with its own cross-training. Cross-training enables teams and individuals from each company to get a clear understanding of the operational and technical details of their partner.

Another method is "secondment," a word seldom used in the U.S. dictionary but used extensively in Europe. The term originated in the British army. When an infantry division would be training to fight alongside a cavalry unit, an officer from the infantry division would be assigned—or "seconded"—to the cavalry unit, to assist in coordination. The seconded officer would learn the procedures, timing, strategies, and idiosyncrasies of the other's command. Today, Fuji-Xerox uses a similar process to ensure functional integration.

At IBM, liaisons are designated before a deal is consummated. The responsibility of these liaisons is to funnel requests for information from the partner into the right area of expertise at IBM—a daunting task for any company unfamiliar with IBM's massive international network.

These seven systems of functional integration can mean the difference between success and failure.

IS OPERATIONAL PLANNING WORTH THE EFFORT?

Frequently, executives ask me: "Why should we spend the time to go through such a long process of operational integration? Isn't there a better [they really mean faster] way?" The answer is very simple. There's a faster way if you skip the details of operations and leave the middle managers out of the loop. But the consequence will be a highly accelerated chance of failure right out of the starting blocks. Wouldn't you rather know where the problems are going to be and cure them before they happen? Alliances are formed to reduce risk; why would you want to throw away this inherent advantage by adding to the risks with poor planning? As the great Chinese strategist Lao-tzu (500 B.C.) said:

> Confront the difficult while still easy. Accomplish the great task with a series of small steps.

Typically, those who want to speed up the venture formation process are more interested in the quantity of deals than their quality.

Understandably, they want action, not planning. In contrast, the alliance architect places success above action, values the achievement of the mission more than the speed of attaining a phantom agreement, and commits the proper resources, neither too little nor too much. Lao-tzu could not have better summarized the meaning of alliance operational planning than in this advice:

> What is rooted is easy to nourish.
> Prevent trouble before it arises.
> Put things in order before they exist.
> Rushing into action, you fail.
> Trying to grasp at things, you lose them.
> Forcing a project to completion, you ruin what is almost ripe.

Inherently, those who rush alliances into action without adequate planning and resource allocation suffer from an illusion that alliances are simply a shortcut to success. According to former Union Carbide top executive William Silvia:

> CEOs often fail to realize that alliances require intensity and commitment. The cooperative venture is not as complex as setting up a new division or establishing a subsidiary, but neither is it as easy as signing a vendor contract. The realm of the extended corporation is foreign to many executives, so they tend to oversimplify the front end design process, often with disastrous consequences.[10]

Once the operational plan is complete, it can be appended to the final agreement if necessary. From the functional plan, the organizational and financial form and structure of the alliance should be self-evident. The legal and tax structure, if required, can then be devised by the technical experts in these fields.

Contribute Missing Elements

Suppose that during the operational planning process you discover that you have found just the right partner—one with great attitudes, compatible strategies, perfect chemistry, and a great fit of cultures—but there are some missing elements—insufficient skills, a lack of a total quality management program, or prior experience in your field of endeavor.

This problem occurred when Gates Energy established its alliance with Jagemann Stamping. Jagemann did not have the necessary statistical process control (SPC) system, but Gates loved Jagemann's commitment to quality and innovation. Because Gates had its own SPC system, it sent two engineers to Jagemann for several days to put the right system in place. This is an excellent example of creating a true double-win environment for the betterment of the alliance. By contributing the necessary missing elements to the alliance, Gates made it work.

Once the operations plan is complete, the last step before finalizing the agreement is to report the implications of the operations planning back to top management. If additional resources or risks will be required, these need to be communicated. Certain perceived advantages and disadvantages may have changed as a result of sweating the details. If there are major deviations from the concepts outlined in the Statement of Principle, these need to be brought to top management's attention.

After top management has given its endorsement to the alliance, final legal agreements can be drafted. Technical details such as licensing, royalties, ownership of technology, confidentiality, and exclusivity should have been addressed in general terms during or prior to the operational planning process; they can now be codified.

THE ULTIMATE AGREEMENT

By engaging in a strong operational planning process, partners can avoid letting the lawyers and accountants get too involved in negotiating points. The 80/20 rule can be used to advantage: Spend 80% of the negotiating time on strategic, operational, and chemistry fit issues, and only 20% on legal and accounting issues. Then, building on A. T. Cross executive John Lawler's advice:

> Resist the lawyer's temptation to squeeze a lot of superfluous information into a legal agreement, because it probably won't be very useful anyway. If you have a cooperative venture and get into arbitration, you'll probably be dealing in a foreign country and foreign precedent will prevail.[11]

Regardless of the length, cost, or detail of the agreement, it is only as valuable as the commitment and fairness of the parties behind it. Dozens of executives in successful alliances echo this advice: If the partners believe they may have to refer to the legal agreement regularly for direction or to solve problems, then the alliance is on the road to failure.

If the three dimensions of fit (strategy, chemistry, and operations) have been adequately addressed and the alliance architects have proceeded this far without major difficulties, they should be well on the road to a potential success.

PART THREE

Managing for Spectacular Results

10

Obtaining Excellent Rewards

Diversity is the grinding wheel that sharpens the strategic edge, sparking creativity.

In January 1990, as the new decade opened, business headlines were filled with announcements of the demise of U.S. Memories, a proposed billion-dollar manufacturing joint venture. The alliance, orchestrated by seven of America's largest technology companies, was to produce dynamic random access memory chips (DRAMs) for each of the partners. Japanese companies controlled 80% of the marketplace, and had driven all but Motorola and Texas Instruments out of the business through a series of price cuts.

A BOLD BUT RISKY VENTURE

Led by Sanford Kane, a former IBM executive, the consortium was composed of IBM, Hewlett Packard, Advanced Micro Devices, Intel, LSI Logic, National Semiconductor, and Digital Equipment. NCR and AT&T were interested in joining. The partners were to put up $500 million in equity, and the rest would be financed through debt.

However, in 1989, just as the effort was coming together, demand for DRAMs began falling off, and the prospective investors became wary. Kane appealed to their strategic needs for chips, maintaining that the United States could not risk being held hostage by Japanese manufacturers in such a critical area of technology. By the end of 1989, demand had dropped 25% and prices had fallen off 40%. These new risks made the alliance partners skittish; the rewards from investment were no longer worth the risks to several of the investors.

Just as the deal began to unravel, Kane developed a revised plan that assumed the lower chip prices, cut the equity investment down from $500 million to $150 million, brought the total project costs down two-thirds to $350 million, and proposed starting the venture with only one manufacturing plant instead of four. Even with the dramatic paring down, a 20% return on investment was projected. However, momentum had turned against the idea, the prospective partners had lost faith, and the venture was never consummated.

Risk management is maintaining the double win. U.S. Memories is an excellent example of how risks should decrease in an alliance, not the reverse. Had U.S. Memories proposed a less optimistic contingency plan in the first place, it's far more likely that the venture would have proceeded. The "big bang, all or nothing" approach by U.S. Memories was more than smart businesses were willing to gamble on in a falling market.

Further, until the last-minute change in the plan, the venture showed it was not adaptable to the changing strategic and operational environment. In other words, even before getting started, it did not have a built-in capacity to be a win/win alliance.

UNDERSTANDING RISK

Risk evaluation is one of the more difficult, least precise elements of alliance analysis. After all, how well can anyone accurately determine the contingencies of the future? The Japanese and Chinese, who consider the future highly indeterminate, establish very flexible strategies that can change in the future. The most repugnant alternative is abdication: doing nothing to evaluate risks and then praying for the best. Unfortunately, however, this approach is too frequently used.

Figure 10.1 is a checklist of some of the risks that should be evaluated in an alliance. Usually, these risks are scrutinized when the alliance commences and never reevaluated later. As the risks change, the driving forces that resulted in the alliance in the first place are changing. The strategic planners and deal makers who conceived the alliance are probably long gone, working on their next deal. The alliance is now left in the hands of the technical experts and operational mechanics.

However, no one ever told the operational managers that it was their responsibility to watch these changing risks, and they were never trained in risk assessment. One of the new strategic duties of alliance champions and managers is risk analysis, because it is highly unlikely that the deal makers can be made to sit still long enough to provide this kind of ongoing support.

Figure 10.1   Checklist for Risk Evaluation

_____ 1. **Market Risk:** Will the market continue to provide opportunities for us to sustain our growth? Beware of entering new markets with new products utilizing new technology.

_____ 2. **Competitive Technology Risk:** Will a competitor develop a technology that will make ours obsolete? Are margins sufficient in the event of a price war?

_____ 3. **Completion or Technical Risk:** Is the venture sufficiently like a predecessor project, technology, or business to ensure that it will work as planned? Are there any new technologies that might throw a monkey wrench into the successful achievement of the venture?

_____ 4. **Cooperative Environment Risk:** What is the chance that someone or something (partner, government, weather, labor unions, subcontractors, transportation, etc.) will stop or slow down the venture? Is there a plan to get around these obstacles?

_____ 5. **Management Risk:** Are sufficient personnel available to carry out the venture? Can proper resources be obtained on a timely and cost-effective basis?

_____ 6. **Political Risk:** Are there governmental regulations, now or pending, that will interfere with success? Will the necessary approvals be issued when needed?

_____ 7. **Resources Risk:** Will the supply of materials or products remain available substantially longer than the amortization of financing? Will the partners have the necessary financial, human, and intellectual resources?

_____ 8. **Capital Risk:** Will inflation, exchange rates, or government policy change the investment's value? What is the chance that our capital will be totally/marginally lost?

_____ 9. **Prospective Partner Risk:** Is the partner strong enough to withstand competitive pressures? Will it be stable and cooperative over the long haul? Will it maintain a strategic perspective? Will conditions for the partner change dramatically and cause a withdrawal of resources or support?

_____ 10. **Compounded Risk:** See Figure 10.2.

Measuring risks and rewards in any business venture is probably as imprecise as predicting next week's weather. There are always unknown variables. It may be impossible to know what new technology a competitor is working on in a laboratory halfway around the world. Will the supply of a certain raw material increase based on a new exploration, driving its price downward, and destroying the market for a synthetic alternative?

Trap

Risk or Uncertainty: Many executives confuse risk with uncertainty. Risk is measured by a probability of variance for a well-defined activity. Uncertainty describes an unknown probability for an ambiguous activity.

Risk is measurable, uncertainty is not.

LIES, DAMNED LIES, AND STATISTICAL ANALYSIS

One of the great problems in risk analysis is trying to accurately evaluate risk. One of the most popular methods is to convert the process into a financial formula that evaluates the payback period on an investment. Variations of this process are discounted cash flow (DCF) and internal rate of return (IRR).

There is substantial statistical validity for these processes; many people stake their careers on these frameworks. DCF and IRR analyses discount the value of a future income stream based on the cost of equity and debt, making a dollar worth more today than a dollar tomorrow. Most capital expenditures in America in the past two decades have been based on this line of analysis.

In Japan, however, these financial formulas are only considered part of the picture. In making a capital equipment decision, in addition to using DCF, the Japanese analyst might also look at total life-cycle costs, as well as the flexibility of using equipment for other purposes, should markets or price points change. Further, other strategic factors might receive considerable weight in the corporate decision-making process. The whole affair is less quantifiable and more intuitive.

The financial formulas and analytic tools we use today have all been developed for the internal corporation. Once the decision falls outside the boundaries of the corporate castle, another set of tools is necessary to augment standard procedures. For example, in the U.S. Memories alliance, the risks were not simply financially quantifiable. Had the Japanese cornered the market for DRAMs, the price may have continued to rise, but Samsung, a Korean competitor, was beginning to drive prices down. At what price should the financial analysis have pegged the future price? Given the 40% fluctuations in price over the course of a year, price–cost analysis was rather difficult. More important than price was the availability of supply and the ability to be competitive in the future. Alliances should have a broad analysis framework, like the five elements of strategic return on investment (STROI)—market potential, organizational strength, competitive advantage, technical innovation, and financial return.

THE COMPOUNDED RISK TRAP

Alliances are the stepchildren of uncertain risks and opportunities. Uncertainty breeds ambiguity, and ambiguity is the seed of business difficulties. The higher the future ambiguity, the higher the probability of failure.

Many inexperienced alliance creators fall into the trap of inadvertently compounding risks. Frequently, in joint ventures that create a new, start-up corporation, none of those forming the joint venture has ever experienced the entrepreneurial agony and ecstasy of a start-up.

An interface is created each time differentiated elements are engaged. What I call the Law of Managing Compounded Risk states: Complexity increases by double the number of new interfaces. Every interface is composed of at least two interface points (Figure 10.2). Whenever *new* elements are introduced, there are always numerous hidden unknowns; hence, the complexity increases by a factor equal to the number of *new* interface points.

An excellent example of this compounded risk trap was a joint venture by an American exhaust component manufacturer in Brazil who secured an order from a European auto manufacturer that had a car assembly

Figure 10.2   Law of Managing Compounded Risk

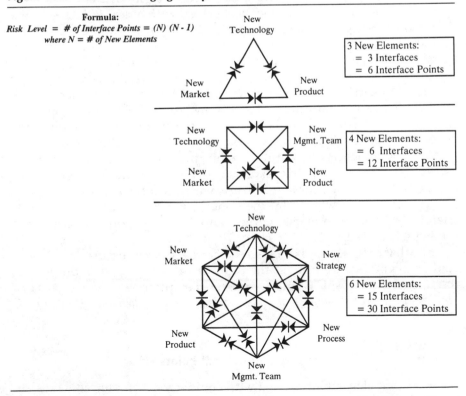

Formula:
$$Risk\ Level\ =\ \#\ of\ Interface\ Points\ =\ (N)\ (N-1)$$
where $N\ =\ \#\ of\ New\ Elements$

New Technology

New Market

New Product

3 New Elements:
= 3 Interfaces
= 6 Interface Points

New Technology

New Mgmt. Team

New Market

New Product

4 New Elements:
= 6 Interfaces
= 12 Interface Points

New Technology

New Market

New Strategy

New Product

New Process

New Mgmt. Team

6 New Elements:
= 15 Interfaces
= 30 Interface Points

Tip

Risk Analysis Rule of Thumb:

Murphy's Law: If something can go wrong, it will—and exactly at the wrong time!

Lynch's Law: Murphy was an optimist, he didn't know about the Law of Compounded Risk.

---

plant in Brazil. The American's new partner was in the metal fabrication business and did not know the automotive marketplace. When the American firm decided to set up a factory with a very new and technologically advanced production process that had been used for only a limited time in the United States, the seeds of failure began to be sown.

Then the decision was made to fabricate with stainless steel, which is a very difficult material. No one in Brazil had experience with this metal for these purposes, and the procurement of the material was improperly handled when specifications were not accurately spelled out in the bid spec. The order for stainless steel was placed with a new Italian supplier that had underbid the competition and did not recognize the problems that would occur. Timing of production was critical: an entire Brazilian automobile assembly line needed the exhaust components.

The exhaust component factory was completed and ready to go. The stainless steel arrived, but when it was placed on the bending machines, it cracked. There was no proper steel anywhere in Brazil, and shipments from Europe or America would take weeks. Attempts to get around the cracking problem failed, and the product could not be delivered on time.

As a consequence, the auto assembly line had to be shut down for nearly a week, at a horrible expense to the car manufacturer. Heavy penalties were in place for late delivery, which cost the Americans dearly. The problem was "solved" by the American firm's going to one of its friendly competitors and asking the competitor to supply the parts—at a predictable markup.

The alliance was built like a house of cards; its architecture was flawed. Had the joint venture limited the number of new risks introduced into the alliance, the result would have been far different. The lesson here: *Start with the fewest number of risks, achieve success, then incrementally add new risks.*

Interfaces: Critical Points

For every new element interacting with another, a set of interfaces is established. Interfaces are always fraught with potential danger because they mark the points in the architecture of the alliance where inherently different systems, frames of reference, language, and methods have to come together. Communication and coordination are inherently discordant at the interfaces; extra management skill, time, and foresight are required.

Managers seldom build in enough slack time or sufficient resources to deal with all the unknowns that pop up unexpectedly at the interface points. As new elements are introduced, the number of new interfaces rises at a faster rate than most management systems are designed to control. Add to the complexity the fact that, typically, these interfaces have never been managed before. When somewhere between three and four *new* elements (creating between six and twelve interface points) are combined, managers have to be acrobats to handle all the interface points, especially since everyone involved is expecting the interfaces to work perfectly the first time.

Once an interface begins to unravel, resources are diverted from other areas, which puts the other interfaces at greater risk. The diverted focus triggers other interfaces to fail, sending the alliance into an often unending, irretrievable downward slide.

The Success of Franchise Alliances

One of the principle reasons for the phenomenal success rate of franchise alliances is that, in actuality, most of the new interfaces are highly structured, controlled, and managed, with risks well controlled in advance. Procedures, methodologies, roles, and systems are in place before the interfaces are actually engaged. There are only two truly "new" interface points to manage: a new location and a new management team.

WHY RISK IS SO VITAL TO SUCCESS

It should not be the partners' intention to eliminate risk entirely. The proper division of risk and reward serves not only the doctrine of fairness in an alliance, but it creates the proper long-term motivation, an absolutely essential ingredient for success. Insurance salespersons know the power of "fear of loss." Bankers would rather make loans to small businesses with the personal guarantee of the owner. Venture capitalists want to keep entrepreneurs lean and mean. What do these three know about risk and reward that is useful to the designer of an alliance?

The insurance salesperson knows that all people fear loss, and, for most people, that fear of loss is a greater motivator than an expectation of gain. People want to protect their interests and will work hard to pay for insurance to prevent losing the assets they have struggled to attain.

The banker, whose professional rules require the acceptance of virtually no risk, dramatically increases the chances of getting a loan repaid in full by requiring a business owner to personally guarantee the company's loan or to secure the loan with a second mortgage on the owner's house. The banker knows from experience that a loan stands a far greater chance of being repaid in full when the material possessions of the entrepreneur are at risk daily, and a business owner will work twice as hard to avoid losing a home and material gains.

In the entrepreneurial world, the venture capitalist will refrain from putting cash directly into the pockets of a struggling entrepreneur through repayments of personal loans or salary increases. Instead, the venture capitalist prefers to channel an investment completely into the company. Even if the entrepreneur has put a home up as collateral for company loans and has every penny of his or her life savings in the company, few venture capitalists will let their investment capital go toward any form of personal repayments. The venture capitalist knows that maintaining these risks will keep the entrepreneur working twice as hard to achieve success and build the value of the enterprise. These illustrations demonstrate the value of *vested interest motivation*, one of the vital principles that increases the chance of success of an alliance.

VESTED INTEREST MOTIVATION

Many alliances fail when they lose their motivation: the top management of the sponsor changes or it becomes too easy to pull back from the venture and deploy resources elsewhere because the "threshold of exit risk" is too low.

This is precisely what happened when a large U.S. chemical company formed a 50/50 joint venture with one of France's leading chemical companies for the manufacture of high-performance adsorbents that were complementary to the French company's standard products.

The joint venture, named TAMIMO, was headquartered in Paris. The French company constructed an integral manufacturing operation within its existing chemical plant in the south of France, supplying all of the raw materials and operating the manufacturing plant. All manufacturing personnel were employees of the French company. The American company contributed the process and manufacturing technology, and marketed the products in Western and Eastern Europe.

The Americans competed with five other producers in the European marketplace. Market prices varied as the market forces dictated. Some products were sold as commodities (razor-thin pricing margins); others could be sold on a value-added basis (better margins). All marketing and sales personnel were employees of the U.S. company.

Because the American company controlled all marketing functions, including pricing the products, the French negotiated a guaranteed 18% return on their plant investment. Each year, negotiations were conducted to establish product transfer prices, which yielded a guaranteed return at various volume points. The French then paid the Americans a 4% royalty on all products produced in the plant. Profits and cash flow were both positive for each company. It would seem the venture had a long future.

However, the French wanted to earn more by participating in the marketing profits. The U.S. company argued that it had taken the market risk, that the French had had no risk, and that the guaranteed return of 18% was enough profit for the French company. Furthermore, the Americans argued, the French also made a profit on the raw materials being sold at market prices to the joint venture.

After many years of debate, the Americans decided to limit the growth of TAMIMO and expand the business in Italy. The already strained relationships became worse and both parties agreed to split up.

Essentially, the uneven risk posture created conditions for conflict. Professor Paul Lawrence of Harvard Business School advises:

> If long-term motivation by top management is desired, then be sure both long-term risk thresholds and long-term reward thresholds are sufficient to keep the partners engaged.[1]

Take away the risk from one of the partners, and the chances are great that the venture will fade away. Before inking a deal, be sure both you and your partner have vested interest motivation sufficient to give the entire team the desire to win.

WHAT AN ATTORNEY CAN'T TELL YOU

If you ask your lawyer about his or her role in helping to form an alliance, the answer will more than likely be: the ability to limit your exposure to risk. This blithe answer is unintentionally deceiving in its simplicity. Managers unwittingly fall into the trap of thinking that the attorney is covering all the elements of risk analysis in the legal agreements.

Lawyers are trained in a system based fundamentally in transactions between the internal corporation and external entities: contracts with suppliers, licensing agreements, governmental regulations, tax consequences, and the dynamics of litigation. The legal system is inherently adversarial. If there is a problem, a good lawyer will attempt to turn the situation around to make the other party responsible (at fault), which is contrary to the mutuality required in effective alliance development.

Your lawyer will look at problems from this perspective and attempt to protect you against *legal* risks. But that is only part of the picture; your lawyer can neither analyze nor protect against *business* risks.

PROTECTING THE CROWN JEWELS

One very important risk, particularly in technology-related deals, is the theft of critical proprietary information. There are three approaches to this problem.

Legal Option. Lawyers will attempt to protect you against theft or misappropriation of intellectual property through a series of legal agreements. If carefully drafted, hopefully they will enable recovery of damages. However, to enforce them may require expensive litigation. Typically, one will see legal papers addressing noncompetition, confidentiality, exclusivity, and licensing. These are basic terms and conditions for most alliances, and are only as good as the money you want to spend to try to enforce them. They are not typically expensive to draft, and they do provide a margin of insurance against theft.

Buffer Zone Option. Rather than reacting after a theft of technology has occurred, the buffer zone strategy is proactive: it attempts to limit access to critical information. One approach gives today's technology to the alliance, but keeps the most advanced R&D in-house, ready for release as the alliance's next generation of product.

Another version of the buffer zone option literally cordons off sections of the facility. Because one-third of Boeing's 747 orders are with Japan, Boeing has formed a joint venture with Mitsubishi to fabricate certain critical wing components. Japan is aggressively interested in penetrating the airplane market, but Boeing is not interested in losing its highly desirable edge as a systems integrator. If there were no joint venture, Boeing would run the risk of having the Japanese develop a competitive industry or losing sales to its European competitor, Airbus. Boeing solved the problem by limiting the meetings its Japanese partners could attend and keeping them from certain confidential areas in the plant.

Interchange Option. A more intriguing manner of protection takes nearly the opposite approach: virtually giving away all the technology for a reciprocal agreement from an ally. This requires a high degree of trust and commitment to the alliance. It is often a second stage of development, after the partners have developed an enormous level of trust.

Frequently, the interchange option is based on a cross-licensing agreement that provides a future flow of any new technology developments to each partner, regardless of who creates them. The Fuji–Xerox joint venture operates this way.

The interchange option bases itself in the premise that there must be a free flow of information to be successful. Although a cross-licensing agreement may be in place, but it is too difficult to accurately determine what you are paying for (i.e., what is informal information? what is formal information?). In the spirit of a true partnership, both sides own the information, and synergistically exchange it for growth.

The strategic alliance between MAX and Stanley Bostitch has successfully operated for 20 years based on this premise. It is reinforced by the presidents of both firms, who meet twice a year, once in Japan and once in the United States—a critical top-level commitment.

Competitive advantage is achieved in this alliance by the constant creation of new ideas and innovations. Critical technical data for product designs are exchanged daily via electronic hookup.

In 1963, 3M licensed its technologies to a joint venture that includes Japan's NEC and Sumitomo as silent partners sitting on the venture's board of directors. The joint venture takes 3M technologies and adapts them to satisfy the local requirements and demands in Japan. Currently, the venture employs about 3,000 people in Japan. One of the most important keys to its success is the tremendous interchange of ideas and general communications between 3M and its joint venture. Douglas R. Hanson, Vice President of Asia-Pacific/International Operations for the $9 billion 3M, explained:

> We log over 5,000 visitor-nights, including Americans who assist the venture, people going to labs, developing strategic plans, and Japanese working in Minneapolis in our labs. We don't differentiate between our Japanese joint venture partners and our subsidiaries; we consider them to be part of 3M and treat them the same.
>
> We have no fear about the Japanese stealing our technology. In my own experience, they have been extremely ethical. As partners we involve them in our strategic planning decisions. We have an outstanding relationship.[2]

But Hanson cautioned, "Remember, 3M is not organized like most companies—we are very flexible and nonhierarchical."

Using the interchange option should not be based on an incredible naivete that condones stealing. You must think through your potential ally's game plan for the future, before deciding that this option makes sense. An innocent Western handshake deal that gives away technology is simply foolish.

SOME UGLY RISKS

While generally few and far between, there are some rather gruesome risks that the alliance architect should be aware of. Some of these have been consciously perpetrated, others have been the result of very poor management, and some have resulted simply from misunderstandings.

The Fake. In this relatively rare occurrence, one company purports to be interested in an alliance in order to induce another company to reveal certain trade secrets, without any intention of actually partaking in a deal.

This occurred in Canada recently, when one company, under the guise of being interested in a potential alliance, stole critical data revealed in good faith during negotiations. Fortunately, Canadian law ruled that the data could not be used and fined the violating company. However, I would not expect a U.S. court to be so just.

Several U.S. companies negotiating in Korea, China, and Japan have reported that they suspected the intention was to fake negotiations for the purposes of larceny. The best protection is good due diligence before negotiations begin in earnest.

The Steal.   Companies accused of stealing technology are presumed guilty of taking valuable information with them after the alliance breaks up. The most publicized cases of this accusation are the Bell & Howell–Canon, Savin–Ricoh, and Micro Power–Seiko joint ventures.

The typical scenario accuses the foreign company of malicious intent. But, upon closer analysis, what really happened was that very different goals, or changes in the strategic environment, prevented the alliance from continuing without changing forms. For example, in the Bell & Howell–Canon deal, Canon had long-term technical development goals, while Bell & Howell saw their Japanese partner as a source for shorter-term advantage. When the companies' strategies became mutually divergent, frictions occurred and the deal broke up, the Americans cried foul. The following two decades were probably the best evidence of the differences between the strategies. Canon continued intensive R&D with numerous new product introductions, while Bell & Howell withered.

Protecting against this option requires understanding the other partner's long-range motives and ensuring that they are satisfied. A partner that gets restless because things aren't meeting the long-term strategy can either adapt or suffer the consequences.

The Squeeze.   This gambit occurs when a small, financially strapped company seeks an alliance primarily to solve its cash-flow woes. Rather than sell a large chunk of equity to a venture capitalist, the business opts for a strategic equity partner that will inject cash by purchasing a very small minority stock position and making a large loan to the business.

Because of the highly tenuous financial condition of the small company, the loan is secured by a collateral position in the technology itself. Some investing companies expect the small company to go belly-up, and will give no mercy when it misses its first loan payment.

Then the squeeze is on. In the most onerous situations, the loan agreement opts for a call on the entire principal payment if one payment is late. If the company is in default, the technology is transferred, completing the squeeze. The small company then is either dead or is forced to sell its remaining assets—at a hefty discount, of course—to the only company that can use the assets: the new acquirer of the technology.

The Float.   The float occurs when an alliance has been negotiated, but, just before launch, one of the partners fails to deliver the committed resources, leaving the alliance in a state of suspended animation, neither dead nor alive. It can go nowhere until a clear decision has been made.

Trap

Environmental Problems: Be very careful of forming joint ventures in developing countries where there is a possibility that land on an industrial site is contaminated. You may get socked with cleanup responsibility later, when environmental laws are passed. Instead, *lease* the land, and let the former owners maintain full responsibility.

Hesitancy is the motivator of this strategy, and it is generally not a premeditated crime, but rather the result of second-guessing or of a lack of full internal commitment. The best defense is to be sure the process of alliance development does not bypass critical elements, such as top- and middle-rank support, and detailed operations planning before the final agreements are signed.

The Bleed-Through.   The problems of bleed-through occur in many purchaser–supplier alliances where the valuable information provided by either the purchaser or the supplier ends up, either purposefully or inadvertently as a result of the alliance, in the hands of a competitor. Hi-tech purchasers are especially concerned that their suppliers, working closely on new products, will let critical information slip out in discussion with a competing company. Similarly, automotive OEM suppliers are concerned that auto manufacturers have given their continuous improvements to the supplier's competition.

These concerns are very real in any alliance of this sort. The best methods of prevention are to limit access to critical information, or to limit the number of alliance personnel that can interact with competitors.

In some cases, bleed-through is actually encouraged on a limited basis, with the desire that it will become a two-way flow, thereby keeping a limited number of competitors always on the leading edge, but giving no one a clear advantage.

KNOWING THE REWARDS IS HALF THE BATTLE

In the final analysis, the gauging of risks is only relative to the rewards that might be achieved. The alliance must always be seeking to minimize mutual risks while maximizing mutual rewards. This is one of the main objectives of maintaining the double win.

The next chapter provides critical insights on knowing how to go after the right results.

11

Achieving Sharp Focus

If you don't know where you're going, . . .
. . . any road will get you there.

—Old New England proverb

. . . you'll end up someplace else.

—Casey Stengel

. . . you're lost.

—Yogi Berra

One of the saddest traps for those creating strategic alliances is the illusion that strategic synergies of the two partners will overcome fuzzy goals. Somehow, the romance of courtship obscures business realities.

The franchise alliance's success both domestically and internationally is due in large part to its capabilities to set very clear and measurable goals, targets, and milestones, all tracked by very accurate systems of measurement. According to Jack Hellriegel, president of International Franchise Management:

> All strategic alliances can learn enormously from the franchise alliance. Franchises gain a great deal of leverage because they customize the alliance structure only upon the initial formation, then replicate the process over and over, literally hundreds of times. The franchise alliance contracts reduce risks by structuring precise responsibilities, clear roles, and very specific targets and goals. Everyone is clear on the mutual objectives; risks are greatly diminished. It is this crispness that makes franchise alliances very tight and extremely successful.[1]

Similarly, real estate joint ventures have a very high level of success for fundamentally the same reason: objectives, roles, and responsibilities are very clear and precise. The systems, procedures, and methods of operation can be carried from one project to another very easily. All the players know what is expected of them.

Achieving a sharp focus on the ultimate objectives of the alliance is absolutely essential for success. Without clarity of objectives, the other factors—risks, roles, and responsibilities—can never fall into place.

SETTING THE RIGHT TARGETS

A top executive from a large machinery company lamented that, in his opinion, alliances don't work. Apparently, his company tried one once with a supplier, prices went up instead of down, and there was little or no innovation between the companies. I asked who had set it up and how it had been managed. He responded that his procurement department had created the alliance, but that neither he nor his staff had gotten involved. When I asked about the specific goals of the alliance, he answered that it was to have been a sole supplier relationship.

From this conversation, it was quite evident that his company did not have a strategic alliance at all—it had an *operating relationship*. The linkage did not serve to achieve clear strategic objectives, it was not supported by top management of both companies, and it was not designed to achieve a continuing win/win result.

This machinery company did not realize that it had fallen into the trap of creating very vague goals for itself. It was like telling a building contractor to construct a building, but not telling him the location or the type of building, and not giving him a set of plans or a budget.

Strategic Return on Investment (STROI)

The company is now reengaging in a second generation of alliances, but this time with a much clearer focus on what it wants to achieve. It is starting at the strategic level by defining the critical strategic return on investment (STROI) targets (see Figure 6.4) for any alliance it considers. After it determines these targets, it will begin assessing the measurable returns and the resources invested (see Figure 6.3).

Rewards from an alliance should be measured against the five strategic return on investment (STROI) dimensions (Figure 6.4). Generally, rewards should not be strictly financial. How each reward is evaluated will be custom tailored for each venture. Strategists should have some quantifiable idea of measuring each of these dimensions.

After setting the targets for strategic return, the company can reasonably engage in negotiations with a prospective partner. By knowing the

Figure 11.1   Comparison of Alliance Mission Statements

Warm Corp. and Sensuous Ltd. intend to create a joint venture to work together to explore the potential of applying concepts of laser cutting and welding technology to the machine industry.

* * *

Alfa Corp. and Beta, Inc. establish this joint venture to use Alfa's patented laser technology and Beta's proprietary instrumentation and process control systems to manufacture and market laser welding systems for the precision tool industry with the intention of capturing 25% of the marketplace by 1995 at a 15% pre-tax profit margin.

desired result, the partners can then engineer (or "imagineer") an operations plan to attain it.

By setting its sights on a measurable strategic return, a company meets the requirements of the rule: If you can't measure it, you can't manage it. Compare the first goal statement in Figure 11.1, which is based on a real alliance proposed by supposedly experienced executives, to the second statement. Had the perpetrators of the first statement been allowed to proceed, they certainly would have ended up someplace else other than where they expected. The initiators of the second statement have a chance of success; but the first statement sounds like a lot of flabby hocus-pocus worthy of a politician looking for votes, not a business seeking results; it is doomed before it starts!

Good strategy must be crisp, precise, timely, and measurable.

TRANSLATING GOALS INTO RESULTS

When the STROI results are clear, the alliance architect's next task is to engineer the tasks in detail to achieve these results. Studies of successes and failures in alliances show two distinct patterns of how this process occurs.

Autopsies of failures reveal a very high correlation between failure of the alliance and failure to complete the "goal transformation process." Many alliances on the failure path tend to start off with a statement like the first example in Figure 11.1, and then never really design a crisp, clear, focused plan for action. The goal transformation process requires three distinct steps:

1. Create distinct, measurable, time-oriented goals using STROI criteria
2. Engineer task structure using project management techniques
3. Assign roles and responsibilities using responsibility charting methodology (see Figure 11.3)

By developing a project management plan, alliances tend to have higher levels of certainty and clarity, which enable alliance managers to make more definite and specific commitments of money, manpower, materials, and market resources. Risks become relatively more predictable and quantifiable, timetables are better adhered to, and roles are more specifically delineated.

Project management orientation enables managers to become focused on performance results. In healthcare, this might mean that a particular intravenous delivery system would be matched with a designated drug, or a specific electronic diagnostic system would be matched with a particular instrument.

On the other hand, alliances that fail the goal translation process tend to deal with much higher levels of uncertainty where the desired tasks, risks, and interim results may not be clear in everyone's mind until well into the venture. For example, in the first statement in Figure 11.1, at the inception of the joint venture, a number of obstacles may need to be overcome and some promising potential solutions may need to be identified. However, it may take years for the solutions to become workable, and the technical team may meet innumerable dead ends until a practical solution is found. Frequently, these "open-ended" ventures are associated with very high-risk R&D alliances that yield lower success rates because of the greater ambiguity and uncertainty levels at conception.

Milestone Management

The more successful high-risk technology development alliances are orchestrated to divide the objectives into very discreet and measurable performance milestones to give the "feel" and manageability of a project. If these milestones and performance criteria are not met, there may be clauses written into the agreements to enable a partner to debark from the alliance or to allow the alliance to terminate.

In mining and oil exploration ventures, the alliance steering committee may review interim development reports at the one-third and two-thirds completion stages or at other critical developmental milestones. If any major impediments loom that require significant increases in capital investment, the steering committee will call a board of directors meeting to determine whether the project should proceed or be abandoned, or

Trap

Tracking and Reporting Systems: Be careful when partners use different project management systems. If one company uses PERT (project evaluation and review technique) and another uses CPM (critical path method) or an in-house method, they will be just enough out of phase to cause confusion.

Figure 11.2 Checklist for Operational Reporting Systems ☑

_____ Schedule Review against Key Milestones
_____ Critical Issues and Deadlines
_____ Monthly and Year-to-Date Financials versus Plan
_____ Steering Committee Members' Activities on the Venture's Behalf
_____ Sales Review and Forecast
_____ Customer Activity, Especially "Target Customers"
_____ Cost and Price Issues
_____ Quality Review
_____ Shipment/Delivery/Completion Reviews
_____ Technical/Manufacturing/Production Problems
_____ Coordination and Teamwork Issues
_____ Next Month's Expectations

whether any of the partners desires to withdraw while the others proceed. Similar provisions are part and parcel of many joint R&D projects in high technology. (Many companies with considerable joint development experience avoid the management difficulties inherent in broad, generalized R&D alliances, leaving those tasks for in-house R&D staffs.) By establishing clear milestones against which to measure progress, and thus helping to bring a project to fruition, the steering committee's role is made far simpler. The committee outlines the framework of interim project reports, conducts periodic performance reviews, ensures that deadlines are met, and reviews the project when complete, to be sure it meets specifications.

Reporting Systems

Establishing an effective reporting system is essential to milestone management. Project evaluation and review should be simple and practical. PERT and CPM will only work if you have the time, the money, and the people to make it work. Otherwise, a simpler, easily managed system should be chosen. Figure 11.2 is a checklist of some of the typical issues that should be considered in developing a reporting system.

If unforeseen problems arise in meeting critical milestones, managers must have a means to get a commitment of resources from the steering committee or the sponsors. This procedure should be planned in advance.

RESPONSIBILITY CHARTING

The last critical step in alliance goal conversion is to be sure there are clear roles and precise lines of responsibility. If lines of authority are not precise, there will be confusion or ambiguity concerning who is responsible for accomplishing a specific task and what exact role the participants should play. The following example from the public sector illustrates this point:

Several years ago, the federal government's General Services Administration brought in a new director from private business, in an attempt to straighten out a rather tangled organization. The new director had not been on the job long when a particularly sensitive problem emerged requiring rapid action. He called in his right-hand man and stated: "I want whoever is responsible for this problem in my office at 2 o'clock this afternoon."

Promptly at 2 o'clock, 17 administrators paraded into the director's office. Puzzled, the director asked his assistant why there were so many people for the meeting. The assistant replied that all 17 were responsible for the problem. The director, somewhat befuddled, explained that this may be how things are handled in a bureaucracy, but, in private business, *one person is responsible,* not an entire organization.

Similarly, designers of the alliance should be cautious not to create a Gordian knot that strangles decision making and operational integrity. This can happen if partners, in an effort to create teamwork, attempt to involve too many people at too many levels in too many decisions. TRW and Fujitsu tried to establish double accounting and reporting systems for their proposed joint venture. Things got so cumbersome, they found it was easier to proceed independently.

Responsibility charting has been designed to reduce the ambiguity at the work group interfaces. One of the first tasks of the steering committee is to clarify roles and responsibilities to prevent people from tripping over each other. This clarification defines how people should act in relation to the other players, and the key decisions they must make. This is a far more functional task than simply assigning titles to positions; it gets to the meat of the critical issue: Who is responsible for what? And how does each working relationship interact with the others?

Richard Beckhard, retired Professor at MIT's Sloan School of Management, has devised an excellent system of responsibility charting to overcome the potential confusion of interlocking management. This technique should be used if there is any chance of an ambiguity of roles, overlapping of functions, confusion as to who is in charge, or mixed loyalties.

Beckhard recommends bringing the teams together to formulate and disseminate the responsibility charts prior to actually making these decisions. Key players should be involved in developing a consensus regarding role assignments, matching each major operational decision or task with the individual or organizational unit necessary to carry it out. Each individual is then assigned a specific functional role (one role per person per task). The categories can and should be modified to suit the needs of a particular situation. As implemented in Figure 11.3, the categories are:

Figure 11.3   Sample Responsibility Chart

Task	Steering Committee	Marketing Company	Manufacturing Company
Develop Operations Plan	R	S	S
Develop Product Specs	L	S	R
Engineer the Product	S	Input	R
Establish Mfg Budget	V	—	R
Manufacture the Product	Input	Info	R
Pricing & Costing	R	S	S
Purchase Materials	Info	—	R
Establish Sales Quotas	Input	R	Info
Train Sales Reps	Info	S	Input
Design Literature	L	R	Input

- Leadership (L) (for carrying out program)
- Keep Informed (Info) (after the decision)
- Input (Input) (before the decision)
- Support (S) (be involved, but not responsible)
- Veto Power (V) (implies Approval Power)
- Responsible (R) (on a day-to-day basis)

Figure 11.3 illustrates the use of this procedure in a joint venture between a marketing company and a manufacturing company that established a small, detached organization for coordination and distribution of its product. (Note that in the task for training sales reps, no entity is held responsible. This task will slip through the cracks, unless someone is assigned. Fortunately, using the responsibility charting process, the problem can be identified early enough to prevent a difficulty.)

In this example, broad tasks are divided between organizations. A further refinement of the charting then splits the broad tasks into specific activities, and assigns one person to be responsible for achieving a specific, measurable result on a day-to-day basis. No more than one person should be responsible for any task or decision; otherwise, each person will assume the other is responsible, and operations will quickly disintegrate.

By engaging in this process of goal transformation, a considerable degree of clarity and focus has been achieved.

EARLY WARNING SYSTEMS

An Early Warning System will identify when problems are beginning to occur. During negotiations, and as soon as operations begin, watch for the signs listed in Figure 11.4.

Figure 11.4   Checklist for Establishing an Early Warning System

_____ **Back Burner:** Someone doesn't give top priority to getting the job done. Look for a lack of "vested interest motivation" in one of the partners or in a key individual.

_____ **Missed Deadlines:** These normally result from insurmountable problems, poor planning, poor management, inadequate resources, or lack of commitment. Watch for a spiraling progression of problems throwing the venture off course.

_____ **Role Confusion and Conflict:** If the team doesn't know its assignments, the job will not get done. The venture champion or manager must clarify roles and expectations immediately.

_____ **Winners and Losers:** If one party thinks it got the short end of the stick, the venture will fail because there is insufficient "vested interest motivation" for success. Realign for parity.

_____ **Cost Overruns:** Early-stage cost overruns may signal problems in risk analysis and planning. Left unattended, the venture may be bled dry of financial resources, creating friction between the partners. Smart managers get on top of these problems immediately.

_____ **Missed Goals or Milestones:** An effective monitoring system determines how well goals and milestones are being met. Any early deviation will be amplified over the long haul. The steering committee should address early deviations immediately.

The last part of tying down the goal transformation process is to be sure that early warning system is simple and effective. Alliance partners must know immediately about any deviations from plan.

If achieving sharp focus is a science, then alliance management, its companion, is an art. The next chapter describes this art.

12

The Secret Art of Management

The critical skill . . . will be that of coordinating units that cannot be commanded but which have to work together.

—Peter Drucker

Running an alliance can be frustrating: coordination must be the rule, diplomacy is a necessity, and the internal politics of allies are often confounding.

The process of managing an alliance is one of the best kept business secrets in the world. It truly has been a mystery because it is not taught in any business school. Neither has it been effectively written down in any books or magazine articles.

In truth, the best understanding of the process comes from those individuals who have been in the trenches for years, honing their skills with fine-tuned precision. As Richard Lembo, Director of International Alliances at GenCorp, said:

> We are usually the last people to write down our experiences, we are so busy putting ventures together. Like folklore, the process is handed down by word of mouth from manager to manager within companies.[1]

When I have read chapters in books or articles purporting to discuss alliance management, I have felt frustrated and dismayed. All too frequently, these were written by someone who had never actually had to manage an alliance; even worse, they were do's and don'ts lists, idealistic platitudes, and fragmented anecdotes, and they assumed favorable conditions. Never did they offer a coherent and realistic approach to alliance management. This chapter presents the necessary frameworks, principles, and management theories for alliance managers to succeed.

THE CRITICAL EDGE

Once an alliance commences, responsibility for success shifts from the strategists, deal makers, and top executives to the champions, alliance managers, and liaisons who, sorrowfully, seldom receive any training to accomplish their often daunting task. It is remarkable how innovative and adaptable some managers have been to make their alliances work. However, for the uninitiated who had been unprepared or unqualified for the task, the result has often been failure, frequently with severe repercussions on their companies or their careers. As retired Union Carbide executive William Silvia said:

> I was thrown into joint ventures and strategic alliances totally unaware of the new management demands I would encounter. It's not like managing in the structured world of a large corporation where authority is clear and decision making is dictated by the policy manual. I was able to adapt successfully, but others were not as fortunate.[2]

Each alliance begins with a mission and purpose. As time marches on, alliance leaders are asked to answer for the alliance, to guide its course, to energize its people. Each new challenge creates an opportunity and presents a problem to solve.

Two Ultimate Goals

There are two ultimate goals in managing an alliance: *achieve the desired strategic returns,* and *maintain a win/win relationship.* Almost deceptively simple in concept, their execution in reality can be exceedingly difficult for the uninitiated. To successfully attain these two goals, the alliance manager must be aware of several critical factors that distinguish the management of cooperative ventures from the normal corporate experience:

1. Managing the extended corporation requires a new and different set of skills and control systems;
2. The role of the middle manager in alliances changes dramatically from tactician to strategist, and from cog in the organizational wheel to team leader;
3. Flexibility will be vital in adapting to change and maintaining a double-win condition that keeps the three dimensions of "fit" in equilibrium;
4. The differences among the partners' strengths, goals, and styles will create conflicts as well as great opportunities for success;
5. Surrounding all actions must be a spirit of cooperation, constantly built and reinforced by the alliance team;

6. The process of governance for the mutual interests of both part-
    ners—a skill that is more normal in politics than in corporations—
    is as critical as achieving the right results.

Successful alliance management requires the mastery of these six distin-
guishing factors by knowing the time-tested principles and processes on
which they are based.

CRITICAL MANAGEMENT CONCEPTS

The greatest obstacle in managing alliances is the lack of a good management framework to bring new managers up to a basic level of competence.
R. Dixon Thayer, Scott Paper's champion of international alliances, expressed this frustration when he said:

> I've spent several years setting up marketing alliances in Latin America; I am
> now relatively proficient at it. But teaching someone else to do it is another
> matter. I have the intuition and the instincts, but we need an effective concep-
> tual framework so that our company can train a cadre of people to operate
> these alliances successfully.[3]

The architecture of the alliance is founded on three essential management principles:

1. Differentiation/Integration;
2. Interface Management;
3. Ambiguity–Certainty Continuum.

Their application will be needed on virtually a daily basis.

WHAT IS DIFFERENTIATION/INTEGRATION?

In earlier chapters, we explored several examples of the differentiation/
integration principle. In Chapter 8, the model of negotiations, based on
10 separate dimensions, differentiated two prospective partners and
demonstrated the impact of greater differentiation on the negotiations.
(See Figure 8.1.) The conclusion was: the greater the differentiation, the
greater the need for integration.

Regardless of the business, tasks for work groups in any organization
are specialized for the purpose of maximizing effectiveness. In a manufacturing plant, marketing and sales serve customers, and production
transforms raw materials into a finished product. Without this type of
specialization, people would be disorganized, mixed up, falling all over

each other, and totally out of harmony. Organizational differentiation looks at the total amount of differences among the specialties between working units. The greater the specialization of tasks, the greater the differentiation. The more unrelated the work groups, the more the differentiation. The more complex the functions are, the more the differentiation. The greater the differences in national or corporate culture, the greater the differentiation.

The more highly differentiated the parts of an alliance, the more the alliance cries to be integrated in order to be successful. For example, when an alliance is composed of an investment banking firm, a gas line owner, and a law firm, and its purpose is to establish a gas commodities clearing house, the three partners look at the world from radically different perspectives. They have highly differentiated skills, needs, frames of reference, and operating procedures. Without very strong integration, the venture will lack the operational synergy, the linkages, the organizational unity, the drive, and the focus to be effective.

Harvard Business School's Professor Paul Lawrence, the foremost authority in this field, has been studying the phenomenon of coordination in complex organizations for over 25 years. His analytic process for differentiation/integration casts light on many of the dark corners of alliances. It can predict problems and prescribe solutions to keep the alliance partners out of trouble. The checklist in Figure 12.1 reviews the most critical dimensions. By carefully analyzing these dimensions before beginning the alliance, the appropriate methods of integration can be designed to make the venture most effective.

In the example in Figure 12.2—a three-way joint venture among a research and engineering firm, a distributor with a worldwide sales force, and a manufacturer—the sponsoring partners were faced with the problem of choosing a venture manager who would have excellent abilities to pull a diverse group of people together and get them to work in a common direction.

Using the differentiation framework, it is obvious that the key job functions have very disparate outlooks on business. Frictions often arise when people with such divergences try to solve problems together. The joint venture manager with the greatest capability to effectively integrate the diverse groups might come from an applications engineering background, or he or she might be a sales engineer with additional experience in manufacturing.

Characteristics of the Integrator

Paul Lawrence found that, to be most effective, the integrators need to feel they are contributing to the important decisions of the organization because of their competence and knowledge, not their positional authority.

Figure 12.1   Checklist for Critical Dimensions of Operational Differentiation ☑️

_____ 1. **Organizational Structure:** How different are the parent's organizations in terms of being hierarchical or collaborative?

_____ 2. **Time Orientation:** Do the partners have radically different pressures on how they utilize time? Does the culture support the long term or short term, or is it vague about time?

_____ 3. **Personal Relationships:** Are there strong personal relationships between the CEOs or other key managers of the partners and within the alliance itself?

_____ 4. **Industry Orientation:** Are the industries of the partners similar or radically different? Do they speak a common language?

_____ 5. **Rate of Change in the Environment:** Is there a significant difference between the partners regarding the speed with which their technological or market environments change?

_____ 6. **Ambiguity/Certainty of Information:** Is there a disparity between the two partners regarding the clarity, preciseness, and specificity of the information needed to be successful in the alliance?

_____ 7. **Management Orientation:** Does top management come from similar or different backgrounds? Marketing? Engineering? Manufacturing? Finance? Law? Government?

_____ 8. **Coordinative Business Culture:** Do the partners have a natural style of management that complements a cooperative alliance? Does their style require them to work closely with other companies, or are they largely independent operators? Do the partners have a tradition of working together? If not, have they had a successful pattern of working with other partners? How will government act?

_____ 9. **Social Culture:** Do the social values and norms of the partners differ widely? Are there major language barriers? Can clashes be expected because of these differences? Have relations with labor been peaceful? Tense? Acrimonious? Productive? How will these relationships affect the alliance?

_____ 10. **Complementary Technical Skills:** Are the technologies and areas of specialized competence similar or compatible? Do the key alliance experts understand each other's technical language?

_____ 11. **Communications:** Are communication styles direct, indirect, bureaucratic, diplomatic? How well do they complement each other?

_____ 12. **Individualism:** Does the corporate or business culture prefer the individual or the team approach to human relationships?

In fact, he learned that, in most cases, these people do not have much positional authority at all. They exhibit most of their influence through personal persuasion; and their persuasion is based on their personalities and their competence as experts. Ultimately, their style can prevent the internal dissension and possible stalemating that can destroy a diverse team.

Figure 12.2   Using the Differentiation Technique

Key Jobs	Organizational Structure	Time Orientation	Personal Relations	Environmental Orientation	Rate of Change	Certainty of Information
Research	Low	Long	Permissive	Science	High	Low
Sales	Medium	Short	Permissive	Customer	High	Medium
Production	High	Short	Directive	Plant	Low	High

Another important characteristic of the integrator is an ability to relate to the diverse perspectives of the often wide variety of specialists in the organization. For example, research and engineering personnel hold a longer-term view that revolves around science, concepts, and technology. This is greatly different from the view of the production manager, whose whole work ethic is built around rapid decisions, efficiency, and practical application. Effective coordinators are able to pull diverse interests together; the managers best suited as coordinators are those who can handle great diversity.

For the champions, the alliance managers, and the corporate liaisons, integrative skills are essential. For example, Liberty Technologies is a small mechanical engineering firm with extensive proprietary knowledge in valve mechanisms. Liberty has a cooperative development and applications agreements with General Electric. Nim Evatt, Liberty's president, is an excellent integrator to manage the relationship between Liberty and GE because he spent nearly 20 years as a GE manager. He knows the ropes, understands the culture, is sensitive to the behind-the-scenes rules and procedures, and can communicate with GE in GE's language and then translate GE's needs back to Liberty's technical staff, thereby minimizing any confusion.

INTEGRATING MECHANISMS

Integration empowers the alliance; without it, the alliance will never hold together. Integration simply cannot be neglected.

Any review of failed alliances will show that, if the partners could not maintain a positive working relationship (the double-win condition) over the long term, the inability to provide adequate integration is one of the most frequent causes. It's worthwhile to review the seven integration mechanisms again:

1. Leadership
2. Teamwork/Role Clarification
3. Control by Coordination
4. Policies and Values

5.   Consensus Decision Making
6.   Resource Commitments
7.   Lateral Liaison

The following sections observe how these impact daily management functioning.

INTEGRATING MECHANISM 1:
LEADERSHIP

There is a continuing debate about whether one company should provide leadership in an alliance and the other company should follow. It echoes the Ted Turner saying (now borrowed by Lee Iacocca): "Either lead, follow, or get the hell out of the way." If neither company is willing to provide real leadership, the alliance will unquestionably fail.

According to Lee Bolman at Harvard's Center for Leadership Effectiveness:

> Leadership is most necessary in situations of uncertainty, conflict, and disagreement. But ironically, it is most difficult to lead when it is needed most. When it is not needed, no one hears a cry for leadership.[4]

In joint ventures, many American companies will want only one leader in the alliance; the other must follow. If the subordinate partner agrees to be subordinate, then there is no problem. However, in many international alliances—particularly in highly developed countries with a long track record of cooperative ventures, like Japan, Germany, France, Italy, and England, among others—the foreign partner will not want second-rate status. Equality will be the objective.

Leadership should actually be intensified by joining forces. In the Ford–Mazda alliance, Ford's small-car design team is led by Mazda, even though the majority of the cars will be built as Fords. Ford recognizes the value of Mazda's skills in compact autos and its ability to shorten the product design cycle to nearly half that of the typical American car company.

What Is Good Alliance Leadership?

There is simply no substitute for good leadership in an alliance. A good strategy, good technology, an accepting market, good lawyers, excessive capitalization—none of these will fill the gap if good leadership is missing. And without leadership, management exists in a vacuum.

When questioned about the success or failure of business alliances, one of the most critical items mentioned by executives is the quality of leadership. It is important to be clear about the differences between leadership and management, for they are related but not the same. They are often referred to synonymously, but there are many important stylistic and substantive distinctions. (See Figure 12.3.)

No alliance will last for long without a strong combination of both of these ingredients, but, between the two, management will flounder without leadership. These distinctions point to an obvious conclusion: To empower the alliance, the people appointed must be able to provide both elements.

One autonomous division of a large U.S. corporation has recently embarked on establishing alliances in the utility industry. The corporation is one of the best managed and most profitable in the world. However, this particular division's internal corporate structure has not reinforced passionate, visionary leaders. None of the alliances is progressing well; they are always running into some obstacle.

The reason (the division is loathe to admit) is that they have no passionate champions to lead the cause. Most of the alliance group are engineers who, during their careers, have held staff jobs, where they were promoted for *not* taking risks. This division cannot empower their alliances because their people are afraid that taking a risk might lead to their termination. Sad.

Companies find the best champions to be seasoned operational veterans with guts and know-how.

Figure 12.3   Leadership and Management: The Critical Distinctions

- Leaders tend to be pioneers; managers are institution builders.
- Leaders like to make things happen; managers follow through, to continue to make them happen.
- Leaders are highly emotional and intuitive; managers are logical and analytical.
- While leaders are creating, managers are problem solving.
- Leadership entails spirit, courage, vision, drive, enthusiasm, imagination, inspiration, selling, breaking through barriers, and overcoming obstacles. Management involves communications, planning, delegating, controlling, coordinating, problem solving, marketing, loyalty, choosing between alternatives, maintaining relationships, and clarifying lines of responsibility.
- Leadership involves risk taking: experimenting with new ideas, creating new opportunities, and driving imagination and teamwork to new limits. Management requires trained people who are willing to do things the right way, to establish an organization that functions the way it is designed. Management keeps the venture on course with the weight of its tasks evenly distributed.
- Leadership, as defined by a leader, is a *"burning, persistent, and focused desire to organize people to win a clear and worthy goal."* Leadership, as defined by a manager, is *"influencing people to achieve a common goal."* The difference is more than subtle, it is passionate and spiritual.
- Success is pursued by the leader methodically, with unrelenting persistence, like a hound dog tracking its prey. Managers provide the consistency and continuity to enable success to be replicated day after day.

The Need for a Leadership–Management Mix

Management and leadership together are like horse and rider. Every team cries for leadership and management, and the partners must know how to provide an experienced, well-trained team with both characteristics.

Leaders must forge clear and distinct values and standards in order to create an alliance culture that holds its strategic objectives as its first priority, supports teamwork to maintain high levels of cooperation and morale, and makes a firm commitment to the alliance's long-term stability.

The forces of organizational gravity are always at work, pulling things down, and the forces of age often bring rigidity, stodginess, and slow responsiveness to organizations. The prescription to prevent organizational gravity and old age from destroying the alliance's competitive vitality requires daily exercise and application of leadership and management. This mixture must be applied fervently and vigilantly, for these forces are relentless in their attack, even on new and growing business alliances. Choosing the right person with the right mix for the right position will be vital to the ultimate success of the venture.

The Nature of the "Champion"

The first time I met insurance executive Scott Welch, I knew immediately he was a champion, and a good one. For three years, this CEO had searched for information on creating a very unique alliance between large insurance agencies and insurance carriers. Welch had reorganized his 90-person agency (at considerable personal expense) to establish the venture. He had driven for an hour that morning to make a 6:30 meeting; he brought his team with him; he was bursting with energy; he had an endless stream of questions.

Scott Welch spoke with an evangelical zeal, thought in innovative terms, and saw no obstacle without solution. The consummation of his alliance would be like finding the Holy Grail, and he had no doubts that his mission would end successfully. You couldn't help liking this man and wanting to join his team. He is the epitome of the classic champion; he will naturally win by the force of his inner spirit.

General Electric's Rob Graber is a similar person. At 5:30 every morning, he is in the gym religiously lifting weights, preparing himself for the task of building alliances. He knows the challenges are great, but addresses each obstacle systematically. Rob Graber is passionate, even when frustrated, but he never gives up. Methodically, he moves forward, even when others get entangled in bureaucracy, red tape, and petty reasons for inaction. Rob is proactive, not reactive. He's committed, not just employed.

The *spirit* of the champion is an important characteristic, not to be given small consideration. The champion's view of success in the alliance is seldom a personal success; it is the victory of a much larger force. Phillip Crosby, one of the great pioneers in implementing total quality management (TQM) in America, is an example of the spirit of the champion. In Crosby's words:

> I was trying to convert the companies I worked for, their suppliers, and the rest of the world to a new way of thinking; any move forward, however slight, was a success. I was like the insurance salesman who, when thrown bodily out of the prospect's home with the dogs chasing and snapping at his heels, marked it down as a "possible."[5]

Most managers are driven by an *ethic of competition*. However, according to Terrence Deal and Allan Kennedy, authors of *Corporate Cultures:*

> [Champions are] driven by an *ethic of creation*. They inspire employees by distributing a sense of responsibility throughout the organization. Everybody performs with tangible goals in sight. There is more tolerance for risk taking, thus greater innovation; more acceptance of the value of long-term success, thus greater persistence; more personal responsibility for how the company performs, thus a work force that identifies personal achievement with the success of the firm.[6]

The force that must really initiate the alliance is the champion. It is far more difficult, if not inappropriate—or worse, ineffective—to "appoint" a champion later. At Texas Instruments, when deciding to develop a new product, the number-one criterion is the presence of a zealous volunteer champion; after that come market potential and project economics as a distant second and third.

Tip

Colin Powell's Rules: General Colin Powell, Chairman of the Joint Chiefs of Staff, was the champion of the powerful strategic alliance that defeated the Iraqi army in one of the world's most lopsided victories. He had several guiding principles worthy of note:

> Avoid letting your ego get so close to your position that, if your position falls, your ego goes with it.
>
> Don't let adverse facts stand in the way of a good decision.
>
> Sweat the details! Share the credit!
>
> Have vision and be demanding.
>
> Don't take counsel of your fears or nay-sayers.
>
> Perpetual optimism is a force multiplier.
>
> You'll never know what you can get away with, unless you try.

The champion is often a CEO, board chairman, executive vice president, or senior manager. According to Peters and Waterman, authors of *In Search of Excellence:*

> He's been there—been through the lengthy process of husbanding, seen what it takes to shield a potential practical new idea from the organization's formal tendency toward negation.[7]

The champion serves on an operational steering committee providing the linkage between the venture and the sponsoring companies. Champions often meet informally among themselves, working out potential problems and ensuring the commitment of their respective organizations.

The champion must provide continuity and support. Unlike deal makers who do not follow through on the maintenance of the venture once the deal is cut, champions do not forsake their offspring.

If the champion must move on to some other job, his replacement should be someone acceptable to all partners, because, in the person-to-person world of the alliance, there is a "marriage" between the people as well as the companies.

The Role of the Alliance Manager

In addition to the champion, an alliance manager with expert management and coordinating skills must be selected from within each company to handle internal operations. The spirit and drive of the champion must be reflected in the choice and behavior of the alliance manager.

A good alliance manager is part zealot and part polished manager—a passionate defender of the new venture, but at the same time strong and smart enough to be a good leader, a good manager, and a good persuader. Not a lunatic or a wild-eyed star-gazer, this person is persuasive, practical, and respected, with strong, consistent, and reliable support from executive champions within the sponsoring companies.

It is essential that the alliance manager, who will be responsible for managing the day-to-day affairs, be a good communicator. Union Carbide's William Silvia, a frequent alliance champion, insists on communication from his alliance managers on a regular basis:

> I don't like surprises. I want [the alliance managers] to keep me informed. Even if there is nothing to report, that's a sign of inaction. And I expected the alliance managers would be in contact with each other regularly between our quarterly operational steering committee meetings.

Godfathers

The "godfather" is typically an aging leader who provides the role model for championing, one who sets the corporate culture for risk taking so that the lower-level champions have corporate support. William Norris of

Control Data perfectly fits this description, having "fathered" over 80 co-operative ventures within his own organization.

INTEGRATING MECHANISM 2:
TEAMWORK/ROLE CLARIFICATION

Teamwork is synonymous with the concept of an alliance; in addition, chemistry derives from trust, which is heavily dependent on excellent teamwork. Take the teamwork out of the alliance, and its very essence is removed. Teamwork empowers the alliance and serves as a fundamental integration mechanism.

Teamwork is not just a trendy word; it is the basis for using chemistry to advantage, it is the manifestation of synergy, and it is often salvation in times of crisis.

As those familiar with teamwork in athletics will attest, teamwork comes from practice, continued working relationships, trust, fairness, consideration, organization, and discipline.

Tip

Guidelines to Support Teamwork

Responsibility: Give individuals within the team sufficient responsibility to gain satisfaction.

Complete Task: Provide team with a complete work task so that, when finished, the team knows it was successful.

Creativity: Allow teams to inject ideas *before* they start tackling a project. Foster creativity by encouraging solutions rather than dictating processes and procedures.

Focus: Maintain oversight without meddling. Focus on results, boundary conditions, and obstacles.

Communications: Provide teams with accurate information and timely feedback.

Resources: Supply proper resources—not too much, which will encourage waste and complex solutions, and not too little.

Big Picture: Keep the team's vision broad so they don't become too ingrained, introverted, or parochial.

Intervention: Put a quick end to ego-centered, antiteam behavior (rumor spreading, us versus them, sacred cows, etc.).

Teamwork creates a harmonious *tension*, like that put on a stringed musical instrument, yielding a resonant note, fusing the requirements for achievement, challenge, creativity, commitment, and human energy into an optimum team experience. The team then has a sense of mastery of its fate, rather than seeming like a victim of circumstance.

For alliances, teamwork is not just a nice value, but a way of life—all for one, one for all. This means fostering a team culture or climate. The team leader will not be an ego-maniac, but a high achiever who sees the highest achievement as pulling a group together so that each person can display his or her best individual talents in a cooperative framework. If there are "superstars," they arise because their team avoided blaming each other, refrained from back-stabbing, and survived without crashing in a crisis.

Teams and Task Forces

To complement the normal structure of the venture's organization, most alliances form task forces and teams when required. Task forces and teams are key elements in the coordinative management style that makes precise use of lateral relations.

As a general rule, task forces and teams are formed when informal contacts alone cannot solve a problem and it is necessary for representatives of three or more organizational groups to be involved in the solution.

Task forces are ad hoc groups formed for a limited time as a temporary network used to shorten communications lines during a time of uncertainty. Task forces must communicate regularly with the established chain of command to integrate information with those having regular line responsibility. (Do not let the regular managers become frustrated because they feel the task force has put them out of the communications loop.)

Teams cross functional lines and are made up of diverse experts or lower-level managers to solve a longer-term or recurring problem, where the resources or expertise to solve the problem are not at top echelons. The team provides functional managers with a broader, temporary, flexible staff to augment their own specialized crew. Assignments to teams should be made on the basis of having relevant information and the authority to make commitments for the functional groups they represent.

Teams and task forces tend to create better coordination and communications at the lower levels of the alliance, as well as between the partners and the venture itself. Task forces and teams will require more human resources—and staff support—to be effective. These staffing and resource support needs are frequently left out of the planning process.

Because it is cumbersome, and often ineffective, to bounce decisions up and down two chains of command to get an alliance decision made, the team approach is clearly a better answer. When the multiple levels of hierarchy are removed, multidisciplinary teams fill the gap. This will, of course, require that the team be empowered by delegating to them clear lines of authority and responsibility.

Managing Conflict

Teamwork is a great idea; everyone supports it, but achieving it is easier said than done. As an alliance brings diverse groups together, each with its own agendas and differing points of view, the team can easily become the natural battlefield for conflict.

Effective integrators will not bury the conflict that emerges among work groups. Instead, conflict *must* be seen as an opportunity to transform tension into creative solutions. Granted, those experiencing the conflict may not naturally gravitate toward this attitude, but a skilled integrator will bring people together, listen carefully, establish a framework to develop mutual understanding, and guide the groups to see the larger picture when developing solutions.

From personal experience, I know this is one of the hardest jobs of an alliance manager. Often, the conflict will be aimed at those "in charge," who will then be called on to fix the problem. This is a nice trap, because if you fix the problem, you have just let the team "disempower" itself. If you don't fix it, you run the risk of having them aim at you until you do. The alliance manager must throw the problem back for the team to accept responsibility for solving.

Integrators should also be firm in clarifying which actions will not be tolerated when conflict emerges. Those who begin by blaming, accusing, or hurling inflammatory remarks should be properly reprimanded. The integrator must not be soft on discipline and must insist on maintaining a corporate culture based upon teamwork.

Conflicts can occur at all levels of the alliance, from the bottom to the top. One quick way to send the alliance into failure is to allow conflict to go beneath the surface and fester. If the problems are not confronted openly, the partners grow farther apart until one abdicates or withdraws or fades into oblivion. Historically, venture managers and sponsor CEOs who are able to bring differences and problems into the open have a better chance of turning the alliance around.

INTEGRATION MECHANISM 3:
CONTROL BY COORDINATION

Unlike the internal corporate organization, alliances cannot be commanded. No one company is in charge; no one is in sole control. Therefore, as Peter Drucker has suggested, the critical skill is *coordination*. Individuals whose skills enable them to coordinate activities through effective communications are the best alliance managers. However, good coordination and communications are not solely the alliance manager's "job." They should be everyone's job, as part of a teamwork function. Otherwise, coordination doesn't work.

Effective coordinators see the big picture, and talk the many languages of the venture. Tri-Wall's Bernie Roth is multilingual and multidisciplinary. He can speak German, break bread with the French, and toast in Yiddish. He has an extensive background in engineering, electronics, manufacturing, and marketing, enabling him to take Tri-Wall's proprietary technology and explain it in marketing terms to the trading-oriented Dutch, but in engineering terms to the detail-oriented Japanese. He did not overpower the differences in culture that contributed to the alliance's effectiveness. He describes himself as an executive willing to get his fingernails dirty. According to Roth, the best coordinators "anticipate problems; not react to them. They must put the grease into the gears before they squeak."

Integrators at the upper echelons use a variety of leadership styles to get the job done, picking a style that matches the current situation. They are able to focus goals into a common vision. They maximize the utilization of diffused resources. The natural integrator is at home in the three dimensions of fit, always looking for ways to maintain the double-win advantage.

Coordinator's Problem-Solving Role

When problems emerge, and they will, the coordinator's role is to manage the decision making, not necessarily to make the decision. (In times of crisis or urgency, the coordinator may become the decision maker.) To be effective in a highly ambiguous environment, with mature people on staff, the integrator will bring key individuals together to build consensus, help the groups mutually diagnose problems, and stimulate creative solutions that maximize meeting each group's needs, while at the same time insisting that the venture's goals be met. Management authority Jay Galbraith says:

> The integrator's role is not to make the best decision, but to see that the best decision gets made. . . . The behaviors of line managers which are described as strong, quick, and decisive would be considered dogmatic, closed-minded, and bull-headed if exhibited by an integrator.[8]

Ernie DeBellis, champion of Foxboro's joint venture in China, would spend hours getting his Chinese managers to stop delegating decision-making upward, until he created a coordinative team culture.

INTEGRATION MECHANISM 4:
POLICIES AND VALUES

Knowing how the differing styles and capabilities of two companies will mesh in an alliance is a key to effective integration. The mission statement created during the negotiations stage is the first step. Still, it is not enough. A set of clear policies regarding corporate interaction is essential. People need to know how decisions will be made, what the priorities are, who will be held accountable, and what rewards will be given.

Many of the policies should emanate from and relate to the operations plan. An effective and clear set of policies replaces the hierarchy of the internal organization, and improves predictability of action. Clear policies and procedures for decision making reinforce trust. People know where they stand and what to expect. The future becomes less ambiguous in an inherently risky environment.

The design of the reporting systems should be carefully considered, to be sure it is performing its integrative function.

Values engender trust, and trust is one of the greatest integrators: it helps cast out corrosive doubt, second guessing, and hesitancy to action, while supporting healthy skepticism. Value structures also guide teamwork and thereby help maintain the alliance's chemistry fit.

INTEGRATION MECHANISM 5:
CONSENSUS DECISION MAKING

Nearly all alliances are built on the premise that decisions, in some way, will be reached by consensus. Consensus is not majority vote, but rather an understanding by all involved that everyone has had a chance to put ideas on the table, and although there may still be some disagreement, the team agrees to move on for the good of the venture.

Making an operational decision in an alliance can be cumbersome if the partners lack teamwork. What should normally be simple and straightforward can become complex and convoluted if the partners do not have a strong common vision for the future of the venture, or disagree regarding over who has what authority. If too much time is needed to make a decision, competitive advantages may quickly slip away while the partners are pondering.

Teamwork within the alliance will be a reflection of teamwork between the top echelons of the venture itself. Coordinating these responsibilities and activities will require some form of board or committee.

The formal decision-making structure varies from alliance to alliance, depending on the legal structure, the frequency and amount of contact needed, and the personal preferences of the sponsors. Corporate joint ventures may have a Board of Directors, which usually meets quarterly, and a Management Committee made up of the top venture managers and one representative (often the executive champion) from each sponsor, which meets between board meetings. Franchise alliances are likely to have a variety of integrating groups, including a Board of Directors representing headquarters, investors, and geographic units, and Advisory Committees on everything from new product development to marketing to technology innovation.

The names are far less important here than their primary functions. (For simplicity, throughout this chapter we will be referring to this coordinating entity with the generic term Steering Committee, to illustrate the coordinative function it serves.)

Steering Committee Purpose

The Steering Committee, an operational committee, is the principal focus of activity of the top alliance management team. It has five major purposes:

1. *Policy Guidance:* to provide direction and support directly to the venture through the sponsors' representatives;
2. *Performance Review:* to measure progress against some mutually agreed-on standards;
3. *Pressure:* in the form of support, planning, and the expectations for performance;
4. *Problem Solving:* in the event there are unforeseen difficulties, resources are needed;
5. *Partnership Relations:* maintenance of communications, understanding, trust, and fairness.

At the outset, the steering committee should set the pace by clearly defining roles and operational reporting channels. The level of operational autonomy of the alliance managers should be specified and agreed on by the steering committee. When problems do arise, the responsibilities for solving those problems should be placed at a preagreed level in the organizational framework. The steering committee maintains high sponsor commitment by focusing on converting goals into specific accomplishments.

Crucial to the ultimate success of the venture are good communications, support, and control by the sponsoring partners. By conducting frequent reviews of the venture, the partners are able to generate confidence and trust in one another, thereby maximizing the ability of the alliance to produce the expected results.

It is the purpose of the steering committee to oversee the total project in general. Its members are responsible for suggesting and approving changes to the operational plan, but the steering committee may not necessarily have the right to reduce its budget without full and complete agreement from the partners.

The number of people on the steering committee can vary, usually ranging from 4 to 8 people. Sometimes, a third party, such as an experienced executive or technical consultant respected by all parties, is included as a neutral member (or mediator if needed).

A prototypical steering committee will be composed of the champions, the alliance manager(s), and operational managers and/or team leaders.

Steering committees usually meet on a regular and predetermined basis, often weekly or biweekly, but usually no less frequently than quarterly, and at any time when requested by a member.

Most steering committees have the authority to call anyone to attend meetings, to have the benefit of that person's input on technical or operational matters.

The Champion's Role

It is absolutely essential to have the champions of the venture represented on the steering committee. They help the venture overcome the following potentially serious problems and pitfalls:

1. Any unclear or unrealistic goals imposed by the sponsor can be clarified and focused. The champion is the policy representative of the sponsoring company and is the venture's primary and regular connection to the sponsor's top decision maker.
2. Many ventures have suffered from poor integration of the venture's products into the sponsoring companies, often because of the "not invented here" syndrome. The champions assume the role of product integrators.
3. In the event the corporate liaison is stymied, the champion helps find internal resources that can assist with the venture.
4. Each sponsor is usually responsible for committing certain support to the venture. The champion is responsible for watching the "people process," making sure quality people are helping the venture achieve its goals and ensuring the venture receives the proper level of corporate attention from the sponsors.

INTEGRATION MECHANISM 6: RESOURCE COMMITMENTS

Allocation of sufficient resources to the alliance is a critical, though often unattended integration mechanism. Like a fast race car with no gas in the tank, the best planned alliance will only succeed with sufficient money, people, materials, and time allocations.

Resources are vital to alliance empowerment. There is a critical mass necessary to enable an alliance to make an impact. Tentativeness in resource allocation will leave the alliance powerless, and thus a failure. If commitments are made, the partners must stick to them or lose trust, causing a downward spiral toward withdrawal.

One U.S. corporation negotiated a technology development alliance with a Swedish company. Right after the successful negotiations, the Swedish managers went into their traditional five-week summer vacation period. The Americans who were to work on the alliance were reallocated to other projects during this period. When the Swedish returned, the Americans were focused on other projects and their bosses did not provide sufficient personnel for all their work assignments. Rather than hire more people or take people from other parts of the organization, everyone was stretched too thin. The alliance never got started and was disbanded shortly thereafter because of a lack of faith in the negotiated commitments.

General Motors has owned 37.5% of Japan's Isuzu Motors Ltd. since the early 1970s. However, this strategic equity partnership has never really delivered on its potential. General Motors considered Isuzu as a supplier, not a real partner. The strategic returns GM received from Isuzu were paltry compared with what could have been received had technical and human resources been added to the formula. Unlike the Ford–Mazda alliance, GM did not integrate small-car design or stimulate joint technical design. GM failed to link Isuzu into critical market structures in a manner that could have empowered Isuzu to become one of Japan's strongest car and truck manufacturers, thus competing head-to-head with Honda, Toyota, and Nissan. Had GM provided real resources to Isuzu, more carefully integrated the operational staffs, and given Isuzu strategic muscle, GM's partner could have been a serious threat to its Japanese competitors, and GM would have reaped hefty rewards. Similarly, GM failed to reintegrate the knowledge and competencies it gained from its Toyota joint venture into its North American operations.

Personnel Selection

Skilled personnel are the most critical of all resources. They will make the critical difference for most alliances, because people are the only resource capable of adapting the alliance to maintain the double-win condition. As a venture gets underway, if the partners find their strategy or structure is not on target, or if changed conditions now place heavy pressures on the venture's stability, skilled managers have a far better chance of success than those of mediocre caliber.

Highly skilled, top-level people whose decisions are valued and trusted by the sponsors constitute an essential ingredient for success. Companies not willing to put top-notch people in charge of the venture are probably lacking some element of the all-important "vested interest motivation."

A lack of commitment to the venture, or a significantly low risk and/or reward ingredient is usually the reason for betting on second-string players!

Tip

Assign Top-Notch People: Business confederations must be treated as though they were start-up companies; weak management will lead down the rapid road to failure.

Remember the essential rule of alliance management: "Far better to have a grade A management team and a grade B product, then a grade A product and a grade B management team."

The second-rate team will be far less capable of guiding the alliance, maintaining a win/win condition, and capturing opportunities.

Many alliances have failed specifically because the sponsoring companies appointed second-rate managers to key positions, figuring the alliance was a good "dumping ground" for people who did not work well in the parent organization. Japanese companies do just the opposite; they commit their *best* people to alliances because they understand both the difficulty of management and the opportunity for great strategic rewards.

Choose personnel whose goals and skills match the needs of the venture, rather than people skilled in a specialty unrelated to the alliance, in the hope that it will become a good training ground. Finding people with excellent integration/coordination skills as well as superb operational management abilities will probably be a most challenging personnel selection task, but is certainly worth the effort.

INTEGRATION MECHANISM 7:
LATERAL LIAISON

Lateral relations reduce the number of decisions referred upward, thereby increasing the capacity of the organization to process information. This function is most useful when the decisions are qualitative in nature, not just numbers-oriented. Its fundamental premise is to utilize direct contact between experts who share a problem, rather than send decisions up and down a cumbersome chain of command, which, in an alliance, can become far more convoluted than in the standard organization.

Peter Drucker says business confederations need to deal person-to-person, to compensate for the cultural differences between partners. Because these partnerships are more highly specialized in a more narrow range of products, the people involved must talk a similar language, regardless of their corporate or national cultural backgrounds.

People whose career paths have included lateral transfers from one department to another will be more effective in managing lateral relations.

Role of Liaisons

Liaisons coordinate when the volume of communication contacts becomes too difficult to manage, especially if information is normally referred upward in the organization, and might tend to become bottlenecked. They serve as "two-way funnels," tracking down and providing relevant information and resources on both sides of the alliance.

Liaisons serve as "buffers" between the venture and the sponsoring organizations. As Norm Alister commented, in *Electronic Business:*

> Liaisons are often the only force capable of keeping the form-shuffling bureaucratic "memo-masters" from tying up the new venture in mountains of red tape.[9]

In IBM's alliances, all requests for information are channeled and supervised through either a project manager or a technical liaison person on either side. No other people may initiate or respond to requests. This limits information slipping over the transom and not being managed effectively. IBM is very careful in its choice of liaison personnel, out of consideration for the different needs and concerns that a smaller partner will have. According to J. William Scruggs, former director of business development at IBM:

> Each of the individuals have great personal knowledge and personal contacts throughout IBM. It could be access to our manufacturing systems, or perhaps IBM has solved a specific technical problem or he could make available some of the things we're doing in terms of software. So it is an efficiency or time-saving concept. The people who are most effective at that tend to have a very broad knowledge of IBM, and they have widespread contacts throughout IBM.[10]

If necessary, the number of liaisons can be increased if the venture becomes rather large. Liaisons can be assigned to specific areas, such as manufacturing, system development, and finance.

Liaisons should have helpful attitudes and lots of contacts. Effective liaisons are the mid-level "interdepartmental deal makers," people who can trade favors and link information. The best ones are organizationally centered, not self-centered. This is not an assignment for a prototypical "organization man" who passes information up and down the chain of command; this is a job for a seasoned insider.

THE PRINCIPLES OF INTERFACE MANAGEMENT

Every manager has had some previous experience with interface management, even without calling it by name. The point of contact between two internal departments—or any differentiated groups, for that matter—is called the interface.

Those in manufacturing know the frustration they experience in dealing with the engineering and production departments. Engineers are often at odds with the production manager because production does not give engineering enough lead time, or production is lowering the quality by cutting corners. Production personnel complain that engineering will not "get practical," and production steams when the sales department promises delivery dates that are not feasible, regardless of how valued the customer might be.

These are examples of "differentiation." Every company composed of more than one department experiences these conflicts, because, when we specialize, we create differences in frames of reference, time perspectives, points of view, needs, values, and operating pressures.

Where the Complexities and Opportunities Lie

Problems and complexities, whether organizational or technological, lie at the interfaces. Interfaces are minefields, but under them are the buried treasures of opportunity. As Kenichi Ohmae, Japan's strategic guru has said, in the *The Mind of the Strategist*:

> In many companies today, functional activities such as design, manufacturing, and sales, which are usually divided from one another organizationally, devote more energy to guarding their own territories than to looking for ways to cooperate. As a result, the full potential for major profit improvement that typically lies in the interfunctional border areas tends to be overlooked.[11]

Mining this ore is an essential task of the alliance manager.

The principle of interface management says it is at this interface where most organizational frictions occur. The role of the coordinator/

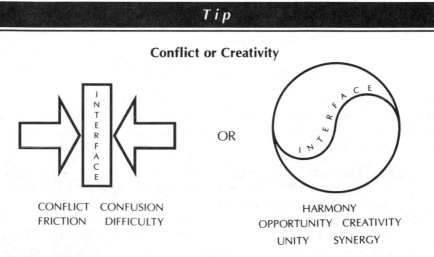

Tip

Conflict or Creativity

CONFLICT   CONFUSION   HARMONY
FRICTION   DIFFICULTY   OPPORTUNITY   CREATIVITY

                                  UNITY   SYNERGY

The mental image we have about interfaces is important. The Western view expects difficulty at the interface, while the Eastern culture foresees opportunity.

integrator is to manage the interface to maximize people's ability to get the job done.

The first task in interface management is to begin identifying the interfaces before the alliance gears up for action. In this way, points of potential conflict can be isolated beforehand, and personnel assigned to the integrator's role can head off potential problems.

USING THE AMBIGUITY/CERTAINTY CONTINUUM

The ambiguity/certainty continuum refers to the relative amount of clarity or fuzziness within the alliance environment. Alliances are designed to overcome risks. When the risks are measurable, specific, and easily defined, there is a modicum of certainty in the risk environment.

In one venture, the partners saw themselves faced with "solving a triple simultaneous equation with all unknowns"—the unknowns were the formulation of the actual product, the kind of machinery that would produce that product, and the market demand—and, in those conditions, we could conclude the alliance would operate in a highly ambiguous environment.

The greater the uncertainty of the task, the greater the unpredictability, and, therefore, the greater the amount of information that must be processed among decision makers to achieve a given level of performance. Similarly, if the companies have not worked together closely, the greater the uncertainty in team relations, the greater the need to focus on and maintain close working relationships. Anyone ever involved in sports competition knows that significant time is needed for any team to "jell." If the partners' teamwork is untested, the organizational structure must adapt to this condition.

Options to Deal with Ambiguity

Conditions of high ambiguity will call for more information to be processed, more collaboration, lower-level decision making, and stronger lateral relations. Partners have three fundamental sets of choices to make, to deal with the situation:

1. *Risk Reduction:* The partners can scale down the venture to a smaller, less risky size, or phase the project into risks that are clearer and more certain to be successfully conquered.
2. *Consolidation:* One partner takes operational control and assumes most of the risk or a certain separable portion of the risk, figuring that the advantages of internal decision making and internal resources outweigh the increased complexity of coordinative sharing of information, decision making, and control. Many highly risky

technology development projects take this approach, leaving early
R&D to their internal staffs, and then, once the technology is ready
for the prototype stage, putting the final applications engineering,
commercial application, and marketing programs into the alliance.

3. *Organizational Integration:* This solution will maximize the resources of the partners in the belief that, without their contributions of knowledge and expertise, the risks will be overwhelming.

If the venture's partners choose the organizational integration solution,
they would begin to analyze their situation by examining some of the
conditions in Figure 12.4.

Few ventures are completely oriented to one end of the spectrum or
the other. The ambiguity/certainty continuum will assist in developing a
set of management functions that relate to the specific conditions within
which the venture is designed to operate.

If some parts of the venture are clear and crisp, as in the production
phase, but other parts are highly ambiguous, as in the marketing phase,
then the production organization may be more centrally organized and
hierarchical in nature, and the marketing organization may be more
collaborative.

As times change, new conditions of ambiguity arise in organizations.
Unanticipated problems, developments outside the organization's control,
and unclear or inadequate information are just some situations that may
drive the venture to reexamine its management functions. Ambiguity

Figure 12.4   The Ambiguity–Certainty Continuum

Ambiguity ←————————————————————→ Certainty

CONDITIONS

Dynamic Change	Stability and Predictability
Innovation Required	Routines Required
Unanticipated Problems	Anticipated Problems
Developments Outside	Developments Within
Organizational Control	Organizational Control
Information Unclear or Inadequate	Information Clear and Adequate

MANAGEMENT FUNCTIONS

Collaborative Management Styles	Hierarchical/Task Management Styles
Decision Making at Lower Levels	Decision Making at Higher Levels
Mature Personnel Needed at All Levels	Mature Personnel at Higher Levels
Looser Structures Needed	Tighter Structures Needed
Shared Decision Making	Decision Dominance of One Partner
Predominant Lateral Information Flow	Predominant Vertical Information Flow

tends to amplify any existing cross-cultural differences between groups, and often is severe enough to drive a wedge between the partners.

Problems and Opportunities in Managing Ambiguity

Ambiguity presents a special condition to a manager: it creates the potential for counterdependence, conflict, and creativity within work groups, all at the same time. Because a situation is unclear, groups will naturally attempt to impose some structure and order. As a result, a group will look to their leader to provide direction, support, and solutions, or they may decide to reject their leader ("We can handle this ourselves"), especially if they do not think the leader is capable. If they feel overwhelmed by the problem, they may feel out of control, and anxiety, frustration, blaming, and confusion will result.

A real dilemma faces the manager at this juncture. On the one hand, ambiguous, complex situations generally call for decentralized decision making and lower-level autonomy; on the other hand, the psychological needs of the team demand structure, direction, and discipline—and the sponsors want performance, not confusion. The manager must do something; if left unchecked and undirected, these highly ambiguous situations, particularly in the earlier stages of an alliance, can lead to the formation of stereotypes and generalizations, which can then escalate into conflict. If unaddressed, these conditions will spread and polarize the alliance right down party lines.

At this point, the manager must intervene with a structured process of problem solving, to redirect the anxiety onto a course of creativity.

Figure 12.5   How to Deal with Ambiguity and Uncertainty

- Delineate several *optional courses of action,* let the group suggest other alternatives, and make the group deal with choosing an alternative they own and to which they will be committed;
- *Restructure the work group* to cope with the ambiguous condition, by decentralizing or recentralizing decision making, increasing or decreasing flow of information, creating more or fewer liaisons, or breaking the desired targets down into smaller, more realistic goals;
- Put *more valid information* into the problem, break assumptions, and put boundaries around the problem by asking what is the worst possible outcome;
- *Break stereotyping* (unfreeze people) by introducing new information that conflicts with old data;
- Display no tolerance for inappropriate blaming, and *reinforce* the alliance;
- Explore more effective methods of *controlling the variables* (i.e., lobby with local officials, employ a specialist, use a more standard formula, and so on);
- *Reduce the number of interfaces* necessary to accomplish the task, thereby reducing complexity and opportunities for confusion.

Figure 12.5 outlines some methods for dealing with ambiguous situations in alliances.

ALL THE PARTNERS MUST BE WINNERS

The two basic objectives of management are to adapt the changing needs of the alliance and to get results. Maintaining the win/win condition is essential: without the presence of this condition, no strategic plan, no legal structure, no formal agreement, and no operational schedule will overcome such a fundamental deficiency. A partner who perceives a losing condition will not perform well and may eventually undermine the alliance itself.

How Uniroyal Created the Double Win

The importance of maintaining the double-win condition is illustrated by a joint venture in the chemical industry, between Uniroyal and Sumitomo, its Japanese partner, which had excess production capacity in Japan. The agreement specified a 50/50 split in the cost of running the plant. Both companies were to receive products from the jointly owned plant at cost, with the Japanese company reaping all benefits from Japanese sales, and the American company selling solely to the export market.

All proceeded well for 20 years, until the bottom dropped out of the Japanese domestic market while export sales continued to thrive. The Japanese, a proud and honorable people afraid of "losing face," never let on that they were on the verge of bankruptcy because of the burden of half the venture's cost. They never asked to renegotiate the agreement.

David Beretta, the American CEO, learned of the condition of the Japanese partner when he read the auditors' end-of-the-year report. Beretta could have done nothing, but, seeing the immediacy of correcting the imbalance, he proposed a more equitable distribution of costs. The new agreement meant less profit for the Americans, but the joint venture continued to be profitable for both parties—a classic and touching win/win condition.

Successful management requires adapting the course of the alliance to ever changing competitive winds, swirling seas of technical innovation, and the ebb and flow of market demands. As strategic objectives, personal relationships, and operational needs evolve, the ultimate purpose of the alliance must adapt accordingly.

PART FOUR

Tools of the Trade

13

How to Find Partners

Friendship founded on business is better than business founded on friendship.

—John D. Rockefeller

According to a survey of 455 CEOs by *Electronic Business* magazine, the most important factor in designing a successful alliance is the selection of the right partner (chosen by 75% of the CEOs).[1] The example of how Tri-Wall found a partner serves to illustrate this process.

When Tri-Wall decided to enter the global market with special triple-wall corrugated paper boxes, Bernie Roth, then Vice President of Strategic Planning, first established his strategy: Find strategic joint venture partners in areas prioritized by market size—continental Europe and the United Kingdom, and then Japan, Australia, and Israel. He was flexible on the issues of timing, and the ideal sequence was desired but not critical.

Roth knew that the United Kingdom would be easier because of lower language and administrative barriers, but he also saw Britain as a much smaller market than Europe, and still "outside," in most Europeans' view. He figured the best location in Europe was in Alsace, on the German–French border, because it was logistically centralized.

ESTABLISH A PARTNER PROFILE

Before he packed his bags and headed to Europe in search of a partner, Roth set his criteria for a good match:

1. A corrugating plant with space to add augmented equipment specified by Tri-Wall;

211

2. The capacity on the corrugating production line to take the Tri-Wall product;
3. High quality standards;
4. Niche marketing capacity with a good sales staff trained in value-added sales;
5. Family ownership, for ease in decision making.

The last factor was very important. Roth's company was a small business; the partner's style had to be entrepreneurial, to enable the partner to see Tri-Wall's vision without interfering layers of bureaucratic decision making. A large commodity paper manufacturer would not do.

Roth hired a small European research firm, but did about 10% of the homework himself, to be sure he was familiar with the techniques and the market.

Do Your Homework

He went to the libraries in major cities—London, Paris, Amsterdam, and Bonn. He looked for data on volume, competing product costs, and product acceptance in a variety of countries and industries within Europe. He looked for key "targets"—manufacturers and distributors in each country. He then planned to make an initial visit to determine mutuality of interest, potential chemistry between CEOs, and local manufacturing costs and constraints among the newly formed Common Market countries.

Before meeting anyone, Roth was clear about the benefits Tri-Wall had to offer sales prospects to speed their acceptance of his offer. While he knew Tri-Wall's product was substantially better than the competing wooden crates, he had devised a plan on how his prospect's marketing staff could convert existing small customers into large orders more rapidly. His unique service plan tracked all trial shipments of goods, inspected trial shipments arriving by ship or air, and reported on the shipment's condition after the package arrived.

Keep on Trying

Roth first decided to try the Alsatian prospect because of the strategic location and the fact that the target firm already made a triple-wall corrugated product (it was not as good as Tri-Wall's, but was better than U.S. imitations). The Alsace plant management liked the concept of the joint venture: it lowered the risk and required less equipment than most new ventures would require, and this company was acclimated to handling large boxes. However, the attempt failed to be consummated in wedlock for nonbusiness reasons.

Tri-Wall's second European target was in Holland. When Roth talked to the Dutch CEO, it soon became evident that he was upset with U.S.

Tip

Advice from Tri-Wall

1. Always promise less than you can deliver—in sales or profits. Had Tri-Wall expressed its real profit expectations—which were quite high—it would not have been credible.
2. Use local talent in each country; send outsiders in to hire, train, coach, and then return home. Tri-Wall had only one full-time American overseas.
3. Avoid major capital expenses. Tri-Wall avoided a paper mill, which was a transaction with too much financial leverage and risk.

---

competitive practices during several recent acquisitions in Holland, and would not consider doing any deal with any American firm.

Use Your Connections

Undaunted, Roth set his sights on the United Kingdom, where Tri-Wall already had a distributor eager to cut the time and cost of ocean freight. The distributor introduced Roth to three firms.

The first firm was not family-owned. Its structure, Roth felt, was too big and monolithic in decision making to be a good match for the smaller Tri-Wall. The second English company was not interested. In the third firm, Roth finally found a match. A two-page Statement of Principle was crafted, and a joint venture alliance agreement followed. The business was a success.

Success Breeds Success

Two years after the U.K. agreement, the original "target" in Holland called Tri-Wall; it liked how Tri-Wall had operated across the Channel. Feeling pressure from U.S. competitors, the Dutch company requested a meeting. Having done his homework on local customs and taboos, Roth wined and dined the previously distraught Dutch CEO, and Tri-Wall speedily inked a deal in the same pattern as had been originally proposed.

The following year, Tri-Wall set its aim toward the Middle East— specifically, the citrus industry in Israel. During a vacation to Israel, Roth visited a corrugator owned by two friendly U.S. companies, which in turn made introductions to an Israeli firm. However, Tri-Wall received a cold shoulder from the Israeli plant operators because the product was "not invented here!"

Persistence was Roth's trademark. A short discussion with the Investment Ministry found a newly established corrugator in Haifa, and its manager quickly got excited about the proposed joint venture. However, his enthusiasm also cost him his job: the company waffled at the proposition, and the manager quit in disgust.

Stay Flexible

Roth decided to take a different tack. He examined the freight and time logistics, and concluded that a box assembly plant in Israel could be supplied with corrugated paper stock from either his U.K. or Holland partners.

Tri-Wall then conducted a market study and saw viability. The following year, Tri-Wall decided to build the box assembly plant. To run the plant, Roth hired the Israeli who had earlier quit his job. Within seven months, the venture was in the black.

Eventually, the previously hesitant Haifa firm came back to Tri-Wall for a joint venture that supplied locally produced corrugated paper to the box assembly plant. This opened up a new set of markets in Greece, Lebanon, Iran, Kenya, and South Africa.

On to the Pacific Rim

Five years after commencing the globalization strategy, Tri-Wall's reputation had spread worldwide. The field sales people were all problem solvers, and new applications were rapidly multiplying around the world as a result of user acceptance and new sales. Tri-Wall created an applications newsletter with international circulation. Two new product areas developed in the United States were rapidly delivered into the international marketplace through the joint ventures.

Roth consummated a similar joint venture in Japan. Within six months, another joint venture was created in Australia. Each one became easier. Although the initial "target" partner didn't work out in each case, patience and having more than one target in a region—and the reinforcement of references provided by already established successful partnerships—eventually brought success.

Within 5 years, Tri-Wall had become a multinational corporation with plants in the United States, the United Kingdom, Holland, Israel, Japan, and Australia. There were no acquisitions, and there was very little additional debt. Sales had grown nearly ten times in this period; profit after taxes jumped from 1% to 10%, and return on investment billowed out to 45%. Gross profit margin for the competition's standard corrugated boxes was 20% to 25%; but for Tri-Wall's specialty product, it was 40% to 45%.

TYPES OF ALLIANCE PARTNERS

Who should your partner be? A carefully selected teammate is essential for maximizing the chances for long-term success, but how should the

Figure 13.1   Checklist for Types of Alliance Partners

_____ **Direct Competitor:** This ally should be chosen when the alternative is cutthroat competition. However, be cautious, because the success of one partner may come at the expense of the other.

_____ **Potential Competitor:** This is an alternative to merger or future competition. Unite to gain market share and to fend off larger direct competitors. A future merger may result, but more often the result is the expansion of product offerings to a larger customer base.

_____ **Parallel Producer:** This type of truly complementary alliance is used to widen or integrate product lines, to capture market share, to trade on relationships, and to take mutual advantage of each partner's strength. Many are formed when highly integrated technology is essential.

_____ **Vertical Integrator:** Rather than be bound by a rigid system of vertically integrated subsidiaries that may not be able to adapt to changing customer needs, many companies use cooperative ventures as a better alternative, linking supply, product, and market functions.

_____ **Technical Developer:** Prohibitive or extremely risky development costs are the prime motivators. Generally, partners occupy parallel but not directly competitive market niches. Research consortia pool direct competitors to give common access to all knowledge developed.

selection be made? Your company has a variety of types of partners to choose from. Figure 13.1 presents an array of these choices.

Knowing who is the right partner is absolutely essential. Otherwise, you will marry the first company that knocks on your door, or worse, your company might overlook the perfect match because someone thought you wanted something else. The smart thing to do is create a good partner profile. (Figure 13.2 is a sample checklist that addresses many issues. Note, however, your own partner profile may be significantly different.)

Once you have established the criteria, you can begin scoring the potential alliance partners on an opportunity matrix, displaying each company in reference to the criteria in the profile. (See Figure 13.3.) If one company stands above the rest, it might make a good match, provided the three-dimensional fits—strategic, chemistry, and operational—prove correct.

WHERE TO FIND PARTNERS

Many large corporations are looking for strategic allies right now. The job titles of those responsible for the selection process often include:

Directors of:
Corporate Planning   Business Development
Strategic Development   Business Alliances
New Enterprise   Mergers and Acquisitions

Figure 13.2   Checklist for Creating a Partner Profile (Example)   ☑

MANAGEMENT STYLE
_____ Compatible Structure, Philosophy
_____ Work Ethic, Operating Style
_____ Strategic Planning, Culture, and Long-Term View
_____ Responsiveness to Opportunities and Threats

MARKETING
_____ Strong Management Team
_____ Consumer Marketing Experience
_____ Development and Maintenance of Competitive Advantage
_____ Consumer-Oriented, Market-Driven
_____ Innovative Market Leader
_____ Understands Brands Management and Market Mix
_____ Proven New Product Success
_____ Track Record of Putting Strategic Thinking into Action

MANUFACTURING
_____ Consistent High-Quality Producer
_____ Production Capabilities
_____ Efficient State-of-the-Art Producer
_____ Technical and R&D Expertise
_____ Willingness to Invest in Production
_____ Develops High Quality Long-Term Suppliers

FINANCE
_____ Strength on P&L Statement and Balance Sheet
_____ Long-Term Perspective
_____ Realistic ROI Expectations

TRADE AND CUSTOMER SERVICES
_____ Strong Trade Relationships
_____ Pan-European Distribution
_____ Customer Service Driven

OTHER ALLIANCES
_____ Successful Alliance Experience
_____ Enthusiastic about Our Company
_____ View Our Company as a High-Priority Partner
_____ Excellent Strategic, Chemistry, and Operations Fit

Small and medium-size companies may not have someone with such a specialized position, but if the company has been involved in strategic alliances, someone is a decision maker. That person may be found in the marketing or R&D department, or in the office of the executive vice president. There is no quick and easy method of finding the right partner; good sleuthing and persistence will yield the best results.

Foreign corporations may provide excellent opportunities. They often have agents who can provide a link to the right person overseas. If,

Figure 13.3   Company Profile and Opportunity Matrix

Step One: PROFILING
Company Profile

Name: ————————————————————————————————

Key Profile Characteristics

Measurement Criteria	Score
A.	
B.	
C.	
D.	
E.	
F.	
G.	
H.	

Step Two: OPPORTUNITY MATRIX

Key Profile
Characteristics Scores

Company	A	B	C	D	E	F	G	H	Total Score
1.									
2.									
3.									
4.									

however, a search for a partner is required, several methods have proven successful for many companies. (See Figure 13.4.)

In foreign countries, your investigation can often begin with the Foreign Service Commercial Officer at the U.S. Embassy in that country. (Try for a breakfast meeting, which should be arranged before you arrive.) Make a prospect list before meeting any prospective partner face-to-face. Create the prospect list from the U.S. Department of Commerce (DOC) resources, plus any information you gather from trade publications, advertisements, trade associations, commercial banks, and government ministries in that country. Consult with other U.S. companies operating in that country; ask their recommendations.

The DOC's primary mission in the 1990s is to promote U.S. exports to improve the balance of payments. Because of this export orientation, DOC officials will bend over backward if they believe a prospective alliance will result in exports rather than imports. Business managers should bear this in mind when seeking assistance. For example, if a manufacturing company is

Figure 13.4   Checklist for Finding International Partners

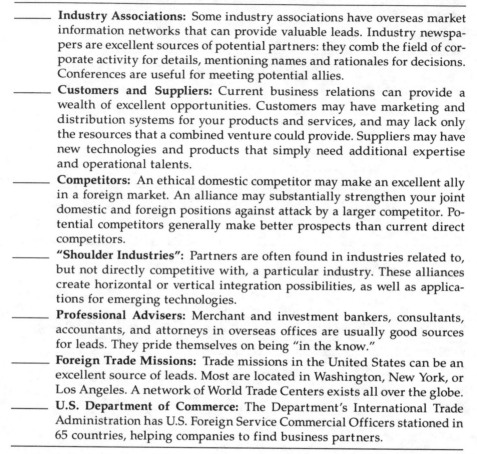

_____ **Industry Associations:** Some industry associations have overseas market information networks that can provide valuable leads. Industry newspapers are excellent sources of potential partners: they comb the field of corporate activity for details, mentioning names and rationales for decisions. Conferences are useful for meeting potential allies.

_____ **Customers and Suppliers:** Current business relations can provide a wealth of excellent opportunities. Customers may have marketing and distribution systems for your products and services, and may lack only the resources that a combined venture could provide. Suppliers may have new technologies and products that simply need additional expertise and operational talents.

_____ **Competitors:** An ethical domestic competitor may make an excellent ally in a foreign market. An alliance may substantially strengthen your joint domestic and foreign positions against attack by a larger competitor. Potential competitors generally make better prospects than current direct competitors.

_____ **"Shoulder Industries":** Partners are often found in industries related to, but not directly competitive with, a particular industry. These alliances create horizontal or vertical integration possibilities, as well as applications for emerging technologies.

_____ **Professional Advisers:** Merchant and investment bankers, consultants, accountants, and attorneys in overseas offices are usually good sources for leads. They pride themselves on being "in the know."

_____ **Foreign Trade Missions:** Trade missions in the United States can be an excellent source of leads. Most are located in Washington, New York, or Los Angeles. A network of World Trade Centers exists all over the globe.

_____ **U.S. Department of Commerce:** The Department's International Trade Administration has U.S. Foreign Service Commercial Officers stationed in 65 countries, helping companies to find business partners.

seeking an ally to market its product in the Pacific Rim, DOC will respond with greater assistance than if the manufacturing company is seeking a low-cost sourcing subassembly manufacturer.

EVALUATING CANDIDATES

Before actually meeting your prospects, do your homework. Know their products, volumes, customer base, and capabilities. When you meet a prospect, you can then ask the right questions.

Mike Van Horn, author of *Pacific Rim Trade*, works closely with companies to establish overseas alliances. During the early stages of opening up discussions he recommends these actions:

- *Get Detailed Information:* Check the company size and the number of employees. Look into the resources and the availability of suitable facilities.
- *Check References:* Talk to companies the prospect does business with. Ask the U.S. Embassy about the prospect's ethics. (The Embassy will do a quick background check.)
- *Evaluate Business Practices:* Get the names and backgrounds of the prospect's principals. Check its current marketing efforts, including sales territories, range of products, types of customers, capabilities of sales or manufacturing force, and the way new products are introduced.[2]

COURTING A PARTNER

The right partner must be interesting, maybe even exciting. Look for more than just strategic strength in a partner. Look beyond partners that can provide a "quick fix" to fill a gap in a product line or that can act as a "sugar daddy" with big bucks. The best partners provide depth of talent to give long-term continuity when business cycles and buying patterns change downstream.

Finding strategic allies is similar to finding a marriage partner. Styles, personalities, and perspectives on life must mesh. Do not be dismayed, if, upon contacting a company to explore a possible alliance, the response is "No." It may mean the wrong person has been approached, or the timing is wrong, or the wrong division of the company has been selected.

It may be presumptuous and imprudent to request an immediate marriage. It is often best to have a "date" first. The "date" may take several forms: mutual work developing a new marketing channel, a contract to supply materials, joint engineering on a new product, and so on. Unless each partner has had considerable experience in alliances, use the simplest form of alliance on the strategic spectrum first. Your company may ask several prospective partners for "dates" and then find them to be poor choices for the future.

In today's world, partners must have the ability to work compatibly where the rules may be continuously evolving. Not every company will be able to handle such enormous changes. Your primary objective will be to find the right partner and the right person within the company—the person who will spearhead the alliance and serve as a champion for its cause. Your own company will also need a champion fully committed to making the alliance work.

Is the Biggest the Best?

The right partner is not necessarily the biggest. In the early 1970s, when Dunkin' Donuts, the U.S. market leader, began establishing franchise

---

T i p

High Standards: Look for a partner that has high standards—world-class standards—so that each company helps the other leapfrog to the top. Look for an alliance in which being better is never enough; where your partner's minimum standard of excellence is their competitors' highest standard.

---

alliances in Japan, it linked up with Sabu, a huge conglomerate, thinking that size would equate with power. However, only 4% of Sabu's sales were in the restaurant segment. In retrospect, Dunkin' Donuts was not a critical part of Sabu's growth strategy.

Dunkin' Donuts' smaller competitor, Mr. Donut, also entered the Japanese marketplace, joining with a relatively unknown company named Duskin. Although far smaller than Sabu, Duskin had a very religious culture and sound values. More importantly, Mr. Donut was considered very important to Duskin's growth. The strategic fit and chemistry were excellent. As could be predicted, 20 years later, Dunkin' Donuts has only 100 outlets in Japan, while Mr. Donut has 700.

14

About Money and Value

Money is not the goal; just the best measure of success.

—Entrepreneurial saying

Money is the goal; just ask the stockholders.

—Investor saying

Money is the resource to gain market share.

—Japanese saying

These three sayings reflect dramatically different perspectives on money. We shall see, through the course of this chapter, how these three perspectives can alter an alliance's method of allocating financial remuneration and can create anxiety among the partners.

PERSPECTIVES ON MONEY

Earlier, I quoted Oscar Wilde: "A cynic is someone who knows the price of everything, and the value of nothing." This statement reflects a potential trap for alliance partners. In the three quotes on money, given above, the dramatic differences in monetary perspectives stem directly from very different implied strategic return on investment (STROI) criteria for alliances. Had these three businesses joined together in an alliance, only a few weeks would pass before they clashed about money matters.

For thousands of years, money has been the universal medium of exchange. Regardless of its universality, money means very different things to different people, and these differences can have a heavy impact on the alliance.

When negotiating an alliance, find out your proposed partner's perspective on money. If it is radically different from yours, it will cause friction and a demand to produce unrealistic results.

Top Line versus Bottom Line

Younger companies may have a tendency to want fast sales growth; older companies may seek strong profit margins. As critical decisions need to be made, younger companies may advocate putting more resources into marketing and sales, and older companies, cutting costs. When well-managed, these differences could be a "dynamite combination," but conflicting differences could be a "dynamite explosion."

Long versus Short Term

Time frames can be the source of much despair unless well-defined. Some corporations think of the long term as anything longer than 5 years, but younger, early-stage companies may view the long term as 2 years or less. Having a clear understanding of how your partner views time and money will help reduce a cause of conflict.

The standard American concept of depreciation is influenced primarily by the total expected life of an asset, the IRS's accepted depreciation schedules, and the need to show profits on the quarterly financial statement. However, the Japanese and Europeans look at depreciation in different terms. Akio Morita, Chairman of Sony, states:

> In our joint venture dealings, we in Japan like to take our depreciation quickly and get on with business, whereas our American partners always want to take their depreciation over a long period on constant value. . . .
>
> Share of market is more important to Japanese companies than immediate profitability. If the purchase of an expensive new piece of machinery will depress short-term profits, but can be expected eventually to increase the company's share of the market, the decision will almost always be made to make the investment in the long-range future of the business.[1]

CAREFULLY DEFINE VALUE

Positive value occurs when something has greater utility than is represented by the price paid for it. Partners need to clarify precisely how they define strategic value, and what measurement systems will be used. If strategic value is not well understood and articulated to each partner, the alliance will chase after totally separate rainbows, neither knowing about the other's incompatible course until too late.

The best mechanism for defining value is the strategic return on investment (STROI) system, which examines five dimensions of value: market, organization, innovation, competitive advantage, and financial. However, regardless of the alliance's strategic goals, unless there is a financial reward somewhere, most ventures will not be worth the risk.

HOW DO YOU MEASURE "GAIN"?

Consider this situation: Suppose your company has proprietary technology and manufactures epoxy resins. You establish a distribution alliance with a partner in Europe who currently sells complementary catalytic resins and agrees to carry your product through his distribution channel without your company's incurring any substantial new fixed costs. You do likewise with his product. To stimulate sales, you discount your product in the European market to gain market share and customer loyalty. Your sales double, as do your profits.

You spent relatively little to establish the alliance, unlike the traditionally expensive method of investing in an overseas sales force, offices, travel, and then a top-notch service force. With the money you saved on setting up the European market, you establish a similar venture in the Pacific Rim. It also does quite well.

To handle the extra production, you add an extra shift, without having to buy any new machinery. Now production efficiency has increased substantially.

Conventional wisdom says you have made a fantastic deal. You created excellent value for your company and your overseas partners. Your domestic sales force is delighted that they have additional product line to offer their customers.

Do You Have an Alliance-Oriented Accounting System?

However, at the end of the year, your chief financial officer has some grim news to report: the profit margins on the overseas sales are razor-thin, just barely enough to cover the overhead costs. He recommends either dropping the alliance, or raising the prices. You are puzzled; everything seemed to be progressing so well. "What happened?" you ask.

Simply put, your accounting system did what typical accounting systems do. Fixed costs were allocated across the board to all sales, thereby reducing the percentage that was previously allocated strictly to your domestic sales (which now show an excellent margin), and increasing the percentage of fixed costs allocated to your overseas sales (which have now absorbed new fixed costs that don't really support those sales).

If yours is a publicly traded company that lives and dies by the quarterly earnings report, this area becomes sensitive, and you begin to reconsider

---

Trap

Beware of Surprise Audits: Rockwell International had a joint venture for making truck axles in Brazil. It had been profitable for a long time. The Brazilian partner was very proud of the association with Rockwell and had Rockwell's logo painted all over the outside of the building and on the smokestack. The logo was displayed throughout the building's interior as well.

Without warning or explanation, Rockwell sent a team of auditors to inspect the books. They found nothing out of the ordinary.

The day after the auditors left, the Brazilian president had every Rockwell logo removed or painted over. He was hurt, and felt the audit was a breach of trust.

---

the alliance strategy. At the next steering committee meeting, you bring your accountant and chief financial officer along to report the grim news. You make it clear that prices must be raised, or sales must increase substantially, or you may have to consider pulling the plug.

The response from your partner is astonishment. Their team thought everything was going great. Aren't you happy with your current profitability? They are perplexed, upset, and a bit angry. A wedge has been driven into the heart of the alliance.

This case is not fictitious; it has happened many times. It illustrates how a system of accounting designed for the *internal* corporation makes an inadequate transition when transferred into the *extended* corporate community. Alliances sometimes need their own custom-tailored financial measurements.

WHAT FINANCIAL MEASURES ARE NEEDED?

Joe Vogel roamed the world establishing ventures for Rockwell International. Holding a doctorate degree in business, he is an expert at complex financial analysis. But he cautions about using many of these methods in every case. For example, Vogel helped establish a venture in Nigeria, where none of the top executives could be U.S. expatriates, and had these comments:

> We were facing Vice Presidents who had elementary school educations and could hardly read. The key issue for us was "How long do we keep our money at risk?" We could have used the sophisticated methods that take pages in the business texts, like discounted cash flow, net present value, internal rate of return, and the like. The financial experts dump on simple ideas, such as "payback period." But in this case, the simple concept was perfectly appropriate. We just did

not want to have our money at risk for too long because we couldn't predict what would happen to the economy or political scene.[2]

Be careful of sophisticated analyses; they are only as good as the assumptions on which they are based.

LEVERAGING ASSETS

Micro Computer-Technology Corporation (MCC), the now decade-old computer research consortium looks for hidden assets. It develops technologies that the original handful of corporate partners, including Digital, 3-M, General Electric, and Westinghouse, did not find commercially attractive. Rather than let the technology go to waste, new partners were added who found uses in the marketplace. With annual expenses over $50 million, the alliance now has 22 shareholders, and MCC has more avenues through which to leverage its knowledge into cash flow.

Ford's joint venture with Tokyo's Central Glass, to produce windshields for Japanese auto manufacturers in the United States, enables Ford to continue high production volumes from its sheet glass plant. It is using an asset to supply its competitors rather than let the asset wallow. Even more importantly, there would have been a lost opportunity cost, should Ford have decided to use its sheet glass exclusively for itself. However, opportunity costs such as this are not accounted for in standard accounting systems.

Take an inventory of various assets in your company that you could leverage more effectively through an alliance. What old machinery, underused technology, proprietary know-how, information, or distribution channel is a potential source of new cash? What looks dead and useless in the context of the internal corporation could be a gold mine outside the walls of the corporate castle.

Create Value by Helping a Supplier

Novellus, one of Silicon Valley's most consistently profitable computer chip manufacturers, uses alliances extensively, unlike many of its very independent competitors. To bring new products to market faster, Novellus has supplier alliances that combine forces with in-house engineers to cut costs, innovate, and reduce bureaucratic entanglements that slow down the design cycle. President Robert Graham maintains: "For this industry to survive, we have to leverage each other's assets."

When a supplier can't justify the cost of additional equipment to serve Novellus, Graham has been known to authorize its purchase for use by the supplier. Novellus is extremely profitable, but if a traditional accountant looked at Graham's decision to *give* equipment to a supplier, it certainly could not be financially justified based on standard return on investment (ROI) criteria. However, when strategic return on investment (STROI) concepts are applied, the rationale becomes quite clear.

Learn New Tricks from Your Supplier

Sometimes, the asset leveraging process in the extended corporate framework can be even more obscure but can contribute highly to the bottom line. For example, in Ford's strategic equity partnership with Mazda, Ford noticed that its partner used proportionately about one-third the number of people to handle accounts payable. Mazda, in a typical Japanese quest for efficiency, gave each clerk full responsibility to process payables, from the point the invoice arrived all the way to cutting the check. Payables were processed in a day or two.

Ford, on the other hand, had an army of clerks. The procedure was assembly-line style, with each person doing a differentiated task: one opened the envelope, the next sorted it, another sought the documentation, and so forth. Processing took substantially more people, and about three to four weeks were needed to complete the cycle. Ford adopted Mazda's system, cutting costs by more than two-thirds. How does one account for this value on the profit and loss statement? Because Ford has a 25% equity ownership in Mazda, the cost savings should really be accounted for as a financial return on the Mazda investment. However, the savings will probably not be accounted for at all, except in the hearts and minds of the executives who know the hidden value of the alliance.

By shifting some engineering out of the internal corporation and into the supplier system, and forming closer supplier alliances, Chrysler saved $900 million. Using the team approach to car design, Chrysler's product development cycle was cut by one year, at enormous additional savings. The value can be great, if you have a method to measure it.

TOTAL LIFE CYCLE COSTS

Reorienting a company's perspective on cost is a fundamental part of understanding value in alliances. When Gates Energy's Mitch Carr began looking at the cost of procured parts, he found his specialized department structure impeded seeing the big picture of the company's total cost needs. The fiefdom approach of the corporate castle caused each specialty to fight for its turf, rather than have an integrated understanding of how cost was really generated.

At Scott Paper, Ted Ramstad, Director of Procurement Processes, has begun looking at total life cycle costs as opposed to the traditional component view of cost. When a paper mill shuts down because of a major part failure, the cost of being out of operation is several hundred thousand dollars a day. When buying items such as large electric transformers, the relatively small incremental investment for a higher reliability, or for an early warning device that will give several days' advance notice before a failure, can provide a gigantic multiple of return on investment.

General Electric Nuclear Energy is reexamining the cost of such small items as pumps for nuclear plants. A failure of a $5,000 pump can cause the shutdown of a nuclear plant, at a cost of over $500,000 per day. When viewed on a *component* basis, procurement managers will accept a low bid and an 18-month warranty. However, on a *total life cycle cost* basis, that pump, if it fails, will really cost over a half-million dollars. By seeing the pump from a larger, systems costs perspective, a redesign for functional redundancy is a very small price to pay for the insurance that it will not or cannot fail.

These examples require a rethinking not only of the relationship a company has with its suppliers, but also of the way costs are measured.

CHALLENGE ASSUMPTIONS

Alliances are, by definition, risky ventures; fuzzy assumptions, outdated data, and generalizations only serve to amplify risks. Too many ventures have failed because too little homework was done on the financial assumptions at the beginning. Alliance managers who ran into problems later on frequently acknowledged that they had not properly learned about the market, the costs of development, the time involved, and the potential problems they would encounter. While no one can realistically expect to accurately predict the future, the more accurate the information, the less the risk.

Good alliance decision making, both before the alliance starts and after it is put into action, will enable participants to engage in wholesome argumentation and debate, honing their thoughts and actions.

Trap

Beware of Over Optimism: My former "resident skeptic," the late A. A. T. ("Pete") Wickersham, cut through overly optimistic presumptions by using his "rules of thumb" whenever he saw a new venture's business plan:

Costs estimated by an entrepreneur will usually run *50% to 100% higher* than projected;

Sales will probably be only *half* of projections;

Time needed to achieve the sales projections will be about *double*.

If these conservative numbers worked, Pete would stoically give his assent. The danger of overzealous estimation should not be regarded lightly.

By ferreting out problems, fuzzy thinking, and idealistic visions, the alliance will perform its first level of "contingency planning."

FORECASTING SALES

Sales forecasts are like weather forecasts—they are bound to be wrong by some factor, and only the future will tell the degree! However, without sales forecasting, it will be next to impossible to project future risk and reward levels.

When sales forecasts are off target (as they probably will be), the discrepancies will be amplified into the future. Therefore, it is worthwhile to make at least two projections—high sales and low sales—and then determine whether the venture is still profitable at the lower figures. Sales forecasts should be updated regularly—while negotiations are going on, and, later, when the alliance is in full operation.

Tri-Wall's Bernie Roth liked to undersell his prospective ally. He would always underestimate sales and overestimate costs. This set a benchmark for his partner's expectations. When sales exceeded the forecast and expenses were lower than estimated, the alliance was far more profitable than people had envisioned. This success helped the chemistry of the deal and enabled the partners to be far more creative and flexible when minor difficulties impacted on the alliance.

TAX CONSIDERATIONS

This section does not attempt to cover all the tax issues; an attorney or accountant should be consulted, particularly because tax codes throughout the world are convoluted and in a constant state of flux. A few thoughts here should keep some things in perspective and help reduce exposure to adverse IRS action, while keeping tax surprises to a minimum.

1. Under no conditions should tax considerations be allowed to "drive" the alliance. The true driving forces should be strategic, with tax considerations then being weighed to improve the profit and cash flow of the parties. No matter how good the tax breaks, these should be of secondary importance.
2. If you are the lead negotiator for your negotiations team, don't let lawyers and accountants use all your time during negotiations, filling your brain with tax and technical issues. Assign one person on your team to handle the administrative issues so that you can devote sufficient time to the strategic and operational issues.
3. If involved in a joint venture that envisions transfer pricing, be sure you have consulted with a good tax accountant, to protect against the IRS's challenging the transfer as a hidden profit. The

IRS is not on your team; it is only interested in finding some taxable transaction; it does not care about economic growth, innovation, balance of trade, or anything else but taxes.

4. Don't make any assumptions about taxes; if involved in a foreign deal, don't let your prospective partner's accountant give you advice. The advice may be in good faith, but it is not reliable for your tax situation or the U.S. Tax Code.

5. Be aware, in international deals, that tax codes define the way financial statements are presented. All balance sheets and operating statements in the free world tend to look alike, but the way in which assets, depreciation, and liabilities are stated can vary radically from country to country.

CURRENCY CONVERSION

In many underdeveloped foreign countries, currency conversion can be a real problem. Taking profits out of Russia, Korea, or India may be difficult, if not impossible.

There have been many devices created to deal with the problem, and there is no "best" way to solve it. Bartering systems have been used effectively. Pepsi takes its profits out of Russia as vodka, which it sells in the United States, turning it into cash. Other companies take the profit as "added value" in their product manufactured overseas, and realize the cash when it is sold in a country where currency conversion is not a problem. Some companies charge for services provided to the alliance; others use licensing fees and royalties.

Try an "Alter-Ego" Loan

Dick Lembo, Director of International Ventures at GenCorp, does a lot of joint venturing in Korea, supplying automobile components to Detroit. Because Korea does not allow expropriation of profits back to the United States, GenCorp finds another United States company with facilities in Korea. GenCorp's Korean profits are then used as a loan to the other company's Korean operations. In the United States, the other company's headquarters, in turn, creates an equal loan (sometimes referred to as an alter-ego arrangement) back to GenCorp, giving GenCorp the cash it would have received from Korea via an indirect but legal method.

HARD VERSUS SOFT CONTRIBUTIONS

Many alliances are formed with a variety of contributions to add to the value creation process. Hard contributions are directly measurable in actual

Trap

Beware of Negative Cash Flows: No matter how enlightened the partners, no matter how extended their long-term perspective: *Negative cash flows are alliance assassins!*

An alliance can remain in a breakeven state far longer than it can when the partners must dip into the till monthly to fund projects. Eventually, the auditors or stockholders will start undermining the alliance. If possible, try to find some way to keep the cash balances from running in the red.

---

dollars, including cash, promissory cash commitments, buildings and land, stock of existing corporations, and the assets and liabilities associated with an ongoing business. Soft contributions are just as valuable, but are not as easily accounted for as cash. They include in-kind commitments of skills, knowledge, services, patents, technology and know-how, licenses, and so forth.

It is relatively easy to weigh the value of a monetary contribution: cash is easy to count. Nonmonetary contributions are far more vague. When negotiating, watch carefully how players contributing hard assets view those contributing soft assets. All too often, hard-asset contributors may see soft-asset players as "getting a free ride," a condition that could lead to future animosity.

"Run to Breakeven"

Reaching "cash flow breakeven" quickly is important for more than just financial reasons. Alliances that continually bleed the parents of cash eventually tend to generate anger in the sponsors. The sooner the venture reaches breakeven, the fewer pressures it will feel from sharpshooting critics.

When the venture is continually in the red (and at least one partner expected it to be in the black), a number of disturbing questions will be asked, including: "Will this manager make the plan?" "If the plan is not achieved, will the entire investment be in jeopardy?" "Where are we going to find more money if it is needed?" If good answers are not forthcoming, the venture may be headed for a crisis.

15

Techniques for
Structure and Control

Organization without cooperation,
Is like a fiddle with one string . . .
Some notes, but not much music.

—Anonymous

The ultimate purpose of structuring is organizational empowerment. All control, apportionment of risks and rewards, legal arrangements, and organizational design should support the empowerment of the alliance.

One of the typical traps for the alliance architect is a desire to jump into the structuring process too early in the sequence. Early structuring of the deal is more appropriate in mergers and acquisitions; it will sour the alliance process. In an acquisition, because all the organizational components already exist, structuring is part of the front end of the process.

On the other hand, in an alliance, deal structuring evolves during the development of the architecture. Form (structure) must evolve from a clarification of functions (strategy and operations). Unlike acquisitions, where the form and structure already exist and only ownership is being transferred, alliances are *created* entities, and their structure must be designed to fit the unique needs of the partners. The structure is chosen only after the basic objectives of the alliance are clearly identified, the risk and rewards are agreed on and apportioned fairly between the partners, and the operating principles are tailored specifically to the needs of the partners.

PURPOSE OF STRUCTURING

The fundamental purpose of structuring is to successfully achieve three goals:

1. Integrate the strategic fit with the operational fit by choosing the right *organizational structures;*
2. Create the proper *leadership* and *management* to drive the venture to success;
3. Fairly apportion the *risks, rewards, resource requirements,* and *responsibilities* of the venture.

Once these issues are clear, further legal and tax issues can be resolved. *Under no circumstances should legal or tax issues drive the deal.* Legal and tax issues should *guide,* but not drive. The driving forces must be strategic; otherwise, the venture will be based on what appears to be a strong legal and tax foundation, when, in reality, it is swimming in a bed of quicksand.

Distribution Issues

Distribution relates to the allocation of "the 4 Rs" of structuring: *responsibilities, resources, risks,* and *rewards.* Ultimately, the central issue in structuring the alliance will be how to distribute these 4 Rs fairly. They will need to be tailored to the particular needs of the alliance; each alliance has its own unique script. Several distribution questions must be weighed during the early stages (Figure 15.1).

The final agreement may be somewhat lengthy, but at the early negotiations stage, most distribution arrangements are conceptually short, basic, and easy to understand. Eventually, as negotiations progress, more detail is examined, organizational issues are discussed, and potential problems are raised for analysis.

Organizational Structure

Partners must decide how to build an organization that will provide effective leadership and management. The first step is to refer to the operations plan to clarify roles and responsibilities, from which the organization will be perfectly clear.

Steering Committee

Control is only useful to the extent that it empowers; when it limits effectiveness, it disempowers. Coordination, the primary form of control, occurs through a steering group, often referred to as a coordinating council

Figure 15.1   Checklist for Structural Distribution: Critical Issues

_____ Who invests **cash**, and how much?

_____ Who invests **time**, and how much?

_____ Who receives **rights** to:

    market or distribute products,

    manufacture products,

    acquire or license technology,

    purchase future products or technology?

_____ Who receives **tax** benefits?

_____ Who is **responsible** for specific accomplishments?

_____ What happens if more **money** is needed?

_____ How are the **profits** (and **losses**) allocated?

_____ How is **confidential information** handled?

_____ What **products** are specifically included/excluded?

_____ What are the **patent** provisions?

_____ What are the guidelines for **transformation, termination**, or **revision**?

_____ What **government regulations** should be considered?

or executive committee (described more fully in Chapter 12). The steering committee's basic functions are intended to maintain a double-win condition for both partners.

Operational decisions in an alliance can be cumbersome if the partners lack teamwork. What should normally be simple and straightforward can become complex and convoluted if the partners do not have a strong common vision for the future of the venture, or disagree regarding the authority to operate the venture. The steering committee is the primary authority for ensuring coordination and teamwork. There can be no teamwork at any level unless there is teamwork at the top echelons of the alliance itself.

Meet Frequently

The formal decision-making structure varies from alliance to alliance, depending on the legal structure, the frequency and amount of contact needed, and the personal preferences of the sponsors. Normally, however, the group will meet at least monthly or every other month, but not less frequently than quarterly. Semiannual meetings allow too much time to pass to catch problems before they swell and burst. Furthermore, the less frequent the meetings, the less interest those assigned to the alliance will have, because they will interpret the lack of meetings as a lack of interest or business activity.

Maintain a Win/Win Condition

To be successful, alliance managers must know how to guide the direction in order to retain the long-term good will and support of the sponsors. Even if the venture is dominated by a shareholder with greater than 50% control, it is important for the venture manager to avoid being heavy-handed and to refrain from driving a wedge between the partners. For example, Professor Peter Killing, of Western Ontario University, tells an exemplary story about a 50/50 venture in which the eight-man board consisted of four executives from the American parent, and four from the German parent, including the general manager, who was a former employee of the German company. The manager made it clear to both parents that, should any issue come to a board vote, he would vote with the German parent executives—even if he disagreed with them—thus creating a 4–4 deadlock. In other words, all issues would have to be negotiated. In 14 years of his administration, no issue had even been put to the board for a formal vote.

In the Shanghai–Foxboro 51/49 joint venture, the American and Chinese managers would not allow an issue to reach the board of directors without having resolved the issue among themselves.

In both these cases the alliance manager successfully builds consensus at every step of the way, maintaining not only harmony but success in a changing strategic environment. The alliance manager must build a "common vision"—a bond of similar perspectives and values about the overall venture—that is shared by the rest of the operational managers, if the alliance is to be effective. If there is no cohesion at the level of the steering committee and the internal management team, there will be no unity at any other level in the venture.

The Right Mix of Autonomy, Support, and Control

To empower the alliance, the structure should provide the proper proportions of *autonomy, support,* and *control,* which will change as the venture grows and develops. One of the franchise alliance's greatest strengths is its ability to get these proportions correct. Once the mix is established, it is able to replicate itself many times over.

Autonomy enables managers to take responsibility and be rewarded for their initiative, but too much autonomy at the wrong times (1) can lead to the venture's failing to satisfy the needs for which it was designed, or (2) may allow the venture to drift too far out of control.

Support is always a critical item; without it, the venture will be undernourished and probably wither.

Control prevents the venture from going awry when the projections are not met, or when the alliance business begins to fail and must be salvaged. At that point, one partner (usually the one with the greatest risk) may need to step in and control the management more carefully. If insurmountable problems emerge, provisions should be made for one party to assume control or buy out the venture.

Power and Control

Companies often have very different views toward power and control. For some, power is perceived simply as the ability to *get things done*. For others, power is the ability to *mold* and *control;* for still others, power translates into a process to *dominate* and *enforce*. These are more than just subtle differences. They are a reflection of the very values, belief structure, and culture of a company. When opposing concepts of power collide in an alliance, sparks will fly. Presumably, these differences have been identified earlier in the negotiations process. If not, the alliance managers must learn to integrate the differences into the alliance itself.

Empowerment or Dominance

An alliance is empowered by its ability to *share* and *expand* power. If one company tends to overemphasize the issue of dominance, it is probable that this dominance will permeate the alliance, placing one member in the superior position, and relegating the other to the inferior position. The ultimate long-term consequences are obvious. Strong egos are too tough to stay in an inferior position for long. All too often, the issue of trust will come into play. The inferior partner will feel the lack of trust by the other, and, in an emerging self-fulfilling prophecy, will act in a manner to justify the lack of trust.

This does not imply that all alliances must operate as 50/50 deals. There can, and often should, be a controlling partner, but there must be a good reason for the division, and both sides must believe it is fair. It is imperative for the more powerful member of the alliance to be sensitive to the needs, values, and style of the other, and for the subordinate member to respect and appreciate the position of the other member.

The opposite condition, where power and control issues are not dealt with sufficiently, is also a problem. It may forewarn a lack of interest or motivation, or it may indicate that the partners, not wanting to offend one another, are treading too cautiously. The alliance itself must be aggressive to be successful.

Power Expanders

One of the most effective methods of bypassing the negative aspects of the control issue is to choose champions and alliance managers who are "power expanders": leaders who create the right conditions to make others around them feel more powerful and effective. This unique trait manages by giving great guidance to subordinates, by focusing on helping subordinates solve their own problems, and by staying out of the subordinates' details unless participation becomes necessary.

HOW TO "CONTROL" AN ALLIANCE

Indeed, alliances can be "controlled," but the methods for controlling the extended corporation are very different from those used for the internal corporation. In the extended corporation, control tends to become an *empowering* process; in the internal corporation, it is generally a *limiting* process. Control tends to be exercised in nine ways:

1. **Control Systems.** By establishing an effective *reporting system* that lets the sponsors know when specific goals are being met, the partner will know quickly how to take corrective action. *Clear responsibilities* ensure specific assignments for results. The adage "If you can't measure it, you can't manage it" should always prevail. Directly *measurable, specific,* and *time-oriented goals* can be monitored, and individuals can be held accountable.
2. **Conception.** By gaining *mutual agreement* at both the top and middle ranks of both partners, all key players share the same "common vision." This empowers people to act as a team and ensures *alignment* of activities. By having an *operations plan* and by *clarifying expectations,* everyone is marching toward the same destination.
3. **Coordination.** Effective coordination is accomplished by using excellent *project management techniques* that break down the tasks of the alliance into discreet process steps. By using individuals with good *integration skills,* teamwork will be enhanced, thereby further providing an empowering form of control.
4. **Communications.** *No alliance ever failed because of too much communications.* With all the advanced technologies to augment face-to-face communications, there is virtually no excuse for failing to communicate. Many companies are now hooked up with Electronic Data Interchange (EDI), video conferencing, and computer networks, to supplement (not replace) face-to-face contact.
5. **"Chemistry."** Those who have experienced good chemistry in an alliance know the irrefutable value and power of this phenomenon in controlling and empowering an alliance. With *integrity as an underpinning,* partners can remain confident that the alliance will not career out of control because of unscrupulous behavior. When good chemistry is combined with a deep *commitment* to a win/win approach, the partners know that, regardless of strategic changes that may blow an ill wind, the alliance will steer a mutually productive course.

Does "Control" Yield Success? According to Japan's Kenichi Ohmae, "Few businesses succeed because of control. Most make it because of motivation, entrepreneurship, customer relations, creativity, persistence, and attention to the 'softer' aspects of organization, such as values and skills."[1]

Always design the control system *after* the empowerment system.

6. **Creativity.** Every cooperative venture should make a supreme effort to develop and support a *creative spirit* dedicated to *flexibility.* Diversity is the magic that energizes the synergistic capacity of the partners. By maintaining a strong *vision* for the final mission, and enabling a level of "experimentation" to exist, the alliance is controlled by expanding its horizons and by facilitating its adaptive mechanisms.

7. **Commitment.** It is truly remarkable how frequently *persistence* leads to success. Commitment is a highly effective control mechanism for an alliance because it is both directive and empowering. *Top-rank support* from both sides of an alliance sets the direction and rewards systems into motion.

8. **Clarity.** When *goals* and *direction* are extremely precise and when *milestones* have been established and are regularly monitored, clarity of direction is set in motion. Add to this an exact *definition* of *roles* and *responsibilities,* and the alliance becomes both empowered and controlled by acting harmoniously.

9. **Consistency.** The last element of control is the consistency or coherency of the value structure of the alliance itself. The alliance's values form the basis for creating the decision-making, achievement, and reward processes that energize people to fulfill their highest performance.

The strength for the alliance comes from using these nine control and empowerment mechanisms together as a whole system. Take away one or two of these methodologies and substitute more arcane and limiting auditing and reporting systems, and the alliance will wither. Executives concerned about their ability to "control" an alliance should embrace these nine methods.

STRUCTURING THE JOINT VENTURE

Unlike more informal types of alliance, a joint venture creates a third corporation and presents several unique issues. However, despite the uniqueness of the joint venture alliance, the same principles bear subtly on all other forms of alliances, even if they are not specifically delineated in a legal document.

Three principles come to bear when partners look to dividing the pie: *operational control, ownership of equity,* and *distribution of rewards.* Each venture will weigh these elements differently.

Operational Control. American companies, more than companies in any other country with the possible exceptions of Germany and Britain, traditionally place the issue of operational control first.

Operational control can be placed in the hands of a minority owner, particularly if that owner is most qualified to contribute effective management resources to the venture. A special consideration is often given for this contribution, in the form of preferential cash returns (i.e., profit sharing) or a larger piece of the equity.

If one partner has only 20% to 25% of the equity of a joint venture, seldom does that partner receive operating control; it is usually considered a passive financial investor rather than a participating partner. (The exception to this rule is when there are three or more partners.)

Ownership of Equity. The holder of the largest risk, or the largest contributor of cash, is often given the largest equity share of a joint venture. (Strategic alliances do not have equity interests, because no separate business entity is created.) If the largest equity owner does not have operational control, there must be a process enabling this "power" member to be involved in the decision making with the "operating" member.

In many international deals, the allies decide that it is not in their mutual best interests to have a superior member and a subordinate. In this case, one of the companies contributes sufficient cash or other assets to create parity.

Distribution of Rewards. The cash flow, tax benefits, and capital appreciation must be divided, with the largest reward usually going to the party making the largest contribution toward the success of the venture. When using a legal partnership structure (instead of a corporation), the cash flow, tax benefits, and capital appreciation can be divided in any manner the partners prefer.

Publicly held corporate sponsors that must satisfy stockholders' demands for quarterly dividends, as well as thinly capitalized entrepreneurial companies, may want short-term cash flow and may give longer-term rewards to partners that desire capital appreciation and balance sheet strength. When using the corporate structure for the joint venture, uneven divisions, common in the partnership structure, are impractical, unless preferred stock and licensing royalties are used.

METHODS OF DIVIDING OWNERSHIP AND CONTROL

Joint ventures are faced with the challenge of dividing ownership and control. Strategic alliances circumvent this problem because each member of a strategic alliance must establish the benefits internally. On the surface, it may appear that the strategic alliance has an easier time dealing with control. However, because the issues are sublimated, the strategic alliance avoids directly addressing the issue, and, as a result, can lack the "punch and power" of a well-designed joint venture. Joint ventures have evolved into three basic frameworks to divide the ownership among the partners: superior/subordinate, equal balance, and majority rule.

Superior/Subordinate Division

Method of Functioning.   This is usually a 51/49 split (or it uses other percentages that give one party clear control of the venture, such as 70/30). In this framework, the equity, operational control, and distribution of rewards generally reflect the majority/minority posture throughout. This structure is used more frequently for high-risk than for low-risk ventures. The board of directors is clearly controlled by the superior partner, and therefore is inherently ceremonial for the passing of information.

Advantages.   The advantages in this format are the clarity of decision making, the ability to make rapid adjustments, and the understanding of who is responsible and in charge. Generally, in the United States, this is the form of choice, but it is not favored in many other countries.

Disadvantages.   The minority party may not have long-term "vested interest motivation," may feel railroaded, and may become passive or disgruntled. Under the worst conditions, the majority party may even take advantage of the minority member, intentionally or unintentionally. The use of the superior/subordinate structure may imply a lack of a clear, unified vision for the venture, or there may not be an effective method of resolving differences. If these are potential problems that are being obscured by a false sense of control, the venture is in serious trouble before it gets started. Should one sponsor's operational skills be absolutely critical to success, when the other sponsor's skills are not necessary, choose this option.

Control Data's William Norris said: "Be sure that one partner is in charge. You can have a 50/50 ownership, but you have to have it very clear who is going to run it." With this method, one sponsor is responsible for operating the venture, and the other sponsors hold the operator accountable for performance.

Use the superior/subordinate approach where there are very crisp and distinct corporate or cultural differences, as between a U.S. company and a company in a small Third World country, especially if the foreign partner has little experience and no strong knowledge of the product or technology, and is agreeable to being a rather passive partner, a financial investor, or a tutored student.

Equal Balance Division

Method of Functioning.   This framework usually provides a 50/50 split in the entire working relationship and assumes 50/50 contribution, decision making, and control. With this division, nothing happens unless there is consensus among the partners: all must agree or hash out their differences until there is agreement. Equal balance assumes that the partners will always be able to work out their differences and that operational managers have excellent human skills to assist the owners in effective consensus decision making. Both companies are represented equally on the board or on steering committees; they set strategy for the joint venture together and make operating decisions together.

Advantages.   The 50/50 arrangement helps promote active engagement by both parties. This format is best suited to companies having a strong common vision for the venture, similar corporate cultures, and, preferably, a congenial personal relationship at the top echelons. Often used when both parties have equally vital contributions of technology and expertise to offer, this method ensures each owner's support, resources, and input, and forces commitment to the success of the venture.

Should a serious problem arise, the sponsors can be ready to adjust, reorient, and adapt faster if they have been fully involved and have understood and supported the decisions that have led to a problem or crisis.

The 50/50 arrangement requires initial trust and common vision among the top managers and continued support as the venture progresses. The venture manager should have good integration skills and should be given a good amount of operational autonomy, to avoid being tied up in red tape.

Disadvantages.   Unfortunately, as seen frequently in partnerships, the equal balance division can have serious drawbacks if not carefully managed. Stalemate may occur among the partners when there is a disagreement. To avoid conflicts, partners may avoid addressing problems.

The equal balance division requires great skill in problem solving and excellent relations among the partners. If an intractable stalemate occurs, divorce or buy-out may be the only solution.

Seldom is there truly a 50/50 division of contribution, leadership, risk, and reward, and often one partner may perceive the other as having failed in the promised contribution, especially when the venture may not be working out successfully.

Some managers believe that the only thing shared control really guarantees is the right to fight. On the other hand, Harvard's Paul Lawrence comments that the equal balance division forces discussions and keeps the partners in an open problem-solving mode. Still, he warns:

> If people cannot seem to get their marching orders clear, if there is vacillation, if the word is inconsistent, if what you are supposed to do depends upon who you ask, then the 50/50 split may not be advisable . . . but the 51/49 split may just temporarily mask more fundamental problems and create a one-up/one-down relationship. If the difficulties are grating now, what happens three years from now when the priorities change?[2]

Parity among foreign partners will often be desirable, because, regardless of their stake, they will be far more likely to want to be considered equals than will traditionally more domineering Americans. Foreign partners are likely to take time to build consensus and to gain commitment—"arm-wrestling over a bottle of wine," as the French call it. According to Gordon Lankton, CEO of Nypro, a $100 million plastics component manufacturer, who has orchestrated several alliances with companies in Asia and Europe:

> Marriage is the oldest type of partnership in the world. Every good marriage has evolved into a real 50/50 partnership. Likewise with business partnerships.
> I never want to be a 49 percent partner . . . every 49 percent partner goes to the table as a second class citizen. . . . Who wants to sit at a table concentrating on issues and developing strategic plans, all the while knowing that he or she really doesn't count as much as the other person? . . . It spells doom for the partnership from day one. . . . Who wants to go to a board meeting that will clearly not be a free and open relationship between equals? Not me. I want everyone present to have the same voice.
> Global strategic partnerships develop out of 50/50 partnerships. As in marriage, the contributions of the partners will not be identical, but they should be equal in importance. One may provide the potential for opening new markets, while the other may provide technology. The secret to success is that both partners recognize their need to contribute equally. Both will strive to do more and to carry more than their 50 percent of the load. This is what pushes the partnership forward.[3]

Tip

How DuPont–Merck Handles 50/50 Control: DuPont–Merck is a 50/50 deal; the two companies operate "Japanese style"—by consensus. If the board ever reaches a deadlock on budgets, the joint venture manager is authorized to run the company at his discretion, as long as he doesn't run it at a loss.

If negotiations about control become adversarial, the alliance will probably be doomed before it starts. Alliances relying heavily on dominance for control may lack the fundamental strategic synergies and operational chemistries needed for long-term success.

Fifty-fifty deals work particularly well when the partners are familiar and comfortable with decentralized decision making, and provide the support and time to manage the relationship.

To avoid stalemating, some equal balance joint ventures, such as Autolatina, a Latin American alliance between Ford and Volkswagen, will have a nonvoting, outside adviser sit in on the steering committee meetings, to ensure that problems are thoroughly addressed in a timely manner and that mutually agreeable solutions are achieved.

Majority Rule Division

Method of Functioning.   This framework, an adaptation of the equal balance method, brings in a smaller shareholder, usually a minority contributing partner, who acts as a tiebreaker in the event that the two other partners stalemate. In this framework, often structured as 49/49/2 or some similar variation, decisions are arrived at by thrashing around a problem until unanimity and consensus occur. Seldom does the partnership actually vote on a business matter. Skilled managers know that the process of good team problem solving serves to build consensus and communications, resulting in stronger teamwork among the partners. The third party is more than a neutral; instead, he or she represents the "greater good" of the alliance itself.

Sometimes, the minority third party is the venture manager, the champion, or a member of the management team. In other circumstances, it is a top executive who sits on both sponsors' boards of directors. Or, the position may be filled by a university professor or professional consultant who, because of technical or market knowledge or connections, can be of great value to its successful operation.

Tip

Third-Party Selection: Use these criteria when choosing a third member in majority rule joint ventures:

- Trusted by both companies;
- Creative under pressure;
- Believes in the alliance;
- Knowledgeable about alliances, or the market, or the technology;
- Can represent the "greater good" of the alliance itself;
- Meets the criteria of an "integrator."

Rules of Thumb for Choice of Equity Splits

- **Superior/Subordinate (51/49):** Use when two highly hierarchical organizations are joining forces. The slower decision making inherent in multilayered organizations is offset by one of the partners' having command and control.
- **Equal Balance (50/50):** Use when two collaborative-style (nonhierarchical) organizations link together. Companies accustomed to consensus decision making have less risk of stalemate; their corporate cultures support teamwork and coordination.
- **Majority Rule (49/2/49):** Use when needing entrepreneurial incentive for the alliance manager or when mating a hierarchical company with a collaborative ("flat") organization. Dissimilar cultures are better integrated with the third-party approach.

  Note: When in doubt about the form to use, the majority rule division is a "universal" approach that will work in virtually all circumstances.

Advantages.   The majority rule framework enables the principal partners to remain actively engaged in the venture, as in the equal balance method, without the problems of stalemated decisions. The third party's role involves pushing for creative solutions and new ideas. When conflicts arise, the third party usually works quietly behind the scenes to diagnose problems and find elegant solutions that meet the conditions of a double win.

The majority rule approach will work well when dissimilar corporate cultures have no past working relationship and one of the partners has a reluctance to accept the subordinate position.

A variation to the majority rule approach is what Union Carbide's William Silvia calls the "silver bullet" technique, which he has used in several international joint ventures. In this circumstance, Union Carbide had parity with a foreign partner, plus one vote that could be used only one time—the "silver bullet." The local venture lawyer also had a silver bullet, but, in the many years of the alliance, it was never used. Silvia speculates that the threat of the silver bullet—which, if used, would have meant the ending of the alliance—was sufficient to keep the parties working in unison.

Disadvantages.   The selection of the right minority party is critical. It may also be difficult to keep the minority/third party sufficiently motivated because it may have too small a stake in the venture. If the structure is multipartied (three or more parties), the operational control mechanisms may become difficult to manage, unless clear lines of authority and decision making are designated.

Multiple Party Ventures

Having several partners in a joint venture permits the organization and its managers to operate at arm's length from the partners. Frank Heffron, of AT&T's Covidea joint venture, says:

> One of the values of having four partners—none of whom control it—is that control really does reside in the management of the partnership. They understand the venture has to be quick and nimble, and I don't think you can do that if you have to check with four people all the time.[4]

There are different versions and variations that combine these methods of division. In international joint ventures in developing countries, operational control and equity control can be quite different. Emerging countries with legal constraints that prevent foreign companies from owning 50% or more of a domestic company have caused the formation of numerous joint ventures in which equity control rests with the third-world company and operational control rests with the larger foreign corporation. Internal cash-flow agreements may allow the foreign company to receive management fees and bonuses based on profit sharing, in addition to the proportionate split of corporate dividends.

In the joint venture between AT&T and Philips, the ownership was divided 50/50, but the five-member board was weighted with three votes for AT&T and two for Philips, which reflected the stronger interest AT&T had in telecommunications switching, compared to Philips, which is a diversified electronics manufacturer. The board had authority to decide all matters except large capital investments, mergers, and acquisitions. AT&T's joint venture in Thailand is a 49/49/2 deal, with the 2% being held by a native Thai who is also an AT&T employee.

Be Flexible for the Future

Difficulties may also arise, particularly later on, when new people join the venture, when the original founders' vision for the venture fades over time, or when market dynamics shift. The proportions that made sense at the beginning may become grossly unfair several years down the road. At that time, adjustments must be made to the proportions or the venture may be on the rocks.

PHASE SHIFTS

It may be advisable to plan to change project managers and sponsor liaisons, if the venture goes through distinct and highly differentiated phases. As in a relay race, where one runner runs the first distance and then passes the baton to the second runner, one partner may be an excellent leader during technological development, and another may be better during the manufacturing and marketing phase. In a real estate venture, a first-phase manager might have construction skills, and a second-phase manager might know marketing, building management, and maintenance.

The Alaska Pipeline joint venture enables each of the owners to rotate operational responsibility annually. The arrangement enables each member to have a broader perspective and understanding of the nature of the alliance.

ADVANCED STRUCTURING TECHNIQUES

Peter Drucker has said that joint ventures are the best tools for making fits out of misfits. The array of alliance structural options—from joint ventures to franchise alliances to equity investments to cross-licensing agreements—provides a myriad of alternatives with which to customize a strategic relationship. The following examples are just a small sample of the diversity available. You may find among these examples a structure that is adequate for your needs, but it would be far better if these concepts triggered creative thinking that influenced your design of an architecture custom-made for the unique needs of your alliance.

Contributive Joint Venture

When Tri-Wall's Bernie Roth began building joint ventures in the paper industry during the late 1960s, he did not know a lot about the architectural structure of a cooperative venture. What he did know was that it had to be a partnership among equals and, foremost, a win/win approach.

Roth also knew that Tri-Wall did not have much money to put up in the venture, and therefore had to leverage its core assets: marketing, sales, know-how, and patents. Because Tri-Wall did not have a world-renowned reputation, the likelihood that a foreign partner would make a substantial investment in either a license or new capital equipment was rather slim. Therefore, if a partner invested in new box-making equipment and the venture failed, the equipment should be usable for other manufacturing functions.

Roth reasoned that, by contributing the key technology and sales expertise to the joint venture, he would induce his partner to make a substantial capital investment and provide expertise in the local marketplace.

The concept called for starting a new joint venture company (JVC), with 50/50 ownership, whose principal purpose was to market the Tri-Wall product in the designated region. Its "lean and mean" staff would be limited strictly to marketing and sales personnel, and a few financial record-keeping and administrative people.

Tri-Wall would invest roughly as much in establishing and supporting the sales organization as the manufacturing partner would invest in machinery and equipment to fulfill Tri-Wall's specifications.

Tri-Wall's cash was expended and irretrievable if the venture failed; the foreign manufacturer had both the added equipment and new manufacturing know-how from Tri-Wall, and this reduced risk served as an inducement to make the commitment. Tri-Wall's patents were licensed to the marketing company, with rights to sublicense all manufacturing of the product to its foreign partner.

The transfer price of boxes from the partner's manufacturing company and the joint venture marketing company was pegged at 1% over manufactured cost. Here, manufactured cost was strictly defined as labor (with productivity standards based on Tri-Wall's U.S. standards) plus materials at published/invoiced prices, plus overhead at a specified ratio to labor costs as found in the manufacturing partner's normal mix. Audit work would be performed by an internationally recognized auditing firm's local branch office, as jointly agreed, and the auditing firm would mediate any transfer cost disputes.

The manufacturing partner had the right to decline incremental production if he could prove that he could make more overall profit on his own products. The life of the agreement was for 15 years, with additional extensions of 10 years by mutual consent.

The board of directors of the JVC was split 50/50, and profits were to be split 50/50. The partners jointly guaranteed the debt of the new company up to an agreed amount, or at a ratio to sales.

The manufacturing partner was to be trained, by Tri-Wall's team, in product manufacturing methods and quality control. Any innovations created by the JVC were jointly owned by both partners, and either partner and the JVC was free to use the technology. New patents on similar products would be licensed to the JVC by Tri-Wall.

Tri-Wall was responsible for recruiting, hiring, managing, and training sales application engineers for the JVC. Deadlocks would be solved by patience and consensus.

Using this contributive joint venture structure, Tri-Wall avoided purchasing a highly expensive paper mill. Any new sales and marketing techniques from foreign markets were integrated back into the United States and then forwarded to the other alliances. The 25-year success of Tri-Wall's ventures is staunch testimony to the effectiveness of its approach.

Revenue-Sharing Joint Venture

One of the world's best selling commercial jet engines is the product of a joint venture between France's government-owned SNECMA and General Electric's Aerospace Division. General Electric formed the venture 20 years ago to break into the European commercial jetliner market, which was out-of-bounds to a strictly American producer. SNECMA manufactured jet turbines for military aircraft, principally the Mirage fighter. By joining together, each contributed strengths the other lacked.

GE and SNECMA compete in military markets, but they operate a joint venture in commercial markets through their joint venture company (JVC), called CFM International. From the structural design of the alliance emerged a relatively simple first product that joined existing components and capabilities from both partners.

CFM's headquarters are in Cincinnati, where GE headquarters its Aerospace Division. Final systems integration therefore occurs close to the partner with the best systems integration skills. CFM also provides expert marketing and sales functions, and has the authority to make pricing and warranty decisions in consultation with its joint advisory committee. All CFM employees are on loan to the joint venture from their parents, which means the coordination between the parents is very high. All CFM staff know the internal procedures of their parents, although the CFM staff can have very split loyalties.

Essentially, with the exception of systems integration, sales, and marketing, CFM, like Tri-Wall, is a shell organization that passes through the JVC product in return for sales. Both GE and SNECMA make all their decisions regarding components, technology, and subsystems independently, according to design specification. CFM ensures the coordinative and integration issues are properly handled as part of its interface management task.

Each company keeps its own core technologies and is totally responsible for its own profit and loss. All revenue coming into CFM is used to pay for the small CFM staff, and the rest is then shared between GE and SNECMA in accordance with the components each of the companies provides.

Spin-Out Joint Venture

The "spin-out" joint venture avoids the risks of a start-up company by taking an existing, usually profitable division from one of the parents and selling 50% of it for cash to the other partner. Union Carbide did just this with its $700 million Carbon Products Division: it sold 50% to Japan's Mitsubishi as part of a strategy to obtain cash to support growth businesses, to utilize Mitsubishi's marketing and technology abilities, and pay down debt.

The JVC is headed by a former Union Carbide division president, Bob Krass. The board of directors is 50% Japanese, and more and more Japanese managers are being transitioned into the operations. In this way, the integration of the Japanese partner will be orderly and organized. Eventually, once the integration is complete, the partners can decide the best course for the venture.

The "dual spin-out," a variant of this approach, takes two divisions, one from each partner, and merges them together into a single joint venture corporation. (See Figure 15.2.)

Chrysler and General Motors used this structure when GM combined its Muncie plant, which primarily manufactures manual truck transmissions, with Chrysler's Syracuse plant, which manufactures components for four-wheel-drive manual transmissions.

GM contributed a plant that was running under capacity. Chrysler brought a plant running at 130% capacity and a backlog of orders to the deal. About 40% of Chrysler's output went to companies other than itself—mainly, to GM. Described by auto officials as a classic win/win, the venture enables Chrysler to shift manual transmission production to the GM plant and concentrate on its core technology—complex transmission casings.

In this arrangement, Chrysler will have two-thirds of the board of directors to GM's one-third, and financially strapped Chrysler avoids the cost of purchasing a new plant.

One- and Two-Way Equity Partnerships

A one-way equity partnership is an alliance in which one partner, usually the stronger of the two, purchases a minority position in the other partner. The purposes are to interlink the two companies for better integration in the alliance and, often, to provide cash to a financially strapped partner. This type of maneuver is very frequent in the electronics industry.

In Japan, the *keiretsu* system is replete with such investments, particularly in the automotive industry. A large systems integrator, such as Toyota or Nissan, will have a series of vertically integrated suppliers, each of

Figure 15.2   Dual Spin Out

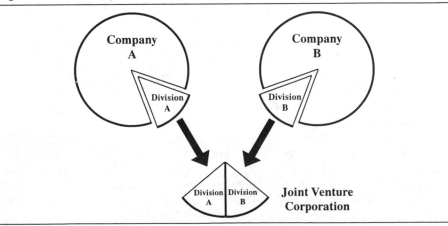

whom is invested in by the larger auto company. This provides excellent cooperation in the supply chain and involves the supplier early on in the design process, thus keeping costs highly competitive.

In the Japanese system, during good times, the suppliers are kept more profitable by their larger procurement partners than their original equipment manufacturer (OEM) counterparts in the United States. In tough economic recessions, the Japanese suppliers are expected to trim profits to the bone, as will the larger parent, to remain competitive. Shareholders expect business to flow from their investment, and dividends are secondary.

In another variant, the two-way equity partnership, stock is exchanged between two relatively equal companies. An example of this strategy is the equity exchange between the American advertising agency, Wells, Rich, and Greene, and France's Boulet, Dru, Dupuy, and Petit (BDDP).

BDDP purchased a 40% position in Wells, Rich, which in turn took a smaller position in BDDP. The primary goal was better access by both companies for their clients in each other's markets. Wells, Rich represented companies such as Ford, Hertz, Sheraton, and IBM in the United States. BDDP represented Polaroid and McDonald's in Europe. A close integration of the two companies would provide each of their clients with better representation on the other side of the Atlantic.

Fourteen months after the initial investment, BDDP liked the engagement and decided to increase its share to 70%, essentially gaining majority control and transforming the alliance into a merger.

Unpopulated Joint Ventures

Some companies prefer to avoid having the separate organization that a joint venture normally embodies, but they benefit from the image it creates and gain from certain tax advantages. This unpopulated joint venture structure creates a shell company that exists for legal and tax reasons, but, in all other respects, acts and serves just like a simple strategic alliance.

In the mid-1970s, after the first oil crisis of the decade, the Halliburton Company and the Linde Division of Union Carbide Corporation decided to form an "unpopulated partnership" to enter the market with a high-pressure nitrogen gas process to stimulate and enhance the production of oil and gas wells. A major competitor of both companies, Big Three Industries, was marketing a similar process and gaining market share.

The negotiating parties agreed to form an alliance. However, Halliburton's management had had some bad experiences with managing joint ventures and was adamant against forming another one.

According to William Silvia, former president of Union Carbide's Catalysts and Services Division, the parties agreed to form a partnership that would provide an easy exit if the relationship didn't work out as originally planned. The partnership, called WELLNITE, capitalized on the two companies' strengths in order to enter the market quickly, before Big Three became dominant.

Halliburton was the largest oil field servicing company in the world, with over 150 service centers in the United States. It had an excellent marketing organization, and manufactured high-quality oil field service equipment. Union Carbide's division contributed the largest industrial gas company in the United States. It was the leading supplier of cryogenic equipment and offered an extensive liquid nitrogen supply system. As a result of the union, WELLNITE was stronger in technology, manufacturing, servicing, and marketing than Big Three and other would-be competitors.

The partners agreed to a 50/50 partnership, directed by an informal board consisting of two senior managers from each company—the general managers and the marketing managers. While personnel were assigned to the partnership, they continued to be employees of the parents, hence the term "unpopulated."

Contributions of capital were shared equally. Sales of equipment, services, and nitrogen from the sponsors to the partnership were at fair market price. All sales and general administrative expenses were billed to WELLNITE, and profits or losses before taxes were divided equally between the parents. WELLNITE is a very successful unpopulated joint venture partnership, still going strong after 15 years.

Joint Venture Franchise Alliance

The franchise alliance is very adaptable to customization. In the insurance industry, a hybrid franchise joint venture is being developed to provide services and bulk buying power to insurance agency groups. McDonald's has also used the hybrid franchise joint venture as part of its global expansion program.

In Thailand, for example, McDonald's was concerned that its potential franchisees did not have the managerial expertise to maintain the proper quality standards of the McDonald's operation. Rather than let the territory lie fallow, or provide an opportunity for competitors to gain early entry, McDonald's decided to develop the promising Thailand market. Departing from its normal franchise pattern, and also avoiding the large capital investment needed to establish a series of wholly owned subsidiaries, McDonald's combined the franchise format with the joint venture structure. (See Figure 15.3.)

By forming a joint venture with a Thai investor group, McDonald's was able to retain significant control of the management and quality control, while sharing the risks with the local investment group. Should the local entrepreneurial talent develop, more than likely there will be a provision for the local managers to buy out the McDonald's portion of the joint venture on an incremental basis sometime in the future.

Figure 15.3   Combining the Joint Venture and Franchise Alliance

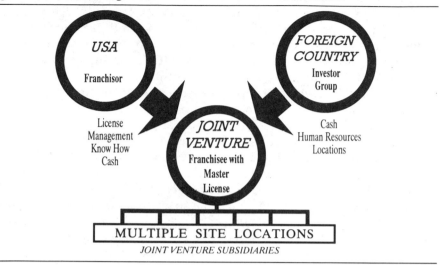

LEGAL STRUCTURE

It is important to understand that the legal form of each alliance will be somewhat different, or even significantly different, depending on the legal and tax rulings of the country of registration. The legal structure should be decided *after* the organizational structure is chosen. Ultimately, competent legal counsel must be involved in the final choice of legal structure.

Joint Venture Corporation.   The corporation is the most sophisticated and mature form of joint venture. It is normally structured as a "stand-alone" business and is often selected when one or more of the following conditions exists:

- When the joint venture is large or complex enough to require a separate organizational entity with its own internal management;
- When it is advisable to contribute cash directly to the joint venture, and, in return for the cash, issue the joint venture partners stock in the new company;
- When the joint venture's purpose is long-term.

This form is the most complicated to design, but, if the venture is large enough, it may also be the easiest to run. Less discussion of the specifics of operations is required among sponsor CEOs, which can then be left to the manager whose full-time assignment is the operation of the details of the joint venture, thus freeing the founding CEOs to focus on strategic issues.

The corporate structure works best when given a certain amount of autonomy in operations, even though it is strategically driven by the founding partners. If strategic conditions change and the joint venture no longer benefits one of the partners, then stock in the joint venture can be sold, or the partner can withdraw from strategic control, while still reaping financial reward from a successful venture.

TriStar Pictures, which originated as a joint venture among HBO, CBS, and Columbia Pictures, was formed in 1982 with $300 million in capital from the founders and has been a notable success. It supplied HBO with an additional source of feature films, gave CBS a source of films and a start in the cable industry, and provided Columbia Pictures with an extra studio and another source of films. TriStar operated on its own, allowing its managers to take advantage of market conditions.

This joint venture was remarkable not so much in what it supplied to the partners, but in how it took shape after 2 years. By 1984, it had issued securities on its own: the three original companies each became 25% owners of Tri-Star, and the remaining 25% was public stock. Subsequent changes in the strategic environment enabled TriStar to adapt after Columbia Pictures was sold to Sony.

Partnership.   The partnership is a legal structure that simply allocates investment, profits, losses, and responsibilities, while maintaining the autonomy of the participants. Smaller, more entrepreneurial companies are more likely to select the partnership form than are large multinational corporations.

The partnership form is most often selected in one or more of these conditions:

- When the alliance is "project-specific" and is expected to last less than 3 to 5 years;
- When a separate business entity is desirable for the alliance, but a separate organization for management of the venture is *not* currently required, but may be needed in the future;
- If high levels of commitment and interaction are necessary.

The partnership form is widely chosen for short-term joint ventures, because it is less complicated, more flexible, and more practical than other forms, in what is often an uncertain environment.

Real estate joint ventures normally select this structure because it allows for equity participation by financial investors on a limited partnership basis, while preserving the management control of the joint venture principals as general partners.

Partnership agreements are adaptable to creative allocations of distribution of the benefits. For example, a minority equity investor may receive a larger share of the distribution of profits, if the partners deem it fair.

Tax considerations are the final reason for choosing the partnership form. Unlike the corporation, the partnership is not taxed doubly—the profits flow directly to the partners.

The partnership form's greatest drawback is the potential for the bleed-through of joint and several liability from one partner to the other, through the partnership. Be very careful to have a properly crafted legal agreement, and be sure *all* employees of the partnership know exactly how their representations of the partnership can be construed in the adversarial environment of a court of law.

Franchise Alliance.   The franchise form is chosen when replicability and very close operational coordination are paramount, but equity sharing is not desirable. Franchises are probably the single most successful form of alliance, with over 500 U.S. franchisors holding over 30,000 separate franchises overseas. Franchise success rates are in the 80% to 90% range over a 5-year period, compared to start-up business successes, which are less than 10% successful after 5 years.

Franchise alliances typically involve the franchisee's making an initial investment (usually ranging from $10,000 to $100,000 per site) to purchase a license, plus additional capital investment for real estate, machinery or equipment, and working capital investments. In turn, the franchisor provides expertise, training, site selection assistance, and economies of scale in procurement of equipment and raw or semiprocessed materials. Sometimes, the franchisor will refrain from marking up supplies, to help the franchisee remain profitable. Royalty payments for the licensee typically range between 3% and 7%. The franchisor uses these payments to maintain the alliance and to grow the technology and remain competitive with new product upgrades. Often, an additional 3% to 5% charge is added by the franchisor for a wide-scale marketing campaign to further the brand image. The franchise alliance is best selected when the following conditions prevail:

- When several or many relatively identical versions of the alliance need to be formed in different regions;
- When there needs to be a common, recognizable identity presented to the customers of each of the alliances;
- When there is proprietary information that needs licensing, and there are specific operational guidelines that cannot be deviated from;
- When there is clearly an imbalance in strength or size between the partners, making it advisable to have a superior/subordinate relationship, but day-to-day operational control must be very close and shared;
- When a joint marketing and/or development program needs to be coordinated and implemented by a single, stronger partner;

- When growth expansion is potentially so great that the equity required to create multiple joint ventures would drain precious financial resources;
- When the degree of change in the business environment is somewhat stable or predictable.

The franchise alliance has the specific advantage of attaining the very tight operational efficiency of a joint venture without the intertwined equity arrangements that can put undue pressure on the participants and drain capital resources.

Equity Partnerhip.   The equity partnership involves a company's purchase of stock in its ally's company, or a two-way exchange of stock by two companies. Because of the resulting intertwining of the two companies, it is commonly referred to as a "partnership," but it is not a partnership in the legal sense of the term.

Equity alliances are extremely common to support various purchaser–supplier relationships, technology development, and marketing alliances. In the most common form, a large corporation with excellent cash reserves makes an investment in a smaller company that is strapped for cash. Because of the investment, the smaller company's products or services are endorsed to a larger marketplace.

For example, Adra Systems, a small, 100-person software developer, had an equity injection from the $13 billion Digital Equipment Corporation, after the two companies had successfully operated a variety of cooperative alliances in marketing and development. The investment strengthened Adra by giving it access to Digital's worldwide marketing, sales, and engineering organization, while providing Digital with a long-term partner to warrant and support customer requests for a single source of integrated engineering solutions.

Typically, the equity partnership's investment will be anywhere between 3% and 30% of the smaller company's outstanding stock. The amount of stock purchased is not intended to be sufficient to control the smaller company, but it usually provides at least one seat on the board of directors, leveraging of strategic capacity, intermingling of operational strengths, and loyalty of personnel. The equity alliance is best used:

- When there is a need to have very close strategic linkage for the long term;
- To preempt another competitor from making an alliance or acquisition;
- As a preacquisition or premerger event, to test the strategic, chemistry, and operational fit;
- When a smaller alliance partner needs cash or other resources for further development and growth;
- In lieu of multi-product formal cross-licensing agreements;

- To instill loyalty of personnel and avoid issues of employees "jumping ship" by legitimizing exchange of personnel.

The "blessing" of the larger corporation gives the small company outstanding leverage for creating value for existing shareholders, or when going public on the stock exchange. There may be options to purchase further equity, should the allies see a value in transforming the alliance into an acquisition in the future.

Contract/Written Agreement Alliance. The written contract alliance is the simplest of all the options. It is used to structure a basic strategic alliance by maintaining an arm's-length relationship between the parties. It outlines how revenue is divided, who is responsible for specific performance, who distributes items, confidentiality, and so forth, but it does not authorize any additional legal layers beyond those issues binding the parties together under contract, and it does not establish a separate business entity for legal or tax purposes. This form is seen frequently:

- For indefinite or shorter-term arrangements lasting under 3 to 5 years, or when there has been no prior alliance relationship and this alliance is essentially seen by both companies as a beginning point that may transform itself into something larger in the future;
- When there is no foreseen need for a separate joint venture organization;
- When daily or extremely close coordination of work is not required for the duration of the project;
- When capital investments are made independently by each of the separate partners within their own companies.

The written contract approach also has the advantage of permitting each company president to continue to run his or her own business with a great deal of autonomy. The character of each company and its individual personality and style require little or no change.

The written contract format is the most common form for simple purchaser–supplier and distribution alliances. Service-based firms with high labor intensity and low capital equipment requirements also use this form of agreement.

Handshake Alliance. Surprisingly, the handshake format is used far more often in strategic alliances than one might imagine, even in today's world of lawyers, liability, and litigation. The handshake form will be seen in these typical circumstances:

- When the written contract form would otherwise be used;
- During an "interim period," before legal documents are drafted but when there is a need to commence a project;

- When partners have so much mutual trust that legal documents seem superfluous.

Generally, however, the handshake form is not recommended over the long haul. People change positions, changes in the economy or the market can put some partners under great financial strain, and memories fade. Add to this human nature's tendency to interpret any agreement to one's own advantage, and it can be easily seen how the handshake form, when used over a long period of time, can end in dispute. (In business law, a handshake can be interpreted as a binding contract.)

To every rule, there are always notable exceptions. In one substantial strategic alliance, a very large chemical corporation joined with a major paper manufacturer and a medium-size plastics company to design, manufacture, and market a new disposable, ecologically safe consumer product. The principals prefer confidentiality, but they confess that there has never been a formal written agreement to consummate the pact, even though nearly $100 million has been spent jointly between them.

CRITERIA FOR CHOOSING A LEGAL STRUCTURE

Choice of a legal structure should be accomplished with the advice of a lawyer. Each alliance is tailored to the specific prevailing circumstances. The following criteria can be used as a general guide in making the decision.

Organization. The number-one driving force in structure should be the proper organization to facilitate alliance effectiveness. Leadership, management, coordination, and support are the real issues that can make or break the alliance. Considerable attention must be given to them, regardless of the legal structure. The management systems should be clearly decided before the legal agreements are formally signed, and the legal form should support the organizational form.

Liability. Choose a structure that provides the necessary protection for the partners.

Simplicity. Use the simplest structure that is capable of meeting your needs. Don't form a corporation if the written contract will do.

Expected Longevity. Alliances intended to last only a few years are probably better advised to use the written contract or partnership form; longer-term ventures are best served when they use the equity, franchise, or corporate structure.

Tax Considerations.   If significant tax shelter is desirable, particularly for technology development, where large losses or R&D investment tax credits are anticipated, a tax lawyer should be consulted for specific advice regarding the ways to maximize use of the tax shelter. A legal structure that maximizes tax shelter may not be the best form to use to maximize other management efficiencies. If significant capital investment is required by both parties, the partnership form may have far better tax effects. However, do not let tax considerations drive the deal.

In the final analysis, the overriding issue in choosing a legal structure is one of organization: What will be the most effective structure for leading and managing?

TERMINATION PROVISIONS

Often, lawyers will counsel their clients that the most important thing to determine about an alliance is its exit strategy. This wisdom is only partially true. An exit is only one of the strategic shifts available. It is more important to consider how the alliance will be transformed over time, as strategic conditions change. The real emphasis should be placed on how to create a flexible structure and how the alliance will be managed rather than exited.

Some lawyers devote a considerable number of pages to termination provisions. Sometimes, up to 80% of the legal documentation will cover issues such as buy-out clauses, prices of the buy-out, how assets and liabilities are to be divided if the venture fails or the partners elect to dissolve the operation, what will happen to key personnel, and who owns trade secrets and patents. Moreover, if a joint venture becomes the signatory for a loan, lending institutions will probably insist on such legal covenants, to provide protection of their collateral. These provisions reflect the 80/20 rule: 80% of the document relates to only 20% of the importance. However, careful "divorce" conditions are essential to prevent litigation, in the event of an adverse change.

REGULATORY CONSIDERATIONS

Every country has its own laws regarding the formation of alliances. For the most part, alliances are far less complex and regulated than acquisitions, particularly if the alliance is a truly competitive weapon (as the overwhelming majority have been), and not a disguise for restraint of trade or price fixing. A full legal analysis is far beyond the scope of this book, but a few points will help put things in perspective.

Antitrust

Antitrust laws have been undergoing major reinterpretation in the United States during the past 10 years, as a result of the global restructuring of the marketplace. The formation of alliances will generally not need governmental approval in the United States, if the combined strength of the partners does not infringe on 25% or more of the world market. Smaller companies not holding dominant market shares will have little to be concerned about.

Any restraint of competition between participants, especially concerning price fixing, geographic division or allocation of markets, and, consequently, depriving the public of the benefits of a competitive marketplace, could be construed to violate the law. Alliances cannot be used to deprive other competitors of a vital resource and cripple competition.

Believing that alliances will play a vital role in promoting growth and international competitiveness in the American economy, the U.S. Justice Department has been systematically removing unwarranted regulatory obstacles. Collaborative research, even among industry giants, is being encouraged more and more, particularly when the research is shared among all the joint venture shareholders.

The Justice Department is open to arguments by potential partners, even in very concentrated marketplaces, particularly if the partners can show gains in production efficiency or the creation of new, competitive technologies. As for purchaser–supplier alliances, the Justice Department regards these as vertical mergers, which, as opposed to horizontal mergers, are not considered serious competitive threats.

Taxation

Unfortunately, tax law has only become more complex and less supportive of business growth than ever before. United States tax regulations are now such a Byzantine labyrinth of convoluted obfuscation that good tax counsel must be consulted, especially in international deals. Tax officials are not interested in the promotion of trade, consumer protection, or business growth, nor are they interested in alliance formation and win/win strategies. They want money and can be relied on to interpret their arcane regulations strictly to their own advantage.

The result has often been to relegate the accounting profession to the role of tax consultants. Instead of finding better ways of understanding how to make companies financially successful, many accountants have now become adjuncts of the IRS, attempting to help companies survive in a torrent of ever changing and increasingly confusing tax regulations, always playing catch-up in a reactive scheme that can never promote proper financial planning and accurate analysis of the impact of strategic moves on the corporate financial picture.

16

Dynamic International Deals

The greater the contrast, the greater the potential. Great energy only comes from a correspondingly great tension between opposites.

—Carl Gustav Jung

Gaining a position in a foreign country is fast becoming a competitive requirement for survival in today's world, for large and small businesses alike. Whether the toehold is a supplier base, a market channel, a manufacturing facility, or a technology development arrangement, the reality is: If you don't gain position, your competitor will—and soon.

NEGOTIATING IN FOREIGN COUNTRIES

The Foxboro Company, a $600 million manufacturer of high-tech precision instruments, recognized the value of establishing an inexpensive but high-quality source of supply in the Far East in 1978. Faced with the possible prospect of future Japanese competition, Foxboro decided to secure a beachhead in China.

Unlike many other companies, Foxboro was not simply looking for cheap labor. The company knew the value of high quality, and much of what was being produced in China was simply not good enough for its high standards. The introduction of poor quality would be devastating to Foxboro's business.

Foxboro spent months combing China for the right partner, one that had the right location, plant facilities, infrastructure, style, and political connections. It was essential that the partner have the critical complementary capabilities relative to Foxboro's market.

The search and ensuing negotiations took four years. By 1982, Foxboro had the deal it was looking for, in Shanghai. The company had taken the time to learn its partner's needs, and to structure any contracts carefully, before jumping into the venture.

Long-Term Incentives

Both the Chinese and Foxboro wanted this venture to be a long-term arrangement. The Chinese were interested in American technical know-how and management skills. The Americans were interested in access to the Chinese market and eventually in a low cost source of supply, but also did not want to see the Chinese as their competitors 10 years hence. Provisions were made for continuing technology transfer to the Chinese over the long haul. Foxboro was clearly interested in maintaining a win/win relationship for years to come, and its Chinese counterparts knew it.

An Almost-Equal Partner

The deal was structured as a 51/49 relationship in favor of the Chinese, the maximum allowed by Chinese law at the time. However, Foxboro negotiated a provision that enabled it to designate any issue it so deemed as a "vital venture issue." For these issues, Foxboro had veto power, which was tantamount to giving Foxboro full control of the alliance.

The individuals who initially negotiated the deal were then involved in ongoing operations to maintain continuity.

Tip

Overseas Negotiations: In developing nations, be prepared to spend an inordinate amount of time to create an unambiguous agreement regarding critical business decisions and practices for the alliance.

- Carefully and consistently avoid unrealistic commitments.
- Have no hidden agendas.
- Obtain your partner's commitment to use U.S. business practices in ongoing operations.
- Provide for long-term continuity of personnel.
- Obtain explicit agreement regarding expatriates' responsibilities, authority, renumeration, and living quarters.
- Keep legalistic aspects until last.

Figure 16.1   Checklist for Preparing an International Deal[1]

_____ **Culture:** Be sensitive to your opposites' culture. Read about their culture during the preparation phase. Ask questions of others who have experience negotiating with individuals of your opposites' culture. Obtain information on local circumstances in the country.

_____ **Personalities:** Find out who your opposites are, who their families are, what their education is, and what makes them tick. Attempt to develop a personal rapport, a base of understanding, and a bank of good will.

_____ **Timing:** Be aware that, in Europe, negotiations may take longer than in the United States. In Japan, negotiations may take even longer than in Europe. In both cases, the reason is the need to thoroughly assess the venture in the context of a long-term relationship rather than a one project deal. The European or Japanese negotiating team will be less interested in a one-time transaction than in a serious long-term relationship.

_____ **Preparation:** Be well-prepared on all issues, especially technical ones. Conduct extensive price, cost and market analysis before the formal negotiation meeting.

_____ **Pricing and Costing:** Do not expect your counterpart, in the beginning of the relationship, to share with you a cost breakdown. Become familiar with applicable tax laws. Such knowledge can lead to significant price reductions.

_____ **Financial Information:** Return on investment (ROI), dividends, and profit as a percent of sales tend to be lower in many countries than in America. Consider this information during the objective-setting process. The tax laws of each country vary widely, resulting in very different representations of the value of assets on the balance sheet, and different methods of reporting expenses and depreciation on the profit and loss statement, even though the format looks just like a U.S.-style set of financials.

_____ **Currency:** Obtain guidance from your controller on the issue of exchange rates and the likely costs or advantages of using a particular currency. Then negotiate the exchange rate as you would any other issue. Watch out for currency conversion problems that may require special government approval. Get the approval before finalizing the deal.

_____ **Win/Win:** Arrange issues in such a manner that your opposite can win a visible share of the issues—possibly while you are winning the big one.

_____ **Negotiating Authority:** If possible, ensure that the head of the other team has the authority to reach agreement on behalf of the firm involved. The position of recorder is a powerful one. Be the recorder or appoint one from your team. However, it is usually best to refrain from using tape recorders or video tapes, because they tend to inhibit frank discussion.

Train, Train, and Train Some More, as a Team

Foxboro knew that its Chinese partner had virtually no knowledge about modern management practices, particularly marketing, sales, and accounting. Foxboro avoided an adversarial, superior stance by taking a tutorial approach.

Foxboro created task forces with representatives from its marketing, legal, accounting, purchasing, inventory, and manufacturing departments. The venture was staffed with bilingual people wherever possible. Teams of Foxboro experts were sent in to train their Chinese partners in management techniques and business know-how as well as technology development. Next, the Chinese were invited to visit the Foxboro facility in the United States. Foxboro believed that it should set an example for its partner to live up to, by exceeding its own part of the agreement.

As a result of this training, Foxboro's Shanghai partner had a greater sensitivity to the American partner's needs. When Foxboro proposed that the Chinese make a significant investment in a customer service capability, to ensure continued growth, the Chinese agreed, and together they built an extensive customer service organization.

Be Aware of the Politics

Politics can be very sensitive in many countries. China was clearly "experimenting" with capitalism at the time, and Foxboro was well aware that the Communist Party was always looking over its partner's shoulder. Foxboro worked at maintaining the high-level contacts that were established during initial negotiations, and found these to be very helpful in keeping the venture on track. When electrical "brownouts" were scheduled for the Foxboro–Shanghai site, the close political relationships and trust that had been established averted several days' plant closings.

What were the results? Foxboro's Chinese partner's quality and production reliability improved constantly; the partner became a sole supplier to Foxboro in 1989. Foxboro now has several joint ventures worldwide, yielding $44 million in sales and contributing very significant profits. When preparing for an international alliance, how can a company be successful? The checklist in Figure 16.1 will help you accomplish this task.[1]

STAFFING THE ALLIANCE

The $9 billion 3M Corporation, headquartered in Minneapolis, has learned a lot about placement of personnel in alliances from its experiences in Japan and Europe.

3M has a cadre of "foreign service employees" with the ability to deal in dual cultures: a Canadian runs the Japanese operations, a Dane runs the

Trap

Career Paths: One large U.S. corporation, a recent entry in the global arena, has a reputation among its managers of marooning people in foreign countries with no clear way back home.

Have a career path for international expatriate managers. Reward them for their skills and achievements, remembering that their role involves integration and empowerment. Because they often give so much credit to others, they may not seem to be the real heroes.

German subsidiary, and a Scandinavian runs the Swiss operations. But 3M adheres to the principle of selecting local nationals for all other management jobs, principally because 3M understands the business and social culture, the complexities of local distribution, and, most importantly, the customers. According to Douglas R. Hanson, vice president of international operations: "We would fail if, as Americans, we did it ourselves."

Be sure to give the alliance your best people. Many deals have failed because they were staffed by second-rate individuals whose motivation and capability were less than adequate to the task. This issue is one that has soured many Japanese–American deals. The Japanese traditionally assign their best people to alliances, an approach that is not frequently reciprocated by their American counterparts.

Managing Information Flow

Different corporate cultures have different thresholds of control; they may have widely varying needs for information and centralization of decision making. These control issues can conflict if a partner has a far different threshold of control.

When a high need for control is overlaid with a need for strong entrepreneurial management, beware of a potentially "hypertensive" environment. High levels of outside corporate control may conflict with an entrepreneurial manager's style, causing friction and frustration. In these circumstances, discussions beforehand are advisable. Columbia University Professor Katheryn Rudie Harrigan comments:

> [Alliances] are especially difficult for managers within firms that instinctively overmanage their subsidiaries and for managers that are unaccustomed to techniques for managing cooperation. When frustrated managers in sponsoring firms slam against the constraints of the matrix organization they created for monitoring their venture, they do not change their control mechanisms. Instead, they layer in more and more people and procedures to solve their personality conflicts with the venture's managers or with their partners by

buffering them from direct contact with them. As the situation grows more hidebound, owners lose track of the original benefits that motivated the venture's formation.[2]

Coordination and Control

Coordination between the partners becomes increasingly more critical in an international deal because the distance between the partners is greater and cultural differences tend to make coordination more complex. This situation is a bit easier in a joint venture because the structure of the venture sets up a separately managed entity whose responsibility is to coordinate between the two partners.

The structural framework of the strategic alliance, because it does not have a separate organization, must rely solely on the skills and commitments of the respective alliance managers. Therefore, in international deals, their time allocation to the alliance will necessarily be higher. The stronger the need to share information and resources between the partners, the more vital this coordination.

Do You Need an Agent?

The best method of handling coordination and providing energy and drive is to have an expatriate manager on-site, working closely with the alliance partner. In many cases, this is unrealistic: the human resources simply may not be available, particularly for smaller companies.

Although it is not the best route, many companies will use agents to represent them on a regular basis. An agent can make a weekly site visit, watch issues such as quality control, provide a hands-on approach to problem solving, act as a translator, and especially communicate face to face to the overseas partner.

Some caution is in order with agents, however. Tri-Wall's Bernie Roth advises a company must be sure to do "due diligence," to ensure that an agent's reputation is impeccable. A poor agent can seriously damage a company's reputation. Be sure that the agent is not working for competitors. Roth suggests that the agent should make a phone call to the hiring company from the partner's office to confirm that the visit has actually been made. He also strongly advises weekly site visits by the agent.

Agents should not be allowed to do all the work. The agent should only be a liaison; the alliance manager should remain in charge. The roles, responsibilities, and limitations of the agent should be very carefully spelled out.

Many agents, up front, will want to negotiate an initial long-term relationship, exclusivity, and large commissions on all sales. Be careful of accepting these arrangements. Regarding the long-term relationship, watch out for any hidden legal obligations. For example, in the Benelux countries

(Belgium, the Netherlands, and Luxembourg), any renewal of a contract beyond 3 years makes the representative virtually a lifetime employee, with stiff legal penalties for severance. Explain that trust is developed through performance. A short-term contract is essential at the beginning, to determine whether the agent is worthy of trust.

Exclusivity and sales commissions can cause problems, if not approached from a long-term perspective. Several years after Foxboro established its Shanghai joint venture, the commissions to its agent were costing the joint venture over $1 million annually and required renegotiation. Commissions can be especially important if the partner arrangement starts as a strategic alliance and then transforms itself into a joint venture or, ultimately, an acquisition. Some companies suggest use of a formula that contains a diminishing rate structure over a period of years, such as a 6% rate in year 1 that diminishes by 1% per year, becoming 0% in year 6.

FOREIGN PERCEPTION OF U.S. LAWYERS

From the foreign perspective, one of the most onerous aspects of doing business in the United States is its vulturous legal system, which provides great incentive for adversarial activity. Many foreign companies see U.S. businesses firmly entrenched in a quagmire of ensnaring legal maneuvers designed to punish rather than reward, to litigate rather than negotiate, to divide rather than unite. It is unquestionably one of the greatest fears and impediments to negotiations.

One major concern was articulated by a Swedish CEO who said: "Lawyers seem to find new ways to insert themselves into every possible transaction in American business, generating huge amounts of paperwork and exorbitant legal fees, and often contributing little to the actual success of the transaction."

Another concern is the litigious nature of the United States system. One of the greatest concerns of foreign companies is a fear that they may become entangled in a morass of lawsuits that will drain their precious time and scarce financial resources. The Swedish president commented, during a negotiations session: " Your product liability laws are just an unbridled intent to soak anyone who touches our product. And the nonreimbursement of legal fees in nuisance suits just amplifies the high cost of legal proceedings."

The final concern is the U.S. liability laws, which hold companies jointly and severally liable for problems, regardless of their proportion of guilt. Recently, for example, one manufacturer was held liable when a worker lost a finger in a machine that lacked a guard on a chain. The machine was manufactured in 1919, 70 years before the accident, and well before OSHA regulations. However, the manufacturer had "deep pockets" in the form of insurance, and was held liable. Another brokerage company held a machine for less than 24 hours during a transaction, but was held liable for a subsequent liability problem because both the manufacturer and the eventual owner did not have deep pockets.

These concerns will result in foreign partners' wanting to register all legal documents in their native jurisdiction, where the laws will be more understandable and acceptable to the foreign partner. Mark Weller, general counsel of AGA Gas, an American subsidiary of a Swedish company, suggests, as an alternative, registering the ventures in a neutral country favorable to business, such as Switzerland. Another alternative he suggests for companies committed to U.S. law is to register in Delaware, whose laws are less litigious than those of many other states. (If you want to scare away a partner, threaten a New York registration.)

Role of Legal Counsel

Do not bring a lawyer to the initial negotiations. Their presence either will turn off open discussion or will force the other side to bring its lawyers, and the negotiations will then be driven by legal issues, not by business issues.

The proper role of a lawyer is as an adviser on the sidelines, providing expert counsel to the business interests. A good lawyer will understand and accept this role. The lawyer must not play a role similar to that of an agent negotiating a contract for a sports figure. Rather, the lawyer is a critical element of a support team providing expert assistance on the nonbusiness issues. In Foxboro's Chinese venture, legal counsel was never present in the negotiations until the final closing. However, he was an integral part of the in-house fourteen-member alliance development team.

In one large U.S. corporation, an executive complained to me that the lawyers were involved in everything. Upon further inquiry, their lawyer said, "We need to be involved at every point and transaction in the business, because we are the 'heartbeat' of the company." This lawyer did not

---

Tip

Legal Documents vs. Operational Agreements: Alliance success does not rest on the quality of the legal documents involved. Ultimately, any cooperative venture's success or failure will be based more on the quality of the operational agreements and on the success of maintaining a win/win condition in the multiple dimensions of strategy, chemistry, and day-to-day operations.

However, don't avoid the legal issues. Be sure to consult (behind the scenes) regularly and early with key advisers.

---

know his role; he was introducing heart-rot into the firm with an ensuing entanglement of paperwork that would eventually strangle the company. Keep the lawyers focused on protecting the company against unreasonable risks; let them know that the customer and the corporate mission must remain preeminent.

One corporation keeps its law firm in control by specifying how many pages may be used for documents. The law firm is provided with a clear Memorandum of Understanding, which guides its work. Without the Memorandum, and a limit on the number of pages, businesses run the risk of having the legal process expand to disproportionate limits. Another method is to put a very strict, but fair, time limit on how long the law firm has to review documents so that work does not expand to fill the time available. This prevents endless fiddling with language, an unprofessional habit exhibited by some attorneys.

What is critical and should not, under any circumstances, be overlooked is the role of the legal team in negotiations. They must remain on the sidelines, advising, consulting, and guiding; they should not be in the middle of the discussions at the front end of the negotiations process. If lawyers are allowed to become the key negotiators early in the deal, then the deal will take on a legal life of its own, reflected in the size and complexity of the legal documents.

Obtain Qualified Counsel

The use of *qualified* legal counsel is essential in international deals. I strongly emphasize the word qualified. There are many good attorneys, but very few are qualified for international work, and even fewer are sensitive to the process of alliance formation.

One of the best ways to kill a deal is to initiate an international deal with a lawyer by your side during initial negotiations, or, alternatively, to send the first written concept of the alliance to your prospective ally in the form of a draft legal document.

TRANSFORM CULTURAL DIVERSITY INTO ADDED VALUE

Alliances have an obligation to capitalize on and exploit differences, not to make the differences tools of destruction. The creative tension that can evolve in an alliance can indeed create synergies.

However, it is truly disappointing how ethnocentrism and egotism—traits sadly indigenous to every culture—can intervene and destroy. Neither a good strategy nor a sound operations plan will overcome this destructive element.

The shattered dreams of many failed foreign exploits are sound testimony to the denial of transforming cultural diversity into added value.

International Negotiations: It is all right to be frank, open, and honest, but be extremely cautious about being too blunt during discussions. Most non-Americans are not accustomed to a blunt approach; it may be misunderstood and disruptive.

Recesses in the negotiation may be required to allow a team to gain approval of a particular proposal. Before such a break, an agreement must be reached on the topic to be discussed immediately following the break. Otherwise, negotiations will become unnecessarily protracted.

When negotiating in Japan, it may be necessary at times to convince the whole group whose activities will be influenced by a proposed transaction.

Americans tend to be uncomfortable with extended silences; many other cultures are not—they feel no compulsion to break a silence. An American's impatience or desire to "hammer out an agreement" results in breaking such extended silences and, frequently, yielding or compromising on the point being discussed. *A good negotiator will be content to allow the silence to run its course, rather than volunteering a concession in order to break the silence.*

Negotiating does not mean "overpowering the opponent" or "squeezing out the last concession." Focus on expanding the pie, and enlarging the opportunities. If problems arise, negotiations must center on maintaining trust, ethics, diplomacy, understanding of the other's perspective, tolerance of differing values, and a willingness to cooperatively resolve any and all differences of opinion.

Among several examples are: An American auto manufacturer that refuses to make right-hand-drive vehicles for export into Japan; an Indian governmental official who denies the value of having an English manager on site to oversee operations; a French chemical company that won't adhere to its partner's production specifications because it isn't the French way; a German engineering firm that insists on controlling an alliance because, it says, Americans are poor engineers. The list could go on. Too many individuals would rather be right than win; they deny the possibility of a better way because their vision is blinded by their ego- and ethnocentrism.

John Poccia, senior vice president of engineering for Stanley-Bostitch, manages his company's alliance with Japan's MAX, a cooperative arrangement involving extensive marketing, technology, and engineering. Poccia will go to trade shows with his partners, to assess new products and customer needs and analyze the opportunities together.

The alliance started twenty years ago as a licensing agreement for technology provided by Stanley-Bostitch to MAX. Soon the Japanese outdistanced their American counterparts and began transferring technology, components, and product to the Americans, still under the original licensing agreement. Poccia comments:

> For a number of years they had better technology, so we became a distributor for them. Now we have improved our contribution to the partnership, which enables them to buy more of our tools to improve our sales in Japan. We needed to bring our QC standards to their level. Licensing of products and royalties is no longer as important as sharing of information.
>
> They are so detail-oriented and take so much time to make decisions through their consensus process. It used to drive us a little crazy. Now, however, we are familiar with their methods and recognize the tremendous value their thoroughness brings to our company.[3]

One of the best tools for understanding the cultural diversity issues is the differentiation–integration process described in Chapter 12. By using this framework, the architecture of the international alliance will be well served.

Style of Doing Business

Differing corporate cultures can create confusion, and sometimes impotence, if not managed by a sensitive leader. Some managers suggest that key members of the management team be sent to one of the other parents for a period of time for "corporate cultural indoctrination" prior to formalizing the venture, to learn how the operational fit will be once the venture is functioning.

In Japan, you can tell the age of a person by whether he is a bureau chief or a group leader; promotions are based on age as much as merit. Most Japanese companies tend to be heavily staffed, sometimes having 30% more people than a similar American company. This creates more convoluted decision making, which sometimes becomes even more prolonged because of decentralized authorities.

In China, or Korea, the style of doing business will be highly related to government policies and to how much the bureaucracy is involved in day-to-day activities. In the transitional countries in Eastern Europe, where there has been no contract law, no marketing system, and no accounting system that understands profit, cost, or price, it is very easy to make assumptions about how well a proposal has been communicated, only to find out after the deal is signed that your partner understood something far different.

Employee Relations

The status of employees is an area for extreme care, when designing the architecture of the alliance. Interaction between people can take on some very difficult dimensions if trouble spots are not recognized far in advance.

For example, in America, a manager who walks the shop floor and talks directly to the factory workers is thought to be "involved, concerned, and in touch." In India, where the caste system still prevails, such actions could put the alliance in deep jeopardy, because the Indian partner has been disgraced and lowered.

Market Conditions

One of the most fatal mistakes any business can make is to assume that customer preferences will be the same in another region of the world. Usually, there will need to be some minor "tailoring" to local tastes, such as when Levi-Strauss had to establish new patterns for jeans to fit the Asian physique. At other times, the changes may have to be major, such as understanding that white is the color of death in many parts of the world. Normally, the best protection against a faux pas is to ask the alliance partner to provide detailed assistance in customizing the product and packaging to the local market.

Another area to consider is distribution networks. For example, in Japan, as is well known, the distribution system is multilayered with numerous middlemen. This obstacle is usually regarded as a detriment, but it also creates opportunities, as A. T. Cross found with its partner in selling quality writing instruments. Cross advertised heavily in Japan. The Japanese, who are great travelers, would purchase large quantities of Cross pens and pencils on their trips to Hong Kong, Hawaii, California, and the Philippines, where prices were significantly lower because of fewer intermediary distributors. John Lawler, Cross's vice president of international operation, estimates that only 50% of the Japanese advertising dollar results in sales in Japan itself, and the other 50% primes the pump for sales outside Japan. Each country will have its own totally unique idiosyncrasies in its distribution system.

Competition must be handled with similar sensitivity. In some countries, competition is naturally cutthroat; in others, it is civil; and in some, it may seem collusive by American standards. The method of competition will have a major impact on the way the strategy and operation of the alliance are handled.

National Culture

Customs, values, and local traditions can often be very difficult for the uninitiated. Simple things like keeping appointments on time can vary dramatically from culture to culture. In Switzerland, Taiwan, and Korea, be exactly on time for meetings, but in Latin America, don't be surprised if you wait for a meeting for an hour and your host waltzes in without apologizing for being late.

Don't try using children in advertising in some European countries. Sex doesn't sell in China, but specifications do.

In other countries, be careful of giving compliments; they might be embarrassing. A compliment toward your host's wife could be interpreted as a request for a liaison, and admiration for a beautiful work of art might be regarded as a request that your host make it a gift to you. Be sure you have studied the culture *before* starting negotiations.

REDUCING RISK THROUGH INSURANCE

Foreign investment can be a risky activity, particularly in undeveloped countries where war or expropriation is a potential hazard. Loans, loan insurance, and loan guarantees are available to small businesses from the U.S. government-backed Overseas Private Investment Corporation (OPIC). It will guarantee loans up to $50 million made by U.S. commercial banks, and provides very reasonably priced insurance against war, expropriation of assets, and inconvertibility of currency. Located in Washington, DC, OPIC has gathered packages of previously fragmented economic and market data from numerous government agencies, which it will provide at very low cost.

MAKING FORCED MARRIAGES WORK

In numerous underdeveloped countries, particularly where there are laws against 51% ownership of companies by foreign investors, the government may play matchmaker by orchestrating a joint venture. Your partner may be hand-picked by a government group that wants to position a local company for growth. These "arranged marriages" can be effective or a disaster, depending on how they are handled.

Due diligence is a critical factor. Be sure to cultivate local business and political connections for yourself. If you leave these to your partner, you may find yourself in an untenable position several years later.

In particular, maintain control of key assets, such as money, auditing, technology, patents, and market access. Be sure you have veto power over key management positions and decisions. Draft the operations agreement carefully and monitor it regularly. Track the alliance's performance in detail. If possible, start with a less risky, less cumbersome structure, such as a purchaser–supplier or distribution alliance; if successful, convert it to a more sophisticated form, such as a joint venture.

SOME PITFALLS

Be particularly wary of forced marriages where the integrity of the partner has not been carefully scrutinized. It is best to know how well their word will hold up under the pressures of financial strain, and their tendency toward greed and personal advantage. Experienced venturers will often say: "If you cannot trust a handshake, even the best-drawn legal agreement will not be adequate protection." Uniroyal's retired chairman, David Beretta, explained his experiences:

> In Japan we entered into a joint venture with the giant Sumitomo chemical company because we needed access to the Japanese market and the raw materials Sumitomo virtually controlled in Japan. They were honorable people, and we relied on that trust extensively, because keeping track of the ever-changing market price of petrochemical raw materials and what we will pay for them is a system of constant negotiation. If we did not deal with honorable people, the venture would have been ruined.
>
> But in Mexico, we had the opposite experience. Mexico's law at that time prevented a foreign company from owning over 40% of an industry classified as petrochemicals; 60% had to be owned by a Mexican national. We found a small company for whom we had been a supplier of chemical intermediates which he in turn then processed. We thought we knew this man; we had done business with him for quite some time, so he was a logical person to go to when we decided we wanted to begin supplying a broader Mexican market. We brought in a portfolio of products, technology, and management.
>
> Soon we spotted a problem when the auditors alerted us to the fact that he was not paying his purchasing manager any salary. His response was: "I don't have to pay him anything, his suppliers pay him!" The second problem we discovered was every time we had a construction project, there was one engineering company that always won the bid. He owned the engineering company too. These were just blatant ways of siphoning off funds. He probably had many other methods we never learned about.[4]

Consider All the Factors

Mike Van Horn, a noted author and consultant who establishes alliances in the Pacific Rim, advises people to avoid making a poor estimate of the start-up time and capital needed to begin overseas alliances. He states:

> Many companies underestimate the administrative complexity of doing international business. Companies often fail to factor in the costs of translating written materials, logos, packaging, slogans, and so on.[5]

Knowledge of the market is vital. Van Horn suggests companies learn about the industry in the target country—its shakers and movers, its leading suppliers, its competitive structure, the customer base, the driving forces, key market factors, and market entry strategies. Too many failures are simply caused by poor planning.

Trading Companies—The "Midwife Alliance"

Many countries have a wide network of trading companies, which essentially act as middlemen and distributors between manufacturers and customers. Most buy goods for cash and sell on terms, with relatively thin margins. Companies new to exporting will often begin overseas operations through a trading company's extensive networks. The most renowned trading companies are Japanese, exemplified by Sumitomo, Mitsui, and Marubeni. The Dutch are also noted for their trading companies.

Because of their extensive networks, trading companies can provide excellent leads for alliances and can serve as intermediaries during negotiations. However, if a trading company is used to "broker" an alliance, be sure it is prepared to step out of the way once the alliance is formed. If it remains as an intermediary, it will impede effective alliance functioning, because it will have no real strategic resources in its internal organization. Be aware, however, they will often continue to want to serve as distributor of the product or to receive a long-term commission for matchmaking. These issues should be negotiated early on, and the long-term effects should be clearly thought through.

How to Use a Translator

The long-term effectiveness of the alliance will be founded on good communications. Language—along with nonverbal, social interaction, cultural sensitivity, and trust—is an essential foundation for communications.

Translators will often be needed, but be careful. Do not use your prospective ally's translator during negotiations. Your own translator will be loyal to your interests and will help clarify translation problems. You may see your translator debate with your prospective partner's translator, to gain a truly accurate representation of what is being said. Do not use students, professors, or amateurs. They may understand conversational English or literature, but will be totally baffled by the technical idioms of your industry. Use the office of the U.S. Department of Commerce in your host country to help find a translator for your needs.

Trap

Knowledge of English: Although many foreign executives understand English, do not assume they understand American culture and values.

Religiously avoid slang and cultural references to sports analogies, such as "quarterbacking," "slam-dunk," and similar terms.

Beware of foreign translations into English. For example, "inspection" in China may mean "teardown" of a piece of equipment, and may put the burden on the American partner to rebuild and recalibrate it.

The Value of Relationships

Human relationships are the foundation for the chemistry fit in an alliance. Throughout the world, this is a universal denominator of alliances. Americans tend to try to lessen this factor, but it is indeed the glue that bonds the alliance in the first place. Mike Van Horn says:

> In foreign countries, they tend to make a friend, then make a deal. They want to get a sense of whether they can trust you. Americans try to make a deal, then make a friend. Then to their horror [they] find they can't trust their partner.[6]

The tightness of relationships can often be misinterpreted. According to Japan's Shoichi Saba, former chairman of Toshiba and member of the Mitsui *keiretsu*, "Japan is not a closed society, but a society of long-term relationships." Therefore, it takes a long time to become part of the social system. This is equally true for the majority of the developed world.

The United States is built on a system that believes adversarial relations will create sufficient checks and balances to prevent one group from becoming too powerful. Our legal, political, and media systems are powerful testimony to this belief. However, other countries have a very different approach to this issue, believing that strong relationships result in a vital, invigorated economy. In the opinion of Kosuke Yamamoto, director general of Japan's Ministry for International Trade and Industry (MITI):

> Unless we get industry together on something, we simply cannot implement a decision. My understanding is that the U.S. Department of Commerce doesn't work as a coordinator between the needs of a society and the market mechanism. It stands on one side and confronts the other.

The critical and overriding rule in any international deal is to turn cultural diversity into an asset. While not easy, with the proper sensitivities, diversity is a gold mine of value.

17

Managing the Details

Anything that won't sell, I don't want to invent.

—Thomas Edison

Edison always built on the base of others' errors and creations, commenting: "I never did anything worth doing by accident, nor did any of my inventions come by accident . . . . I start where the last man left off."

MANAGING THE TECHNOLOGY TRAP

This is an important principle of technology development in an alliance. Engineers who are not willing to build on the knowledge of their counterparts on the other side of an alliance should not be allowed near the alliance in the first place. Their "chemistry" is wrong to start with, and their negative, myopic attitude will poison any cooperative relationship faster than a dose of arsenic.

A Condition Sure to Result in Failure

The worst trap in technology development is not inherently in the technology itself, but in the market that will accept the new product. The customer base and the new technology must be wed together, consecrated by the high priests of the alliance. If this marriage does not take place, terrible consequences are inevitable.

Tip

Marketing Costs: Rule of Thumb: Market development will cost at least as much and take as much time as technology development.

TIME: TECHNOLOGY'S BIGGEST ENEMY

Napoleon said he could always make up lost ground, but not lost time. In a development project, time is the biggest enemy. It translates into lost money, particularly when coordination slips and people and production lines must grind to a halt because something unexpected has ruined the best planned schedule.

In a new development program, it is virtually impossible to recover from the combined problems of learning new methods, coordinating with new team members, integrating new technologies, and making up for a major delay in schedule.

The number of design changes that occur from new concept development to manufacturing engineering to final production can be enormous. Every design change, especially if made later in the development cycle, has a snowballing effect on changes to tooling, parts supply, production planning, and budgeting. The ratchet effect of design changes can chaotically leverage time and budgets by a multiple of two or three times the initial projection. (See Figure 10.2, the Law of Compounded Risk.)

THE START-UP PLAGUE

The inherent problem, no matter how it is approached, is that technology development is essentially a start-up business problem. It has all the indigenous problems of a start-up; its multiple risks increase geometrically as additional risks are added. Figure 17.1 is a lighthearted insight into typical problems of start-up joint technology development ventures.

No matter how simple a project looks on the surface, turbulent waters lie underneath. When Fram Corporation, a leading aftermarket maker of auto air and oil filters, decided to become a manufacturer of replacement windshield wiper blades, the project looked rather simple. With Fram's tremendous distribution system, great profits were projected. However, the technique of keeping the blades in place was not as simple as it appeared. Blades came loose, the metal frames scratched windshields, and Fram was faced with covering the cost of damaged autos. The company quickly withdrew from the market, leaving a legacy of lawsuits and a damaged reputation.

Figure 17.1   A Humorous Look at Start-Up Risks

1. **Staffing:** No major start-up technology development project can be completed on time or with the staff that started it (unless they've done it together before).
2. **Completion:** Projects progress quickly until they become 90% complete; then they spend inordinate time and resources making the last 10%.
3. **Goals:** One advantage of fuzzy objectives is that they let you avoid the embarrassment of estimating corresponding costs.
4. **Momentum:** When times are tough, something will go wrong. When things just can't get any worse, they will. When things appear to be going better, you have obviously overlooked something.
5. **Flexibility:** If the project objectives are allowed to change freely, the rate of change will always exceed the rate of progress.
6. **System Completion:** No system is ever completely debugged. The better the attempt to debug the system, the higher the chance of inevitably introducing new bugs that are even harder to find.
7. **Planning:** Carelessly planned ventures will take three times longer to complete than expected; a carefully planned project will take only twice as long.
8. **Progress:** Teams detest progress reports because they vividly demonstrate their lack of progress.
9. **Reporting:** The more reports required to manage a project, the more entangled the problem becomes.
10. **Marketing:** Technical people will neither appreciate nor understand the exorbitant time and money necessary to bring their new idea to market. Every customer objection will be met with rejection and/or ridicule.

In any technology development alliance, the very reason for forming the alliance is because none of the partners has ever traveled on this path before. Because no one has ever successfully created the new technology, on the positive side there are new concepts, applications, processes, and solutions. On the negative side lie many hidden traps, pitfalls, and difficulties no one has yet found. Yet the pitfalls are always underestimated.

No Room for Failure

When everyone tries to make up lost time, time is being shaved off every incremental function. Because the functions have never been performed before, they are fraught with unknown difficulties. Instead of having the flexibility of an expanded schedule that allows some room for error, the schedule has now been tightened.

Throwing experienced people into the situation usually doesn't solve the problem; the "tried and true" systems are not necessarily the right ones for the new situation, and the individuals assigned to the alliance are seldom dedicated solely to this task and become "double hatted" with their normal duties plus the alliance.

Trap

Six Phases of Improper Technology Development

1. Enthusiasm
2. Disillusionment
3. Panic
4. Search for the presumed guilty
5. Punishment of the innocent
6. Praise and reward for the nonparticipants

How Changes Add to Confusion

Mandatory changes affect form, fit, and function. Every mandatory change wreaks havoc on production, scheduling, procurement, inventory control, and marketing functions. The later in the schedule the changes occur, the worse the problems. Typically, the burden piles up like a log jam in a river until it bursts and crashes down in a cascading torrent of aggravation, animosity, and finger pointing. As the marketing program falls out of alignment with the production schedule, distributors cancel orders, customers become furious, and the sales department screams that millions of dollars are being lost.

Downward Spiral

It doesn't take a genius to know the outcome: With less time to handle unexpected difficulties, Murphy's Law becomes Lynch's Law. (Murphy didn't know about the Law of Compounded Risk.) Problems only amplify each other. The first problem creates a delay or draws away resources and attention. This results in another problem, such as rework, which requires even more resources.

Throwing additional resources at the problem only brings in new people who seldom have a real understanding of the essential difficulties, thereby creating further conflict. By now, everything has gone to hell. In march the auditors and top brass, who now make every little function a "priority" with a consequent shift in emphasis for all personnel, thus further confusing everyone involved.

Witch Hunt

Soon after, the auditors and bean counters are introduced into the game. They demand reports and numbers, make everyone work overtime, thus causing resentment, and shift focus away from the real priorities. Attention becomes centered on those individuals who "caused" the problem. There is no acknowledgment that the system was destined to fail from the very beginning.

When the technology development program begins to slip off schedule or go over budget, and when the prototypes fail to perform adequately, the first activity is a finger pointing at the other team; after all, they really didn't understand the objectives in the first place. Ultimately, the blame is laid on the fact that it was an alliance, and a faulty conclusion is reached: "We should have done it ourselves."

MANAGING MOTIVATION

Thomas Watson, IBM's founder, once said that management's primary job was managing motivation. Given the entangling problems inherent in technology development, every alliance architect is faced with a dilemma: if you look at all the problems, your mind will be trapped in the negative, thinking of all the ways it can't be done. If entrepreneurs thought this way, there would be no invention, no innovation.

Creation is given birth by people who are in a perpetual state of *enlightened* dissatisfaction. Take the enlightened, visionary, can-do element away, and cynicism results.

The development team must be kept within the boundaries of the real world, but they must not become overwhelmed with difficulties. For

---

Tip

The Best Ways to Reduce Technology Risks

- Be sure "the dog will eat the dog food."
- Avoid multiple risks.
- Step back one step from the leading edge.
- Develop in increments, like the Japanese. Avoid revolutionary technology unless you're sure it won't be cataclysmic.
- Try the "hot rod" approach: Have a very basic first design or core technology, and add new adaptations or modules to the core.
- Be careful of single applications. Develop technologies that can be adapted for multiple markets.
- KISS: Keep it simple, stupid.
- Use milestone management.
- Choose technical people who have good integration skills to manage the technology interfaces.

Tip

Technology Transfer Is a People Process: According to Gerald McAchran, Director of Venture Capital at Monsanto, the key to technology transfer is people and relationships.

Look for employees who have a strong network of people and outside experts who are essential in helping alliance partners implement the integration process.[1]

---

example, if the engineers are informed about the difficulties of the sales and prospecting process, the engineers may begin to lose faith by becoming consumed with problems outside of their realm of expertise.

THE MARKETING CONNECTION

One of the most widespread fatal flaws in technology development is a failure to understand its intimate connection to the marketplace. New concepts must be related to real customers, not to a vague market. Roy Bonner, formerly of IBM, is emphatic on this point:

> Too many times I see market studies that are oblivious to who the first customer is going to be. Technical people need to know what is being brought to the market that is truly wanted by the customer—what problem does it solve? What is new, unique, and better than what exists now?
>
> Most entrepreneurs are myopic about pricing. They must understand the benefit/cost analysis from both the customer's and the manufacturer's standpoint, yet most don't have a clue about how to be responsive to customer needs. The critical question must be asked: How does the customer perceive the appropriate value?
>
> Technical developers must understand the customer's needs in detail. They must talk to the decision-makers who will buy the product, not middle men! Know the precise reason for buying.[2]

The checklist in Figure 17.2 will help to refine the link to the customer.

The first aspect of technology development is actually market development, to determine whether the technology concept is correct in exact detail, from the customer's perspective. Bonner further comments:

> The bean counters will keep you profitable, but the top line will keep you in business. All accounting is founded on the tactical efficiency of using resources, but does nothing to expand how resources were created, nurtured, or leveraged. Only develop the product when you fully understand the customer, the specifications, and the price points.

Figure 17.2   Checklist for Technology Development

_____ Can it be scaled up?

_____ Will the government approve it?

_____ Will the customer buy it?

_____ What does the customer really want? What are the terms and conditions of a sale?

_____ Does it integrate well with existing systems?

_____ Is it easy to use? From whose perspective?

_____ Who will buy it? Can it be sold? By whom? What does the sales force need to know to sell it?

_____ Does the market need to be developed? At what price? How long will it take? Forever?

_____ How many risks are in the development? What will be the impact of compounding these risks?

New technology?	New sales force?
Multiple technologies?	New development team?
New manufacturing process?	New knowledge?
New product?	New skills?
New subcomponents?	New partners?
New market?	Multiple partners?
Multiple markets?	

_____ Is there a design prototype? Does it work? Has it been field-tested?

_____ Is there a production prototype? Has a pilot production process been designed? Tested?

Concurrent Development

The entire process must result in the parallel development of technology, manufacturing, engineering, purchasing, marketing, and finance. According to Richard Sandberg, Senior Industrial and Manufacturing Engineer at Allied Signal Aerospace:

> Concurrent development is a team effort. It incorporates concepts where people working on a project are empowered to make decisions without having to check with multilayers of management prior to making the decisions. This implies a trust in the team, and a willingness to delegate.
>
> In concurrent development, the critical driving forces are customer requirements, quality, cost, and schedule; precisely in that order.[3]

Technology development, probably the riskiest of all alliances, is fraught with unknowns. The alliance must manage risk by lessening the number of risks, getting the design *right* early in the development cycle, using very effective teamwork, and providing enough flexibility in the schedule to absorb many of the unknowns.

PURCHASER–SUPPLIER ALLIANCES

The phenomenal growth of strategic alliances between purchasers and suppliers over the past 3 years is a notable example of a silent revolution affecting manufacturing and service industries worldwide. The changes are profound, and alliances are redefining the fundamental role of procurement. Traditional views of the purchasing role as a *component procurement* and *contract audit* function are being enlarged by the more *strategic* and *systems-oriented* perspective.

Procurement as a Strategic Weapon

In concert with these changes, suppliers are having to make major adjustments in their thinking, management styles, and methods of responding to purchasers' new standards and operational requirements. According to Professor David Burt, an expert authority on procurement at the University of San Diego, procurement is now being recognized as a vital weapon in a corporation's strategic arsenal. He states:

> Over the past 50 years, the value of purchased materials and services [from outside suppliers] has grown from 20 percent to 56 percent of the selling price of finished goods. A similar change has occurred in the supplies and services purchased by nonmanufacturing organizations such as banks, hospitals, and governments. Purchasing professionals are their companies' managers of its "hidden factories"—the facilities and expertise available at supplier firms.[4]

Unfortunately, the strategic implications of alliances, in the executive suite as well as at the purchasing managers' and the supplier's representatives' levels, have been largely overlooked. When an alliance does make sense, purchasing managers and suppliers are often shoved into the breach unprepared for their new roles. Moreover, effective organizational responses have been poorly documented, and the learning of those who have successfully muddled through the alliance management process has seldom been communicated to others who could have benefited most.

DRIVING FORCES

The alliance revolution in procurement is not driven by some faddish trend, but by the combination of four very strong underlying business

Figure 17.3   Driving Forces for Procurement Alliances

Quality: Heavy emphasis on material and performance improvements and higher product reliability.

Speed: Need for rapid delivery of new product innovations to the market.

Cost: Cost-effectiveness programs to lower production/assembly costs.

Engineering: New design techniques for early-stage development and continuous product improvements.

forces at work in the manufacturing, engineering, and marketing sectors, as illustrated in Figure 17.3. The combination of these four forces has fostered closer working relationships between purchasers and suppliers. Purchasing managers should be alert to these four forces at work in their own companies, because they will signal future changes required in their purchasing organizations.

Quality Management Requires Alliances

According to W. William Lindner, vice president of purchasing and distribution at Union Carbide's Chemical and Plastics Company in Danbury, Connecticut:

> If you make a commitment to quality, each supplier must know how the purchaser will use the supplier's product, which means a closer relationship between the purchaser and supplier.[5]

Ford's quality program led to a drastic cut in the number of its component makers, resulting in a much closer relationship with the remaining base of preferred suppliers. Quality management experts advocate close alliances with suppliers, but few programs truly capitalize on their potential.

NEW MANAGEMENT STYLES FOR PURCHASING

The alliance trend does not require purchasing managers to reject their fundamental teachings. There will always be a use for the component-oriented, short-term supply contracts, combined with healthy doses of skepticism and an auditor's sense of distrust.

However, when business conditions necessitate an alliance, an additional set of management dimensions will prevail. The purchasing manager's role expands enormously, beyond traditional boundaries, by encompassing strategic and systems management functions.

According to David Archer, at Boothroyd-Dewhurst, the pioneers in design for manufacturing and assembly engineering techniques, in traditional purchaser-supplier relations, design engineers are evaluated for their quickness and their ability to keep parts costs within budget; manufacturing engineers, for design, scheduling, and budget performance; and purchasing managers, for obtaining the lowest price from vendors. Departments isolate a few numbers that are relatively easy to obtain.

In the new realm of alliances, internal incentives must foster teamwork within the purchasing company's own departments. Engineering, manufacturing, purchasing, quality control, and even marketing should participate in determining new, more encompassing measurements of success, not just from each individual department's perspective, but also from the broader business perspective. Such factors as product cycle costs, scrap, reliability, lower service and warranty costs, time-to-market, less overall manufacturing/assembly cost, and team (versus individual) performance are typical measurement criteria in alliances.

Selecting Personnel Suited to the New Role

An alliance represents a major shift: from a "components" to a "systems" approach, from a "cat-and-mouse" to a "teamwork" game, from a tactical to a strategic perspective. Some purchasing managers will adapt quickly and well; others will require considerable time and retraining.

The purchasing manager must recognize his or her new role as a "systems integrator," and the supplier's salesperson should similarly assume a far broader role.

Reporting can be confusing in this less hierarchical, less formal partnering system. Personnel must be chosen who can handle the subtleties of cross-corporate communications and interdepartmental teamwork. Plan on using specially designated liaison personnel who are properly selected and trained for facilitating communications. IBM selects liaisons based on their track record of being "interdepartmental deal makers" with multidisciplinary backgrounds. Liaisons keep alliances from getting caught in the paper-shuffling game.

Purchaser–supplier alliances should not just look for price reductions. From the purchaser's perspective, clarify the costs of late delivery, poor quality, and inflexible supply. Otherwise, purchasing managers get stuck in the belief that the lowest price is the best cost.

Toyota takes an intense interest in its preferred supplier alliances, which, in turn, help Toyota retain its position as the world's low-cost carmaker. Using its highly skilled manufacturing/engineering team, Toyota helped its U.S. supplier, Flex-N-Gate, double its productivity, while cutting lead times 94%, inventories 98%, and defects 91%.[6]

According to Professor Burt: "Historically, buyers have been 'price takers,' or bid receivers, largely relying on competitive market forces to help them obtain a 'fair and reasonable' price."[7] A purchaser–supplier alliance can result in substantial improvements in price, quality, service, technology, and innovation. A purchaser–supplier alliance can also be integrated into a total quality management (TQM) program to produce defect-free incoming materials.

DESIGN'S IMPACT ON COST

One of the most critical areas for reducing cost occurs *before* the product design stage. As demonstrated in Figure 17.4, while the cost of actually designing a product is only 5% of the price, a whopping 70% of the price is determined by the design itself. Motorola estimates that 80% of a product's costs are fixed by the time the first prototype is built.

Figure 17.4   Impact of Design on Cost (Ford Motor Company)

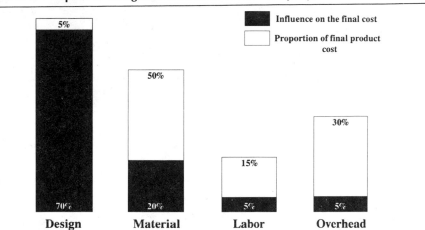

The obvious path is to influence the design at the very earliest possible stage. This requires extensive teamwork at the front end of conceptualization of a product.

Getting suppliers involved earlier has major implications for companies. Purchasers can get in front of the problem, becoming proactive rather than reactive. This earlier involvement changes the relationship from a standard supplier arrangement into an alliance. The majority of engineers focus internally on technology, performance, and reliability, paying relatively little attention to supplier capacity. According to Professor Burt:

> The design stage is frequently the only point at which a majority of the cost of making an item can be reduced or controlled. If costs are not controlled here, they may be built in permanently, resulting in an expensive, noncompetitive product. Later cost reductions are a poor substitute for having the lower cost design from the beginning.[8]

At Xerox, early supplier involvement, when combined with volume leverage from a smaller supplier base, netted cost reductions of 10% per year. At Ford, design-for-manufacturing techniques with early supplier involvement in new car design are reported to exceed $1 billion in savings.

Alliances between purchasers and suppliers create value in the supply chain. Procurement is indeed a powerful strategic weapon.

PART FIVE

Achieving Success

18

Getting Started

Extraordinary results flow from persistant visionaries committed to unreasonably worthy goals.

In the competitive marketplace of the 1990s, companies will have to reexamine all of their baseline assumptions about the future and about what makes them competitive. For a company to be strong in the global marketplace, it must look at alliances as one of the more powerful strategic weapons in its arsenal.

The alliance architect's task is to custom-design a venture that must focus on continuously devising win/win methods to adapt the alliance so that it maintains the three dimensions of fit—strategy, chemistry, and operations. The stage should be set for doing a number of things right at the beginning of the alliance.

SUPPORT DYNAMIC STRATEGIC FIT

It is all too easy for people to assume that their skills and capabilities, which were so effective in running an internal department, will carry them successfully into alliances. Alliance management processes are often far different.

Companies with high levels of internal teamwork, and flexible, non-bureaucratic decision making, will probably find the transition far more comfortable. Similarly, companies that are fundamentally systems integrators and rely strongly on the value brought by their supply base will find alliances much easier than will those who are highly vertically integrated.

Obtaining Top-Rank Support

Having the corporate high priests "sprinkle holy water" on the corporate alliance strategy is absolutely essential. Without close and intense executive support, the alliance, by definition, is probably not strategic.

At IBM, alliances must be blessed by the corporate executive committee. At Corning and Ford, top brass get to know and support their counterparts, which creates a climate of cooperation. By endorsing teamwork, the corporation also supports internal teamwork, cross-training, and integration, building an important skills base to make alliances more effective.

Superficial Support: Not Enough

In a few instances, corporations have naively jumped on the alliance bandwagon. In their annual reports, they have espoused the need to establish alliances and have delegated the authority to form such alliances to middle managers. However, tragically, some of these CEOs wouldn't know an alliance if they woke up in bed with one. Their subordinates, the middle managers who courageously forge the linkages, can't even get a meeting with top management to explain what they did. The high priests are too busy with meetings, reports, and trying to digest their latest acquisition's money loss.

Needless to say, their alliances are faltering because of the executive committee's "flavor-of-the-month" mentality. It won't be long before these companies abandon the alliance approach and broadly announce that cooperation doesn't work. Further, they will probably shoot the brave troops who gallantly tried to forge the linkages, and will hang anyone who tries to learn why they failed.

Getting the Architecture Right

The process of developing the alliance is far more important than many executives want to believe. Some deal makers secretly harbor the hope that a shotgun marriage will be sufficient; they can then plunder on to the next deal, never looking back to see what havoc lies in their wake. The dreadful legacy of failed acquisitions is terrible testimony to this attitude. Unfortunately, many of the consummate deal makers of the past decade are already becoming the scourge of alliances. Astute executives will spot this problem.

Designing the processes, methodologies, fits, integration mechanisms, operational interfaces, and reporting systems is a task that should not be done haphazardly. Alliances are designed to be strategic and flexible, which requires more than superficial commitment and thought.

Creating a Flexible Structure

Asian business strategy is predicated on the belief that much of the future is indeterminate. It is important to lay out a plan and a strategy for the future, but there are always unforeseen twists and turns of fate.

Strategy must remain fluid enough to respond to unpredicted problems as well as emerging opportunities. To successfully make transitions, the organizational structure and the legal agreements must have built-in adaptive mechanisms.

Being Clear About Objectives

Know the expected strategic return on investment (STROI) for your company as well as for your partner. Only by being clear about these objectives can you define the elements of victory and set out a workable set of operational plans to achieve them.

For example, Nabisco's alliances are aimed at deriving 25% to 30% of sales from new products (less than 4 years old). Mike Richmond, director of alliances for Kraft Foods, makes sure that key milestones, expectations for performance, time frames, objectives and user–supplier advantages are very specifically defined before any formal or legal agreements are signed. There is no question about the value of the alliance before it becomes official.

Maximizing Driving Forces

Alliances tend to last longer and perform better when there are strong strategic forces keeping the venture together. In a franchise alliance, the structure of the alliance itself requires both partners to have complementary strengths and weaknesses, which, like a magnet, keep them together. Additional driving forces are profit, growth, and the need for continued competitive advantage. 3M shares its strategic plans with its Japanese allies, NEC and Sumitomo, in order to find more effective ways to align the strategic driving forces and further cement the relationship, which is now entering its fourth decade.

Preparing for Internal Realignments

No company should ever expect to introduce a strategic alliance into its midst without making internal changes to procedures and policies. Adding an alliance is like bringing a new child into a family. Organizational patterns must change.

Alliance architects should think through precisely what strategic realignments may occur, how to create the right rewards systems, how to streamline decision making, and how to create more effective internal lines of communications.

BUILD EXCELLENT CHEMISTRY AND RELATIONSHIPS

How many people who will be intimately involved in an alliance have had training? Corporations train people in every other skill—engineering, finance, sales—but, tragically, seldom in the field of architecture or management of alliances. Then executives wonder why the alliance failed. Japanese and German companies make a far greater commitment to training than their American counterparts. For example, the typical Japanese company spends 6% of its payroll on training, compared to 2% in the United States.

The rules of engagement are different outside the corporate castle walls. The team of champions, alliance managers, and liaisons, along with those negotiating the deal, should be properly trained for their complex roles. In this way, they will share the same language, frames of reference, and processes. By the same token, it is quite fair and reasonable to insist that a prospective partner have a trained team as well, to avoid setting up the partner for failure.

After selecting key personnel, seriously consider engaging in a team-building session to jump-start the alliance by clarifying roles, defining key priorities, focusing efforts, and establishing workable reporting systems. A neutral outsider is often called on for a team-building session as the project begins to get underway. This neutral third party should be agreed on by all partners.

Harvard's Harry Levinson urges the use of a sophisticated team-building program to enhance the venture's chance of success. He recommends that, during this process, several key points should be covered, including the mission of the venture, the expectations each member has of the other, the problems they should anticipate, and how the problems will be resolved. Levinson warns:

> If people are not brought together at first to get on the same wavelength, they will take more time later. Many managers don't realize this; they get started on the task, and forget focusing on the team.[1]

Dow Chemical's success in joint ventures is, in part, attributable to its own cross-training of managers to communicate and coordinate across internal corporate boundaries. These skills are then easily adapted to joint venture situations, using functional teams led by people with good integrative skills.

Creating Internal Teamwork

When Gates Energy decided to embark on supplier alliances to combat stiff Japanese competition, it had to look at itself squarely. Gates didn't like what it saw: poor internal teamwork, inadequate communications, fragmented specialists failing to see the big picture of the real needs of the company, scant support for the supplier base. This frank analysis led to dramatic changes in internal teamwork, which then enabled Gates to succeed in moving rapidly toward its goal of becoming a low-cost, high-quality producer.

Integrating Teams

Teamwork in an alliance begins with negotiations. "The problem with negotiating the deal 'by throwing documents over the transom' is that it creates an 'us-versus-them' atmosphere that is antithetical to the very process of building teamwork," states David Kitscher of GE's Corporate Research and Development.[2]

When Sonoco, the world's largest producer of composite packaging materials, formed a 50/50 joint venture with Britain's Composite Metal Box by spinning out existing divisions, one of the first priorities was to interchange staffs. The joint venture's chairman of the board alternates from one partner to the other. At the middle management level, both companies identified people who were effective integrators to work on the unification, with plenty of cross-training and interchange of information.

Make use of integrating methods such as secondment (cross-assignment) and cross-training. Require site visits to the other company's location.

Tightening Personal Relationships

An essential ingredient of the glue that binds the alliance together is the trust that top and middle management have in each other as individuals. Companies do not trust or distrust companies; people form the bonds of trust.

John Poccia, senior vice president of engineering at Stanley-Bostitch, personally visits his Japanese counterpart at least two or three times a year. Mazda's president, Yoshihiro Wada, meets frequently with Ford officials, and the joint senior management strategy group meets every eight months. Corning chairman Jamie Houghton nurtured a very tight personal fondness for Samsung's B. C. Lee. When Lee passed away, Houghton interrupted a very busy schedule to fly to Korea for the funeral. Not only do these personal bonds build trust, but they also send a powerful signal to middle managers regarding ethics, commitment, and support for the alliance.

Fighting for the Other Company

If you have a true vested interest in your partner's winning, as should be the case, then you will pledge to fight as hard for your partner's winning as for your own. When your partner wins, you do also. Often, this requires the alliance manager to *represent the interests of the alliance first* and those of the parent company second, and to be rewarded by the parent company for such behavior.

Office furniture manufacturer Herman Miller, Inc. increased the price paid to one vital strategic supplier, to ensure a strong partner. Gates Energy gave Jagemann Stamping a statistical process control system. As allies, Lam Research and computer chip equipment maker Novellus service each other's equipment to keep their mutual customer base satisfied.

Maintaining Middle-Rank Support

"People support what they help create" is the motto for all alliance formation and operation. The middle managers' roles change significantly, once they shift from the internal to the extended corporation, where they become leaders of teams and are faced with being far more aware of corporate strategy than ever before.

These managers must also be reinforcing creativity within the alliance and continually seeking to expand the size of the pie. At 3M and Corning, years of technical development between differentiated research teams and with outside corporations has created corporate cultures that reinforce middle management integration and initiative.

Capitalizing on Diversity

Diversity is the spice of life and the power of an alliance. It can also be a destructive element if trust is not present. The greater the ambiguity of the project and the rate of change of forces acting on the alliance, the greater the chance of diversities becoming corrosive.

It is essential to maintain trust through personal relationships, commitment to critical values, and strong leadership to manage diversity in times of uncertainty. At Colgate-Palmolive, supplier alliances are viewed from a win/win perspective. If Colgate spends one dollar for quality assurance, and its supplier spends an equal amount, but the supplier's dollar is more valuable or productive than Colgate's, then Colgate will seek to increase the burden on the supplier, but will help foot the bill.

Choosing the Right People

Assign the best people to the alliance. Know their past assignments, their character, their skills. Be sure the type of personnel will mesh within the operational framework of the venture. Reject any candidates who do not meet the quality standards of the desired team. Find individuals who can lead without being anointed or without wearing gold stripes on their sleeves; their capacity to motivate will not depend on their ability to hire, fire, or promote.

Key operating personnel should have previous experience in at least two of the venture's functional specialties, in order to ensure effective integration and respect of authority by demonstrating a reasonable degree of competence. For these reasons, the role of the integrator is not a good selection for a new, unseasoned management trainee.

Addressing the People Issue

When pacemaker manufacturer Cordis linked with Dow to market a Dow-developed fiber for kidney dialysis, the joint venture grew at a feverish rate. The venture was unable to add human resources fast enough, so Dow helped its partner by supplying personnel to the alliance. Dow supplied marketing executives who were expert in commodity sales, not in specialized medical supplies. They were used to selling tanker loads of chemicals in bulk sales, not high-technology customized equipment.

To add to the problem, manufacturing people with continuous process manufacturing experience were put into jobs where manufacturing was more job-shop, specialty oriented. Sales and customer relationships suffered. Eventually, Dow bought out Cordis, which was by then only a shell of its former self. Most probably, Dow was not intent on destroying the venture, but was instead the victim of its own ignorance or indifference.

Developing Career Paths

Key personnel must be devoted to the alliance first and foremost. If their priorities are focused in other corporate directions, internal management problems are inevitable. Alliances are frequently outside the normal career paths of those appointed to staff them. Unless the venture can provide long-term growth opportunities, the sponsors should not let a venture manager become an anomaly, a marooned organizational outcast. Alliance assignments should be part of an employee's regular career path.

Some experienced venturers suggest that some of the middle management positions in alliances should be for a relatively short term, to enable a cross-pollination of new and creative ideas that may be carried back to the sponsoring companies. However, sponsors must avoid making an alliance a "revolving door"—an assignment for a brief period of time, before returning to the parent company, or a "one-way street" from which the employee can return only if victorious. One major U.S. company, relatively new to alliances in the global marketplace, has a tendency to maroon its managers in foreign lands, with no way back to a position in the United States once they are assigned abroad. Managers are, understandably, reluctant to take overseas assignments.

Harvard's Professor Paul Lawrence says that, because alliance integrators often attain high degrees of performance by indirection, they often fail to receive the credit they deserve for making things happen. To compensate for this inequity, some cooperative ventures provide additional motivational incentives for key managers by offering a share in the venture's profits.

Using Flexible Legal Agreements

The legal process all-too-often destroys rather than builds trust. Good business strategy must guide the legal process, not vice versa. The lawyer's role must be to keep the deal legal, avoid unreasonable risk, avoid potential for future litigation, and build both the soundness of the business strategy and the effectiveness of the alliance.

Bob Teutsch, vice president and chief legal counsel for Dobbs International, advocates that legal counsel must first really understand the purpose and mission of the alliance well, and then find creative methods of managing reasonable risks. He believes that in-house corporate counsel is more likely to understand this purpose and is paid to deal with reasonable risks, whereas out-of-house counsel is independent and therefore has to seek zero risk by being overly cautious.[3]

SUPPORT SUPERB OPERATIONAL MANAGEMENT

Designing Management into the "Front End"

One of America's largest corporations has made a major commitment to growing by alliances. Behind the scenes, corporate spokespersons admit that a significant number of the alliances are not performing up to expectations. The principal reason is that this corporation does not really understand how to manage alliances. The alliances are, for the most part, strategically sound and well-structured, but the deal makers make a fatal mistake by not concerning themselves with the methods, processes, mechanisms, and frameworks for management until after the alliances are underway. Fragmenting the front end from the back end of a deal creates organizational schizophrenia.

Little do they realize that, once the ignition key is turned, the vehicle will be traveling in the wrong direction; as soon as problems arise, the management mechanisms for fixing the problems are far from adequate. Failures and frustrations grow into anxiety; trust spirals downward; the alliance's problems become so severe that saving it requires immense resources—if it can be saved at all.

Success comes from the prevention of problems. Design the management system up front; don't try to fix it later. Good management is built in at the beginning, like total quality management, not checked at the back end after the partners find the alliance isn't working right.

Clarifying Responsibilities

Without clear lines of authority, decision making will be severely hampered, teamwork will falter, and performance will suffer. The responsibility charting process described in Chapter 11 can be used to gain sharp focus. This process should happen on a macrolevel before the alliance is negotiated, and on a microlevel before launching actual operations.

Having Strong Champions

Passionate individuals with vision, values, and commitment are essential to making alliances happen. Champions must be empowered to talk to everyone; they cannot be tied to the ball and chain of command. Keep champions glued to their deals for the long term.

Do not duplicate one corporation's mistake: after the deal makers had decided an alliance was necessary, and after finding a partner and commencing negotiations, they looked on my checklist of essential ingredients to make sure they hadn't missed anything.

They spotted the line that said they needed a champion. Off they went in search of a champion who would bring back the Holy Grail. No one volunteered, so someone was appointed. This designated soul, now empowered by the almighty corporate fathers, was expected to have religion, to believe in the cause, to fight for the truth and righteousness of the alliance, and to inspire the confidence of the allies. The champion's level of effectiveness was quite predictable.

In contrast, IBM initiates most of its strategic alliances at the operational level, not from headquarters, to ensure it has a champion. Then it requires executive committee approval to ensure top-rank support.

Converting Expectations to Goals

Expectations are unstated imaginings of what people would like to see. As long as they remain unstated, expectations are "time bombs" that will require a crisis or frustration to trigger them.

The solution is to put all the expectations out in the open, turn each into a goal, and then set forth a plan to achieve each goal. In this way, expectations become a powerful tool to focus energy and empower people to meet the needs of the alliance.

Identifying Critical Incidents Up Front

Prepare for the worst things. Good luck stems from excellent preparation. Union Carbide's William Silvia comments:

> I never want surprises. The best alliance managers anticipate problems well in advance. I recommend performing a critical incident analysis before finalizing any cooperative venture. Then you know what to expect from your partner. This is essential to trust and good chemistry. It also reduces the possibilities for divorces later on.[4]

Developing Contingency Plans

Each partner should know its own role, risks, and responsibilities, should problems occur. Particularly in fast moving markets and highly risky ventures, a strong contingency plan may spell the difference between success and failure.

William Lauer, the operations manager for an alliance in the food service industry, handles the ever changing daily conditions of the restaurant trade by training his staff well. Before every major event, he advises his team to anticipate every problem that could realistically ruin the affair. Employees are expected to work closely together as a team; if one of the problems crops up, each knows how to move quickly to remedy the problem. During the event, Lauer roams the dining room and kitchen floors watching for any small indication that a problem is emerging—cold food, slow pick-up of orders, a waitress becoming burdened by the needs of a special table, a refrigerator beginning to lose temperature, and a myriad of other minor problems that are constantly brewing. At the first sign of a problem, he pounces like a cat on a mouse, taking firm, corrective action.

Have three plans ready to go at all times: an optimistic plan, a conservative plan, and a "Black Sunday" plan. With each adverse turn of business events, some aspect of one of the plans can be counted on to help save the day. The worst case plans don't necessarily need to be written down, but, when the enemy attacks, the troops need to know their battle station assignments.

Establishing an Early Warning System

After the critical incidents and contingency plans are identified, an early warning system should be developed to give advance notice of their arrival. The early warning system approach has been used effectively by many alliance managers. Figure 18.1 lists the typical signals cited by managers as warnings of an impending problem.

Figure 18.1   Critical Incident Early Warning Indicators

- **Back Burner:** When one or more of the parties doesn't give top priority to getting the job done, look for a lack of vested interest motivation in one of the partners or in a key individual.
- **Missed Deadlines:** This will normally be the result of insurmountable problems, poor planning, or poor management. If it occurs, watch for a spiraling progression of problems throwing the venture off course.
- **Role Confusion and Conflict:** If the team doesn't know its assignments, the job will not get done. The venture manager is responsible and must clarify roles and expectations immediately.
- **Winners and Losers:** If one party thinks it got the short end of the stick, the venture will fail because the structure is wrong and there is insufficient vested interest motivation for continued success. Realign for parity.
- **Cost Overruns:** Early-stage cost overruns may signal serious problems in risk analysis and planning. Left unattended, the venture may be bled dry of financial resources, creating friction between the partners. Smart managers get on top of these problems immediately.
- **Missed Goals, Milestones:** An effective monitoring system determines how well goals and milestones are being met. Any early deviation will be amplified over the long haul. The steering committee should address early deviations immediately.
- **Missing Communications:** Establishing good communications is essential, and venture managers must be held accountable for this function. Be careful, don't shoot messengers bearing bad news, for this will only stifle good communications.

BEWARE OF THE DEADLY SINS

The seeds of destruction are usually sown before the legal agreements are signed, because someone, in a rush to get the deal signed, sealed, and delivered, left critical elements out of the architectural design of the alliance. It's like forgetting to put windows in a building or not letting the concrete set long enough before putting up the walls. You'd never do it in a building; don't do it in an alliance, unless you are willing to pay the penalty later.

ISSUE OF GOVERNANCE

Decisiveness is a critical factor. Alliances should not become cumbersome, unwieldy, bureaucratic behemoths. Time is one of the greatest opponents of those who play the field of risk. To defeat time requires decisiveness—an ability to make timely and correct decisions. Before deciding to embark on the alliance course, get a clear view of how your company will deal with the joint decision-making process needed to make an alliance successful.

What kind of people inside your organization will facilitate decisive decision making?

It is important to differentiate between the decisive leader and the "hip shooter." The decisive leader consults with staff members, receives ample early warning signals, plans for contingencies, and acts accordingly. The hip shooter makes quick decisions but bases them on inaccurate, untimely, or incomplete information. The decisive leader empowers others; the hip-shooter is unconcerned about empowering anyone.

IBM's former chairman and CEO, Thomas Watson, Jr., looked for intelligent people with "common sense" when he was at the helm of IBM:

> Common sense allows managers to make a decision, but too much intellectual depth may allow them to see too many variables—and therefore make *no* decision.[5]

DESIGN FOR SUCCESS

At the outset, create the right architecture for succeeding. Mike Richmond, Director of Alliances at Kraft Foods, has attributed Kraft's success to its having made a systematic commitment:

> We are dedicated to a win/win relationship with our allies. We have regular and frequent reporting with go/no milestones so we don't do something wrong forever. Senior management is intimately involved. It is important to dedicate sufficient resources, especially committing key employees. And we provide for sufficient social interaction to build respect and trust.[6]

Get Started on the Right Foot

Considerable attention should be paid to getting an alliance launched the right way, to set the trends, directions, velocity of achievement, and confidence level. Make sure you are ready, and allow enough time for managing the interfaces. Follow up on inquiries, questions, and complaints. Make sure things work the first time.

People Make a Difference

The diversity between corporate cultures produces *creative tension*—one of the alliance's finest assets. However, this tension can easily degenerate into conflict, which, in turn, produces combative behavior. A very moderate level of friendly competition can actually be potentially healthy by creating a level of tension for focusing energy.

The critical issue is not inherently the *differences and contradictions*, but the manner in which conflict is *elevated* into creative problem solving. It may seem paradoxical, but in the contradictions lies the truth. What seems to conflict is often really a crystallization of two different and seemingly opposite dimensions of the same whole.

Personality Traits

The job of managing business is managing morale. Sony CEO, Akio Morita, said:

> I was taught that scolding subordinates and looking for people to blame for problems was useless. The proper thing is to make use of the motivations you share with people to accomplish something that will be to the advantage of both.[7]

This attitude is vital, if an alliance is to function effectively. Seek the following qualities in the people who will be intimately involved in the alliance:

- *Humor* tempers conflict and channels energy into creativity. All alliances are "change processes" which, by their very nature, tend to create conflict. Look for managers who know the *delicate* role of humor—how it provides energy and triggers creativity. It can be used to break the ice, establish rapport, foster teamwork, and help transcend cultural boundaries.
- *Persistence* and dedication to winning are vital leadership factors. Preference should be given to those who do not accept defeat easily and, when faced with defeat, rebuild their plans, act creatively, and move forward to the coveted prize of success.
- *Leadership* in an alliance often requires directing without having full authority, because there is often no direct line of command across corporate boundaries. Humility, diplomacy, and the ability to ask the right questions to make others think of the solution tend to be most effective traits. Humble people tend to set a good example for others, often by "getting their hands dirty."
- *Power expanders* are leaders who create the right conditions to make others around them feel more powerful and effective. A power expander will generally focus on helping subordinates solve their own problems, and stay out of subordinates' details unless necessary. It is vital that the champions of the alliance play this role once the alliance has begun. Otherwise, their passion can become an impediment by focusing all the leadership onto the champion and away from effective delegation to the alliance team.

SUPPORT YOUR PARTNER

Mike Van Horn, a San Francisco-based authority on Pacific Rim alliances, advocates providing intense support to a partner from the outset:

It's essential to build strong confidence in the alliance at the very beginning. Don't hesitate to validate the alliance by providing impeccable technical support and backup to the customers. Put in joint appearances with customers. Respond to questions and requests as rapidly as possible, even on very short notice. Make early adjustments or refinements in your product or service, to correct problems, improve market fit, and meet competitive responses. Build your reputation for excellence in the market.

Build close relationships, visit your partner frequently, and have your partner visit your U.S. facility regularly. Also, give serious consideration to linking your other strategic partners together to leverage multiple strengths.[8]

The inner harmony of the alliance—maintaining the three-dimensional fit (strategy, chemistry, and operations)—must be evident in both the negotiations phase and the operations phase of the alliance. It is a critical process that must be designed into the architecture to maintain the double-win condition. These techniques should not be superficial artifices cunningly devised for the moment, but must represent a fundamental set of values inherent in the alliance itself. Essentially, the continuing management of the alliance is simply an extension of the process of win/win set into place when the alliance is being developed.

19

Going with the Flow

The winds and the waves are always on the side of the ablest navigators.

—Edward Gibbon

After an alliance is launched, management's ultimate goal is to maintain a win/win condition in an ever changing world where strategic forces are always in flux and operational conditions are shifting. Change is inevitable and not always predictable; it creates problems and opportunities. There are methods to ensure that changes are handled effectively and opportunistically.

EARLY PREVENTION OF PROBLEMS

Every alliance will run into problems; they go with the territory because, by definition, business partnerships tackle elements of the unknown. Whenever there are risks, there are bound to be anxieties and conflicts.

Solving the Problems When They Occur

Effective venture managers and integrators should have excellent abilities for solving more than just mechanical and technical problems; they need to be able to solve personal conflicts as well. Figure 19.1 provides basic rules for alliance problem solving.

Figure 19.1   Operational Problem Solving "Rules of Thumb"

Rule 1:   Deal with Problems Quickly.
Some problems seem to solve themselves or go away, and are replaced by bigger problems. If the problem festers and conflict gets in the way of everyday operations, the venture manager must act—sometimes very subtly, sometimes abruptly.

Rule 2:   Work Through Problems Together.
Placing blame on the other party will doom the venture. Unless the problem is urgent and time is crucial, most venture managers will let their staff talk out the problem in detail, enabling a full discussion of the issues. Good integrators seem to have exceptional listening skills, enabling people with a problem to talk it through carefully. Once the problem is clearly spelled out, the integrator will guide a discussion of alternatives, and carefully generate a consensus decision to gain an acceptance by the entire team.

Rule 3:   Make a Commitment to Action.
Don't procrastinate. Once the solution is found, effective managers are neither passive nor shy. They take the initiative, turn on the heat, and aggressively pursue the objective. They are "deadline driven." Commitments are made, milestones set, and results achieved.

Rule 4:   When in Doubt, Communicate.
No alliance has ever failed because of over communications. Establish clear, accurate, and timely communications. Effective managers will be sensitive to communications across corporate boundaries, ensuring the right person is doing the talking to the right people. They are also aware that certain specialists may be junior in the management hierarchy, but their closeness to operational problems gives them the best perspective.

Rule 5:   Keep Your Partner Whole.
Fight for your partner's best interest. Demonstrate you care about your partner's winning. Don't hold your partner hostage in a conflict.

The best way to limit operational problems is to take strong preventive action, a result of careful planning far ahead of time. Evaluate potential problems regularly. Have venture managers meet frequently with their key advisory teams to discuss potential problems before they occur. The old adage: "An ounce of prevention is worth a pound of cure," still prevails. Determine what factors are likely to create problems. If the problems seem very likely to occur, ask whether the problems are surmountable or insurmountable.

Reevaluate the risks, break them down into manageable components, and organize for a succession of incremental victories. One venture manager suggested this was analogous to the riddle: "How do you eat an elephant." The answer: "One bite at a time."

If Problems Persist

If operational problems go unchecked, sponsoring companies become anxiety ridden, often jumping into the middle of the venture management picture, demanding reports, sending in investigators, and tightening financial controls. Then the venture manager's ability to function worsens, decision making becomes more difficult, and a downward spiral dooms the alliance.

Sponsors, when faced with such a condition, should call a "summit" meeting of all the partners, to address the problems and a set of solutions that will constructively bring the venture back on course. Nipping at the heels of the alliance manager will probably have negative effects.

Expect a Crisis

Alliances can be expected to have crises, like any other start-up businesses going through a growth cycle. When crises happen, use the principles of the three-dimensional fit to isolate the root cause; evaluate whether the failure is strategic (such as a change in market conditions), chemistry-related (one of the partners has lost interest or commitment), or operational (the problem is in leadership, management, support, marketing, or production). Many operational problems can be solved without structural or strategic realignments, simply by bringing teams together for problem-solving sessions.

Perhaps a structural redesign will be required to make the form fit the newly adjusted functions, with a redivision of risks, rewards, and management. Strategic problems, usually the most vexing of all, may call for a complete reevaluation of the venture and either a restructuring along the strategic spectrum of options, or terminations.

EXPLOITING THE CHEMISTRY FACTOR

Good chemistry is both a cause and a result of a successful alliance. Chemistry is a potent tool deriving its strength from the unification of common business goals and psychological harmony.

Chemistry works on two levels. At the first, more rational level, each partner trusts the other.

Beyond this elemental rationale, at a second level, something else happens. When together in a room, trying to solve a problem, minds in harmony, tend to become elevated, excited, and creative, for some reason best explained as "psychic." "Synergy" or "dynamic tension" occurs and it works. When structure and strategy are in harmony, when trust and integrity are foundations, when enthusiasm and desire are heightened, and when leadership and management enhance human effectiveness, chemistry is in action.

Those who have experienced chemistry know the power of this force; it creates a dynamic environment for a "sixth sense" to emerge enabling the design of unique, creative solutions. When unleashed, chemistry enables partners to generate new answers to problems that would never be found alone.

Using chemistry in creative problem solving is one of the greatest advantages strategic alliances have over more traditional business structures. Inherently, the alliance provides a staff of experts available to tackle unique and seemingly insurmountable problems. Without strong inspirational champions and alliance managers who can bring expert resources to the table in a coordinated and harmonious manner, chemistry in problem solving may go untapped.

MEASURING STRATEGIC RETURN ON INVESTMENT

Every alliance should be evaluated against very tough criteria to determine on a regular basis, whether it is achieving its designed objectives. The principal audit that should be performed on a regular basis must measure strategic return on investment (STROI). In Chapter 6, the five elements of STROI were outlined: market strength, organizational capability, innovative capacity, competitive advantage, and financial gain. An annual audit process should be undertaken using an independent third party who is experienced in operational auditing, capable of objectively assessing the impact of the alliance, and able to make professional recommendations for improvement.

Perform Regular Reviews

Quarterly alliance steering committee meetings should form the basis of the regular review. Some companies use video conferencing facilities when distance makes it prohibitive to have many people attend the meeting. Champions should be intimately involved in these reviews with their alliance managers, to check on progress, problems, and new opportunities.

Perform Autopsies

Just because an alliance "failed" doesn't mean cooperative ventures should never be done again. Most alliance "failures" are double failures: the first is the failure itself, the second is that an autopsy wasn't done and nobody learned anything. It's like saying "I got burned on the stove so I'm not going to cook any more."

Instead, take Thomas Edison's perspective: "There is no such thing as failure, only results." Perform an autopsy, get back in the ring, and try again.

A number of journalists, commenting on the "failure rate" in alliances, have sounded alarm bells for those considering alliances. Unfortunately, these superficial examinations are prone to gross generalizations and sensationalism. Ironically, the long-term successful alliances are often taken for granted; the failures make better grist for the journalists' mill.

There has been very little truly scholarly analysis of the failure rates of alliances, and most of what has been done has been a study of symptoms, not causes. Without a clear understanding of the architecture of alliances, it is very difficult to determine the real causes for failure.

Failure or Transformation?

Too many scholars don't clearly understand the difference between a failure and a transformation. For example, one academic study examined 50 "terminations" of "failed" joint ventures in the chemical industry over a 25-year period.[1] When the transformations were separated from the failures, the resulting data were very enlightening, as can be seen from Figure 19.2.

While this analysis cannot be predictive of any single alliance, and only relates to one industry, it is instructive to note that "failed" joint ventures were the result of external conditions or uncontrollable risks, whereas the "transformations" enabled the continuance of the operations in another form. They were certainly not "failures" as had been presumed. When these 50 ventures terminated, transformations outdistanced failure by a factor of 2 to 1.

Figure 19.2   Analysis of Terminations in the Chemical Industry over a 25-Year Period

TRANSFORMATIONS

52%	Purchased by parent or other
8%	Merged into parent or other joint venture
8%	Broken up by antitrust
68%	**Sub-total**

FAILURES

20%	Adverse market changes
8%	Research efforts unsuccessful
2%	Obsolete facilities
2%	Bankruptcy of one parent
32%	**Sub-total**
100%	**Total**

The Seeds of Destruction

Of all the failures I have seen, had the deal makers used the principles and procedures outlined in this book, 80% to 90% could have been predicted in advance, and the alliance could have been either aborted before it started or remedied before it was launched. The *seeds of destruction are sown before the legal agreements are signed,* and can be predicted.

HOW MANY ALLIANCES ARE "TOO MUCH?"

Beware of agglomerating so many alliances that your corporation is like an uncontrolled octopus. Several large companies have tried this approach, one had over eighty alliances, with spotty results. Another large U.S. corporation privately admits that many are not working, not because the strategy was wrong, but because they don't know how to manage them. They did not build good management into the front end, and they don't have a clear method of measuring their success.

These companies had similar problems when they tried the acquisitions game. And they took the same problems. However, they did not understand alliances well enough to handle the impending morass. The reality is that too many top executives have become entranced by making deals and bored with maintaining them. Too many companies have more deals than they can possibly manage, because their deal makers were rewarded for the number of deals they made, not for successful results that resulted in their aftermath.

Now that the acquisition-happy deal makers of the 1980s have had their sources of cash dry up, they are jumping helter-skelter into the alliance game; and are tragically repeating their errors of the past—"six-gunning" deals to death and putting notches on their guns, with no consideration of whether their deals are really successful.

Do a Few Good Alliances Well

We need fewer deal makers and more architects who are concerned about the ability of the alliance to withstand the test of time. Do only a few good deals, not hundreds. Ed Austin, vice president of procurement at Hughes Aircraft, says all Hughes alliances are functioning well. He attributes their success to doing only a few alliances, and doing them well. A senior group vice president at Hughes is intimately involved in all of its alliances.

TRANSFORMATION

Opportunities exist at favorable points in time; when time passes, so do many opportunities. Changes are bound to occur—industries change;

people move to other positions; the sponsors' businesses change direction, expand, and contract; competition is always maneuvering for advantage; and the alliance itself is changing as it matures.

If the owners expect the alliance to succeed over the long haul, its designers must enable the organization to continually adapt and flow with the times. It must maintain its strategic synergy, its trust and integrity, its operational leadership, its risk/reward balance, and the vested interest motivation of its partners, all within a dynamic, ever changing, strategic environment. Like the proverbial oak tree in a gale, the rigid venture will probably be uprooted, while the more flexible venture, bending with the winds of change, has a higher likelihood of survival. This is the art of managing the double win and the three dimensions of fit—strategy, chemistry, and operations.

Use the Strategic Spectrum Effectively

The alliance is simply a *structure* used to achieve a strategic objective; it is *not the objective* itself. To become locked into using one form of the alliance structure when it no longer meets the strategic and operational needs of the partners is a mistake.

The original agreement should be written flexibly enough to acknowledge that business interests do not remain stable over time. This will allow the partners to modify the structural form to meet new circumstances. Sponsors should refer to the strategic spectrum and find a new form that will most closely match the new needs.

For example, Honeywell sold its equity interest in its strategic partnership with Yamatake, but maintains close ties, thereby transforming the relationship into a nonequity strategic alliance. Other companies have transformed their joint ventures into acquisitions. The rule of thumb is: Use whatever structural form is the most effective means of accomplishing the objective; when another means is more appropriate, shift gears. By understanding the nature of transformation, alliance architects have a far greater range of options for adapting the structure than is provided by lawyers, who think only in the limited frame of reference of "exit clauses."

Watch for Shifts in Strategic Environment

Strategic fit is probably the most important to monitor, because when the strategic driving forces for one of the partners change significantly, the alliance will be under pressure to adapt. Every joint enterprise exists in a "strategic environment." As the strategic environment changes or competitive pressures shift, the mission of the alliance may also shift to become more valuable to one of the sponsors and less to another.

However, changes to the structure may be futile if it is no longer to the advantage of either partner to be part of an alliance. Try as the partners may, they might discover that no longer is the alliance the right structure for the strategic environmental conditions. A multitude of conditions could cause the partners to rethink the viability of the venture:

- **International Price/Political Changes:** Many ventures that were initially motivated to form international alliances will find, when the host nation changes laws and monetary rates of exchange, that the motive for formation will change drastically.
- **Change in Technology:** Technological changes can provide superior competitive advantage, as long as the process remains on the cutting edge.
- **Competitors Entering Market:** Good business strategy is based on good competitive strategy. A formidable competitor can cause a realignment within the venture.
- **Market Changes:** Fundamental market changes cannot always be predicted. When they occur, all firms within an industry will see shifts in their own strategic underpinnings.
- **Production Costs:** Production cost changes can have the same basic impact as changes in the market.
- **Strategic Realignments:** Within any industry, major and minor players are always jockeying for position.

If, however, the strategic environment makes less radical course changes, then only minor changes to the structure and operational aspects of the venture may be in order.

Be Alert for Changes in the Operational Environment

Even if strategic conditions remain somewhat stable, the alliance may suffer strains from operational conditions that cannot be corrected simply by mutual discussions and problem solving. Some operational conditions may require a minor restructuring of the alliance; other more serious problems may result in a more drastic change, such as termination or acquisition. Some of these possible situations affecting operational "fit" are:

- **Internal Financial Problems:** When one partner gets into financial difficulties, it automatically increases the risk to the alliance and therefore to the other partner.
- **Production and Marketing Costs:** Even the best forecasters cannot predict the complexities created by nature's elements and politicians.

Be Sensitive to Changes in Chemistry and Relationships

Human relationships, trust, integrity, and values are essential to maintaining the win/win condition in an alliance. When forces intervene that change chemistry, the alliance must make adaptations. These include:

- **Desire:** There is no guarantee that this important ingredient of organizational chemistry will last eternally.
- **Change of Key Personnel:** Leadership and management are key elements to the success of any cooperative agreement. Without the right people committed to the enterprise, continued allegiance may be difficult at best.
- **Lack of Commitment and Support:** Without commitment and support, no venture will survive. If the support or commitment is withdrawn, changes must be made.
- **Conflicting Organizational Values:** What is important to a company today can often change dramatically if other conditions change and have an impact on the venture.

Merger or Acquisition

Strategic alliances have served as excellent interim vehicles to test the strategic and operational fit of two companies before a merger or acquisition occurs. Sometimes, this is done by spinning out a separate division as a test bed for the merger or acquisition. Other ventures prefer using the equity partnership as part of a phased acquisition.

If the alliance is successful, the chances of a merger's being successful are far more likely than if the partners never worked together at all. If the alliance is too tense or fails, then relatively little was risked and the companies can continue on their own separate ways.

Licensing

Some cooperative ventures eventually determine that there is not a close need to work together. A friendly, arm's-length relationship is all that is needed by many companies.

Some joint ventures and strategic alliances are converted to simple licensing agreements when one of the partners' strategic interests diverge from the purposes of the alliance or when anticipated markets stagnate. In these events, one partner may desire to purchase the rights to the product or technology. Licensing can provide a safe and relatively low-risk method of cooperation, requiring little capital investment. Licensing can also provide excellent royalty income (but without the up-side advantages of high returns, synergy, and strategic value).

Stay Flexible and Be Creative

Business alliances are intended to be flexible institutions—they are arrangements of convenience and opportunity. More often than not, the designers of an alliance are anticipating a future transition that will place their organization in a strategically stronger position.

Anticipate changes in operations. For example, a commitment to continuous improvement will require partners to continually adapt to new standards and processes.

Alliances can take advantage of the "novice effect," similar to that which occurs when middle-age professionals change careers (i.e., Louis Pasteur in bacteriology, and Francis Crick in DNA) and make major innovations by connecting old knowledge with new paradigms.

Great synergy is built on a foundation of teamwork and creativity. Creativity is the offspring of being in a constant state of enlightened dissatisfaction. When the great architect, Frank Lloyd Wright, was asked which of the many edifices he had designed was his favorite, he replied: "My next one!"

20

Growth Strategy for the Future

All things move, and nothing stays.

—Heraclitus

Alliances are, unquestionably, one of the most important weapons in a business's strategic arsenal. Alliances extend a corporation's boundaries and potentialities to new limits by finding new synergies and leveraging precious resources for competitive advantage.

However, alliances do have their detractors, and it is worthwhile to examine some of their views.

ARE ALLIANCES A DEMON AT OUR DOORSTEP?

Myth: A creative invention, often a lie or a half-truth, disguised as the truth. An unproven belief without a determinable basis in fact, accepted uncritically and used to justify a position.

There are numerous myths circulating about alliances. Some of these myths are perpetrated by unknowledgeable journalists seeking attractive headlines rather than in-depth explorations of truth. Another source of the mythology is scholars who have given alliances a glancing analysis as a secondary aspect of another field of endeavor. One criticism presumes the formation of business alliances dulls our competitive instinct and will ruin America's strategic vitality by stifling competition and damaging consumerism. Others proclaim that alliances are detrimental because they give away critical technology to other countries without sufficient rewards in return.

These proclamations play well in Washington, enabling politicians to rant and rave about how joint ventures will hurt our economy, thereby diffusing the real issue. Without citing evidence of where cooperation has inherently thwarted our competitive desire, the proclamations have a nice conspiratorial ring that invariably creates headlines. Making business alliances the new demon at our doorstep has the same superficial allure as Japan-bashing.

Such commentaries are in stark contrast to Japan's top strategic mind, Kenichi Ohmae, a strong advocate of alliances. He maintains that the real suspicion regarding alliances comes from Western fear that alliances are "Trojan horses" whose real effect will be to let foreigners invade our own markets. Ohmae states:

> This is dangerous thinking. Defeatism is infectious. . . . This fear of Trojan horses implies a management group's belief in its inability to structure an alliance intelligently or to execute it well. . . . In most cases, doing it on your own is harder, more expensive, and more time-consuming than doing it with a suitable partner. But the benefits of an alliance remain benefits in theory only unless managers are willing to make the necessary effort.[1]

These myths, and the hard realities, deserve some investigation.

Myth 1. Cooperation Is Anticompetitive

This argument asserts that businesses forging alliances are engaged in anticompetitive behavior, and maintains that collaboration is a retreat from competition.

The Reality. Most alliances are *not* formed between competitors. They are bonds between parallel producers, purchasers and suppliers, different industries, isolated markets, or companies that share risks and enormous capital expenses.

Cooperation is not the opposite of competition; cooperation is simply a competitive weapon. Cooperation does not make business fat and flaccid any more than teamwork makes an athletic team lethargic.

The evidence strongly indicates that alliances between large direct competitors are very short-lived. Companies with highly differentiated strengths and weaknesses make much better partners.

Myth 2. Collaboration Is Collusion

Proponents of this myth maintain that only local rivals battling in industries under intense market pressure can create real innovation and upgrading of products and technologies. These advocates say that alliances are a modern equivalent of the reemergence of cartels. (If you want to prey on the paranoic instincts of our society, just promote any conspiratorial theory and watch the politicians line up for investigations, publicity, and headlines.)

The Reality.   There is sufficient truth to this argument to be convincing on the surface, but the argument confuses cooperation with collusion by implying that the purpose of alliances is to control prices and manipulate markets. People holding this view make a fundamental mistake: they see collaboration as automatically taking on the sadistic structure of a cartel—a grievous misuse of capitalism. They have fallen victim to a case of flawed, two-dimensional thinking based on the assumption that competition and cooperation are at opposite ends of a linear spectrum. The Japanese know quite differently.

Such a paranoic view is as myopic as believing that "power naturally corrupts." Like the use of power, collaboration can be used to magnify competition, or it can be used unethically to obliterate it.

A closer look finds that successful alliances combine the strengths of one partner to offset the weaknesses of the other partner and allow both to compete more effectively against a larger adversary. Companies that are already dominant in their markets seldom choose alliances.

Cooperative ventures are one of the best mechanisms for rapid response to highly demanding and ever changing markets. Even universities engage in collaboration with industry, for mutual exchange of important developmental technology. In the packaging industry, centers at North Carolina State and Rutgers are engaged in helping industry design safer, more recyclable, and biodegradable materials.

Successful alliances are built on a strong sense of ethics and are designed for long-term returns. It is extraordinary how many ventures involving millions of dollars are initially consummated by nothing more than a handshake. Economic pirates do not make good partners.

Cooperation is a positive response to intense competition. It eliminates needless bureaucracy. Alliances are the natural process of competitive capitalism becoming more efficient in response to competition, as the Japanese have so effectively demonstrated.

Myth 3. Alliances Are the Defeatist Retreat of a Declining Economy

This myth postulates that the rugged individualism of competition is presumably the best route for industrial and consumer advancement; alliances and mergers reduce a company's risk, thereby enabling it to avoid the painful steps of becoming truly competitive.

The Reality.   Strength comes from using competitive weapons effectively, including using cooperative ventures as a substitute for cumbersome vertical integration.

American companies have bought vertical integration through a voracious acquisition spree, often resulting in ossified technological and marketing structures. Vertical integration worked well at the beginning of the century, when technology and markets were slower to change, but it has been disastrous during the latter part of this century.

Unfortunately, advocates of this myth also fail to grasp the historic precedents of business collaboration in the early development of America's economic history. As described earlier, joint ventures were our most formidable competitive weapon in the first half of the 1800s, when they were used to grow our most vital new industries—textiles, shipping, mining, railroads—before the corporate legal structure was invented.

Business alliances have continued to be an excellent route for emerging industries to gain a beachhead in new markets with new technologies. This is precisely why high-tech companies, like their early-stage industrial counterparts of the previous century, have become one of the greatest proponents of strategic alliances.

We love to perpetuate the historic illusion of the rugged individualist as entrepreneur, but, in reality, the courageous whaling voyages of the 1800s were not initiated by sea captains working independently, but by consortia of businessmen spreading their risks among many ships on many voyages. The oil, railroad, mining, and electrical industries grew the same way.

Myth 4. Collaboration Reduces Innovation

Advocates of this position believe innovation results not from cozy and warm alliances where risks have been minimized, but from fierce competitive pressures and challenges. Close collaboration dulls the creative juices; inherently, cooperation is not an effective competitive tool.

The Reality. This argument touches on enough raw intuition to postulate a superficially convincing rationale. However, business alliances seldom exist in a warm and fuzzy environment in which flabby CEOs conduct business from their easy chairs, with a portable telephone in one hand and a martini in the other, as some critics like to imply.

Collaboration arises as the offspring of unacceptably high risks, where a company typically will not compete at all without a partner to share those risks. When risk is eliminated or substantially diminished, then one of the partners will typically choose to *acquire* the other partner or the alliance itself, thereby terminating the collaboration.

Risk for business is like stress for individuals: too much begets anxiety, too little begets lethargy, and the right amount stimulates innovation. Collaboration does not reduce innovation; alliances are created to reduce risks to economically justifiable levels and to stimulate innovation by taking advantage of synergies.

THE TIME IS NOW

Arguably, the optimum way of the future—the way that has spurred the phenomenal revival of Japanese industry, the extraordinary success rate of franchise alliances, and the 25% annual growth of Walmart—is not through acquisitions, but through a carefully devised strategy combining internal growth with outside alliances, customized to suit a company's unique capacities and characteristics.

Growth comes not solely from serving the customer well, but also from having sufficient margins to feed expansion and investment, and to fuel further competitive advantages. Properly designed, alliances can help attain many of these objectives.

Core Competencies

The formula for the successful business of the 1990s will incorporate a hidden weapon: the capacity to *integrate unique internal core competencies with the external capabilities of allies.* By unleashing the power of organizational linkages, both internal and external to the company, the successful executive will bring new meaning to the statement that "a chain is as strong as its weakest link."

New competitive opportunities will unfold as companies examine their core competencies and find new linkages for using them in new fields.

New core competencies will emerge from the synergies created by the *differentiated* functions of the alliance partners, and the real power of the alliance will be in the manner in which these capabilities and processes are *integrated* and *delivered* along the value chain.

Adding value for the customer is fundamental to every competitive strategy, whether value be price, performance, service, or uniqueness. For companies whose strategies are tied to the profit maximization school of strategic thought, alliances will be a temptation for off-loading internal business activities that don't look like they make a sufficient contribution to profit. More often than not, this will be a tragic mistake leading, in the long term, to a rotting of the corporate core as internal strengths are whittled away and peddled either to the highest bidder or to a present ally, who will then be tempted to become a future competitor.

Companies must continue to *add value* and *gain internal competencies* from alliances, instead of the converse. The alliance process should not become a mechanism to create a financial shell by substituting alliances for corporate core competencies. Alliances should be built *around* the core, should *support* the core, not *divide* the core.

Be Clear about Strategy and Goals

An alliance is a process, not an edifice; alliances are not the goal; they are only a means to a greater strategic end. It is not the *form,* but the *function* that counts. Know the ultimate goal clearly, communicate the goal to everyone, and stop all action superfluous to its attainment.

A shared vision of a clear strategic mission for the alliance is essential. In Ruskin's words:

> Failure is less frequently attributable to either insufficiency of resources or lack of persistence, than to a confused understanding of the actual objective.

In the old hierarchy, the CEO was the chief corporate strategist. In the "extended" corporation of networked alliances, strategic thinking and implementation become more decentralized. Middle managers are far more responsible for integrating strategic planning with strategic implementation. CEOs and their boards of directors must first understand and then empower this process.

Strategy in this new world is analogous to a sailing race in a fluid, dynamic environment of wind, sea, and other competitive racers, where navigation requires a continued series of course corrections and trimming of the sails. Strategy no longer resembles a chess game on a stable playing field with static rules in a world of bricks, mortar, and money. Navigation in a sea of change will be the natural state of doing business.

CEOs' New Role

Alliances cause the CEOs' role to shift from being captains and key decision makers to master architects and capacity builders, from emperors to empowerors. Emphasis will be placed on building staff and line capabilities to create new systems, processes, and infrastructures. The CEOs' role will certainly not be diminished, but it will be very different. Their leadership regime will focus on seeing that core values and best processes are effectively leveraged throughout their companies—not by policy manuals but by action.

A firm commitment to organizational integration is essential for alliances to be successful. This integration must happen first at the top echelons, between the senior executives of the alliance partners, *and then* within the corporate management team. Internal alliance development between SBUs (strategic business units) has been a long neglected management objective, for which many of the approaches discussed herein will be of great use. A group of executives in one very large U.S. corporation recently estimated that more effective SBU integration would result in a 15% to 50% increase in sales revenues and a large increase in bottom-line profits.

The CEOs' role in managing alliances will take valuable time. Executives consistently underestimate the time coordination takes. If this time is too precious to spare, it cannot be effectively delegated to subordinates without great risk. Therefore, CEOs should concentrate on doing a few alliances well, rather than scattering numerous efforts to the wind.

Three-Dimensional Fit

Managing alliances means focusing equally on the three dimensions of fit—strategy, chemistry, and operations. For many CEOs, managing chemistry—the quality of their relationships—will be an uncomfortable role at first, especially for CEOs who look "downward" into the "vendor" supply chain.

This perception of suppliers as "lesser entities" must change if companies truly believe in providing superior value to their customers and making real commitments to rapid delivery of quality goods and services.

New Roles for Middle Management

As decisions are pushed farther down the corporate hierarchy, the role of the middle manager changes dramatically. Middle managers become tasked with *strategic implementation* (with a far stronger focus on the larger needs of the business) and *operational integration* of cross-corporate teams. Senior executives, on the other hand, become more involved in redesigning the fundamental infrastructures that will support decentralized speed, flexibility, coordination, and integration.

For many middle managers, making this transition will be tumultuous. They were not trained for this new role. Intangible issues will emerge—fear of failure, career patterns in jeopardy, the anguish of tackling a project that has many unknowns. People can become anxiety-ridden in a new, highly ambiguous entrepreneurial environment. Top management must address these amorphous issues directly.

Managing alliances can be a difficult task, and not all managers have the requisite skills and perspectives to be successful. Most essential is having the right attitude: continuing to maintain the delicate balance of a win/win condition by seeing the alliance as its own unique, goal-oriented entity with a mind, a heart, and a soul.

Trust and Relationships

The quality of human relationships is far more important in implementing strategy than most academic authorities are willing to acknowledge. Trust is one of the essential ingredients for alliance success, and it is built on ethical dealings.

At this critical time in history, when communism has met its demise, capitalism is beginning to redefine itself, and a fundamental element among many businesses is a reaffirmation of core values, including ethical dealings with others. Greed, corruption, and narrow self-interest will always exist—and will sometimes prevail—but the ethical business world still survives, and in the future may even thrive.

Alliance champions must foster relations expressed as "us and the team," not "us versus them." Management relationships are the glue that unites and aligns the alliance.

Values

Values become the internal guidance system that leads the alliance to its goals and keeps the companies congruent.

Values are fundamental to maintaining a win/win condition. As strategic and operational conditions change and as new people come into the alliance, values are a stabilizing factor to assist the management of change. Blowouts are far less likely with a strong, mutually held value structure in place.

"Value-driven" alliances create certainty and predictability, thereby building trust, whereas "conditions-driven" alliances are not predictable, changing endlessly with every whim and quirk of fate, creating ambiguity, uncertainty, and distrust.

Excellent leadership is most necessary in situations of uncertainty and rapid change, where conflict and disagreement are naturally prevalent. Yet it's hardest to lead when it's needed the most. Value structures give people a road map through ambiguity and uncertainty.

Find the Right Partner

Look for strong partners, tough partners, partners that want to grow and demand results. A lean and mean partner, one used to competitive battles, is usually better than a fat and rich partner that will not contribute a fair share of the work, but instead will placate with money and then demand rapid financial rewards.

Stay tough, hard-nosed, and results-oriented to keep the alliance partners committed and ready to act rather than react. Don't assume your partner will do all your work for you. Clarify your roles and responsibilities early and often. When you get the big picture clear, and the details right, success is at hand. As the famous architect Mies Van der Rohe said: "God resides in the details." And, by all means, sweat the details *before* signing the legal agreements.

Don't make the fatal, but oft-repeated assumption that two partners really understand the meaning of an alliance in similar terms. Even if your company develops an excellent capability to manage alliances, it is naive at best to believe your partner has a similar understanding or capability.

New Measurements and Rewards

The traditional measures and control systems of the old "internal" corporation—the "corporate castle"—will miss the mark when applied outside the castle walls in the "extended" corporation. Be prepared to put in place more integrated, "big-picture" measures and controls that consider such things as total life-cycle cost, strategic return on investment, "top-line" management, integrated sales and service costs, target costing, and maximum product life-cycle profitability. These measures focus on customer value and organizational capability.

Internal reward systems will also change. The individual "superstar" performers will fade and architects and capacity builders committed to empowerment, infrastructure, and integration will shine.

Building Flexible Organizations

In the old strategic system, brute strength and profit were paramount for gaining competitive advantage. In the new, ever changing global market, the race will go not to the largest, but to the swiftest and most adaptive. Flexibility is derived from an organization's ability to integrate strategy, operations, and human energy by building a unified capability to add value for its customers. Money and market share will always be important, but knowledge, organizational facility, and the capacity to innovate will separate the real winners from the also-rans. In a world of ambiguity and uncertainty, flexibility is essential for successful management.

Flexibility comes from driving decisions down to the level where the expertise lies, where the people are closest to the customer, and where the problems and opportunities exist. Seasoned alliance veterans strongly suggest the human element is vital here, in order to abandon cultural bondage, to be willing to engage in lots of give and take, and to provide for things that may likely go wrong. And above all, communicate, communicate, and then communicate some more.

The creation of flexibility in organizations, particularly when attempted by the behemoths, is not a quick or simple task. Changing corporate culture is difficult and time-consuming; companies with a heritage of command-style control may only grudgingly accept coordination-style control systems. However, on the bright side, many companies have found that the alliance development process is equally effective in developing *internal* bonds and alliances between divisions and departments. According to Gates Energy's Mitch Carr:

If you want to create alliances, you've got to be committed and patient—but it pays off in the long run. As a result of our alliance program, we've found benefits to our own teamwork as well. We recently surveyed our departments, and learned our internal relationships have never been better.[2]

Corporate cultures can and do change, but only when executives intensify their efforts, shifting focus to management by *values* and *processes*. Often, this cultural change can be accelerated by the development of an alliance that spurs and reinforces internal changes to support nonrigid cultures.

Top managers will have to make a long-term investment to design and build the organization of the future, and to buffer the best alliance managers from the ruthless pressure of the quarterly earnings report. Flexibility also implies simplicity. Avoid complex reporting systems, cumbersome procedures, and difficult decision making.

Alliances offer a wonderful opportunity to bring the right combination of people and circumstances together to make synergy and breakthroughs a reality.

A New Paradigm for Deal Makers

It is unfortunate, in many respects, that the lawyers and investment bankers who orchestrated many of the merger and acquisition failures of the 1980s will set their sights on the alliance realm, without shifting their frames of reference, value systems, and operational imperatives. They will bring all the baggage and shortsightedness that caused 80% failure rates in the acquisitions game, and superimpose this "hit-and-run" process on alliances, with predictable consequences. The mentality that allows corporate divisions to be bought and sold like commodities on a stock exchange, and the revolving-door policies for corporate executives can devastate efforts to build stable alliances.

Similarly, corporate deal makers must avoid the tendency to see alliance development shortsightedly as the latest "flavor of the month" or as an opportunity to put another notch on the handle of their gun. Deal makers must intimately involve the future alliance managers in the negotiations process, and be sure the alliance can be managed effectively before closing the deal. Integrating the "front end" of the deal with the "back end" is essential to success.

Ideally, executives will put an end to these ramrod approaches and pay greater attention to their roles as alliance architects. Alliance formation is both an art and a science; it must be directed from within the company and not subcontracted out to investment bankers, lawyers, and accountants.

Deal makers should remain close to their alliances over the long haul and be rewarded not for the *quantity* of deals, but for their *success* rate.

The Successes and Failures

Many mistakes will be made in forming and managing alliances. The most fundamental mistake will be an assumption that alliances will "cure" weaknesses. If internal problems exist, an alliance will only amplify them rather than fix them. Alliances should be used primarily to augment strengths.

Using the methods outlined in this book, probably a full 80% to 90% of all the failures of alliances could have been predicted well in advance.

THE GREAT CORPORATE ADVENTURE

The word *venture* is derived from *adventure*. Alliances are a voyage through the realms of challenge and the lands of opportunity. Like every adventure, cooperative ventures cross uncharted waters, face canyons of doubts, encounter storm clouds of conflict, and sometimes confront danger head-on. Regardless of success or failure, it is vital to learn something from every adventure, because, in reality, there is no such thing as failure, only results. In the words of Theodore Roosevelt:

> Far better to dare mighty things,
> To win glory 'tho checkered by disaster;
> Than to take rank with those poor spirits
> Who've made mediocrity their master.
> Neither enjoying nor suffering much,
> Always choosing to be discreet;
> While they wallow in fog and grey twilight,
> Knowing neither victory nor defeat.

Alliances are not an easy solution, but, like marriage, they are wonderful when they work. They can be controlled, not through domination, but through inspired conception and careful coordination.

Mutual advantage is the name of the alliance game. Alliance management must be flexible enough to change as strategic and operational conditions change. Alliances keep rolling over, taking new forms, making transitions to reflect new global situations.

The ultimate measure of success will not be the alliance's longevity nor its quarterly earnings report, but its long-term strategic value.

The business weaponry of the future will rely not primarily on money nor size of organization, but in the ability to innovate new products and services, to adapt fluidly to rapidly emerging opportunities, to continually create greater value by leveraging core competencies, and to create synergies by integrating corporate diversity.

Appendix
Statement of Principle

Each Statement of Principle should be tailored to meet the specific needs of each individual alliance. However, most contain references addressing the ten issues detailed below:

1. **Spirit of the Venture.** The operating principles or values that will engender communication and trust within the alliance.

2. **Purpose, Goal, Strategic Mission, and Value.** Briefly, why the alliance is being formed, and its perceived mission. What is the strategic rationale of the participants? Beyond money, what are the expected rewards (new product, new market, technology, etc.)? What is the presumed strategic fit?

3. **Realm of Activity.** What scope of product and services will be provided? What specific projects will be included and excluded from the venture? What are the target markets (i.e., regions, user groups, etc.) for the venture? Are any markets excluded from the venture, to remain the domain of the partners?

4. **Key Objectives, Responsibilities, and Operational Milestones.** The specific objectives and targets to be achieved by the alliance; when to expect achieving these objectives; any major obstacles anticipated; and the point at which the alliance will be self-supporting. A human resources philosophy for operations should be outlined. Details of responsibilities should be described later, in an Operational Plan.

5. **Method of Decision Making.** Each alliance will have its own unique decision-making process. Who has the authority to make what types of decisions in what circumstances? Who reports to whom? Is a Board of Directors or Steering Committee to be established? Will one company have operating control? If so, it should be designated at this point.

6. **Technology Inputs; Resource Commitments and Requirements.** Commitment of specific skills, technologies, products, distribution systems, or services of value to the parties. These may include "soft" resources—licenses, knowledge, R&D, a sales force, contacts, production facilities, inventory, raw materials, engineering drawings, management staff, access to capital, the devotion of specific personnel for a certain percentage of their time, and so on. Sometimes, these "soft" resources should be quantified with a financial figure so that a monetary value can be affixed and valued along with the cash commitments.

7. **Financial Philosophy.** What type of financial returns are the sponsors seeking? When do they expect to see the returns? What happens if more cash is needed or the returns are not forthcoming when expected? What are the perceived risks? What are the expected financial commitments (cash, equity, staged payments, loan guarantees, etc.)? What borrowing, entry into equity markets (e.g., public offerings, private placements), or purchase of stock in one of the partners is anticipated? In the event that the sponsors need to make additional cash infusions, what will happen to the alliance? How will cost overruns be handled? Pricing and costing procedures should be mentioned, if applicable.

8. **Project-Specific Subjects.** These include: raw material sourcing; services from parents; licensing; agents and distributors; rights products, distribution, licensing; exclusions; confidentiality/noncompetition, patent provisions; and assets.

    If the venture has purchase and supply provisions, which specific products, services, raw materials, or resources will be purchased from or sold to the owners? Will there be any licensing issues? Will one company serve as agent or distributor? Who will receive rights to particular products, distribution, or licensing? What products, regions, or technologies are specifically excluded from the alliance? Are there any confidentiality/noncompetition or patent provisions? Who has the rights to new products and inventions?

9. **Anticipated Structure of the Alliance.** This section describes the intended structure (written contract, corporation, partnership, or equity investment). Regardless of the legal form, any terms, percentages, or formulas for exchange of stock, if required, should be spelled out. Headquarters location and use of facilities can be mentioned.

10. **Transformation.** What will happen if strategic or operational changes occur? How will the partners respond if the alliance's objectives are not achieved? Is there an anticipated evolution to the venture, such as buy-out, going public, sale to third party, or acquisition? What happens if there has to be a termination, separation, or liquidation?

Endnotes

CHAPTER 1

1. Barrett & Steele, *Providence Journal,* Nov. 3, 1991.
2. Fumio Kodama, "Japanese Exchange for Process Innovation," *Les Novelles: Journal of Licensing,* Sept. 1990, p. 114.
3. Jerry Wasserman, Interview, Nov. 1989.
4. Jean Pierre Ergas, Speech at Packaging Strategies Conference, April, 1990.
5. Michael Bonsingnore, Interview, Nov. 1989.
6. Peter Schauvoir, "Strategic Alliances in Asia Pacific, *Journal for Corporate Growth,* 6:2, 1990, pp. 5–11.
7. David Beretta, Interview, Oct. 1989.
8. Confidential Interview.
9. Frederick G. Withington, quoted in "Failed Marriages," Laurie P. Cohen, *The Wall Street Journal,* Sept. 1984, p. 1.
10. David N. Burt, Warren E. Norquist, Jimmy Anklesaria, *Zero Base Pricing* (Chicago, IL: Probus Publishing Company, 1990) vii.
11. William Lundberg, Interview, Aug. 1992.
12. James Sharp, Interview, Dec. 1991.

CHAPTER 2

1. Survey conducted by the author during alliance seminars.
2. John Hellriegel, Interview, Oct. 1991.
3. Peter Drucker, "The Shape of Industry to Come," *Industry Week,* Jan.11, 1982, pp. 55–59.
4. Joseph Badarocco, *The Knowledge Link* (Boston, MA: Harvard Business School Press, 1991).

CHAPTER 3

1. Gordon Lankton, "50/50 Alliances or Nothing," *CHIEF EXECUTIVE* magazine, May, 1990, p. 37.
2. *Ibid.*, p. 38.
3. Bernard Roth, Interview, July 1990.
4. Alexander Giacco, "Making Joint Ventures Work," *Chemical Week*, Aug. 17, 1983, p. 34.
5. *Ibid.*

CHAPTER 4

1. Roy Bonner, Interview, March 1989.
2. Richard Hayes, quoted in "Strategic Partners," Norm Alister, *Electronic Business*, May 15, 1986, p. 54.

CHAPTER 5

1. Kenichi Ohmae, *The Mind of the Strategist* (New York: McGraw-Hill, 1990) p. 37.

CHAPTER 6

1. Robert Lynch, *The Practical Guide to Joint Ventures and Corporate Alliances*, (New York: John Wiley, 1990) p. 56.
2. George Cioe, Interview, May 1987.

CHAPTER 7

1. William F. Silvia, Interview, Oct. 1990.
2. Herbert Granath, quoted in "Friendly Ties," John Marcom, *The Wall Street Journal*, Nov. 8, 1985, p. 115.
3. Bernard Roth, Interview, April 1992.
4. Stephen Covey, *Seven Habits of Effective Leaders* (New York: Simon & Schuster, 1989) 32.
5. William Norris, Interview, June 1984.
6. Richard Girard, Interview, May 1991.
7. Michael Bonsignore, Interview, Nov. 1989.
8. John Lawler, Interview, Oct. 1990.
9. David Berretta, Interview, Oct. 1990.
10. Mitch Carr, Interview, March 1991.
11. Mihalyi Czikszentmihaly, *Flow, The Psychology of Optimal Experience* (New York: Harper & Row, 1990) p. 4.
12. Denis Waitley, *The Double Win* (New York: Berkeley Books, 1986) 25, 69.
13. Covey, see note 4, pp. 72 & 92.
14. Covey, see note 4 (William George Jordan quote) and James Allen, *As a Man Thinketh* (Philadelphia, PA: Running Press, 1989).

CHAPTER 8

1. Denis Waitley, *The Double Win* (New York: Berkeley Books, 1986) p. 103.
2. Paul Moffat, Interview, Nov. 1991.
3. Theodore Ramstad, Interview, Dec. 1991.
4. Richard Lembo, Interview, Oct. 1991.
5. John Poccia, Interview, Oct. 1989.
6. Timothy Collins, & Thomas Doorley, *Teaming Up for the 90's* (Homewood, IL: Business One Irwin, 1991) 298.
7. Neil Humphrey, *The Art of Contrary Thinking* (Cleveland, OH: Caxton Press, 1971).
8. Robert W. Edwards, Interview, Sept. 1988.
9. Akio Morita, *Made in Japan* (New York: Penguin Books, 1986) 94.
10. Excerpted from IBM Code of Conduct.
11. Roy Bonner, Interview, August 1988.
12. Dana Callow, Interview, Aug. 1987.
13. Ernest DeBellis, Interview, Nov. 1991.

CHAPTER 9

1. Paul D. Broude, "Emerging Business Update," Newsletter, Law firm of O'Connor, Broude & Aronson, Spring 1992.
2. Frank Little, Interview, Oct. 1991.
3. William F. Silvia, Interview, Oct. 1991.
4. Roy Bonner, Interview, March 1989.
5. John Hellriegel, Interview, Oct. 1991.
6. A.A.T. "Pete" Wickersham, Interview, Sept. 1989.
7. Edwin Martin, Jr., *Corporate Partnering* (New York: Practicing Law Institute, 1986) 15.
8. John Lawler, Interview, Oct. 1990.
9. Paul Lawrence, Interview, Oct. 1991.
10. William F. Silvia, Interview, Oct. 1991.
11. John Lawler, Interview, Oct. 1990.

CHAPTER 10

1. Paul Lawrence, Interview, Oct. 1991.
2. Douglas Hanson, Interview, Oct. 1989.

CHAPTER 11

1. John Hellriegel, Interview, Oct. 1991.

CHAPTER 12

1. Richard Lembo, Interview, Oct. 1991.
2. William Silvia, Interview, Oct. 1991.
3. R. Dixon Thayer, Interview, Oct. 1991.
4. Lee Bolman, presentation, ASTD RIChap., Nov. 1991.
5. Philip B. Crosby, *Let's Talk Quality* (New York: Penguin Books, 1989) 40.

6. Terrence Deal, & Alan Kennedy, *Corporate Cultures* (Lexington, MA: Addison Wesley, 1982) 41–42.

7. Thomas J. Peters, & Robert H. Waterman, *In Search of Excellence* (New York: Warner Books, 1982) 208.

8. Jay Galbraith, *Designing Complex Organizations* (Lexington, MA: Addison Wesley, 1973) 97–98.

9. Norm Alister, "Strategic Partners," *Electronics Business*, p. 50, May 15, 1986.

10. William Scruggs, "Strategic Partners," p. 52.

11. Kenichi Ohmae, *The Mind of the Strategist* (New York: McGraw-Hill, 1990) 27.

CHAPTER 13

1. Strategic Alliance Survey, *Electronic Business*, p. 38, March 30, 1992.

2. Mike Van Horn, Interview, Aug. 1991.

CHAPTER 14

1. Akio Morita, *Made in Japan* (New York: Penguin Books, 1986) 180, 206.

2. Joseph Vogel, Interview, March 1991.

CHAPTER 15

1. Kenichi Ohmae, *The Mind of the Strategist* (New York: McGraw-Hill, 1990) 128.

2. Paul Lawrence, Interview, Oct. 1991.

3. Gordon Lankton, "50/50 Alliances or Nothing," *CHIEF EXECUTIVE* magazine, May, 1990, p. 37.

4. Frank Heffernan, quoted in "Friendly Ties," *The Wall Street Journal*, Gupta Udayan, Nov. 8, 1985, p. 1.

CHAPTER 16

1. Adapted from Burt et al., *Zero Base Pricing* (Chicago, IL: Probus Publishing Company, 1990) p. 304.

2. Kathryn Rudie Harrigan, *Managing for Joint Venture Success* (Lexington, MA: Lexington Books, 1986) 189.

3. John Poccia, Interview, Oct. 1989.

4. David Beretta, Interview, Oct. 1990.

5. Mike Van Horn, Interview, Aug. 1991.

6. Mike Van Horn, Interview, Aug. 1991.

CHAPTER 17

1. Gerald McAchran, Address: Spin Out Conference, Philadelphia, Oct. 15, 1992.

2. Roy Bonner, Interview, March 1989.

3. Richard Sandberg, Interview, July 1992.

4. David N. Burt, Warren E. Norquist, Jimmy Anklesaria, *Zero Base Pricing* (Chicago, IL: Probus Publishing Company, 1990) viii.

5. W. William Lindner, Interview, March 1991.

6. James Treece, "Lessons GM Could Learn for(?) Its Supplier Shake-Up," *Business Week*, Aug. 31, 1992, p. 29.

7. David Burt, Interview, Nov. 1991.

8. David N. Burt, Warren E. Norquist, Jimmy Anklesaria, *Zero Base Pricing* (Chicago, IL: Probus Publishing Company, 1990) p. 27.

CHAPTER 18

1. Harry Levinson, Interview, March 1987.
2. David Kitscher, Interview, Oct. 1991.
3. Robert Teutsch, Interview, March 1992.
4. William F. Silvia, Interview, Oct. 1991.
5. Thomas Watson, Jr., Address: Brown University, May 1986.
6. Michael Richmond, Interview, April 1990.
7. Akio Morita, *Made in Japan* (New York: Penguin Books, 1986) 12.
8. Michael Van Horn, Interview, Aug. 1991.

CHAPTER 19

1. Richard J. Thompson, "Competitive Effects of Joint Ventures in the Chemical Industry," Dissertation, University of Massachusetts, Dec. 1970.

CHAPTER 20

1. Kenichi Ohmae, *The Borderless World*, (New York, Harper, 1991) 134.
2. Mitch Carr, Interview, March 1991.

Index